DISCOVERING
The AMERICAN PAST

DISCOVERING
The AMERICAN PAST
A Look at the Evidence

SECOND EDITION

Volume II: Since 1865

William Bruce Wheeler

University of Tennessee

Susan D. Becker

University of Tennessee

HOUGHTON MIFFLIN COMPANY   Boston

Dallas   Geneva, Illinois   Palo Alto   Princeton, New Jersey

Acknowledgments

CHAPTER TWO

Sources 1–10: From Roger L. Ransom and Richard Sutch, *One Kind of Freedom: The Economic Consequences of Emancipation*. Copyright 1977. Reprinted by permission of the publisher, Cambridge University Press.

Source 13: Pages 64–69 from *W. E. B. DuBois: A Biography* by Virginia Hamilton. (Crowell) Copyright © 1972 by Virginia Hamilton. Reprinted by permission of Harper & Row, Publishers, Inc.

CHAPTER FOUR

Source 1: Sunken Gardens. Smithsonian.

Source 3: Negrito tribesman. Library of Congress.

Source 5: Igorot tribesmen. Library of Congress.

Source 9: Igorot dance and spectators. Library of Congress.

Source 12: American school. National Archives.

Acknowledgments continue following page 363.

Cover photograph courtesy Kenneth M. Newman/The Old Print Shop, New York.

Printed in the U.S.A.
Library of Congress Catalog Card Number: 89-080972
ISBN: 0-395-43299-5

ABCDEFGHIJ-B-9543210/89

CONTENTS

PREFACE

The response of students and teachers to the first edition of *Discovering the American Past: A Look at the Evidence* (1986) has been extremely gratifying, thus warranting a second edition of the book. That response has confirmed our suspicion that students have a strong desire to learn about United States history *and* will put forth considerable effort to do so, provided that the nation's history is presented in a way that they find both challenging and stimulating. Students appear to enjoy "doing history" rather than simply being told about it. In other words, students respond to the challenge to be *active learners,* and not merely passive vessels into which information is poured.

We began this book with an urgent desire to tap the already existing interest students have in the past and a firm belief that the study of American history can contribute to an understanding of the contemporary world. It does this in two important ways: (1) it can put the present in perspective by giving us an appreciation of the trends, forces, and people who served to shape contemporary American life, and (2) it can teach us the skills we need in order to examine and analyze our present environment and culture. Our goals in this book, then, are to interest students in historical issues and to help them develop and sharpen the crucial skills that people need to live in today's society.

Those of us who are historians find ourselves surrounded by a wealth of primary evidence that can be used to reconstruct American history. This evidence ranges from the more traditional sources such as letters, newspapers, public documents, speeches, and oral reminiscences to the less traditional sources such as photographs, buildings, statistics, film scripts, and cartoons. Moreover, as historians we know how exciting it can be to sort and analyze this evidence, arrange it in various ways, formulate a hypothesis, and arrive at a probable explanation for at least a part of our collective past.

In *Discovering the American Past,* we have tried to present a series of historical issues and events so as to engage students' interest in a wide variety of different types of primary evidence. We have also tried to provide a good mixture of types of historical situations and a balance among political, social, diplomatic, intellectual, and cultural history. In addition, each type of historical evidence is combined with an introduction to the appropriate methodology in an effort to teach students a variety of research skills. As much as possible, we have tried "to let the evidence speak for itself" and have avoided leading students to one particular interpretation or another. In this book, then, we have created a kind of historical sampler that we believe will help students learn the methods and skills historians use, as well as help them learn historical content. This approach is effective in many different classroom situations including seminars, small classes, and large lecture classes with discussion sections.

Each chapter is divided into six parts: The Problem, Background, The Method, The Evidence, Questions to Consider, and Epilogue. We have made a major alteration in the format of the book for this edition. "The Problem" section this time begins with a brief discussion of the central issues of the chapter and then states the questions students must answer. Then, a "Background" section has been added, to help students understand the historical context of the problem. The format of the remaining sections is the same as in the first edition. The section called "The Method" gives students suggestions for studying and analyzing the evidence. "The Evidence" section is the heart of the chapter, providing a variety of primary source material on a particular historical event or issue. The section called "Questions to Consider" focuses students' attention on specific evidence and on linkages among different evidence material. The "Epilogue" section gives the aftermath or the historical outcome of the evidence—what happened to the people involved, who won the election, the results of a debate, and so on.

In response to student and faculty reactions to the first edition, we have made many changes in content. Exactly one-third (seven of twenty-one) of the chapters are new, either replacing those that students and faculty found less stimulating or, in some cases, adding chapters to fill certain gaps in the first edition. Volume I begins with a new chapter on Europeans' first encounters with American Indians. Chapter 6 is also new, on debates about universal male suffrage at the New York State constitutional convention in 1821. In Volume II, we have added new chapters on American imperialism (Chapter 4), the Progressives and child labor regulation (Chapter 6), the decision to drop the atomic bomb (Chapter 8), the Second Red Scare and the 1947 hearings of the House Committee on Un-American Activities (Chapter 9), and politics and television during the presidential election of 1988 (Chapter 11). In addition to these new chapters, all the chapters from the first edition have been rethought, discussed, revised, and tested in classrooms.

An Instructor's Manual suggests ways that might be useful in guiding students through the evidence, questions students often ask, and a variety of ways in which the students' learning may be evaluated.

Finally, we would like to thank the many people who have helped us in our effort. Our colleagues at the University of Tennessee have been extremely supportive—offering suggestions, reading chapter drafts, and testing the new chapters in their own classes. We would like to thank especially Cathy Matson, Paul Bergeron, John R. Finger, Michael J. McDonald, Charles W. Johnson, and Jonathan Utley. Connie Lester offered invaluable assistance on the Instructor's Manual. Helping to prepare the manuscript were Cynthia Ogle, Jill Finger, Tracy Phelps, and Lisa Medlin. During the spring of 1989, Bruce Wheeler was a Brown Visiting Professor at the University of the South. While there, people who assisted him in preparing the manuscript included Sondra Bridges, Minnie Childers, Jim Jones, and Cathy Young. Finally, colleagues at other institutions who reviewed chapter drafts made significant contributions to this edition, and we would like to thank them for their generosity, both in time and in helpful ideas and suggestions. These reviewers were:

Kathleen Berkeley
University of North Carolina, Wilmington
Nancy H. Bowen
Del Mar College
Carolle Carter
Menlo College
John C. Chalberg
Normandale Community College

George Q. Flynn
Texas Technological University
Carl J. Guarneri
St. Mary's College of California
Thomas Hietala
Grinnell College
John V. Jezierski
Saginaw Valley State College
Charles McCormick
Fairmont State College
Clay McShane
Northeastern University
James Matray
New Mexico State University
John K. Nelson
University of North Carolina, Chapel Hill
Gregory Schmidt
Winona State University
Jason H. Silverman
Winthrop College
Daniel Blake Smith
University of Kentucky
Deborah White
Rutgers University
John Scott Wilson
University of South Carolina

As with the first edition, we dedicate this book to our colleagues at our own university and elsewhere who seek to offer a challenging and stimulating academic experience to their students, and to those students themselves, who make those efforts worthwhile.

RECONSTRUCTING RECONSTRUCTION: THE POLITICAL CARTOONIST AND THE NATIONAL MOOD

THE PROBLEM

The Civil War took a tremendous toll on North and South alike. In the defeated South, more than one-fourth of all men who had borne arms for the Confederacy died, and an additional 15 percent were permanently disabled. Indeed, in 1865 Mississippi spent one-fifth of the state's total revenue on artificial arms and legs for Confederate veterans. Combined with the damage to agriculture, industry, and railroads, the human cost of the Civil War to the South was nearly catastrophic. For its part, the North had suffered frightful human losses as well, although proportionately less than those of the South.

And yet the Civil War, although appalling in its human, physical, and psychological costs, did settle some important issues that had plagued the nation for decades before that bloody conflict. First, the triumph of Union arms had established the United States as "one nation indivisible," from which no state could secede.[1] No less important, the "peculiar institution" of slavery was eradicated, and African Americans at last were free. In truth,

1. In response to President Benjamin Harrison's 1892 appeal for schoolchildren to mark the 400th anniversary of Columbus's discovery with patriotic exercises, Bostonian Francis Bellamy composed the pledge of allegiance to the American flag, from which the phrase "one nation indivisible" comes. In 1942, Congress made it the official pledge to the flag, and in 1954, Congress added the words "under God" in the middle of Bellamy's phrase.

CHAPTER 1

RECONSTRUCTING
RECONSTRUCTION:
THE POLITICAL CAR-
TOONIST AND THE
NATIONAL MOOD

although the Civil War had been costly, the issues it settled were momentous.

The victory of the United States, however, raised at least as many questions as it settled. There was the question of what should happen to the defeated South. Should the states of the former Confederacy be permitted to take their natural place in the Union as quickly and smoothly as possible, with minimum concessions to their northern conquerors? Or should the North insist on a thorough reconstruction of the South, with new economic and social institutions to replace the old? Tied to this issue was the thorny constitutional question of whether the South actually had left the Union at all in 1861. If so, then the southern states in 1865 were territories, to be governed and administered by Congress. If not, then the Civil War had been an internal insurrection and the president, as Commander in Chief, would administer the South's re-entry into the Union.

Perhaps the most difficult question the Union's victory raised was the status of the former slaves. To be sure, they were no longer in bondage. But should they possess all the rights that whites had? Should they be assisted in becoming landowners; if not, how would they earn a living? Should they be allowed to vote and run for elective office? Indeed, no more complex and difficult issue confronted the country than the "place" of the newly freed slaves in the nation.

In all these questions, public opinion in the victorious North was a critical factor in shaping or altering the policies designed to reconstruct the South. Earlier democratic reforms made it unlikely that either the president or Congress could defy public opinion successfully. Yet public opinion can shift with remarkable speed, and political figures forever must be sensitive to its sometimes fickle winds.

Who shapes or reflects public opinion? In this chapter you will be examining and analyzing the work of one person who attempted to shape and reflect public opinion in the North: editorial cartoonist Thomas Nast (1840–1902). Clearly Thomas Nast was not the *only* person who attempted to influence or reflect public opinion in the North. In this chapter, however, you will be concentrating on his work, principally to see the influence of public opinion on governmental policy.

BACKGROUND

By early 1865, it was evident to most northerners and southerners that the Civil War was nearly over. While Grant was hammering at Lee's depleted forces in Virginia, Union general William Tecumseh Sherman broke the back of the Confederacy with his devastating march through Georgia and then northward into the Carolinas. Atlanta fell to Sherman's troops in September 1864, Savannah in December, and Charleston and Columbia, South Carolina, in February 1865. Two-thirds of Columbia lay in ashes. Meanwhile, General Philip Sheridan had driven the Confederates out of the Shenandoah Valley of Virginia, thus blocking any escape attempts by Lee and further cutting southern supply routes. The Union naval blockade of the South was taking its fearful toll, as parts of the dying Confederacy were facing real privation. Hence, although northern armies had suffered terrible losses, by 1865 they stood poised on the brink of victory.

In the South, all but the extreme die-hards recognized that defeat was inevitable. The Confederacy was suffering in more ways than militarily. The Confederate economy had almost completely collapsed, and Confederate paper money was nearly worthless. Slaves were abandoning their masters and mistresses in great numbers, running away to Union armies or roaming through the South in search of better opportunities. In many areas, civilian morale had almost totally deteriorated, and one Georgian wrote, "The people are soul-sick and heartily tired of the hateful, hopeless strife. . . . We have had enough of want and woe, of cruelty and carnage, enough of cripples and corpses."[2] As the Confederate government made secret plans to evacuate Richmond, most southerners knew that the end was very near.

Yet, even with victory almost in hand, many northerners had given little thought to what should happen after the war was over. Would southerners accept the changes that defeat would almost inevitably force on them (most especially the end of slavery)? What demands should the victors make upon the vanquished? Should the North assist the South in rebuilding after the devastation of war? If so, should the North dictate how that rebuilding, or reconstruction, should take place? What efforts should the North make to ensure that the former slaves were receiving the rights of free men and women? During the war, few northerners had seriously considered these questions. Now that victory was within their grasp, they could not avoid them.

One person who had been wrestling with these questions was Abraham Lincoln. In December 1863, the president announced his own plan for reconstructing the South, a plan in keeping with his later hope, as expressed in his second inaugural address, for "malice toward none; with charity for all; . . . Let us . . . bind up the nation's wounds."[3] In Lincoln's plan, a southern state could resume its normal activities in the Union as soon as 10 percent of the voters of 1860 had taken an oath of loyalty to the United States. High-ranking Confederate leaders would be excluded, and some blacks might gain the right to vote. No mention was made of protecting the civil rights of former slaves; it was presumed that this matter would be left to the slaves' former masters and mistresses.

To many northerners, later known as Radical Republicans, Lincoln's plan was much too lenient. In the opinion of these

2. The letter probably was written by Georgian Herschel V. Walker. See Allan Nevins, *The Organized War to Victory, 1864–1865*, Vol. IV of *The War for the Union* (New York: Charles Scribner's Sons, 1971), p. 221.

3. The full text of Lincoln's second inaugural address, delivered on March 4, 1865, can be found in Roy P. Basler, ed., *The Collected Works of Abraham Lincoln,* Vol. VIII (New Brunswick, NJ: Rutgers University Press, 1953), pp. 332–333.

CHAPTER 1

RECONSTRUCTING
RECONSTRUCTION:
THE POLITICAL CAR-
TOONIST AND THE
NATIONAL MOOD

people, a number of whom had been abolitionists, the South, when conquered, should not be allowed to return to its former ways. Not only should slavery be eradicated, they claimed, but freed blacks should be assisted in their efforts to attain economic, social, and political equity. Most of the Radical Republicans favored education for African Americans, and some advocated carving the South's plantations into small parcels to be given to the freedmen. To implement these reforms, Radical Republicans wanted detachments of the United States Army to remain in the South and favored the appointment of provisional governors to oversee the transitional governments in the southern states. Lincoln approved plans for the Army to stay and supported the idea of provisional governors. But he opposed the more far-reaching reform notions of the Radical Republicans, and as president he was able to block them.

In addition to having diametrically opposed views of Reconstruction, Lincoln and the Radical Republicans differed over the constitutional question of which branch of the federal government would be responsible for the reconstruction of the South. The Constitution made no mention of secession, reunion, or reconstruction. But Radical Republicans, citing passages in the Constitution giving Congress the power to guarantee each state a republican government, insisted that the reconstruction of the South should be carried out by Congress.[4] For his part,

however, Lincoln maintained that as chief enforcer of the law and as Commander in Chief, the president was the appropriate person to be in charge of Reconstruction. Clearly a stalemate was in the making, with Radical Republicans calling for a more reform-minded Reconstruction policy and Lincoln continuing to block them.

President Lincoln's death on April 15, 1865 (one week after Lee's surrender at Appomattox Court House)[5] brought Vice President Andrew Johnson to the nation's highest office. At first, Radical Republicans had reason to hope that the new president would follow policies more to their liking. A Tennessean, Johnson had risen to political prominence from humble circumstances, had become a spokesperson for the common white men and women of the South, and had opposed the planter aristocracy. Upon becoming president, he excluded from amnesty all former Confederate political and military leaders as well as all southerners who owned taxable property worth more than $20,000 (an obvious slap at his old planter-aristocrat foes). Moreover, Johnson issued a proclamation setting up provisional military governments in the conquered South and told his cabinet he favored black suffrage, although as a states' rightist he insisted that states adopt the measure voluntarily. At the outset, then, Johnson appeared to be all the Radical Republicans wanted, far preferable to the more moderate Lincoln.

Yet it did not take Radical Republi-

4. See Article IV, Section 4, of the Constitution. Later Radical Republicans also justified their position using the Thirteenth Amendment, adopted in 1865, which gave Congress the power to enforce the amendment ending slavery in the South.

5. The last Confederate army to give up, commanded by General Joseph Johnston, surrendered to Sherman at Durham Station, North Carolina, on April 18, 1865.

cans long to realize that President Johnson was not one of them. Although he spoke harshly, he pardoned hundreds of former Confederates who quickly captured control of southern state governments and congressional delegations. Many northerners were shocked to see former Confederate generals, officials, and even former Confederate vice president Alexander Stephens returned to Washington. The new southern state legislatures passed a series of laws, known collectively as black codes, that so severely restricted the rights of former slaves that they were all but slaves again. Moreover, Johnson privately told southerners that he opposed the Fourteenth Amendment to the Constitution, which was intended to confer full civil rights on the newly freed slaves. He also used his veto power to block Radical Republican Reconstruction measures in Congress and seemed to do little to combat the general defiance of the former Confederacy (exhibited in many forms, including insults thrown at Union occupation soldiers, the desecration of the United States flag, and the formation of organized resistance groups such as the Ku Klux Klan).

To an increasing number of northerners, the unrepentant spirit of the South and Johnson's acquiescence to it were nothing short of appalling. Had the Civil War been fought for nothing? Had more than 364,000 federal soldiers died in vain? White southerners were openly defiant, African Americans were being subjugated by white southerners and virtually ignored by President Johnson, and former Confederates were returning to positions of power and prominence. Radical Republicans had sufficient power in Con-

gress to pass harsher measures, but Johnson kept vetoing them, and the Radicals lacked the votes to override his vetoes.[6] Indeed, the impasse that had existed before Lincoln's death continued.

In such an atmosphere, the congressional elections of 1866 were bitterly fought campaigns, especially in the northern states. President Johnson traveled throughout the North, defending his moderate plan of Reconstruction and viciously attacking his political enemies. However, the Radical Republicans were even more effective. Stirring up the hostilities of wartime, they "waved the bloody shirt" and excited northern voters by charging that the South had never accepted its defeat and that the 364,000 Union dead and 275,000 wounded would be for nothing if the South was permitted to continue its arrogant and stubborn behavior. Increasingly, Johnson was greeted by hostile audiences as the North underwent a major shift in public opinion.

The Radical Republicans won a stunning victory in the congressional elections of 1866 and thus broke the stalemate between Congress and the president. Armed with enough votes to override Johnson's vetoes almost at will, the new Congress proceeded rapidly to implement the Radical Republican vision of Reconstruction. The South was divided into five military districts to be ruled by martial law. Southern states had to ratify the Fourteenth Amendment and institute black suffrage before being allowed to take their formal places in the Union.

6. Congress was able to override Johnson's vetoes of the Civil Rights Act and a revised Freedmen's Bureau bill.

CHAPTER 1

RECONSTRUCTING
RECONSTRUCTION:
THE POLITICAL CAR-
TOONIST AND THE
NATIONAL MOOD

The Freedmen's Bureau, founded earlier, was given additional federal support to set up schools for African Americans, negotiate labor contracts, and, with the military, help monitor elections. Only the proposal to give land to blacks was not adopted, being seen as too extreme by even some Radical Republicans. Congressional Reconstruction had begun.

President Johnson, however, had not been left completely powerless. Determined to undercut the Radical Republicans' Reconstruction policies, he issued orders increasing the powers of civil governments in the South and removed military officers who were enforcing Congress' will, replacing them with commanders less determined to protect black voting rights and more willing to turn the other way when disqualified white southerners voted. Opposed most vigorously by his own secretary of war, Edwin Stanton, Johnson tried to discharge Stanton. To an increasing number of Radicals, the president would have to be removed from office.

In 1868, the House of Representatives voted to impeach Andrew Johnson. Charged with violating the Tenure of Office Act and the Command of the Army Act (both of which had been passed over Johnson's vetoes), the president was tried in the Senate, where two-thirds of the senators would have to vote against Johnson for him to be removed.[7] The vast majority of senators disagreed with the president's Reconstruction policies, yet they feared that impeachment had become a politi-

cal tool that, if successful, threatened to destroy the balance of power between the branches of the federal government. The vote on removal fell one short of the necessary two-thirds, and Johnson was spared the indignity of removal. Nevertheless, the Republican nomination of General Ulysses Grant and his subsequent landslide victory (running as a military hero, Grant carried twenty-six out of thirty-four states) gave Radical Republicans a malleable president, one who, although not a Radical himself, could assure the continuation of their vision of Reconstruction.[8]

By 1872, a renewed Democratic party believed it had a chance to oust Grant and the Republicans. The Grant administration had been rocked by a series of scandals, some involving men quite close to the president. Although honest himself, Grant lost a good deal of popularity by defending the culprits and naively aiding in a cover-up of the corruption. These actions, along with some of his other policies, triggered a revolt within the Republican party, in which a group calling themselves Liberal Republicans bolted the party ranks and nominated well-known editor and reformer Horace Greeley to oppose Grant for the presidency.[9] Hoping for a coalition to defeat Grant, the Democrats also nominated the controversial Greeley.

7. See Article I, Sections 2 and 3, of the Constitution.

8. Southern states, where the Democratic party had been strong, in 1868 either were not in the Union or were under the control of Radical Reconstruction governments. Grant's victory therefore was not as sweeping as it first appears.

9. See Volume 1, Chapter 10, for a discussion of Greeley's position on the emancipation of slaves in 1862.

Greeley's platform was designed to attract as many disparate groups of voters as possible to the Liberal Republican–Democratic political fold. Greeley favored civil service reform, the return to a "hard money" fiscal policy, and the reservation of western lands for settlers rather than for large land companies. He vowed an end to corruption in government. But the most dramatic part of Greeley's message was his call for an end to the bitterness of the Civil War, a thinly veiled promise to bring an end to Radical Reconstruction in the South. For their part, Radical Republicans attacked Greeley as the tool of die-hard southerners and labeled him as the candidate of white southern bigots and northern urban Irish immigrants manipulated by political machines. They took one of Greeley's phrases, "Let us shake hands over the bloody chasm" (a phrase with which Greeley intended to state his hope for an end to sectional hostilities), and warped that utterance almost beyond recognition. By contrast, Grant was labeled as a great war hero and a friend of blacks and whites alike. The incumbent Grant won easily, capturing 55 percent of the popular vote and 286 electoral votes. Greeley died soon after the exhausting campaign.

Gradually, however, the zeal of Radical Republicanism began to fade. An increasing number of northerners grew tired of the issue. With their commitment to full civil rights for African Americans never strong, they had voted into office Radical Republicans more out of anger at southern intransigence than out of any lofty notions of black equality. Hence northerners said little when, one by one, southern Democrats returned to power in the states of the former Confederacy.[10] As a mark of how little their own attitudes had changed in the years since the Civil War, white southerners labeled these native Democrats "Redeemers." Yet, as long as southern Democrats made no overt moves to subvert the rights of African Americans, most northerners were willing to put the whole agony of Reconstruction behind them. Hence, although much that was fruitful and beneficial was accomplished in the South during the Reconstruction period (most notably black suffrage and public education), some of this was to be temporary, and many opportunities for progress were lost. By the presidential election of 1876, both candidates (Rutherford B. Hayes and Samuel Tilden) promised an end to Reconstruction, and the Radical Republican experiment, to all intents and purposes, was over.

It is clear that northern public opinion from 1865 to 1876 was not static but was almost constantly shifting. This public opinion was influenced by a number of factors, among them speeches, newspapers, and word of mouth. Especially influential were editorial cartoons, which captured the issues visually, often simplifying them so that virtually everyone could understand them. Perhaps the master of this style was Thomas Nast, a political

10. Southerners regained control of the state governments in Tennessee and Virginia in 1869, North Carolina in 1870, Georgia in 1871, Arkansas and Alabama in 1874, and Mississippi in early 1876. By the presidential election of 1876, only South Carolina, Louisiana, and Florida were still controlled by Reconstruction governments.

CHAPTER 1

RECONSTRUCTING
RECONSTRUCTION:
THE POLITICAL CAR-
TOONIST AND THE
NATIONAL MOOD

cartoonist whose career, principally with *Harper's Weekly,* spanned the tumultuous years of the Civil War and Reconstruction. Throughout his career, Nast produced more than 3,000 cartoons, illustrations for books, and paintings. He is credited with originating the modern depiction of Santa Claus, the Republican elephant, and the Democratic donkey. Congratulating themselves for having hired Nast, the editors of *Harper's Weekly* once exclaimed that each of Nast's drawings was at once "a poem and a speech."

Apparently Thomas Nast developed his talents early in life. Born in the German Palatinate (one of the German states) in 1840, Nast was the son of a musician in the Ninth Regiment Bavarian Band. The family moved to New York City in 1846, at which time young Thomas was enrolled in school. It seems that art was his only interest—one teacher admonished him, "Go finish your picture. You will never learn to read or figure." After unsuccessfully trying to interest their son in music, his parents eventually encouraged the development of his artistic talent. By the age of fifteen, Thomas Nast was drawing illustrations for *Frank Leslie's Illustrated Newspaper.* He joined *Harper's Weekly* in 1862 (at the age of twenty-two), where he developed the cartoon style that was to win him a national reputation, as well as enemies: He received praise from Abraham Lincoln, Ulysses Grant, and Samuel Clemens (also known as Mark Twain, who in 1872 asked Nast to do the illustrations for one of his books so that "then I will have good pictures"). On the other hand, one of Nast's favorite targets, political boss

William Marcy Tweed of New York's Tammany Hall, once shouted, "Let's stop these damn pictures. I don't care so much what the papers say about me—my constituents can't read; but damn it, they can see pictures!"

It is obvious from his work that Thomas Nast was a man of strong feelings and emotions. In his eyes, those people whom he admired possessed no flaws. Conversely, those whom he opposed were, to him, capable of every conceivable villainy. As a result, his characterizations were often terribly unfair, gross distortions of reality, and more than occasionally slanderous. In his view, however, his central purpose was not to entertain but to move his audiences, to make them scream out in outrage or anger, to prod them to action. The selection of Nast's cartoons in this chapter therefore is typical of the body of his work for *Harper's Weekly*: artistically inventive and polished, blatantly slanted, and brimming with indignation and emotion.

Your task in this chapter is to analyze Nast's cartoons and read the appropriate material in your textbook to answer the following questions:

1. How did Nast attempt to influence public opinion in the North regarding Reconstruction?
2. Did Nast change his views regarding Reconstruction between 1865 and 1876? Did public opinion change? How (if at all)?
3. How did public opinion in the North, as reflected in the work of Thomas Nast, influence public policy (if at all)?

To complete the assignment, you should do the following:

1. Read the introduction to this chapter and supplementary texts carefully to identify the principal issues of Reconstruction. You should make a list of those issues.
2. Examine closely the cartoons presented to determine where Nast stood on those issues.
3. Compare where public opinion in the North stood on those issues *at different times* during Reconstruction with how Nast stood *at different times*.
4. Compare shifting public opinion with changing government policies regarding Reconstruction, in an attempt to measure the impact of public opinion on policymakers.

Public opinion is not always easy to measure. But we do have certain clues. Election results, for example, are a good gauge of public opinion, as are audience responses to speakers (recall the audiences that President Johnson faced in 1866). As you read, looking for public opinion, be sensitive to these clues.

THE METHOD

Although Thomas Nast developed the political cartoon into a true art form, cartoons and caricatures had a long tradition both in Europe and America before Nast. English artists helped bring forth the cartoon style that eventually made *Punch* (founded in 1841) one of the liveliest-illustrated periodicals on both sides of the Atlantic. In America, Benjamin Franklin is traditionally credited with publishing the first newspaper cartoon in 1754, the multidivided snake (each part of the snake representing one colony) with the ominous warning "Join or Die." By the time Andrew Jackson sought the presidency, the political cartoon had become a regular and popular feature of American political life. Crude by modern standards, these cartoons influenced some people far more than did the printed word.

As we noted, the political cartoon, like the newspaper editorial, is intended to do more than objectively report events. It is meant to express an opinion, a point of view. Cartoons often praise or ridicule. Those who create them want to move people, anger them, make them laugh, or spur them to action. In short, political cartoons are poor devices for learning what is happening, but they are excellent devices for portraying popular reaction to what is happening.

How, then, can we analyze political cartoons? First, cartoons almost always portray events. As you examine the cartoons in this chapter, try to determine what event is being portrayed. Often a cartoon's caption, dialogue, or other clues will help you discover the event in question. By careful scrutiny, you can discern what the car-

CHAPTER 1

RECONSTRUCTING
RECONSTRUCTION:
THE POLITICAL CAR-
TOONIST AND THE
NATIONAL MOOD

toonist's opinion of the event is. Is the cartoonist approving or disapproving? How did you reach that conclusion?

Examine the people in each cartoon. Is the cartoonist aiming for a true likeness? Is he or she portraying the people sympathetically or unsympathetically? Nast often placed his characters out of their historical context (in Roman circuses, for example). Why did he do this? What did he intend to show? Sometimes cartoonists accentuate their subjects' physical features. Why do they do this?

After you examine a cartoon in detail, try to determine the message the cartoonist is trying to convey. What reactions does he or she hope those who see the cartoon will have? What do you think people's reactions might have been at the time the cartoon was published?

Before you begin the exercises in this chapter, familiarize yourself with both the method discussed above and Nast by making a "trial run" on one of Nast's cartoons on another subject, that of public subsidy of private schools.

In 1868, the New York state legislature ruled that public funds could be made available to private schools. Most of the schools that benefited from this law were parochial schools of the Roman Catholic Church. Shortly thereafter, Roman Catholics complained about the compulsory use of the King James Version of the Bible in public schools.

The cartoon in Source 1 appeared in *Harper's Weekly* on September 30, 1871. It graphically shows Nast's opinion on the issue. Examine the cartoon carefully. How are Roman Catholic clergymen portrayed? In the upper right, who is the woman being led to the gallows, and who is leading her? To the left of that, who are the adults at the top of the cliff, and what are they doing? In what condition are the public schools? What is Tammany Hall (upper left), and what is the building intended to look like? In the foreground, what is stuck in the largest child's coat? What are the children's reactions? Finally, what was Thomas Nast's opinion of Tammany Hall? The Irish Americans? The New York state legislature? The Roman Catholic Church? What feelings was Nast trying to elicit from those who saw this cartoon?

As you can see, a political cartoon must be analyzed to the most minute detail to get the full meaning the cartoonist is trying to convey. From that analysis, one can discover the creator's full meaning or message and can imagine the emotions the cartoon was likely to evoke.

Now you are ready to begin your analysis of the Reconstruction period through the cartoons of Thomas Nast. As you analyze each cartoon, be aware of the collective message of *all* the cartoons. Most subscribers to *Harper's Weekly* saw all the cartoons. What was their general reaction likely to be?

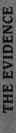

THE EVIDENCE

Sources 1 through 13 from Morton Keller, *The Art and Politics of Thomas Nast*
(New York: Oxford University Press, 1968), plates 108; 55 and 56; 22; 17; 27; 32;
47; 50; 38; 196; 197; 155; and 209, respectively. Courtesy of the publisher.

1.

THE AMERICAN RIVER GANGES.

THE PRIESTS AND THE CHILDREN.—[See Page 915.]

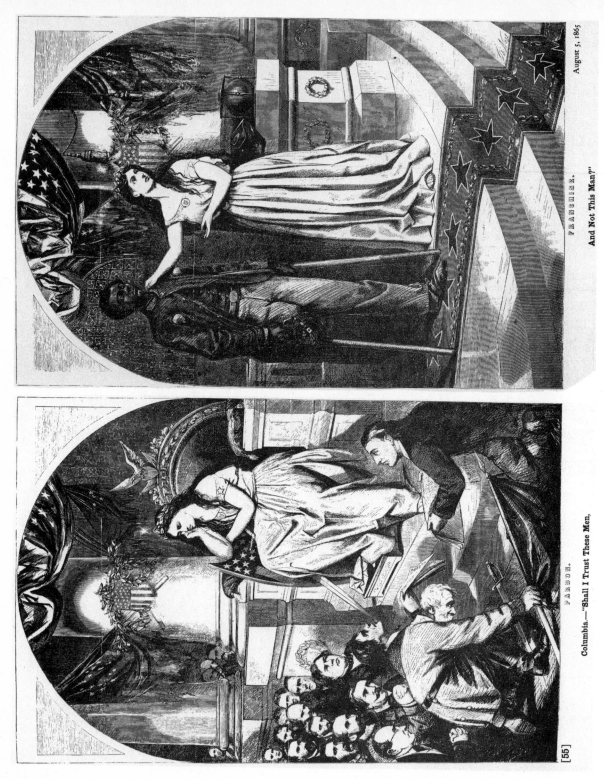

2.

August 5, 1865

FRANCHISE.

"And Not This Man?"

PARDON.

Columbia.—"Shall I Trust These Men,

[55]

[12]

THE CONTRAST OF SUFFERING ANDERSONVILLE & FORTRESS MONROE.

TREASON MUST BE MADE ODIOUS.

June 30, 1866

March 30, 1867

Amphitheatrum Johnsonianum—Massacre of the Innocents
At New Orleans, July 30, 1866.

4.

[14]

September 5, 1868

"This Is a White Man's Government."

"We regard the Reconstruction Acts (so called) of Congress as usurpations, and unconstitutional, revolutionary, and void."—*Democratic Platform.*

6.

The Modern Samson.

October 3, 1868

August 3, 1872

Baltimore 1861–1872.

"Let Us Clasp Hands over the Bloody Chasm."

CHAPTER 1

RECONSTRUCTING
RECONSTRUCTION:
THE POLITICAL CAR-
TOONIST AND THE
NATIONAL MOOD

8.

September 7, 1872

The Whited Sepulchre.

Covering the monument of infamy with his white hat and coat.

April 13, 1872

The Republic Is Not Ungrateful.

"It is not what is *charged* but what is *proved* that damages the party defendant. Any one may be accused of the most heinous offenses; the Saviour of mankind was not only arraigned but convicted; but what of it? Facts alone are decisive."—*New York Tribune*, March 13, 1872.

CHAPTER 1

RECONSTRUCTING
RECONSTRUCTION:
THE POLITICAL CAR-
TOONIST AND THE
NATIONAL MOOD

10.

March 14, 1874

Colored Rule in a Reconstructed (?) State.

(THE MEMBERS CALL EACH OTHER THIEVES, LIARS, RASCALS, AND COWARDS.)

COLUMBIA. "You are aping the lowest whites. If you disgrace your race in this way you had better take back seats."

September 26, 1874

The Commandments in South Carolina.

"We've pretty well smashed that; but I suppose, Massa Moses, you can get another one."

CHAPTER 1

RECONSTRUCTING
RECONSTRUCTION:
THE POLITICAL CAR-
TOONIST AND THE
NATIONAL MOOD

12.

December 9, 1876

The Ignorant Vote—Honors Are Easy.

13.

October 24, 1874

A Burden He Has To Shoulder.

And they say, "He wants a third term."

14.

Source 14 from J. Chal Vinson, *Thomas Nast, Political Cartoonist* (Athens: University of Georgia Press, 1967).

A review of the process you must use to complete this exercise is helpful. First, identify the principal issues of the Reconstruction period. Second, determine where Nast stood on each issue. Third, determine the extent to which Nast's cartoons reflect a changing public opinion in the North regarding Reconstruction. And fourth, compare shifting public opinion with governmental policy changes in an attempt to measure the impact of public opinion on government policies.

The process readily lends itself to a chart:

Issues:

_____

Nast's Position:

_____

How Northern Public Opinion Changed, As Reflected by Nast's Cartoons:

_____

Impact of Public Opinion on Government:

_____

A close reading of the introduction to this chapter and supplementary texts will provide the data for the first row, and an examination of Nast's cartoons will help you fill in the second row. Then, by comparing the first and second rows, you should be able to answer the question of how Nast's cartoons can be used to gain insight into shifts in northern public opinion regarding Reconstruction. The fourth row will require you to compare public opinion (as reflected in Nast's work) with your reading on shifting Reconstruction policies.

Sources 2 through 4 represent Nast's views of Reconstruction under President Andrew Johnson. Sources 5 and 6 deal with an issue crucial to Radical Republicans. Sources 7 and 8 focus on the presidential election of 1872, and Sources 9 through 13 evaluate Radical Reconstruction in its latter years. You will be examining these cartoons in these four groupings to determine shifts in northern public opinion regarding Reconstruction.

Source 2 must first be examined for its symbolism. Who is Columbia? What emotions do her two different poses suggest? Who are the people asking for pardon in the first frame? Now look carefully at the black man in the second frame. Who does he represent? Can you formulate one sentence that summarizes the message of both parts of Source 2?

Source 3 is more complex: two drawings within two other drawings. If you do not already know what purpose Andersonville and Fortress Monroe served, consult a text on this time period, an encyclopedia, or a good Civil War history book. Then look at the upper left and upper right outside drawings. Contrast the appearance of the man entering with the man leaving. Now examine the lower left and lower right outside drawings the same way. What was Nast trying to tell? The larger inside drawings explain the contrast. What were the conditions like at Andersonville? At Fortress Monroe? What did the cartoonist think were the physical and psychological results?

Source 4 also must be examined for its symbolism. Who is the emperor? What is the amphitheater intended to

CHAPTER 1

RECONSTRUCTING
RECONSTRUCTION:
THE POLITICAL CAR-
TOONIST AND THE
NATIONAL MOOD

represent? Who is the person in the lower left intended to represent? On July 30, 1866, several blacks attending a Radical Republican convention in New Orleans were shot and killed by white policemen. How did Nast react to this event? What did he think caused it? How is President Andrew Johnson portrayed with regard to what is taking place?

Each of the three people standing in Source 5 represents part of the Democratic Party coalition, and each has something to contribute to the party. Can you identify the groups that the man on the right and the man in the center represent? What do they offer the party? Notice the facial features of the man on the left as well as his dress, particularly the hatband from Five Points (a notorious slum section of New York City). Who is this man supposed to represent, and what does he give the party? Notice what the black man lying on the ground has dropped. What does he represent? What is he reaching for? What is happening in the background of the cartoon?

Source 6 also explores the question of rights for freed blacks, this time within the setting of the well-known story of Samson and Delilah. Who is Nast's Delilah, and what has she done? Who are her supporters at the left? What other things do they advocate? Now look carefully at the figure in the upper right-hand corner. Who is he? What has he promised African Americans? What has he done?

Sources 7 through 9 were published just before the presidential election of 1872. Who is the plump little man with the white beard and glasses who appears in all three cartoons?

What part of this character's campaign did Nast find especially objectionable? Why? What is wrong with what the character is trying to do? (Because these cartoons show many reasons for Nast's disgust, it is helpful to keep a list as you study each cartoon separately.) On the other hand, who is portrayed in Source 9? To whom is he linked?

Sources 10 through 13 reflect Nast's thinking in the latter years of Reconstruction. Sources 10 and 11 portray his opinion of Reconstruction in South Carolina, presided over by Radical Republican Governor Franklin J. Moses (caricatured in Source 11). How are African Americans pictured (compare to Sources 2, 5, and 6)? To whom are African Americans compared in Source 12? What does this say about Nast's opinion on Reconstruction? Source 13 portrays President Ulysses Grant (compare to Sources 4 and 9). How is he pictured?

The last cartoon (Source 14) shows Nast's opinion of the South in 1876, near the end of Reconstruction. What scene was Nast re-creating? What is the significance of this scene? How is the black man depicted? What was Nast trying to show? How would you compare or contrast this cartoon with Sources 10 through 12? What does this tell you about Nast's views?

You should now return to the central questions asked earlier and to your text on Reconstruction. How did Nast attempt to influence public opinion in the North regarding Reconstruction? Did Nast change his views on Reconstruction? Did the general public in the North change its views? How did public opinion in the North influence public policy on Reconstruction?

EPILOGUE

Undoubtedly Nast's work had an important impact on northern opinion of Reconstruction, the Democratic Party, Horace Greeley, the Irish Americans, and other issues as well. Yet gradually northern ardor began to decline as other issues and concerns eased Reconstruction out of the limelight and as it appeared that the crusade to reconstruct the South would be an endless one. Radical Republicans, who insisted on equality for the freed slaves, received less and less attention, and southern Democrats, who regained control of southern state governments, were essentially allowed a free hand as long as they did not obviously violate the Constitution and federal law. By 1877, the South was once again in the hands of white Democrats.

Yet as long as African Americans did not insist on their rights, white southern leaders allowed them to retain, in principle, all that the Civil War and Reconstruction had won. In other words, as long as black voters did not challenge the Redeemers, they were allowed to retain their political rights. Economically, many African Americans gradually slipped into the status of tenant farmer, sharecropper, or even peon. The political structure, local courts, and law-enforcement agencies tended to support this arrangement. For his part, African American leader Booker T. Washington was praised by white southerners for urging that blacks seek education and economic opportunities but not "rock the boat" politically in the white-controlled South. Finally, in the late 1880s, when white southerners realized that the Reconstruction spirit had waned in the North, southern state legislatures began instituting rigid segregation of schools, public transportation and accommodations, parks, restaurants and theaters, elevators, drinking fountains, and so on. Not until the 1950s did those chains begin to be broken.

As the reform spirit waned in the latter years of Reconstruction, Nast's popularity suffered. The public appeared to tire of his anger, his self-righteousness, his relentless crusades. The new publisher of *Harper's Weekly* sought to make the magazine less political, and in that atmosphere there was no place for Nast. He resigned in 1886.

Nast continued to free-lance for a number of magazines and tried unsuccessfully to start his own periodical, *Nast's Weekly*. Financially struggling, he appealed to friends, who influenced President Theodore Roosevelt to appoint Nast to a minor consular post in Ecuador. He died there of yellow fever in 1902.

Yet Thomas Nast was a pioneer of a tradition and of a political art form. His successors, people such as Herbert Block (Herblock), Bill Mauldin, Oliphant, and even Garry Trudeau ("Doonesbury"), have continued to prick the American conscience, fret and irritate newspaper readers, and assert through their art the proposition that no evildoer can escape the scrutiny and ultimate justice of the popular will. Sometimes these successors are effective, sometimes not.

CHAPTER TWO

WASHINGTON AND DUBOIS: AFRICAN AMERICAN ALTERNATIVES IN THE NEW SOUTH

THE PROBLEM

By 1895, when African American spokes-man and educator Booker T. Washington delivered his much-publicized Atlanta Exposition address, southern blacks had been free for thirty years. Yet in many ways their situation had barely improved from that of servitude. Economically, few had been able to acquire land of their own, and the vast majority continued to work for white landowners under various forms of labor arrangements and sometimes under outright peonage.[1] Political and civil rights had been

guaranteed under the Fourteenth and Fifteenth Amendments to the Constitution (ratified in 1868 and 1870, respectively), yet those rights often were violated, and, beginning in the early 1890s, southern states began a successful campaign to disfranchise black voters and to institute legal segregation through legislation that collectively became known as Jim Crow laws.[2] In some ways more threatening, violence against African Americans was increasing and in most cases going unpunished. Between 1889 and 1900, 1,357 African Americans were lynched in the United States, the

1. Whatever names were given to these labor arrangements (tenancy, sharecropping, etc.), in most of the arrangements a white land-owner or merchant furnished farm workers with foodstuffs and fertilizer on credit, taking a percentage of the crops grown in return. For a fascinating description of how the system worked, see Theodore Rosengarten, *All God's Dangers: The Life of Nate Shaw* (New York: Alfred A. Knopf, 1974).

2. The term "Jim Crow," generally used to refer to issues relating to African Americans, originated in the late 1820s with white minstrel singer Thomas "Daddy" Rice, who performed the song "Jump Jim Crow" in blackface makeup. By the 1840s, the term was used to refer to racially segregated facilities in the North.

vast majority in the states of the former Confederacy. In 1898, in New Bern, North Carolina, one white orator proposed "choking the Cape Fear River with the bodies of Negroes." In truth, by the 1890s it had become evident that Lincoln's emancipation of southern slaves had been considerably less than complete.

For African Americans in the South, two spokesmen for their race offered significantly different alternatives to improving their situation. Booker T. Washington, a former slave who had earned an education and had become a celebrated educator and author, offered southern blacks one option. Massachusetts native and Harvard-educated W. E. B. DuBois (pronounced DuBoys') generally opposed Washington's alternative and offered a contrasting vision. And, as you will see, there were other options for southern

blacks as well, principally that of abandoning the states of the former Confederacy for opportunities elsewhere.

In this chapter you will be analyzing the situation that southern African Americans faced in the years after Reconstruction and identifying and evaluating the principal options open to these people. How were southern African Americans faring economically? Were they making progress in terms of land ownership, economic betterment, and education? What alternatives did Washington and DuBois offer African Americans? Were there other options they did not mention? Finally, based on your examination of the evidence and use of your historical imagination, which alternative do you think was the better one for African Americans at the turn of the twentieth century?

BACKGROUND

The gradual end of Reconstruction by the federal government left the South in the hands of political and economic leaders who chose to call themselves "Redeemers." Many of these men came from the same landowner and planter-lawyer groups that had led the South prior to the Civil War, thus giving the post–Reconstruction South a high degree of continuity with earlier eras. Also important, however, was a comparatively new group of southerners, men who called for a "New South" that would be highlighted by increased in-

dustrialization, urbanization, and diversified agriculture.

In many ways, the New South movement was an undisguised attempt to imitate the industrialization that was sweeping through the North just prior to, during, and after the Civil War. Indeed, the North's industrial prowess had been one reason for its ultimate military victory. As Reconstruction gradually came to an end in the southern states, many southern bankers, business leaders, and editors became convinced that the South should

CHAPTER 2

WASHINGTON
AND DUBOIS:
AFRICAN
AMERICAN
ALTERNATIVES
IN THE NEW
SOUTH

not return to its previous, narrow economic base of plantations and one-crop agriculture but instead should follow the North's lead toward modernization through industry. Prior to the Civil War, many of these people had been calling for economic diversification, but they had been overwhelmed by the plantation aristocracy that controlled southern state politics and that had used that control to further its own interests. By the end of Reconstruction, however, the planter elite had lost a good deal of its power, thus creating a power vacuum advocates of a New South could move into.

Nearly every city, town, and hamlet of the former Confederacy had its New South boosters. Getting together in industrial societies or in chambers of commerce, the boosters called for the erection of mills and factories. Why, they asked, should southerners export their valuable raw materials elsewhere, only to see them return from northern and European factories as costly finished products? Why couldn't southerners set up their own manufacturing establishments and become prosperous within a self-contained economy? And if the southerners were short of capital, why not encourage rich northern investors to put up money in return for promises of great profits? In fact, the South had all the ingredients required of an industrial system: raw materials, a rebuilt transportation system, labor, potential consumers, and the possibility of obtaining capital. As they fed each other's dreams, the New South advocates pictured a resurgent South, a prosperous South, a triumphant South, a South of steam and power rather than of plantations and magnolias.

Undoubtedly the leading spokesman of the New South movement was Henry Grady, editor of the Atlanta *Constitution* and one of the most influential figures in the southern states. Born in Athens, Georgia, in 1850, Grady was orphaned in his early teens when his father was killed in the Civil War. Graduating from his hometown college, the University of Georgia, Grady began a long and not particularly profitable career as a journalist until in 1879, aided by northern industrialist Cyrus Field, he purchased a quarter interest in the Atlanta *Constitution* and became that newspaper's editor. From that position, he became the chief advocate of the New South movement.

Whether speaking to southern or northern audiences, Grady had no peer. Addressing a group of potential investors in New South industries in New York in 1886, he delighted his audience by saying that he actually was glad the Confederacy had lost the Civil War, for that defeat had broken the power of the plantation aristocracy and had provided the opportunity for the South to move into the modern industrial age. Northerners, Grady continued, were no longer unwelcome: "We have sown towns and cities in the place of theories, and put business above politics . . . and have . . . wiped out the place where Mason and Dixon's line used to be."[3]

To those southerners who envisioned a New South, the central goal was a

3. Grady's speech is in Richard N. Current and John A. Garraty, eds., *Words That Made American History,* Vol. II (Boston: Little, Brown and Company, 1962), pp. 23–31.

harmonious, interdependent society in which each person and thing had its clearly defined place. Most New South boosters stressed industry and the growth of cities because the South had few factories and mills and almost no cities of substantial size. But agriculture too would have its place, although it would not be the same as the cash-crop agriculture of the pre–Civil War years. Instead, New South spokesmen advocated a diversified agriculture that would still produce cash crops for export but would also make the South more self-sufficient by producing food crops and raw materials for the anticipated factories. Small towns would be used for collection and distribution, a rebuilt railroad network would transport goods, and northern capital would finance the entire process. Hence each part of the economy and, indeed, each person would have a clearly defined place and role in the New South, a place and role that would ensure a piece of the New South's prosperity for everyone.

But even as Grady and his counterparts were fashioning their dreams of a New South and selling those dreams to both northerners and southerners, a less beneficial, less prosperous side of the New South was taking shape. In spite of the New South advocates' successes in establishing factories and mills (for example, Knoxville, Tennessee, witnessed the founding of more than ninety such enterprises in the 1880s alone), the post–Reconstruction South remained primarily agricultural. Furthermore, most of the farms were worked by sharecroppers or tenant farmers who eked out a bare subsistence while the profits went to the landowners or the banks. This situation was especially prevalent in the lower South, where by 1890 a great proportion of farms were worked by tenants: South Carolina (61.1 percent), Georgia (59.9 percent), Alabama (57.7 percent), Mississippi (62.4 percent), and Louisiana (58.0 percent). Hence, even as factory smokestacks were rising on portions of the southern horizon, a high percentage of southerners remained in agriculture and in poverty.

Undeniably, African Americans suffered the most. More than four million African American men, women, and children had been freed by the Civil War. During the period of Reconstruction, some advances were made, especially in the areas of public education and voter registration. Yet even many Radical Republicans were reluctant when it came to the issue of giving land to the former slaves. Thus most African Americans were forced to either take menial, low-paying jobs in southern cities or work as farmers on land they did not own. As poor urban laborers or as tenant farmers, African Americans were dependent on their employers, landowners, or bankers and prey to rigid vagrancy laws, the convict lease system, peonage, and outright racial discrimination. Moreover, the end of Reconstruction in the southern states witnessed a reimposition of rigid racial segregation, at first through a return to traditional practices and later (in the 1890s) by state laws governing nearly every aspect of southern life. For example, voting by African Americans was discouraged, initially by intimidation and then by more formal means, such as poll taxes

CHAPTER 2

WASHINGTON
AND DUBOIS:
AFRICAN
AMERICAN
ALTERNATIVES
IN THE NEW
SOUTH

and literacy tests. African Americans who protested or strayed from their "place" were dealt with harshly: between 1880 and 1918, more than 2,400 African Americans were lynched by white southern mobs, each action being a grim reminder to African Americans of what could happen to those who challenged the status quo. For their part, the few southern whites who spoke against such outrages were themselves subjects of intimidation and even violence. Indeed, although most African American men and women undoubtedly would have disagreed, the African Americans' relative position had in some ways deteriorated since the end of the Civil War.

Many New South advocates openly worried about how potential northern investors and politicians would react to this state of affairs. Although the dream of the New South rested on the concept of a harmonious, interdependent society in which each component (industry, agriculture, and so forth) and each person (white, black) had a clearly defined place, it appeared that the African Americans were being kept in their "place" largely by intimidation and force. Who would want to invest in a region in which the status quo of mutual deference and "place" often was maintained by force? To calm northern fears, Grady and his cohorts assured northerners that the African Americans' position was improving and that southern society was one of mutual respect between the races. "We have found," Grady stated, "that in the summing up the free Negro counts more than he did as a slave." Most northerners believed Grady because they wanted to believe Grady,

because they had no taste for another bitter Reconstruction, and in many cases because they shared the white southerners' prejudice toward African Americans. Grady was able to reassure them because they wanted to be reassured.

Thus for southern African Americans, the New South movement had done little to better their collective lot. Indeed, in some ways their position had deteriorated. Tied economically either to land they did not own or to the lowest paying jobs in towns and cities, subjects of an increasingly rigid code of racial segregation and loss of political rights, and victims of an upswing in racially directed violence, African Americans in the New South had every reason to question the oratory of Henry Grady and other New South boosters. Jobs in the New South's mills and factories generally were reserved for whites, so the opportunities that European immigrants in the North had to work their way gradually up the economic ladder were closed to southern blacks.

How did African Americans respond to this deteriorating situation? In the 1890s, numerous African American farmers joined the Colored Alliance, part of the Farmers' Alliance Movement that swept the South and Midwest in the 1880s and 1890s. This movement attempted to reverse the farmers' eroding position through the establishment of farmers' cooperatives (to sell their crops together for higher prices and to purchase manufactured goods wholesale) and by entering politics to elect candidates sympathetic to farmers (who would draft legislation favorable to farmers). Many feared, however, that this increased militancy of farmers—white and black—would produce a political backlash that would leave them even worse off. Such a backlash occurred in the South in the 1890s with the defeat of the Populist revolt.

Booker T. Washington and W. E. B. DuBois offered African Americans two other alternatives, competing strategies to meet the economic, social, and political problems they faced. And, as African American men and women soon discovered, there were other options as well.

Essentially, your task in this chapter is to analyze the evidence to answer the following central questions: (1) What situation did African Americans in the South face in the years after Reconstruction? (2) What were the principal options available to these people (including the two strategies advocated by Washington and DuBois, respectively)? (3) Which option do you think was the better one for African Americans at the turn of the twentieth century?

THE METHOD

In this chapter the evidence is arranged in three clusters:

1. Eleven sets of statistics that together with the background section from this chapter and reading in your text will give you a good idea as to the situation southern African Americans faced.
2. Two speeches, one delivered by Washington in 1895 and the other (only a portion of which is reproduced here) by DuBois in 1906. Both are considered famous American speeches.
3. One statistical set, from combined United States census reports from 1880 to 1920, designed to show you another option available to southern African Americans.

This is not the first time you have examined statistics or speeches. Indeed, our society is inundated daily with statistics that we must absorb,

analyze, and understand. At the same time, we are bombarded by speeches delivered by politicians, business figures, educators, and others, most of whom are trying to convince us to adopt a set of ideas or actions. As we listen to such speeches, we invariably weigh the options presented to us, often using other available evidence (such as statistics) to help us make our decisions. One purpose of this exercise is to help you think more critically and use evidence more thoroughly when assessing different options.

It is logical to begin by assessing the situation of southern African Americans in the post–Reconstruction South. Sources 1 to 10 plus your reading will enable you to do this. Collectively, what was that situation? Use each source, plus your other reading, to prove your thesis.

Next, define the alternatives open to southern African Americans in the

CHAPTER 2

WASHINGTON
AND DUBOIS:
AFRICAN
AMERICAN
ALTERNATIVES
IN THE NEW
SOUTH

late nineteenth and early twentieth centuries. For that information you must go to the speeches of Washington and DuBois. Both men were black, and both wanted their race completely integrated into the political, social, and economic mainstream of American life. Yet each had a different idea of how that goal could be accomplished. Read each speech carefully, looking for the particular method espoused. A rough chart is helpful:

Then examine Source 14 for another option open to southern African Americans.

Once you have carefully defined the options Washington and DuBois presented and evaluated the other evidence, you will be ready to use your historical imagination and the evidence to determine which was the better option.

What African Americans Should Do

Washington	
DuBois	

THE EVIDENCE

Sources 1 through 10 from Roger L. Ransom and Richard Sutch, *One Kind of Freedom: The Economic Consequences of Emancipation* (Cambridge, London and New York: Cambridge University Press, 1977), pp. 5; 85; 183; 184; 227–228; 30; 29; and 28, respectively.

1. Comparison of Per Capita Output and Material Income Measures, Slaves on Large Plantations in 1859 with Black Sharecroppers in 1879.

	Plantations with 51 or More Slaves, 1859	Black-Operated Sharecropped Family Farms, 1879	Percentage Change, 1859–1879
Expressed in 1859–1860 dollars per capita			
Total output	147.93	74.03	− 50.0
Product of labor	78.78	41.39	− 47.5
Material income	32.12	41.39	28.9

2. Population and Land Ownership in Georgia, by Race: 1870–1880.

	White				Black			
Year	Population	Acres Owned	Percentage of Total	Acres Per Person	Population	Acres Owned	Percentage of Total	Acres Per Person
1870	638,926				545,142			
1874		34,196,870	99.0			338,769	1.0	
1876		35,313,351	98.7			457,635	1.3	
1880	816,906	36,792,243	98.4	45.04	725,133	586,664	1.6	0.81

3. Value of Assets Held in Rural Counties of Georgia, by Race: 1876.

	Whites		Blacks	
Asset Class	Value (Thousands of Dollars)	Percentage of All Assets Held	Value (Thousands of Dollars)	Percentage of All Assets Held
Land	$ 84,613	50.1	$ 922	21.6
City and town property	15,906	9.4	441	10.4
Money and liquid assets	21,335	12.6	84	2.0
Kitchen and household furniture	8,279	4.9	450	10.6
Horses, mules, hogs, etc.	21,086	12.5	238	5.6
Plantation and mechanical tools	2,337	1.4	121	2.8
All other property	15,314	9.1	2,003	47.0
Aggregate taxable wealth	$168,870	100.0	$4,259	100.0

CHAPTER 2

WASHINGTON
AND DUBOIS:
AFRICAN
AMERICAN
ALTERNATIVES
IN THE NEW
SOUTH

4. Inputs of Capital on Farms, by Race and Tenure, Cotton South: 1880.

Type of Farm	Average Value of Farm Implements Per Acre Reported in Crops ($)		Number of Untilled Acres Per Tilled Acre	
	White	Black	White	Black
Small family farms	$1.80	0.79	$2.72	0.63
Owned	2.25	1.28	4.01	2.02
Tenanted	0.90	0.66	0.88	0.37
Rented	0.80	0.64	1.65	0.42
Sharecropped	0.93	0.67	0.69	0.34
Medium-scale farms	1.08	0.69	3.92	1.40
Owned	1.15	0.67	4.43	1.58
Tenanted	0.83	0.71	2.23	1.31
Large farms	1.04		2.23	

5. Number of Acres of Cropland Per Worker on Family Farms, by Race and Tenure, Cotton South: 1880.

Form of Tenure	Acres of Crops Per Worker	
	White	Black
Owner-operated farms	12.5	6.6
Rented farms	14.5	7.3
Sharecropped farms	11.7	8.0
All farms	12.4	7.5

6. Value of Output Per Worker and Value of Output Per Family Member on Small Family Farms, by Type of Farm, Tenure, and Race of Farm Operator, Cotton South: 1880.

Type of Farm	Value of Output Per Worker ($)		Value of Output Per Family Member ($)	
	White	Black	White	Black
Small family farms	$255.74	$159.62	$81.35	$63.57
Owned	283.70	155.78	88.12	58.11
Tenanted	212.47	160.40	70.87	64.67
Rented	260.19	159.51	88.02	67.63
Sharecropped	200.69	160.81	66.64	63.30

7. Distribution of Male and Female Workers, Ten Years and Older, by Occupation, Five Cotton States: 1890.

Occupation	Males		Females	
	% Black	% Native White	% Black	% Native White
Agriculture	73.6	70.3	62.2	51.4
Laborer	41.9	22.1	56.3	30.7
Farm operator	31.7	48.2	5.9	20.7
Nonagriculture	26.4	29.7	37.8	48.6
Low-skilled	19.2	8.4	34.8	23.0
High-skilled	7.3	21.3	3.0	25.6
Total	100.0	100.0	100.0	100.0
Number gainfully occupied	985,280	801,369	515,894	120,750

8. Percentage of Persons Unable to Write, by Race and Age Group, Five Cotton States: 1870, 1880, 1890.

Age and Race	1870	1880	1890
10–14 years			
Black	78.9%	74.1%	49.2%
White	33.2	34.5	18.7
15–20 years			
Black	85.3	73.0	54.1
White	24.2	21.0	14.3
Over 20 years			
Black	90.4	82.3	75.5
White	19.8	17.9	17.1

CHAPTER 2

WASHINGTON
AND DUBOIS:
AFRICAN
AMERICAN
ALTERNATIVES
IN THE NEW
SOUTH

9. Public Schools by Race of Students and Number of Children Five to Seventeen Years Old in Alabama, Georgia, and Mississippi: 1871, 1873.

	Whites			Blacks		
State, Year	Number of Public Schools	Number of Children Aged 5–17	Number of Children Per School	Number of Public Schools	Number of Children Aged 5–17	Number of Children Per School
Alabama, 1871	2,399	184,441	76.9	922	165,601	179.6
Mississippi, 1871	1,742	131,570	75.5	860	156,424	181.9
Georgia, 1873	1,392	228,866	164.4	360	207,167	575.5

10. Public School Enrollment of Blacks in Four Cotton States: 1871–1880.

State, Year	Number of Students	Enrollment as Percentage of School-Age Population	Enrollment as Percentage of Black Population 5–17
South Carolina			
1871	33,834	27.0	23.2
1875	63,415	41.6	36.9
1880	72,853	43.4	34.5
Georgia			
1873	19,755	13.2	9.5
1874	42,374	24.2	19.8
1880	86,399	37.4	33.7
Alabama			
1871	54,336	33.7	32.8
1875	54,595	31.6	29.6
1880	72,007	42.3	34.1
Mississippi			
1871	45,429	n.a.	29.0
1875	89,813	50.8	48.2
1880	123,710	49.2	53.3

Source 11 from A. F. Raper, *The Tragedy of Lynching* (Chapel Hill: University of North Carolina Press, 1933), p. 481.

11. Lynchings of African Americans, 1889–1900.

Year	Number Lynched	Year	Number Lynched
1889	95	1895	112
1890	90	1896	80
1891	121	1897	122
1892	155	1898	102
1893	155	1899	84
1894	134	1900	107

Source 12 from Louis R. Harlan, ed., *The Booker T. Washington Papers* (Urbana: University of Illinois Press, 1974), Vol. 3, pp. 583–587.

12. The Standard Printed Version of Booker T. Washington's Atlanta Exposition Address.

[Atlanta, Ga., Sept. 18, 1895]

Mr. President and Gentlemen of the Board of Directors and Citizens:

One-third of the population of the South is of the Negro race. No enterprise seeking the material, civil, or moral welfare of this section can disregard this element of our population and reach the highest success. I but convey to you, Mr. President and Directors, the sentiment of the masses of my race when I say that in no way have the value and manhood of the American Negro been more fittingly and generously recognized than by the managers of this magnificent Exposition at every stage of its progress. It is a recognition that will do more to cement the friendship of the two races than any occurrence since the dawn of our freedom.

Not only this, but the opportunity here afforded will awaken among us a new era of industrial progress. Ignorant and inexperienced, it is not strange that in the first years of our new life we began at the top instead of at the bottom; that a seat in Congress or the state legislature was more sought than real estate or industrial skill; that the political convention or stump speaking had more attractions than starting a dairy farm or truck garden.

A ship lost at sea for many days suddenly sighted a friendly vessel. From the mast of the unfortunate vessel was seen a signal, "Water, water; we die

CHAPTER 2

WASHINGTON
AND DUBOIS:
AFRICAN
AMERICAN
ALTERNATIVES
IN THE NEW
SOUTH

of thirst!" The answer from the friendly vessel at once came back, "Cast down your bucket where you are." A second time the signal, "Water, water; send us water!" ran up from the distressed vessel, and was answered, "Cast down your bucket where you are." And a third and fourth signal for water was answered, "Cast down your bucket where you are." The captain of the distressed vessel, at last heeding the injunction, cast down his bucket, and it came up full of fresh, sparkling water from the mouth of the Amazon River. To those of my race who depend on bettering their condition in a foreign land or who underestimate the importance of cultivating friendly relations with the Southern white man, who is their next-door neighbour, I would say: "Cast down your bucket where you are"—cast it down in making friends in every manly way of the people of all races by whom we are surrounded.

Cast it down in agriculture, mechanics, in commerce, in domestic service, and in the professions. And in this connection it is well to bear in mind that whatever other sins the South may be called to bear, when it comes to business, pure and simple, it is in the South that the Negro is given a man's chance in the commercial world, and in nothing is this Exposition more eloquent than in emphasizing this chance. Our greatest danger is that in the great leap from slavery to freedom we may overlook the fact that the masses of us are to live by the productions of our hands, and fail to keep in mind that we shall prosper in proportion as we learn to dignify and glorify common labour, and put brains and skill into the common occupations of life; shall prosper in proportion as we learn to draw the line between the superficial and the substantial, the ornamental gewgaws of life and the useful. No race can prosper till it learns that there is as much dignity in tilling a field as in writing a poem. It is at the bottom of life we must begin, and not at the top. Nor should we permit our grievances to overshadow our opportunities.

To those of the white race who look to the incoming of those of foreign birth and strange tongue and habits for the prosperity of the South, were I permitted I would repeat what I say to my own race, "Cast down your bucket where you are." Cast it down among the eight millions of Negroes whose habits you know, whose fidelity and love you have tested in days when to have proved treacherous meant the ruin of your firesides. Cast down your bucket among these people who have, without strikes and labour wars, tilled your fields, cleared your forests, builded your railroads and cities, and brought forth treasures from the bowels of the earth, and helped make possible this magnificent representation of the progress of the South. Casting down your bucket among my people, helping and encouraging them as you are doing on these grounds, and to education of head, hand, and heart, you will find that they will buy your surplus land, make blossom the waste places in your fields, and run your factories. While doing this, you can be sure in the future, as in the past, that you and your families will be surrounded by the most patient, faithful, law-abiding, and unresentful people that the world has seen. As we have proved our loyalty to you in the past, in nursing your children, watching by the sick-bed of your mothers and fathers, and often following them with tear-dimmed eyes to their graves, so in the future, in our humble way, we shall stand by you with a devotion that no foreigner can approach, ready to lay down our lives, if need be, in defense of yours, interlacing our industrial, commercial, civil, and religious life with yours in a way that shall make the interests of both races one. In all things that are purely social we can be as separate as the fingers, yet one as the hand in all things essential to mutual progress.

There is no defense or security for any of us except in the highest intelligence and development of all. If anywhere there are efforts tending to curtail the fullest growth of the Negro, let these efforts be turned into stimulating, encouraging, and making him the most useful and intelligent citizen. Effort or means so invested will pay a thousand per cent interest. These efforts will be twice blessed—"blessing him that gives and him that takes."

There is no escape through law of man or God from the inevitable:—

"The laws of changeless justice bind
   Oppressor with oppressed;
And close as sin and suffering joined
   We march to fate abreast."

Nearly sixteen millions of hands will aid you in pulling the load upward, or they will pull against you the load downward. We shall constitute one-third and more of the ignorance and crime of the South, or one-third [of] its intelligence and progress; we shall contribute one-third to the business and industrial prosperity of the South, or we shall prove a veritable body of death, stagnating, depressing, retarding every effort to advance the body politic.

Gentlemen of the Exposition, as we present to you our humble effort at an exhibition of our progress, you must not expect overmuch. Starting thirty years ago with ownership here and there in a few quilts and pumpkins and chickens (gathered from miscellaneous sources), remember the path that has led from these to the inventions and production of agricultural implements, buggies, steam-engines, newspapers, books, statuary, carving, paintings, the management of drug stores and banks, has not been trodden without contact with thorns and thistles. While we take pride in what we exhibit

CHAPTER 2

WASHINGTON
AND DUBOIS:
AFRICAN
AMERICAN
ALTERNATIVES
IN THE NEW
SOUTH

as a result of our independent efforts, we do not for a moment forget that our part in this exhibition would fall far short of your expectations but for the constant help that has come to our educational life, not only from the Southern states, but especially from Northern philanthropists, who have made their gifts a constant stream of blessing and encouragement.

The wisest among my race understand that the agitation of questions of social equality is the extremest folly, and that progress in the enjoyment of all the privileges that will come to us must be the result of severe and constant struggle rather than of artificial forcing. No race that has anything to contribute to the markets of the world is long in any degree ostracized. It is important and right that all privileges of the law be ours, but it is vastly more important that we be prepared for the exercise of these privileges. The opportunity to earn a dollar in a factory just now is worth infinitely more than the opportunity to spend a dollar in an opera-house.

In conclusion, may I repeat that nothing in thirty years has given us more hope and encouragement, and drawn us so near to you of the white race, as this opportunity offered by the Exposition; and here bending, as it were, over the altar that represents the results of the struggles of your race and mine, both starting practically empty-handed three decades ago, I pledge that in your effort to work out the great and intricate problem which God has laid at the doors of the South, you shall have at all times the patient, sympathetic help of my race; only let this be constantly in mind, that, while from representations in these buildings of the product of field, of forest, of mine, of factory, letters, and art, much good will come, yet far above and beyond material benefits will be that higher good, that, let us pray God, will come, in a blotting out of sectional differences and racial animosities and suspicions in a determination to administer absolute justice, in a willing obedience among all classes to the mandates of law. This, coupled with our material prosperity, will bring into our beloved South a new heaven and a new earth.

Source 13 from Virginia Hamilton, ed., *The Writings of W. E. B. DuBois* (New York: Thomas Y. Crowell Co., 1975), pp. 64–69.

13. DuBois's Niagara Address, 1906.

The men of the Niagara Movement coming from the toil of the year's hard work and pausing a moment from the earning of their daily bread turn toward the nation and again ask in the name of ten million the privilege of a hearing. In the past year the work of the Negro hater has flourished in the land. Step by step the defenders of the rights of American citizens have retreated. The work of stealing the black man's ballot has progressed and the fifty and more representatives of stolen votes still sit in the nation's capital. Discrimination in travel and public accommodation has so spread that some of our weaker brethren are actually afraid to thunder against color discrimination as such and are simply whispering for ordinary decencies.

Against this the Niagara Movement eternally protests. We will not be satisfied to take one jot or tittle less than our full manhood rights. We claim for ourselves every single right that belongs to a freeborn American, political, civil and social; and until we get these rights we will never cease to protest and assail the ears of America. The battle we wage is not for ourselves alone but for all true Americans. It is a fight for ideals, lest this, our common fatherland, false to its founding, become in truth the land of the thief and the home of the Slave—a by-word and a hissing among the nations for its sounding pretensions and pitiful accomplishments.

Never before in the modern age has a great and civilized folk threatened to adopt so cowardly a creed in the treatment of its fellow-citizens born and bred on its soil. Stripped of verbiage and subterfuge and in its naked nastiness the new American creed says: Fear to let black men even try to rise lest they become the equals of the white. And this is the land that professes to follow Jesus Christ. The blasphemy of such a course is only matched by its cowardice.

In detail our demands are clear and unequivocal. First, we would vote; with the right to vote goes everything: Freedom, manhood, the honor of your wives, the chastity of your daughters, the right to work, and the chance to rise, and let no man listen to those who deny this.

We want full manhood suffrage, and we want it now, henceforth and forever.

Second. We want discrimination in public accommodation to cease. Separation in railway and street cars, based simply on race and color, is un-American, undemocratic, and silly. We protest against all such discrimination.

Third. We claim the right of freemen to walk, talk, and be with them that wish to be with us. No man has a right to choose another man's friends, and to attempt to do so is an impudent interference with the most fundamental human privilege.

Fourth. We want the laws enforced against rich as well as poor; against Capitalist as well as Laborer; against white as well as black. We are not more lawless than the white race, we are more often arrested, convicted and

CHAPTER 2

WASHINGTON
AND DUBOIS:
AFRICAN
AMERICAN
ALTERNATIVES
IN THE NEW
SOUTH

mobbed. We want justice even for criminals and outlaws. We want the Constitution of the country enforced. We want Congress to take charge of Congressional elections. We want the Fourteenth Amendment carried out to the letter and every State disfranchised in Congress which attempts to disfranchise its rightful voters. We want the Fifteenth amendment enforced and no State allowed to base its franchise simply on color.

The failure of the Republican Party in Congress at the session just closed to redeem its pledge of 1904 with reference to suffrage conditions [in] the South seems a plain, deliberate, and premeditated breach of promise, and stamps that party as guilty of obtaining votes under false pretense.

Fifth. We want our children educated. The school system in the country districts of the South is a disgrace and in few towns and cities are the Negro schools what they ought to be. We want the national government to step in and wipe out illiteracy in the South. Either the United States will destroy ignorance or ignorance will destroy the United States.

And when we call for education we mean real education. We believe in work. We ourselves are workers, but work is not necessarily education. Education is the development of power and ideal. We want our children trained as intelligent human beings should be, and we will fight for all time against any proposal to educate black boys and girls simply as servants and underlings, or simply for the use of other people. They have a right to know, to think, to aspire.

These are some of the chief things which we want. How shall we get them? By voting where we may vote, by persistent, unceasing agitation, by hammering at the truth, by sacrifice and work.

We do not believe in violence, neither in the despised violence of the raid nor the lauded violence of the soldier, nor the barbarous violence of the mob, but we do believe in John Brown, in that incarnate spirit of justice, that hatred of a lie, that willingness to sacrifice money, reputation, and life itself on the altar of right. And here on the scene of John Brown's martyrdom we reconsecrate ourselves, our honor, our property to the final emancipation of the race which John Brown died to make free.

Our enemies, triumphant for the present, are fighting the stars in their courses. Justice and humanity must prevail. We live to tell these dark brothers of ours—scattered in counsel, wavering and weak—that no bribe of money or notoriety, no promise of wealth or fame, is worth the surrender of a people's manhood or the loss of a man's self-respect. We refuse to surrender the leadership of this race to cowards and trucklers. We are men; we will be treated as men. On this rock we have planted our banners. We will never give up, though the trump of doom find us still fighting.

And we shall win. The past promised it, the present foretells it. Thank God for John Brown! Thank God for Garrison and Douglass! Sumner and Phillips, Nat Turner and Robert Gould Shaw,[4] and all the hallowed dead who died for freedom! Thank God for all those today, few though their voices be, who have not forgotten the divine brotherhood of all men, white and black, rich and poor, fortunate and unfortunate.

We appeal to the young men and women of this nation, to those whose nostrils are not yet befouled by greed and snobbery and racial narrowness: Stand up for the right, prove yourselves worthy of your heritage and whether born north or south dare to treat men as men. Cannot the nation that has absorbed ten million foreigners into its political life without catastrophe absorb ten million Negro Americans into that same political life at less cost than their unjust and illegal exclusion will involve?

Courage, brothers! The battle for humanity is not lost or losing. All across the skies sit signs of promise. The Slav is rising in his might, the yellow millions are tasting liberty, the black Africans are writhing toward the light, and everywhere the laborer, with ballot in his hand, is voting open the gates of Opportunity and Peace. The morning breaks over blood-stained hills. We must not falter, we may not shrink. Above are the everlasting stars.

4. Robert Gould Shaw was a Massachusetts white man who during the Civil War commanded African American troops. While leading those soldiers into battle, Shaw was killed on July 18, 1863.

CHAPTER 2

WASHINGTON
AND DUBOIS:
AFRICAN
AMERICAN
ALTERNATIVES
IN THE NEW
SOUTH

Source 14 from Bureau of the Census, *Historical Statistics of the United States, Colonial Times to 1970* (Washington, D.C.: Government Printing Office, 1975), Vol. 1, p. 95.

14. Estimated Net Intercensal Migration* of Negro Population by Regions 1870–1920 (by Thousands).

	1910–1920	1900–1910	1890–1900	1880–1890	1870–1880
New England[1]	12.0	8.0	14.2	6.6	4.5
Middle Atlantic[2]	170.1	87.2	90.7	39.1	19.2
East North Central[3]	200.4	45.6	39.4	16.4	20.8
West North Central[4]	43.7	10.2	23.5	7.9	15.7
South Atlantic[5]	−158.0	−111.9	−181.6	−72.5	−47.9
East South Central[6]	−246.3	−109.6	−43.3	−60.1	−56.2
West South Central[7]	−46.2	51.0	56.9	62.9	45.1

*A net intercensal migration represents the amount of migration that took place between United States censuses, which are taken every ten years. The net figure is computed by comparing in-migration with out-migration to a particular state. A minus figure means that out-migration from a state was greater than in-migration.
1. The following states are included in New England: Maine, New Hampshire, Vermont, Massachusetts, Rhode Island, and Connecticut.
2. The following states are included in Middle Atlantic: New York, New Jersey, and Pennsylvania.
3. The following states are included in East North Central: Ohio, Indiana, Illinois, Michigan, and Wisconsin.
4. The following states are included in West North Central: Minnesota, Iowa, Missouri, North Dakota, South Dakota, Nebraska, and Kansas.
5. The following states are included in South Atlantic: Delaware, Maryland, District of Columbia, Virginia, West Virginia, North Carolina, South Carolina, Georgia, and Florida.
6. The following states are included in East South Central: Kentucky, Tennessee, Alabama, and Mississippi.
7. The following states are included in West South Central: Arkansas, Louisiana, Oklahoma, and Texas.

QUESTIONS TO CONSIDER

Sources 1 through 11 provide you with some information about the economic and educational progress of southern African Americans roughly from emancipation to the turn of the century. How did these people fare with respect to the following factors:

1. Output on African American-operated sharecropper farms? How did this compare with output on large plantations?
2. Land ownership? At what rate was African American land ownership in Georgia increasing?
3. Value of assets owned in rural Georgia in 1876? Could you make another column to denote the percentage, in terms of value, of each asset class African Americans held? How would you go about doing this?
4. Value of farm implements and number of untilled acres, as compared to whites? Why is the number of *untilled* acres important?
5. Amount of crops per acre, as compared to whites?
6. Occupational distribution of male and female workers?
7. Illiteracy? What does this statistic really show?
8. Public schools and enrollment? What do these statistics really show?
9. Lynching of African Americans?

The statistics and other evidence show portions of the *reality* that former slaves faced; the two speeches represent the *reactions* to that reality. What was Washington's response to the reality confronting the former slaves? How did he propose to rectify the problems he saw? How did he support his argument? What did Washington conceive the role of southern whites in African Americans' progress to be?

Before you consider DuBois's speech, think a moment. Be willing to use some inference. How would southern whites have greeted Washington's speech? Southern blacks? What about northern blacks? Northern whites? To whom was Washington speaking?

Now move on to DuBois's speech. How does DuBois differ from Washington with respect to goals? Timing? Tactics? Tone? How does he support his arguments? To whom was DuBois speaking? Use inference again. How would each group named above have greeted DuBois's address?

Next examine Source 14. What do the statistics show? How does migration change over time? Can you tell why such a change took place? What does this tell you about southern African Americans' reaction to the alternatives Washington and DuBois articulated?

It is now time to assess the various options open to southern African Americans in the late nineteenth and twentieth centuries. To determine which option was the better one, you will have to answer the following questions:

1. How do I define "better?" More realistic? More morally defensible? Better in the long range? Better in the short range?

CHAPTER 2

WASHINGTON
AND DUBOIS:
AFRICAN
AMERICAN
ALTERNATIVES
IN THE NEW
SOUTH

2. What would happen if southern African Americans adopted Washington's alternative? How long would it take for them to realize Washington's goals?

3. What would happen if southern African Americans adopted DuBois' alternative?

4. Would white assistance be necessary to Washington? To DuBois? How did each man perceive the roles of the federal government and the federal courts? How did the government and courts stand on this issue at the time? [*Clue:* What was the Supreme Court decision in *Plessy v. Ferguson* (1896)?]

No one living in the latter part of the twentieth century can assess with absolute objectivity which of the options available to African Americans in the South almost a century before was the better one. Nor is it possible to put ourselves completely in the shoes of these men and women. Yet a thorough examination of the positive points and liabilities of each option can give us a closer approximation of which alternative was the more attractive one. As you do this, do not neglect the statistical evidence or the material provided in the Background section of this chapter or in other material you read.

EPILOGUE

For the advocates of a New South, the realization of their dream seemed to be just over the next horizon, always just beyond their grasp. Many of the factories did make a good deal of money. But profits often flowed out of the South to northern investors. And factory owners often maintained profits by paying workers pitifully low wages, which led to the rise of a poor white urban class that lived in slums and faced enormous problems of malnutrition, poor health, family instability, and crime. To most of those who had left their meager farms to find opportunities in the burgeoning southern cities, life there appeared even worse than it had been in the rural areas. Many whites returned to their rural homesteads disappointed and dispirited by urban life.

For an increasing number of southern African Americans, the solution seemed to be to abandon the South entirely. Beginning around the time of World War I (1917–1918), a growing number of African Americans migrated to the industrial cities of the Northeast, Midwest, and West Coast. But there too they met racial hostility and racially inspired riots.

But at least in the North, African Americans could vote and thereby influence public policy. By the late 1940s, it became clear that northern urban African American voters, by their very number, could force American politicians to deal with racial discrimination. By the 1950s, it was evident that the South would have to change its racial policies, if not willingly then by force. It took federal courts, federal marshals, and occasionally federal troops, but the crust of discrimination in the South began to be broken in the 1960s. Attitudes changed slowly, but the white southern politician draped in the Confederate flag and calling for resistance to change became a figure of the past. Although much work still needed to be done, changes in the South had been profound, laying the groundwork for more changes ahead. Indeed, by the 1960s the industrialization and prosperity (largely through in-migration) of the Sunbelt seemed to show that Grady's dream of a New South might become a reality.

By this time, of course, both Washington and DuBois were dead. Washington had stubbornly clung to his notion of self-help, although he realized privately that whites could use him as an apologist for the status quo and a supporter of racial segregation. He died in Tuskegee, Alabama, in 1915. For his part, DuBois had grown more and more embittered, turning toward Marxism and Pan-Africanism when he believed "the system" had failed him and his people. He died in Africa in 1963.

Yet in their time both men were giants, important and respected figures. Although publicly at odds, they both privately dreamed of an America in which African Americans would enjoy the full rights of citizens. In an era in which few people would champion the causes of African American people, Washington and DuBois stood as heroic figures that time has only partially tarnished.

HOW THEY LIVED:
MIDDLE-CLASS LIFE, 1870–1917

In the 1870s, Heinrich Schliemann, a middle-aged German archaeologist, astonished the world with his claim that he had discovered the site of ancient Troy. As all educated people of the time knew, Troy was the golden city of heroes that the blind poet Homer (seventh century B.C.) made famous in his *Iliad* and *Odyssey*. Although archaeologists continued to argue bitterly about whether it was really Troy or some other ancient city that Schliemann was excavating, the general public was fascinated with the vases, gold and silver cups, necklaces, and earrings that were unearthed.

Not only the relics and "treasure" interested Americans, however. As the magazine *Nation* pointed out in 1875, these discoveries offered an opportunity to know about Troy as it had actually existed and to understand something about the daily lives of the inhabitants. Nineteenth-century Americans were intensely curious about the art, religion, burial customs, dress, and even the foods of the ancient Greeks. "Real Trojans," noted a magazine editor in 1881, "were very fond of oysters." (He based his conclusion on the large amounts of oyster shells uncovered at the archaeological digs.)

Material culture study is the use of artifacts to understand people's lives. In this exercise, you will be looking at some artifacts of the late nineteenth and early twentieth centuries—advertisements and house plans—to try to reconstruct the lives of middle-class white Americans during a period when the country was changing rapidly. What were Americans' hopes and fears during this era? What were their values?

BACKGROUND

The age from approximately 1870 to 1900 was characterized by enormous and profound changes in American life. Unquestionably the most important changes were the nation's rapid industrialization and urbanization. Aided and accelerated by the rapid growth of railroads, emerging industries could extend their tentacles throughout the nation, collecting raw materials and fuel for the factories and distributing finished products to the growing American population. By 1900, that industrial process had come to be dominated by a few energetic and shrewd men, captains of industry to their friends and robber barons to their enemies. Almost every conceivable industry, from steel and oil to sugar refining and meat packing, was controlled by one or two gigantic corporations that essentially had the power to set prices on the raw materials bought and the finished products sold. In turn, the successes of those corporations created a new class of fabulously rich industrialists, and names like Swift, Armour, Westinghouse, Pillsbury, Pullman, Rockefeller, Carnegie, and Duke literally became almost household words as much for the notoriety of the industrialists as for the industries and products they created.

As America became more industrialized, it also became more urban. In the past, the sizes of cities had been limited by the availability of nearby food, fuel, and employment opportunities. But the network of railroads and the rise of large factories had removed those limitations, and American cities grew phenomenally. Between 1860 and 1910, urban population increased sevenfold, and by 1920, more than half of all Americans lived in cities.[1] These urban complexes not only dominated the regions in which they were located but eventually set much of the tone for the entire nation as well.

Both processes—industrialization and urbanization—profoundly altered nearly every facet of American life. Family size began to decrease; the woman who might have had five or six children in 1860 was replaced by the "new" woman of 1900 who had only three or four children. The fruits of industrialization, distributed by new marketing techniques, could be enjoyed by a large portion of the American population. Electric lights, telephones, and eventually appliances virtually revolutionized the lives of the middle and upper classes, as did Ford's later mass production of the Model T automobile.

The nature of work was also changed because factories required a higher degree of regimentation than did farm work or the "putting out" system. Many industries found it more profitable to employ women and children than adult males, thus altering the

1. The census defined *city* as a place with a population over 2,500 people. Thus, many of the cities referred to in this exercise are what we would call towns, or even small towns.

home lives of many of the nation's lower-middle and lower-class citizens. Moreover, the lure of employment brought millions of immigrants to the United States, most of whom huddled together in cities, found low-paying jobs, and dreamed of the future. And as the cities grew grimy with factory soot and became increasingly populated by laborers, immigrants, and what one observer referred to as the "dangerous classes," upper- and middle-class Americans began to abandon the urban cores and retreat to fashionable suburbs on the peripheries, to return to the cities either in their automobiles or on streetcars only for work or recreation.

Industrialization and urbanization not only changed how most Americans lived but how they *thought* as well. Faith in progress and technology was almost boundless, and many felt that America was about to enter a golden age of universal prosperity in which all problems could be solved by science and technology. The poor, especially the immigrant poor, were seen as biologically inferior, and most people believed that the industrial barons had reached their exalted positions less through shrewdness and ruthlessness than by virtue of their biological preeminence. It followed, then, that efforts to help the less fortunate through charity or government intervention were somehow tampering with both God's will and Darwinian evolution. In such a climate of opinion, the leaders of gigantic corporations became national heroes, superior in prestige to both preachers and presidents. Voices of dissent were often ignored or brushed aside, and evidence of the ex-

cesses of the industrial barons (as when steel magnate Henry Clay Frick imported a genuine throne from Europe so he could be comfortable while reading the *Saturday Evening Post*) were viewed as merely the just rewards for superiority and toil. Many young boys read the rags-to-riches tales of Horatio Alger, and girls learned to be "proper ladies" so that they would not embarrass their future husbands as they rose in society together.

Social critics and reformers of the time were appalled by the excesses of the "fabulously rich" and the misery of the "wretchedly poor." And yet a persistent belief in the opportunity to better oneself (or one's children's position) led many people to embrace a kind of optimistic attitude and to focus on the acquisition of material possessions. What we would call the middle class was also expanding rapidly. New consumer goods were pouring from factories, and the housing industry was booming. Middle-class families emulated the housing and furnishing styles of the more wealthy, and skilled blue-collar workers and their families aspired to own modest suburban homes on the streetcar line.

After 1900, widespread concern about the relationship of wages to the cost of maintaining a comfortable standard of living led to numerous studies of working-class families in various parts of the country. In 1909, economist Robert Coit Chapin estimated that a family of five needed an annual income of about $900 to live in a decent home or apartment in New York City. A follow-up study of Philadelphia in 1917 estimated that same standard of living at approximately $1,600. Yet the average annual pay of adult male wage workers during these years only ranged from $600 to $1,700. There are several other factors that affected family income, however. Average wages are misleading, since skilled workers earned significantly more than unskilled or semiskilled workers. Even within the same industry and occupation, midwestern workers earned more than northeastern workers, and southern workers earned the lowest wages of all. Adult women workers, 80 percent of whom lived with families as wives or unmarried daughters, added their wages (approximately $300 to $600 a year) to the family income, as did working children. Many families, especially those of recent immigrants, also took in boarders and lodgers who paid rent.

Finally, the cost of land and building materials was much more expensive in large cities than in smaller cities and towns. In his investigation of New York, Chapin found that 28 percent of working-class families in nine upstate cities owned their own homes, compared with only 1 percent in New York City. Another study in 1915 also sharply illustrated regional differences in home ownership. Twenty percent of Patterson, New Jersey, silk workers were homeowners, but only 10 percent of Birmingham, Alabama, steelworkers. Nineteen percent of Milwaukee's working-class families owned their own homes, compared to 4.4 percent of Boston's working-class families. Nor were all these homes in the central city. Working-class suburbs expanded along streetcar lines or were developed near industries on the fringes of a city, such as the suburb of Oakwood just outside Knoxville, Tennessee.[2] In this community near textile mills and a major railroad repair shop, house lots measuring 50 × 140 feet sold for less than $100; most homes were built for under $1000. Nearly half of the one thousand families who moved to Oakwood between 1902 and 1917 came from the older industrial sections of Knoxville.

Completely reliable income and cost statistics for early twentieth-century America do not exist, but it seems reasonable to estimate that at least one-fourth of working class families owned or were paying for homes and that many more aspired to home ownership. But fully half of all working-class families, usually concentrated in large cities, lived in or near poverty and could not hope to own their own homes. Those with middle-class white-collar occupations were more fortunate. Lawyers, doctors, businessmen, ministers, bank tellers, newspaper editors, and even school teachers could— through careful budgeting and savings—realistically expect to buy or build a house.

Although technological advances and new distribution methods put many modern conveniences and new products within the reach of all but the poorest Americans, the economic growth of the period was neither constant nor steady. The repercussions from two major depressions—one in 1873 and one in 1894—made "getting

2. Knoxville's population in 1900 was 32,637; the city had experienced a 237 percent growth in population from 1880 to 1900.

ahead" difficult if not impossible for many lower middle-class and blue-collar families. Furthermore, at times everything seemed to be changing so rapidly that many people felt insecure. Yet within middle-class families this sense of insecurity and even fear often coexisted with optimism and a faith in progress.

One way to understand the lives of middle-class Americans during the post–Civil War era is to look at the *things* with which they surrounded themselves—their clothes, the goods and services they bought, and even their houses. Why did such fashions and designs appeal to Americans of the late nineteenth and early twentieth centuries? What kind of an impression were these people trying to make on other people? How did they really feel about themselves? Sometimes historians, like archaeologists, use artifacts such as clothes, furniture, houses, and so forth to reconstruct the lives of Americans in earlier times. Indeed, each year many thousands of tourists visit historic homes such as Jefferson's Monticello, retrace the fighting at Gettysburg, or stroll through entire restored communities such as Colonial Williamsburg. But historians of the post–Civil War period may also use advertisements (instead of the products or services themselves) and house plans (instead of the actual houses) to understand how middle-class Americans lived and what their values and concerns were.

Every day Americans are surrounded, even bombarded, by advertising that tries to convince them to buy some product, use some service, or compare brand X with brand Y. Tele-vision, radio, billboards, magazines, and newspapers spread the message to potential consumers of a variety of necessary—and unnecessary—products. Underlying this barrage of advertisements is an appeal to a wide range of emotions—ambition, elitism, guilt, and anxiety—and a whole new "science" has arisen, called market research, that analyzes consumers' reactions and predicts future buying patterns.

Yet advertising is a relatively new phenomenon, one that began to develop after the Civil War and did not assume its modern form until the 1920s. P. T. Barnum, the promoter and impresario of mid-nineteenth-century entertainment, pointed the way with publicity gimmicks for his museum and circuses and, later, for the relatively unknown Swedish singer Jenny Lind (Barnum created such a demand for Lind's concert tickets that they sold for as much as $200 each). But at the time of the Civil War, most merchants still announced special sales of their goods in simple newspaper notices, and brand names were virtually unknown.

Businesses, both large and small, expanded enormously after the Civil War. Taking advantage of the country's greatly improved transportation and communications systems, daring business leaders established innovative ways to distribute products, such as the mail-order firm and the department store. Sears Roebuck & Co. was founded in 1893, and its "wish book," or catalogue, rapidly became popular reading for millions of people, especially those who lived in rural areas. Almost one thousand pages long, these catalogues offered a dazzling variety of consumer goods and were filled with testimonial letters from satisfied customers. Lewis Thomas from Jefferson County, Alabama, wrote in 1897,

> I received my saddle and I must say that I am so pleased and satisfied with my saddle, words cannot express my thanks for the benefit that I received from the pleasure and satisfaction given me. I know that I have a saddle that will by ordinary care last a lifetime, and all of my neighbors are pleased as well, and I am satisfied so well that you shall have more of my orders in the near future.

And from Granite, Colorado, Mrs. Laura Garrison wrote, "Received my suit all right, was much pleased with it, will recommend your house to my friends. . . ."

For those who lived in cities, the department store was yet another way to distribute consumer goods. The massive, impressively decorated buildings erected by department store owners were often described as consumer "cathedrals" or "palaces." In fact, no less a personage that President William Howard Taft dedicated the new Wanamaker's department store in Philadelphia in 1911. "We are here," Taft told the crowd, "to celebrate the completion of one of the most important instrumentalities in modern life for the promotion of comfort among the people."

Many of the products being manufactured in factories in the late nineteenth and early twentieth centuries represented items previously made at home. Tinned meats and biscuits, "store-bought" bread, ready-made clothing, and soap—all represented the impact of technology upon the functions of the homemaker. Other products were new versions of things already being used. For example, the bathtub was designed solely for washing one's body, as opposed to the large bucket or tub in which one collected rainwater, washed clothes, and, every so often, bathed. Still other products and gadgets (such as the phonograph and the automobile) were completely new, the result of a fertile period of inventiveness (1860 to 1890) that saw more than ten times more patents issued than were issued during the entire period up to 1860 (only 36,000 patents were issued prior to the Civil War, but 440,000 were granted during the next thirty years).

There was no question that American industry could produce new products and distribute them nationwide. But there *was* another problem: how could American industry overcome the traditional American ethic of thrift and create a demand for products that might not have even existed a few years earlier? It was this problem that the new field of advertising set out to solve.

America in 1865 was a country of widespread, if uneven, literacy and a vast variety of newspapers and magazines, all competing for readership. Businesses quickly learned that mass production demanded a national, even international, market, and money spent on national advertising in newspapers and magazines rose from $27 million in 1860 to more than $95 million in 1900. By 1929, the amount spent on advertising had climbed to more than $1 billion. Brand names and catchy slogans vied with one another to capture the consumer's interest. Consumers could choose from among many biscuit manufacturers, as the president of National Biscuit Company reported to his stockholders in 1901: "We do not pretend to sell our standard goods cheaper than other manufacturers of biscuits sell their goods. They always undersell us. Why do they not take away our business?" His answer was fourfold: efficiency, quality goods, innovative packaging, and advertising. "The trademarks we adopted," he concluded, "their value we created."

Advertising not only helped differentiate one brand of a product from another, it also helped break down regional differences as well as differences between rural and urban lifestyles. Women living on farms in Kansas could order the latest "New York-style frocks" from a mail-order catalogue, and people in small towns in the Midwest or rural areas in the South could find the newest furniture styles, appliances, and automobiles enticingly displayed in mass-circulation magazines. In this era, more and more people abandoned the old ways of doing things and embraced the new ways of life that resulted from the application of modern technology, mass production, and efficient distribution of products. Thus, some historians have argued that advertising accelerated the transition of American society from one that emphasized production to one that stressed consumption.

The collective mentality, ideas, mood, and values of the rapidly changing society were reflected in nearly everything the society created, including its architecture. During the period from approximately 1865 to 1900, American architects designed public buildings, factories, banks, apartment houses, offices, and residential structures, aided by technological advances that allowed them to do things that had been impossible in the past. For instance, as American cities grew in size and population density, the value of real estate soared. Therefore it made sense to design higher and higher buildings, taking advantage of every square foot of available land. The perfection of central heating systems; the inventions of the radiator (1874), the elevator (1850s), and the flush toilet; and the use of steel framing (1880s) allowed architects such as William LeBaron Jenney, Louis Sullivan, and others of the Chicago school of architecture to erect the modern skyscraper, a combined triumph of architecture, engineering, ingenuity, and construction.

At the same time, the new industrial elite were hiring these same architects to build their new homes—homes that often resembled huge Italian villas, French chateaux, and even Renaissance palaces. Only the wealthy, however, could afford homes individually designed by professional architects. Most people relied on contractors, builders, and carpenters who adapted drawings from books or magazines to suit their clients' needs and tastes. Such "pattern books," published by men like Henry Holly, the Palliser brothers, Robert Shoppell, and the Radford Architectural Company, were extremely popular. It is estimated that in the mid-1870s, at least one hundred homes a year were being built from plans published in one women's magazine, *Godey's Lady's Book,* and thousands of others were built from pamphlets provided by lumber and plumbing fixture companies and architectural pattern books. Eventually, a person could order a complete home through the mail; all parts of the prefabricated house were shipped by railroad for assembly by local workers on the owner's site. George Barber of Knoxville, Tennessee, the Aladdin Company of Bay City, Michigan, and even Sears Roebuck & Co. were all prospering in mail-order homes around the turn of the century.

From the historian's viewpoint, both advertising and architecture created a wealth of evidence that can be used to reconstruct our collective past. By looking at and reading advertisements, we can trace Americans' changing habits, interests, and tastes. And by analyzing the kinds of emotional appeals used in the advertisements, we can begin to understand the aspirations and goals as well as the fears and anxieties of the people who lived in the rapidly changing society of the late nineteenth and early twentieth centuries.

Unfortunately, most people, including professional historians, are not used to looking for values and ideas in architecture. Yet every day we pass by houses and other buildings that could tell us a good deal about how people lived in a particular time period as well as something about the values of the time. In this chapter you will be examining closely both advertisements and house plans to reconstruct partially how middle-class Americans of the late nineteenth and early twentieth centuries lived.

THE METHOD

No historian would suggest that the advertisements of preceding decades (or today's advertisements, for that matter) speak for themselves—that they tell you how people actually lived. Like almost all historical evidence, advertisements must be carefully analyzed for their message. Advertisements are intended to make people want to buy various products and services. They can be positive or negative. Positive advertisements show the benefits—direct or indirect, explicit or implicit—that would come from owning a product. Such advertisements depict an ideal. Negative or "scare" advertisements demonstrate the disastrous consequences of not owning the product. Some of the most effective advertisements combine both negative and positive approaches ("I was a lonely 360-pound woman before I discovered Dr. Quack's Appetite Suppressors—now I weigh 120 pounds and am engaged to be married!"). Advertisements also attempt to evoke an emotional response from potential consumers that will encourage the purchase of a particular product or service.

Very early advertisements tended to be primarily descriptive, simply picturing the product. Later advertisements often told a story with pictures and words. In looking at the advertisements in this chapter, first determine whether the approach used is positive, negative, or a combination of both factors. What were the expected consequences of using (or not using) the product? How did the advertisement try to sell the product or service? What emotional response(s) were expected?

The preceding evaluation is not too difficult, but in this exercise you must go even further with your analysis. You are trying to determine what each advertisement can tell you about earlier generations of Americans and the times in which they lived. Look at (and read) each advertisement carefully. Does it reveal anything about the values of the time period in which the advertisement appeared? About the roles of men and women? About attitudes concerning necessities and luxuries? About people's aspirations or fears?

House plans also must be analyzed if they are to tell us something about how people used to live. At one time or another, you have probably looked at a certain building and thought, "That is truly an ugly, awful looking building! Whatever possessed the lunatic who built it?" Yet when that building was designed and built, most likely it was seen as a truly beautiful structure and may have been widely praised by its occupants as well as by those who merely passed by. Why is this so? Why did an earlier generation believe the building was beautiful?

All of us are aware that standards for what is good art, good music, good literature, and good architecture change over time. What may be pleas-ing to the people of one era might be considered repugnant or even obscene by those of another time. But is this solely the result of changing fads, such as the sudden rises and declines in the popularities of movie and television stars, rock 'n' roll groups, or fashionable places to vacation?

The answer is partly yes, but only partly. Tastes do change, and fads such as the hula-hoop and the yo-yo come and inevitably go. However, we must still ask why a particular person or thing becomes popular or in vogue at a certain time. Do these changing tastes in art, music, literature, and architecture *mean* something? Can they tell us something about the people who embraced these various styles? More to the point, can they tell us something about the *values* of those who embraced them? Obviously they can.

In examining these middle-class homes, you should first look for common exterior and interior features. Then look at the interior rooms and their functions, comparing them with rooms in American homes today. You must also try to imagine what impression these houses conveyed to people in the late nineteenth and early twentieth centuries. Finally, you will be thinking about all the evidence—the advertisements and the house plans— as a whole. What is the relationship between the material culture (in this case, the advertisements and the house plans) and the values and concerns of late-nineteenth- and early-twentieth-century Americans?

Sources 1 through 3 from Sears Roebuck & Co. Catalogues, 1897 and 1902.

1. Children's Reefer Jackets (1897) and Children's Toys (1902).

SEARS ROEBUCK & CO. INC

85¢

$1.50

24171

24172

REEFER JACKETS FOR CHILDREN FROM 1 TO 5 YEARS OLD.

Do not forget to mention age and color desired when ordering.

Reefer Jackets for little toddlers, from one to four years, nobby, stylish little coats at little bits of prices. As usual S. R. & Co. will save you money on these goods.

DRESSED SAILOR DOLLS.

Sailor Girl Dolls.

No. 29R735 Sailor Girl Doll, bisque head, flowing hair, solid eyes, dressed to represent a girl in sailor costume. A very pretty doll. Length, 13 inches.
Price, each.................50c

Sailor Boy Dolls.

No. 29R739 Sailor Boy Doll, dressed to represent a boy in sailor costume, companion doll to sailor girl. Length, 13 inches.
Price, each.................50c

The Penny Saver.

No. 29R147 A perfect registering bank; no key, no combination. Each time a cent is dropped into the bank the bell rings and the register indicates. Opens automatically at each 50 cents. The total always in sight. They are attractive and interesting to children. The mechanism is made of steel, and will not break or get out of order. It is highly interesting to children, and for this reason will encourage them to save. Shipping weight, 5 pounds. Price, each........85c

[59]

2. Boys' Wash Suits and Girls' Wash Dresses (1902).

BOYS' WASH SUITS.

The extraordinary value we offer in Boys' Wash Suits can only be fully appreciated by those who order from this department. A trial order will surely convince you that we are able to furnish new, fresh, up to date, stylish and well made wash suits at much lower prices than similar value can be had from any other house.

NOTE.—Boys' wash suits can be had only in the sizes as mentioned after each description. Always state age of boy and if large or small of age.

Boy's Wash Crash Suit, 35 Cents.

Navy Blue and White Percale Wash Suit, 40 Cents.

38R2128
98c

38R2130
$1.39

38R2131
$1.48

GIRLS' WASH DRESSES.

AGES FROM 4 TO 14 YEARS.

WHEN ORDERING please state Age, Height, Weight and Number of Inches around Bust.

SCALE OF SIZES, SHOWING PROPORTION OF BUST AND LENGTH TO THE AGE OF CHILD

Age	4	6	8	10	12	14
Bust	24	27	28	29	30	31
Skirt length	18	20	22	24	26	28

No. 38R2126 GIRLS' DRESS. Some made of Madras and some made of ginghams in fancy stripes and plaids, round yokes, "V" shape yokes, some trimmed with braid, ruffles and embroidery. We show no illustration of this number on account of the differ-

3. Hip Pad and Bustle, 1902.

Parisienne Hip Pad and Bustle.

No. 18R4880 The Parisienne Hip Pad and Bustle, made of best tempered, black enameled, woven wire with hip pads of padded cloth. Perfect in shape, and light in weight. Very durable.

Price, each,..**40c**

If by mail, postage extra, each, 10 cents.

Source 4 from 1893 and 1886 Advertisements.

4. Corset (1893) and Bathing Suit (1886).

DOCTORS RECOMMEND REAST'S PATENT

INVIGORATOR CORSETS.

FOR LADIES, MAIDS, BOYS, GIRLS, AND CHILDREN.

Dr. M. O. B. NEVILLE, L.R.C.P., Edin. Medical Officer of Health, says, Nov. 1st, 1890:—

"From a scientific point or view, I am of opinion that your Corset is the only one that gives support without unduly compressing important organs. Its elasticity, in a great measure, prevents this. I am satisfied, by its support of back and shoulders, that it is a material help to expanding the chest."

"Mrs. WELDON'S FASHION JOURNAL," says July '90:—

"Undoubtedly supplies a long-felt want for ensuring an upright form and graceful carriage, COMBINES ELEGANCE of FORM WITH COMFORT. It renders a corset what it should be, comfort, and support to the wearer, strengthening the spine, expanding the chest, and giving necessary support without tight lacing or undue pressure."

PRICES.

Child's under 5 years, 3/4; Boys' and Girls' over 5 years, 4/6; Maids, 5/6; Ladies', 6/6, 8/6, 12/9, 18/6, 22/6, 63/-.

SOLD BY ALL DRAPERS, OR SEND P.O. TO
REAST, 15, CLAREMONT, HASTINGS, ENGLAND.
FOR LICENSE FOR MANUFACTURING, OR SALE OF AMERICAN PATENT APPLY AS ABOVE.

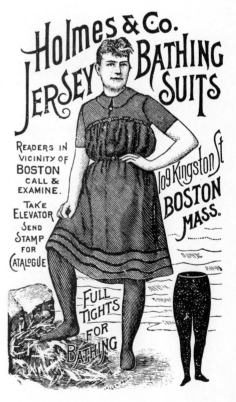

Holmes & Co. JERSEY BATHING SUITS

READERS IN VICINITY OF BOSTON CALL & EXAMINE. TAKE ELEVATOR SEND STAMP FOR CATALOGUE

109 Kingston St BOSTON MASS.

FULL TIGHTS FOR BATHING

Sources 5 and 6 from Sears Roebuck & Co. Catalogues, 1897 and 1902.

5. Ladies Coats (1902)

No. 17R149
$13.50

No. 17R152
$9.50

No. 17R151
$7.95

LADIES' LONG COATS
...OR AUTOMOBILES.

WHEN ORDERING, please state bust measure and length of sleeves, measured from under the arm to wrist, also the color you desire. Sizes are from 32 to 42 inches around bust. Shades or sizes different or larger than regular stock garment will be made to order at 20 per cent above the regular price quoted in catalogue and cash in full in advance. It takes about two weeks to make a special.

THESE GARMENTS ARE TOO HEAVY TO BE SENT BY MAIL.

No. 17R149 LADIES' AUTOMOBILE JACKET OR OVERCOAT. Made of all wool kersey, strictly tailor made; large collar and lapels made of South American beaver, otherwise called nutria; double breasted front trimmed with fancy buttons; side pockets stitched several times; bell sleeves; half tight fitting back; 36 inches long; facing in front made of same material; lined throughout with satin. Colors, black or castor. Price, each.............. **$13.50**

No. 17R151 LADIES' AUTOMOBILE OR OVERCOAT. Made 42 inches long, tailor made; large storm collar and lapels buttoning high at the neck; side pockets; several rows of stitching on collar, lapels, and cuffs; double breasted front; half tight fitting back; trimmed with kersey straps and fancy buttons; facing in front made of the same material; lined throughout with black mercerized sateen. Color, black only. Price, each........... **$7.95**

No. 17R152 LADIES' AUTOMOBILE OR OVERCOAT. Made of all wool kersey; storm collar, lapels buttoning at neck; silk stitching on collar, lapels and around the bottom as well as on the cuffs; double breasted front trimmed with fancy buttons; side pockets; half tight fitting back; facing in front made of same material; lined throughout with fine satin; watch pocket on inside. Made 42 inches long. Colors, black or tan. Price, each........ .... **$9.50**

6. Ladies' Toiletries, 1897.

Perfumes.

D 1027 Sears, Roebuck & Co.'s Perfume Extracts have given great satisfaction to everyone who has used them. They are sweet and lasting perfumes, put up in handsome packages. We import these perfume extracts in bulk from the flower gardens of France, and put them up ourselves in different sized bottles. By this method we can afford to give the choicest full strength perfume in a pretty bottle for a low price.

Lilac Blossoms.	Moss Rose.	Lily of the Valley.
Musk.	New Mown Hay.	Violet.
Indian Violet.	White Rose.	Wh'te Hellotrope.
Ylang Ylang.	English Violet.	Sweet Clover.
Jasamine.	Crab Apple.	Mignonette.
Sweet Pea.	Tea Rose.	Tuberose.
Wood Violet.	Shandon Bells.	Rose Geranium.
Carnation Pink.	Jockey Club.	Meadow Blossom.
Columbia Bouquet.		

Put up in glass stoppered bottles, 1 cz., each...**25c**
Put up in glass stoppered bottles, 2 oz., each...**48c**
Put up in glass stoppered bottles, 4 oz., each...**89c**
Put up in glass stoppered bottles, 8 oz., each.**$1.60**

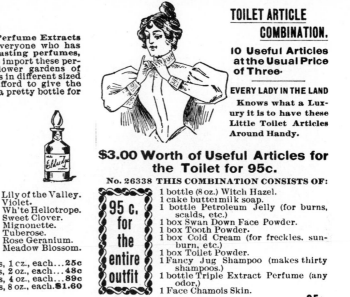

TOILET ARTICLE COMBINATION.

10 Useful Articles at the Usual Price of Three.

EVERY LADY IN THE LAND Knows what a Luxury it is to have these Little Toilet Articles Around Handy.

$3.00 Worth of Useful Articles for the Toilet for 95c.

No. 26338 THIS COMBINATION CONSISTS OF:

95 c. for the entire outfit

1 bottle (8 oz.) Witch Hazel.
1 cake buttermilk soap.
1 bottle Petroleum Jelly (for burns, scalds, etc.)
1 box Swan Down Face Powder.
1 box Tooth Powder.
1 box Cold Cream (for freckles. sunburn, etc.)
1 box Toilet Powder.
1 Fancy Jug Shampoo (makes thirty shampoos.)
1 bottle Triple Extract Perfume (any odor,)
1 Face Chamois Skin.

The Entire Outfit for .... **95c.**

Source 7 from an 1884 Advertisement.

7. Beauty Advice Book.

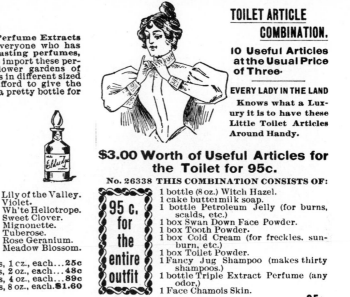

A SCRAP-BOOK FOR "HOMELY WOMEN" ONLY.

We dedicate this collection of toilet secrets, not to the pretty women (they have advantages enough, without being told how to double their beauty), but to the plainer sisterhood, to those who look in the glass and are not satisfied with what they see. To such we bring abundant help.

CONTENTS. Part 1--Part 2.

Practical devices for ugly ears, mouths, fingertips, crooked teeth. To reduce flesh, etc. How to bleach and refine a poor skin. Freckles, Pimples, Moles, etc. Mask of Diana of Poictiers. Out of 100 Cosmetics, which to choose. How to make and apply them for daylight, evening, and the stage (one saves two thirds, and has a better article by making instead of buying Cosmetics). What goes to constitute a belle. Madame Vestris's methods for private Theatricals. How to sit for a photograph successfully, and other toilet hints.

Send $1.00, 2 two-cent stamps, and an envelope addressed to yourself.

BROWN, SHERBROOK, & CO.,
27 Hollis Street, Boston, Mass.

Source 8 from a 1912 Advertisement.

8. Massage Cream for the Skin.

Sources 9 and 10 from Sears Roebuck & Co. Catalogues, 1897 and 1902.

THE EVIDENCE

9. Ladies' and Men's Hats.

LATEST DESIGNS IN STYLISH TRIMMED HATS.

AT 99 CENTS, $2.35, $3.25 AND UPWARDS.

WE SUBMIT ON THESE FOUR PAGES, the very newest effects in fashionable trimmed hats made especially for us from original designs, the same styles as will be shown by fashionable city milliners in large cities; styles that it will be impossible for you to secure in the stores in smaller towns, such goods as can be had only from the big millinery emporiums in metropolitan cities and there at two to three times our prices. These illustrations are made by artists direct from the hats, but it is impossible in a plain black and white drawing to give you a fair idea of the full beauty of these new hat creations. We ask you to read the descriptions carefully, note the illustrations and send us your order with the understanding that if the hat, when received, is not all and more than we claim for it, perfectly satisfactory, you are at liberty to return it to us at our expense and we will immediately return your money.

Wonderful Value.

99c

$1.95

No. 39R101 Is a black dress shape fancy straw, slightly raised on the left. Very tastefully trimmed in the front with six large muslin roses and shaded foliage. Trimmed high to the right is a large rosette consisting of silk finished pink mull in half wheel effect, same extending all around the crown and falling over the back and caught on bandeau with loops of the same material. A very stylish young or middle aged ladies' hat. Shape can be ordered only in black or white, trimmings in any color desired, but looks very handsome as described. Price, each....... ......99c

No. 39R107 This is a hand made fancy straw braid dress hat, drooping slightly to front and back. The wire frame is covered with an imported hand made straw braid, trimmed fully to the left with artistically designed rosettes draped in plume effect. The entire crown is covered with an imported tinted foliage and buds. The facing is neat drawn work of narrow folds of pink silk finished mull, and the bandeau is covered with nicely made loops of the same material. An exceedingly becoming and effectively designed hat. Can be ordered in all colors. Price, each.................. ....$1.95

...HAT DEPARTMENT...

DO NOT BE SATISFIED WITH ANY STYLE HAT when you can have at no additional expense a hat that will be becoming and at the same time stylish and in good form. Different sections of the country have their styles, due mainly to their difference in occupation and environment. If you live on a ranch and want the proper hat for such a life, we have it. If you wish the fashionable derby or stiff hat, we can supply this.

OUR LINE OF SOFT AND FEDORA SHAPES CANNOT BE EXCELLED.

VALUE. We can sell you a hat at almost any price, but by our manufacturer to the wearer plan we are able to sell to you at almost the same price your home merchant pays for the same quality. We want your order, because we can save you 25 to 40 per cent, and at the same time fill your order with NEW, CLEAN, UP TO DATE GOODS.

MEN'S DERBY OR STIFF HATS, $1.50.

No. 33R2010 Young Men's Stiff Hat, in fashionable shape. Is a very neat block, not extreme, but stylish. Crown, 4¾ inches; brim, 1¾ inches. Fine silk band and binding. Colors, black or brown. Sizes, 6¾ to 7½. Price, each.... $1.50 If by mail, postage extra, 34 cents. **A Fashionable Block in Men's Stiff Hats for $2.00.**

Men's Large or Full Shape Stiff Hats.

No. 33R2040 A style particularly suited to large men. A shapely, staple hat, as shown in illustration. Crown, 5¼ inches; brim, 2¼ inches. Fine silk band and binding. Sizes, 6¾ to 7⅝. Color, black only. Each..... $1.50 If by mail, postage extra, 34 cents.

Our Men's $2.25 Quality Full Shape Hat.
No. 33R2046 Men's Full Shape Hat, same style and dimensions as the above, in the high grade non-breakable stock, with very fine silk band and binding; imported leather sweatband. Color, black only. Sizes, 6¾ to 7¾. Price, each............. $2.25
If by mail, postage extra, 34 cents.

10. Men's Underwear.

MEN'S UNDERWEAR.

ASTONISHING TEMPTATIONS FOR ALL MANKIND.

QUALITIES THAT WILL SURPRISE YOU,

PRICES THAT WILL CONVINCE YOU.

MAKE A CHANGE, Off with the Old, on with the New. Prudence suggests it, your health demands it. Our prices protect you from over profit paying. We handle more Underwear and Hosiery than any one concern in the World. We save you nearly 50 per cent. on your purchases and give you better values than you could possible obtain anywhere else either wholesale or retail. Every garment we quote is guaranteed to be exactly as represented or money refunded. **EVERY PRICE WE QUOTE IS A REVELATION.**

OUR TERMS ARE LIBERAL. All goods sent C. O. D., subject to examination, on receipt of $1.00, balance and express charges payable at express office. **Three** per cent. Discount allowed if cash in full accompanies your order. **Nearly All Our Customers Send Cash in Full.**

Ventilated Health Underwear.

Summer Weight Balbriggan.

No. 2830 Men's Ventilated Natural Gray Mixed Summer Undershirts. The most comfortable as well as the most healthful balbriggan underwear ever made; fine gauge and soft finish; fancy collarette neck, pearl buttons and ribbed cuffs; ventilated all over with small drop stitch openings. Highly recommended by the best physicians as conducive to good health. Sizes 34 to 42 only. Price each..**$0.58**

MEN'S FANCY UNDERWEAR.
Men's Striped Balbriggan Underwear, 41 Cents.

No. 16R5078 Men's Fine Fancy Balbriggan Undershirts, knit from fine Egyptian cotton, made in a very narrow ½-inch alternating white and blue stripe. A very pretty garment that never fails to give satisfaction. Fast color. Trimmed with collarette neck and pearl buttons. Perfect fitting ribbed cuffs. Never retails for less than 50 to 65 cents. Stitched throughout with never-rip seams. Sizes, 34 to 44 breast measure.
Price, each......................**41c**

Source 11 from an 1893 Advertisement.

11. Shaving Soaps.

WILLIAMS' SHAVING SOAPS have enjoyed an unblemished reputation for excellence—for over HALF A HUNDRED YEARS—and are to-day the *only* shaving soaps—of absolute purity, with well-established claims for healing and antiseptic properties.

"CHEAP" and impure Shaving Soaps—are composed largely of refuse animal fats—abound in scrofulous and other disease germs—and if used —are almost sure to impregnate the pores of the skin—resulting in torturing cutaneous eruptions and other forms of blood-poisoning.

This view shows face—as shaved daily for years—with the famous WILLIAMS' Shaving Soap—always soft—fresh —bright and healthy. Not a sore or pimple in over 20 years of Shaving Experience.

This view shows the effect of being shaved ONCE with an impure—so-called "Cheap" Shaving Soap. Blood-poison— caused by applying impure animal fats to the tender cuticle of the face.

MR. CHAS. A. FOSTER,

34 SAVIN STREET,

BOSTON, MASS., writes:

"Never again will I allow a Barber to shave me unless I am *sure* he is using the only safe and reliable shaving soap made—namely **WILLIAMS'**. The other day—being in a hurry—I went into a shop near the Boston and Maine depot—to get a shave.

"I noticed a rank odor when the lather was put on my face, and asked the Barber if he used WILLIAMS' Shaving Soap. He said, 'No—I do not—because it costs a little more than other kinds.'

"A few days after this experience—my face was all broken out—terribly sore and smarting like fire.

"I consulted my Physician who told me it was a bad case of 'BARBER'S ITCH'—caused by the use of the Cheap Shaving Soap—containing diseased animal fats.

"I have suffered the worst kind of torture for two weeks—but I have learned a lesson."

Qu–?

Ask your Barber if *he* uses WILLIAMS'. Take no chances. Blood-poisoning—in some form or other is the almost sure result of using a cheaply made and impure Shaving Soap. While shaving—the pores of the Skin are open—and quickly drink in—any of the disease germs which may be contained in the diseased animal fats—so largely used in all "cheap"—inferior Toilet and Shaving Soaps. Ask for WILLIAMS'—and *insist* that you have it—and enjoy a feeling of SECURITY—as well as of comfort—while shaving or being shaved.

In providing for the safety and comfort of visitors—it has been officially ordered that

WILLIAMS' SHAVING SOAPS

shall be used EXCLUSIVELY—in all of the Barber Shops located on the Grounds of the World's Columbian Exposition. Thus AT THE VERY START—it receives the highest possible Honor.

 **WILLIAMS' "JERSEY CREAM" TOILET SOAP.**

Something new with us. The result of 50 years of costly and laborious experiment. Send for circular.

A most exquisite—healing and beautifying toilet soap. Containing the rich yellow cream of *our own herd* of imported Jersey Cattle. A full size cake mailed to any address for 25c. in stamps.

Do not fail to try it. Ask your Druggist—or send to us.—Address,

The J. B. Williams Co., Glastonbury, Conn., U. S. A.

"WILLIAMS' SOAPS have for a foundation—over half a hundred years of unblemished reputation."

Source 12 from a 1908 Advertisement.

12. Safety Razor.

"Shave Yourself"

"The man who shaves himself before breakfast in the morning has a pleasure which is never known by those whose faces are not familiar with the razor or for whom it is wielded by another.

"The operation creates a sense of cleanliness, opens one's eyes to things as they are, dissipates the cobwebs in the brain which accumulate during the night, and assists in establishing amicable relations with the world for the beginning of the day."

Well lathered, you can shave yourself with the "GILLETTE" in three to five minutes any and every morning in the year at a fraction of a cent per day. The blade of my Razor, the "GIL-LETTE," is the only new idea in Razor Blades for over 400 years. This double-edged, thin-as-a-wafer blade is held by the Gillette frame in a perfectly rigid manner (which avoids all possibility of vibration), thus ensuring a comfortable, safe and uniform shave — which conditions are not obtainable with any other make of razor.

With the "GILLETTE" a slight turn of the handle adjusts the blade (which is always in position) for a light or close shave with a soft or hard beard.

The "GILLETTE" holder triple silver plated will last you a lifetime, and when the blades become dull, throw away and buy —

10 Brand New Double-Edged "GILLETTE" Blades for 50c.

No blades re-sharpened or exchanged. The price of the "GILLETTE" set is $5.00 everywhere.

Sold by the leading Jewelry, Drug, Cutlery and Hardware Dealers.

Ask for the "GILLETTE" and booklet. Refuse all substitutes and write me to-day for special 30-day free trial order.

King C Gillette

Care of Gillette Sales Co.

279 Times Building, New York City.

Gillette Safety **Razor**
NO STROPPING. NO HONING.

Source 13 from a 1912 Advertisement.

13. Watch Chains.

ROBERT HILLIARD
The Famous Actor, now Appearing in New York
in "The Argyle Case," Wears a Waldemar

These are the watch chains now worn by men who set the styles

When a man buys a watch chain he chooses a *pattern* to suit his individual taste—but he wants a *style* which will always be in good taste.

A watch chain is the only piece of jewelry worn universally by men. It is the most prominent piece a man can wear. Every man with any regard for his personal appearance wants his watch chain right.

SIMMONS CHAINS
TRADE MARK

are always "correct" in style. That is one reason why first-class jewelers have handled them for forty years. A man in the smaller cities and towns can be just as sure as a New Yorker that he is getting the "proper thing" if he buys a *Simmons Chain*.

Waldemar and Dickens are the most popular styles this year. Lapels, vests and fobs are also in good taste. For women there are chatelaines, neck, eyeglass and guard chains and bracelets.

The beauty of design and finish and the satisfactory service of the *Simmons Chains*, have made them a standard among well-dressed men and women.

The surface of a *Simmons Chain* is not a wash or plate. It is a rolled tube of 12 or 14 karat *solid gold*, of sufficient thickness to withstand the wear of years.

If your jeweler hasn't *Simmons Chains* write us for Style Book—make your selection and we'll see that you are supplied.

DOUGLAS FAIRBANKS
The Popular Actor who Made a Great
New York Success in "Officer 666,"
Wearing a Dickens

R. F. Simmons Co.   (Established 1873)   177 N. Main St., Attleboro, Mass.
Look for SIMMONS stamped on each piece—your protection and guarantee for wear.

Source 14 from 1899 and 1916 Advertisements.

14. Smith & Wesson (1899) and Colt (1916) Revolvers.

Source 15 from an 1891 Advertisement.

15. One-Volume Book.

NONE ARE TOO BUSY TO READ

IN ONE VOLUME.

"The Best Fifty Books of the Greatest Authors."

CONDENSED FOR BUSY PEOPLE.

BENJAMIN R. DAVENPORT, EDITOR.

NO EXCUSE FOR IGNORANCE.

Born 1564.   William Shakespeare.   Died 1616.

THIS WORK of 771 pages covers the whole range of Literature from Homer's Iliad, B. C. 1200 to Gen. Lew. Wallace's Ben Hur, A. D. 1880, including a Brief Biographical Sketch and FINE FULL-PAGE PORTRAIT OF EACH AUTHOR. Every one of the Fifty Books being so thoroughly reviewed and epitomized, as to enable the READERS OF THIS VOLUME TO DISCUSS THEM FULLY, making use of Familiar Quotations properly, and knowing the connection in which they were originally used by their Great Authors.

THIS BOOK is made from material furnished by Homer, Shakespeare, Milton, Bunyan, Dickens, Stowe, Gen. Lew. Wallace. and the other great authors of thirty centuries.

BY IT A LITERARY EDUCATION MAY BE ACQUIRED WITHIN ONE WEEK, ALL FROM ONE VOLUME.

A BOOK FOR BUSY AMERICANS.

TIME SAVED. MONEY SAVED.

KNOWLEDGE IN A NUTSHELL.

NEW YORK WORLD, March 15th.—"The book is one destined to have a great sale, because it supplies, IN THE FULLEST SENSE, A LONG FELT LITERARY WANT."

Born 1783.   Washington Irving.   Died 1859.

Opinions expressed by practical, busy and successful self-made men, as to the great value and merit of Mr. Davenport's condensations:

Mr. PHILIP D. ARMOUR writes: "I am pleased to own 'Fifty Best Books.' It certainly should enable the busy American, at small expenditure of time, to gain a fairly comprehensive knowledge of the style and scope of the authors you have selected."

GEN. RUSSELL A. ALGER writes: "I have received the beautiful volume. It is surely a very desirable work."

GOV. JOSEPH E. BROWN, of Georgia, writes: "You have shown great power of condensation. This is eminently a practical age; men engaged in the struggle for bread have no time to enter much into details in literature. What the age wants is to get hold of the substance of a book. This work entitles you to be understood as a benefactor."

Born 1812.   Charles Dickens.   Died 1870.

BOSTON DAILY GLOBE, April 2, 1891.—"Men of the present generation have not time to wade through from 2,000 to 3,000 pages of any of literature's standard volumes, and as a result they do not undertake it at all, and are often placed in an embarrassing position."

BUFFALO EXPRESS, March 1st.—"The Best Fifty Books of the Greatest Authors. Condensed for Busy People," edited by Benjamin R. Davenport, deserves high praise. It not only gives busy people an introduction to literature, but takes them to its very sanctum sanctorum and bids them be at home. The editor has selected his best fifty books with the advice of the most eminent literary men in England and America. These masterpieces, from Homer's 'Iliad' to Lew. Wallace's 'Ben Hur,' he has condensed into one volume of 771 pages, working in all of the famous passages and supplying a narrative in good, straightforward, unpretentious English. The story of each book is accompanied with a brief biographical sketch and a portrait of each author. No matter how familiar one is with any of these fifty books, be it for instance, 'Don Quixote,' 'Rasselas,' 'Les Miserables,' 'Paradise Lost,' or any other, he will be forced to admit, after reading the dozen pages devoted to each one in this condensation, that there is little, if anything, to add, either with regard to plot, characters, scenes, situations, quotations, or anything else that is ever discussed by people. The result of days or weeks of reading will be the possession of hardly one single bit of information or one tangible idea concerning the book in hand that is not to be acquired by reading the dozen pages in this condensation within a half hour."

SOLD BY SUBSCRIPTION ONLY.   AGENTS WANTED EVERYWHERE.

CANVASSERS who desire to represent a book which sells rapidly and without argument should send for CIRCULARS. Books forwarded, postage paid, to any address upon receipt of price.

Fine English Muslin, Sprinkled Edges, $3 75.   Full Sheep, Library Style, Marbled Edges, $4.75.
Seal Russia, Gilt Edges, $6.75.

19th CENTURY BOOK CONCERN, 40 Exchange St., Buffalo, N. Y.
[1891]

Source 16 from a 1906 Advertisement.

16. Correspondence School.

What are You Worth
From The NECK UP?

It is estimated that the average man is worth $2.00 a day from the neck *down*—what is he worth from the neck *up?*

That depends entirely upon training. If you are trained so that you can plan and direct work you are worth ten times as much as the man who can work only under orders.

The **International Correspondence Schools** go to the man who is struggling along on small pay and say to him, "We will train you for promotion right where you are, or we will qualify you to take up a more congenial line of work at a much higher salary."

What the I. C. S. says it can do, it *will* do. It has already done it for others and will do it for *you,* if you only show the inclination.

Thousands of ambitious men, realizing this fact, have marked the I. C. S. coupon, and multiplied their wages many times. During March, 403 students voluntarily reported an increase in salary and position as the direct result of **I. C. S.** training.

In this day of demand for leaders, a young man ought to be ashamed to be satisfied with small wages when he has the I. C. S. ready to qualify him for a higher salary.

Mark the coupon at once and mail it. You need not leave your present work, or your own home, while the I. C. S. prepares you to advance.

Back your *trained hand* with a *trained head!* It pays big. This coupon is for you. *Will you use it?*

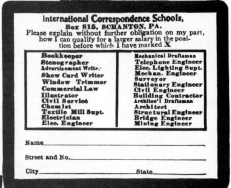

International Correspondence Schools,
Box 815, SCRANTON, PA.
Please explain without further obligation on my part,
how I can qualify for a larger salary in the position before which I have marked X

Bookkeeper	Mechanical Draftsman
Stenographer	Telephone Engineer
Advertisement Writer	Elec. Lighting Supt.
Show Card Writer	Mechan. Engineer
Window Trimmer	Surveyor
Commercial Law	Stationary Engineer
Illustrator	Civil Engineer
Civil Service	Building Contractor
Chemist	Architec'l Draftsman
Textile Mill Supt.	Architect
Electrician	Structural Engineer
Elec. Engineer	Bridge Engineer
	Mining Engineer

Name_____

Street and No._____

City_____ State_____

Source 17 from a 1906 Advertisement.

17. Typewriter.

A Course in Practical Salesmanship
Tuition FREE~All Expenses Paid

IN these times of keen business rivalry, the services of the Trained Salesman command a high premium.

The Oliver Sales Organization is the finest body of Trained Salesmen in the world. It is composed of picked men, and is under the guidance of Sales Experts.

In less than ten years it has placed the Oliver Typewriter where it belongs—in a position of absolute leadership.

Its aggregate earnings are enormous and the individual average is high.

The scope of its activities is as wide as civilization and the greatest prizes of the commercial world are open to its membership.

The organization is drilled like an army. It affords a liberal education in actual salesmanship, and increases individual earning power many per cent, by systematic development of natural talents.

Its ranks are recruited from every walk of life. Men who had missed their calling and made dismal failures in the over-crowded professions have been developed in the Oliver School of Practical Salesmanship into phenomenal successes.

The Oliver Typewriter puts the salesman in touch with the men worth knowing—the human dynamos who furnish the brain power of the commercial world.

Because every Business Executive is interested in the very things the Oliver stands for—economy of time and money—increase in efficiency of Correspondence and Accounting Departments.

The OLIVER Typewriter
The Standard Visible Writer

is simple in principle, compactly built, durable in construction, and its touch is beautifully elastic and most responsive.

In versatility, legibility, perfect alignment, visibility, etc., it is all that could be desired in a writing machine.

It's a constant source of inspiration to the salesman, as every day develops new evidence of its wide range of usefulness.

Just as the winning personality of a human being attracts and holds friends, so does the Oliver, by its responsiveness to all demands, gain and hold an ever-widening circle of enthusiastic admirers.

If you wish to learn actual salesmanship and become a member of the Oliver Organization, send in your application **immediately,** as the ranks are rapidly being filled.

You can take up this work in spare time, or give us your entire time, just as you prefer.

Whether you earn $300 a year, or **twelve times** $300 a year, depends entirely upon **yourself.**

We offer to properly qualified applicants the opportunity to earn handsome salaries and to gain a knowledge of salesmanship that will prove of inestimable value.

Can you afford to vegetate in a poorly-paid position, when the way is open to a successful business career?

Address at once.

THE OLIVER TYPEWRITER CO., 161 Wabash Ave., Chicago

WE WANT LOCAL AGENTS IN THE UNITED STATES AND CANADA.
PRINCIPAL FOREIGN OFFICE—75 QUEEN VICTORIA ST., LONDON.

Source 18 from a 1908 Advertisement.

18. Life Insurance.

Don't Depend on Your Relatives When You Get Old

If you let things go kind o' slip-shod *now*, you may later have to get out of the 'bus and set your carpet-bag on the stoop of some house where your arrival will hardly be attended by an ovation.

If you secure a membership in the Century Club this sad possibility will be nipped in the bud. It is very, very comfortable to be able to sit under a vine and fig-tree of your own.

The Club has metropolitan headquarters and a national membership of self-respecting women and men who are building little fortunes on the monthly plan. Those who have joined thus far are a happy lot—it would do your heart good to read their letters.

We would just as soon send our particulars to you as to anybody else, and there is no reason in the world why you shouldn't know all about everything. You'll be glad if you do and sorry if you don't.

Be kind to those relatives—*and to yourself*.

Address, stating without fail your occupation and the exact date of your birth,

Century Life-Insurance Club
Section O

5, 7 and 9 East 42d Street, New York

RICHARD WIGHTMAN, Secretary

Source 19 from 1881 and 1885 Advertisements.

19. Bicycles and Tricycles.

COLUMBIA BICYCLES

The Art of wheelmanship is a gentlemanly and fascinating one, once acquired never forgotten, which no young man should neglect to acquire.

The Bicycle is practical everywhere that a buggy is, and enables you to dispense with the horse and the care and cost of keeping him. It is destined to be the prevailing light, quick, ready conveyance in country towns.

The Youth take to bicycles like ducks to water. They ride it quickly, easily, safely and gracefully. They can get more pleasure out of it than out of a horse, a boat, and a tennis or cricket outfit all together.

Parents should favor bicycle riding by their boys, because it gives them so much enjoyment, makes them lithe and strong, keeps them from evil associations, and increases their knowledge and their self-reliance. There is no out-door game or amusement so safe and wholesome.

The above paragraphs are but fragmentary suggestions; ask those who have ridden; read "The American Bicycler" (50 cts.), the "Bicycling World" (7 cts. a copy), our illustrated catalogue (3-ct. stamp).

The Columbia bicycles are of elegant design, best construction, fine finish, and are warranted. They may be had with best ball-bearings, finest nickel plate, and other specialties of construction and finish, according to choice.

The Mustang is a less expensive, plain and serviceable style of bicycle made by us for boys and youths.

Physicians, clergymen, lawyers, business men of every class, are riding our Columbias in nearly every State and Territory to-day, with profit in pocket, with benefit in health, and with delightful recreation. The L.A.W. Meet at Boston brought 800 men together on bicycles; but the **boys,** who outnumber them, and who have their own clubs and associations in so many places, were at school and at home. Why don't every boy have a bicycle?

Send 3-cent stamp for our 24-page illustrated catalogue and price-list, with full information.

THE POPE M'F'G CO.,
598 Washington Street,
BOSTON MASS.

COLUMBIA BICYCLES.

FOR HEALTH—BUSINESS—PLEASURE.

"Having examined somewhat carefully the 'wheels' of England and France, I do not believe that a better roadster is made in the world than the 'Expert Columbia.'"—ALONZO WILLIAMS, Professor of Mathematics, Brown University, Providence, R. I.

"A contractor and builder in Pennsylvania writes: 'I am using my 'wheel' night and day to make business calls, and conveying hardware and other things. . . . I would not exchange my bicycle for the best horse in the country.'"—*The Wheelman.*

"From the practical results which I determined by subjecting the different qualities of steel from which it is constructed to the recognized standard of Government tests, I am free to assert that you may justly claim that the 'Columbia' *has not its equal in quality of material and finish*; all of which is shown in the tabulated results in your possession."—F. J. DRAKE, U. S. Inspector of Material.

"A LADY'S TESTIMONY.—A recent recruit from the fair sex, in bearing evidence as to the utility of the tri cycle, writes: 'My sister and myself have just returned from a tour, having ridden from Leeds to Woodbridge (Suffolk), and home again by Halstead and Walden (Essex), or a total of 470 miles whilst we have been away; and, as we have had such a successful time of it in every respect, we intend having another tour next year.'"—*The C. T. C. Gazette.*

EVERY BOY AND MAN SHOULD HAVE A

COLUMBIA BICYCLE.

"I want to lift my voice in favor of the 'wheel' as a thing of beauty, as an instrument of pleasure, and as one of the most practical of modern inventions, looking towards practical ends."—REV. GEO. F. PENTECOST.

"But the bicycle and tricycle are not only enjoyable modes of locomotion, they are also without a peer in their hygienic capacity."—DR. S. M. WOODBURN.

EVERY LADY SHOULD RIDE A

COLUMBIA TRICYCLE.

"I am of the opinion that no exercise for women has ever been discovered that is to them so really useful. Young and middle-aged ladies can learn to ride the tricycle with the greatest facility, and they become excellently skilful. The tricycle is, in fact, now with me a not uncommon prescription, and is far more useful than many a dry, formal, medicinal one which I had to write on paper."—B. W. RICHARDSON, M. D., F. R. S.

Illustrated Catalogue Sent Free.

THE POPE M'F'G CO., Principal Office, 597 Washington St., Boston, Mass.

[1885] BRANCH HOUSES: 12 Warren St., New York; 179 Michigan Ave., Chicago.

Source 20 from 1882 and 1896 Advertisements.

20. Photographic Supplies (1882) and Gramophone (1896).

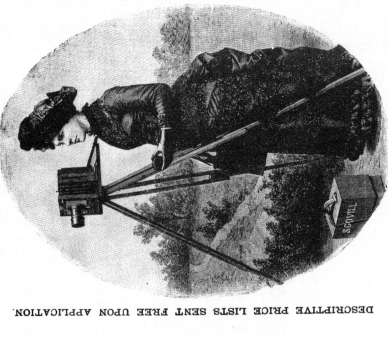

21. Ford Automobile and Electric Car for Women.

FORD RUNABOUT
"Built for Two"

Two's company and a crowd frequently spoils a motoring trip.

When you have a large car you feel like filling up the seats—seems stingy for two to usurp so much luxury; so your tonneau is always full. Everybody's happy but—

Did you ever feel as if you'd just like to go alone—you and she—and have a day all your own? Go where you please, return when you please, drive as fancy dictates, without having to consult the wishes or the whims of others?

Ford Runabouts are ideal for such trips. Just hold two comfortably; ride like a light buggy, control easily and you can jog along mile after mile and enjoy the scenery.

Of course you can scorch if you want to—40 miles an hour easily—but you won't want to. You'll get used to the soft purr of the motor and the gentle motion of the car over the rolling country roads and—well, it's the most luxurious sensation one can imagine.

"**We've enjoyed motoring** more since we've had the Ford Runabout than we ever did before," says one lady whose purse can afford anything she desires. "Got the big car yet, but 'two's company,' and most times that's the way we go."

$600,
F.O.B. Detroit

Model N. 4 Cyl. 15 H.P.

FORD MOTOR COMPANY,
25 Piquette Ave., - Detroit, Mich.

BRANCH RETAIL STORES—New York, Philadelphia, Boston, Chicago, Buffalo, Cleveland, Detroit and Kansas City. Standard Motor Co., San Francisco, Oakland and Los Angeles, distributors for California. Canadian trade supplied by Ford Motor Company of Canada, Walkerville, Ont.

The Automobile for Women

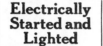

| Electrically Started and Lighted | Inter-State | Controls Itself Pumps Its Own Tires |

THE advent of the Inter-State, with its marvelously simple mechanism, its electrical self-starter and its self-controller has brought a revolution in motoring. Now the powerful and magnificent Inter-State starts and obeys the will of the woman driver as readily, as easily and as simply as an electric coupe. Without moving from the driver's seat or shifting gears she starts the engine by a turn of the switch — regulates the mixture by a simple movement of the lever on the steering column, and the magnificent Inter-State is under way

No labor to start the Inter-State

and under perfect and absolute control, with no more trouble than turning on an electric light. The Inter-State electric self-starter is **part of the system** and **built into it,** and the motor dynamo turns the engine itself until it picks up under its own power.

Electric Lights as in Your Own Home

ONE of the greatest features of the Inter-State is its electric light system—not a single light or two—but an entire and reliable system, front —side—rear, all correlated and so arranged that by a turn of the switch, without leaving the driver's seat, any or all of the lights may be turned on in all their brilliancy. No more gas tanks, no more oil filling, no more lamp trimming or adjusting. The system is simply perfect. The front head-lights are provided with a dimming feature so that driving in city streets may be done with a medium diffused light.

Any or all lights on by turning switch

Write Today for Art Catalog

This describes fully the six 40 and 50 H. P. completely equipped Models which cost from $2,400 to $3,400. Gives complete details of all the equipment and features, and also shows the Inter-State Models 30-A and 32-B, 40 H. P., costing $1,750 and $1,700 respectively.

THAT greatest nuisance of motoring—tire pumping—is *totally eliminated* with the Inter-State equipment. Any woman can attach the valve to the tire, turn on the pump and in a few minutes have tires just as solid and as perfectly filled as if done by the greatest tire expert in the world.

The Inter-State *does* the work. You *direct* it. There is nothing to it at all and you are forearmed for any emergency with the complete and thorough equipment of the Inter-State.

Inter-State Tire Pumping—No Work

Motoring Now All Pleasure

THIS great car performs all the labor itself— electrically self-started—electric lights and ignition, tire pumping and the automatic regulation of fuel consumption.

For the first time in the history of the automobile, electricity plays its *real part* in the entire mechanism. The Inter-State Electric System is really the *nerve system* commanding the energy and motion of the powerful steel muscles that make the Inter-State such a masterpiece of construction. Every conceivable accessory and feature is built into or included in the Inter-State. The Inter-State is truly the *only complete car* in this country or abroad —and this statement is made advisedly.

The *Only Complete Car*—Equipment and Features Unequalled

INTER-STATE AUTOMOBILE COMPANY, Dept. X, Muncie, Indiana

Boston Branch: 153 Massachusetts Avenue   *Omaha Branch:* 310 South 18th Street

Source 22 from a 1906 Advertisement.

22. Automobile Speed and Distance Meter.

Avoid a Trip to the
Police Court

Miles per Hour
KNOW
how fast

Distance
Traveled
KNOW
how far

Flexible
Driving
Shaft
attaches
to Front
Wheel.

The fine amounts to little—it's the hours of delay, the inconvenience and possible humiliation for you and for those in your company that try the patience and spoil the pleasure of the whole trip.

All this can positively be avoided by equipping your car with

The Warner
Auto-Meter
(Registers Speed and Distance)

This little instrument always *tells the truth.* It registers with ABSOLUTE ACCURACY from ¼ mile to 60 miles per hour. It attaches to any Automobile made.

Without it you never know your *exact speed* — and the temptation to go a little faster and a little faster is almost irresistible—you know how it is. And you know, too, what happens to you and your party when you *think* you are going 8 miles an hour and the Policeman's stop watch says 15.

Don't guess yourself into trouble—KNOW and keep out of it. The Warner Auto-Meter is your salvation.

And it's your ONLY salvation.

Because the Warner Auto-Meter is the only speed indicator which is sensitive enough to be absolutely and unfailingly accurate at *speeds under 10 miles an hour.*

Because it's the only one which works perfectly in all positions and at all angles, on rough roads or smooth, up hill or down.

Because it's the only one which changes with the *speed alone* and in which the indicator does not dance back and forth from the jar of the car.

The Warner Auto-Meter is the only speed indicator which is actuated by the same fixed, unchangeable Magnetism which makes the Mariner's Compass reliable FOREVER under all conditions.

No one else can use Magnetism to determine the speed of an Automobile, though it's the only *positive* and *sure* way. Because there is just one way in which Magnetism can successfully be used for this purpose and *we have Patented that way.*

There is nothing about the Warner Auto-Meter which can give out, or wear out, or get out of adjustment. It is the only speed-indicator made without cams, plates or levers, and in which there is *no friction.* Friction wears away the cams and levers in other speed indicators, which are necessarily so small that *1-1000 of an inch* wear will throw out the reading from *one to five miles per hour.*

One Warner Auto-Meter will last a lifetime. It is as sensitive as a Compass and as *Solid as a Rock.* Otherwise it couldn't stand our severe service-test, which is equivalent to a trip of

160,000 Miles at 50 Miles per Hour on Granite Pavements Riding Solid Tires.

The practical Warner Testing Machine is shown in Fig. 1. The wheel connection of the Auto-Meter is attached to a shaft running

Figure 1

200 revolutions per minute. Across this shaft lies a plank which is hinged at one end and has the Auto-Meter attached to the other. Brazed to the shaft is a knob of steel, which at every revolution "bumps" the plank, giving to the Auto-Meter *200 shocks per minute* while it is showing a speed of *50 miles per hour.*

Each one of these shocks is more severe than would be suffered in an entire season's riding. After running 10 hours a day for THREE MONTHS, actual tests show the Auto-Meter to be recording the speed with the same accuracy as at first within 1-1000 of 1%, or less than *6 inches per mile.*

No other Speed Indicator on Earth could Stand this Test.

This is why we sell each Auto-Meter on a **10 YEARS GUARANTEE** and why we gladly renew any Auto-Meter (which has not been injured by accident) if the Magnet (the HEART of the instrument) is less accurate than 1-10 of 1% after 10 years use.

We will gladly tell you more about this wonderful instrument if you will write us.

If you write TODAY we will send you something every motorist will prize—our **Free Book—"Auto Pointers."**

The Warner Instrument Co.,   104 Roosevelt St., Beloit, Wis.

(The Auto-Meter is on sale by all first-class dealers and at most Garages.)

23. Stove (1884) and Washer and Wringer (1908).

ASK YOUR DEALER FOR THE
"GLENWOOD"

WITH PATENT MAGIC GRATE.

There is nothing more essential to the healthy happy
home than well cooked food—which you may always be
sure of by using the Glenwood Range. 100 styles!
Illustrated Circular and Price List sent free.
WEIR STOVE CO., Taunton, Mass.

The Electric Washer and Wringer

Washing

YOU can now have your washings done by electricity.
The 1900 Electric Washer Outfit (Washer, Wringer and Motor complete) does all the heavy work of washing and wrings out the clothes.
Any electric light current furnishes the power needed. You connect up the washer the same way you put an electric light globe into its socket. Then all there is to do to start the washer is—turn on the electricity. The motion of the tub (driven by the electricity) and the water and soap in the tub wash the clothes clean. Washing is done quicker and easier, and more thoroughly and economically this way than ever before.

30 Days' FREE Trial—Freight Prepaid

Wringing

Servants will stay contented—laundry bills will be saved—clothes will last twice as long—where there is a 1900 Electric Washer to do the washing.

These washers save so much work and worry and trouble, that they *sell themselves.* This is the way of it—

We ship you an Electric Washer and *prepay the freight.*

Use the washer a month. Wash your linens and laces—wash your blankets and quilts—wash your rugs.

Then—when the month is up, if you are not convinced the washer is all we say—don't keep it. Tell us you don't want the washer and that will settle the matter. We won't charge anything for the use you have had of it.

This is the *only* washer outfit that does *all* the drudgery of the washing—*washes* and *wrings* clothes—saves them from wear and tear—and keeps your servants contented.

Our Washer Book tells how our washers are made and how they work. Send for this book today.

Don't mortgage your pleasure in life to dread of wash-day and wash-day troubles with servants. Let the 1900 Electric Washer and Wringer shoulder your wash-day burden—save your clothes and money, and keep your servants contented.

Write for our Washer Book at once. Address—

The 1900 Washer Co. 3133 Henry Street, Binghamton, N. Y. (If you live in Canada, write to the Canadian 1900 Washer Co., 355 Yonge Street, Toronto, Ont.)

Source 24 from 1909 and 1913 Advertisements.

24. Vacuum Cleaner (1909) and Bathroom Closet (1913).

Why stir up the Dust Demon to Frenzy like this?

SIWELCLO Noiseless Siphon Jet **CLOSET**

The Noiselessness of the Siwelclo Is an Advantage Found in No Other Similar Fixture.

This appeals particularly to those whose sense of refinement is shocked by the noisy flushing of the old style closet. The Siwelclo was designed to prevent such embarrassment and has been welcomed whenever its noiseless feature has become known. When properly installed it cannot be heard outside of its immediate environment.

Every sanitary feature has been perfected in the Siwelclo—deep water seal preventing the passage of sewer gas, thorough flushing, etc.

The Siwelclo is made of Trenton Potteries Co. Vitreous China, with a surface that actually repels dirt like a china plate. It is glazed at a temperature 1000 degrees higher than is possible with any other material.

The most sanitary and satisfactory materials for all bathroom, kitchen and laundry fixtures are Trenton Potteries Co. Vitreous China and Solid Porcelain. Your architect and plumber will recommend them. If you are planning a new house or remodeling, you ought to see the great variety and beauty of design such as are shown in our new free booklet "513 **Bathrooms of Character.**" Send for a copy now.

The Trenton Potteries Co.
Trenton, N.J., U.S.A.

The largest manufacturers of sanitary pottery in the U.S.A.

The Man
always wonders why some way of cleaning can't be found without tormenting him with choking clouds of dust.

You can Escape all this for $25

EVERY MAN AND WOMAN

The Woman
thinks she is performing praiseworthy and necessary work in an unavoidable manner.

should now realize that such laborious and tormenting "cleaning" methods, not only are absolutely unnecessary, but are **a relic of barbarism**, **a mockery and a farce.** "Cleaning" with broom and carpet-sweeper merely scatters more of the dirt over a wider area. Old dirt has to be *rehandled again and again*. The house is never thoroughly clean. Disease germs are left to multiply, then are sent flying to infect all those whose powers of resistance may be lowered.

THE IDEAL VACUUM CLEANER

(Fully Protected by Patents)

Operated by Hand puts no tax on the strength.
Price $25

Or by Electric Motor, at a cost of 2 cents per hour.
Price $55 or $60

"IT EATS UP THE DIRT"

literally sucks out all the dust, grit, germs, moths and eggs of vermin that are *on* the object as well as *in* it—gobbles them down into its capacious maw, never to trouble you again.

This machine places in your hands a method of cleaning carpets, rugs, curtains, upholstery, wall decorations, etc., that hitherto has been limited to the very rich. It does exactly the same work as the Vacuum Cleaning systems that cost from *$500 up—and does it better and with more convenience.*

The Ideal Vacuum Cleaner is the perfection of the Vacuum Cleaning principle.

OPERATED BY HAND

Weighs only 20 pounds. Anybody can use it. Everybody can afford it. Compared with sweeping

It is ease itself.

It is absolutely dustless.
Every machine guaranteed.

Our free Illustrated Booklet tells an interesting story of a remarkable saving in money, labor, health, and strength. Send for it to-day.

The American Vacuum Cleaner Company
225 Fifth Avenue, New York City

PRICE $55 and $60

PRICE $25.00

25. Musical Organ.

CARPENTER,

"LIBRARY ORGAN."

Containing the Celebrated Carpenter Organ Action.

Something Entirely New! The Æsthetic Taste Gratified!

THIS IS ONLY ONE OF ONE HUNDRED DIFFERENT STYLES.

THIS effective and beautiful design in the modern Queen Anne Style is intended to meet the demands of those desiring an instrument of special elegance, and in harmony with the fittings and furnishings of the Study or Library Room, combining as it does, in a substantial and tasteful manner, the Organ, the Library cases, and the cabinet for bric-a-brac and articles of virtu.

It is well adapted to find favor in homes of culture and refinement, and will be championed by the music lover and connoisseur.

The composition is one of well balanced proportions, chaste subordination of ornamentation, and of artistic arrangement in constructive details, imparting to the design a rich simplicity and substantial worth

This beautiful organ contains the Celebrated Carpenter Organ Action. The action is to an Organ what the works are to a watch. The merits of the Carpenter Organ were fully proved on page 158 of the YOUTH'S COMPANION of April 20th, to which special attention is directed.

A beautiful 80-page Catalogue, the finest of its kind ever published, is now ready and will be sent free to all applying for it.

Nearly all reliable dealers sell the Carpenter Organs, but if any do not have them to show you, write to us for a Catalogue and information where you can see them. DO NOT BUY ANY ORGAN UNTIL YOU HAVE EXAMINED "THE CARPENTER." In writing for a Catalogue always state that you saw this advertisement, in the *Youth's Companion.*

Address or call on E. P. CARPENTER, Worcester, Mass., U. S. A.

Source 26 from a 1909 Advertisement.

26. Reed and Rattan Furniture.

ESTABLISHED 1826

Heywood-Wakefield

TRADE MARK

FACSIMILE OF OUR TAG

THE name *Heywood-Wakefield* appearing on Reed and Rattan Furniture signifies quality, style, and workmanship, that individualizes our brands of goods and has made them world-renowned. The best in Rattan Furniture is *not* the best unless it bears the tag *Heywood-Wakefield*

Our furniture enhances the beauty of any home. Its presence lends an influence of dignity, comfort, and artisticness that harmonizes with any color treatment or architectural effect. So numerous are the styles made by us in Reed and Rattan Furniture, covering every known desire for the household, club, or hotel, and to which our design creators are constantly adding new effects in shapes and patterns, that you are practically sure of possessing, when selecting our goods, ideas that are exclusive and original.

We are also producers of the well-known line of *Heywood* *Wakefield* go-carts and baby carriages. Made in every conceivable style, including our celebrated collapsible, room-saving go-carts.

We have prepared attractive illustrated catalogs showing and describing our Reed and Rattan Furniture. Before purchasing, *write for catalog G.*

We also furnish, free, interesting catalog of our go-carts and baby carriages. If interested, *write for catalog 7.*

Write to our nearest store.

HEYWOOD BROTHERS AND WAKEFIELD COMPANY

BOSTON, BUFFALO, NEW YORK,
PHILADELPHIA, BALTIMORE,
CHICAGO, SAN FRANCISCO,
LOS ANGELES, PORTLAND, ORE.

J. C. PLIMPTON & CO., Agts.
LONDON AND LIVERPOOL, ENG.

Style 6830 B

[82]

27. Houses in New York (1887) and Tennessee (1892). Exterior View and Floor Plan.

* * * This marvelous house has been built more than 300 times from our plans; *it is so well planned* that it affords ample room even for a large family. 1st floor shown above; on 2d floor are 4 bedrooms and in attic 2 more. Plenty of Closets. The whole warmed by one chimney.

Large illustrations and full description of the above as well as of 39 other houses, ranging in cost from $400 up to $6,500, may be found in "SHOPPELL'S MODERN LOW-COST HOUSES," a large quarto pamphlet, showing also how to select sites, get loans, &c. Sent postpaid on receipt of 50c. Stamps taken, or send $1 bill and we will return the change. Address, BUILDING PLAN ASSOCIATION. (Mention this paper.) 24 Beekman St. (Box 2702.) N. Y.

A Complete Home should be so designed as to combine Comfort, Convenience, Durability and Style.

We design and furnish plans of just such homes, and publish **Artistic Dwellings**. The Beauty & Completeness of these Designs, combining so many new features, has given this book a wonderful sale, and hundreds of **Beautiful Homes** are being built in all parts of our land from its designs. Price postpaid, **$2.00**. *Prospectus and Sample Pages FREE.*

The "Cottage Souvenir," a book of 172 pages, 8½ x 11 inches, containing a great variety of **Designs** and **Plans** of — costing from **$500 to $10,000.**

Geo. F. Barber & Co.
—— ARCHITECTS ——
Knoxville, Tenn.

Source 28 from a *Ladies' Home Journal* Advertisement, 1909.

28. Advice for Couples Buying a Home.

This is the house the young couple saved and paid for in five years.

A Young Couple
Were Married 5 Years Ago

He had a moderate salary. They started simply and saved. But they didn't skimp. They gave little dinners and heard the best lectures. In five years they had saved enough to pay for the house at the head of this page.

Another Young Couple Were Married, Too

They put by $7 a week, and the house at the bottom of this page is now theirs, —entirely paid for. A third young couple's income was $16 per week. They saved $8 of it, and bought and paid for the house at the bottom of this page.

How these and 97 others did it, step by step, dollar by dollar, is all told in the great series, "*How We Saved For a Home,*"— 100 articles by 100 people who saved for and now own their own homes on an

Average Salary of $15 a Week: None Higher Than $30

This great series will run for an entire year in

The Ladies' Home Journal

For ONE DOLLAR, for a year's subscription, you get the whole series.

THE CURTIS PUBLISHING COMPANY, PHILADELPHIA, PA.

This is the house saved for on $7 a week and now all paid for.

This is the house paid for out of a salary of $16 per week, saving $8.

Sources 29 through 32 from *Palliser's Model Homes*, 1878.

29. Cottage for a Mill Hand at Chelsea, Mass. (Cost $1,200).

This is a very attractive design, and intended to give ample accommodation at a low cost for an ordinary family.

The cellar is placed under the Kitchen and Hall, which was thought in this instance to be sufficient to meet all requirements, though it is generally considered, in the Eastern States at least, to be poor economy not to have a cellar under the whole house, as it only requires about one foot in depth of additional stone work to secure a cellar, it being necessary to put down the stone work in any case, so that it will be beyond the reach of frost. The Kitchen is without a fire-place, the cooking to be done by a stove, which, if properly contrived, is a very effective ventilator, and preferred by many housekeepers for all Kitchen purposes.

The Parlor and Dining-room or general Living-room are provided with the healthy luxury of an open fire-place, and we know of no more elegant, cleanly and effective contrivance for this purpose than the one adopted in this instance; they are built of buff brick, with molded jambs and segment arch, and in which a basket grate or fire dogs can be placed for the desired fire, and in this way large rooms are kept perfectly comfortable in cold weather without heat from any other source. These fire-places are also provided with neat mantels constructed of ash, and which are elegant compared with the marbelized slate mantel, which is a sham, and repulsive to an educated taste.

On entering nearly every house in the land we find the same turned walnut post at the bottom of the stairs with tapering walnut sticks all the way up, surmounted with a flattened walnut rail having a shepherd's crook at the top; however, in this instance it is not so, but the staircase is surmounted with an ash rail, balusters and newel of simple, though unique design; and now that people are giving more attention to this important piece of furniture, we may look for a change in this respect.

This house is supplied with a cistern constructed with great care, the Kitchen sink being supplied with water by a pump, and there is no more easy method of procuring good water for all purposes of the household.

For a compact, convenient Cottage with every facility for doing the work with the least number of steps, for a low-priced elegant Cottage, we do not know of anything that surpasses this. Cost, $1,200.

Mr. E. A. Jones of Newport, Ohio, is also erecting this Cottage with the necessary changes to suit points of compass. Such a house as this if tastefully furnished, and embellished with suitable surroundings, as neat and well-kept grounds, flowers, etc., will always attract more attention than the uninviting, ill-designed buildings, no matter how much money may have been expended on them.

It is not necessary that artistic feeling should have always a large field for its display; and in the lesser works and smaller commissions as much art may find expression as in the costly façades and more pretentious structures.

30. Floor Plan of Cottage for a Mill Hand.

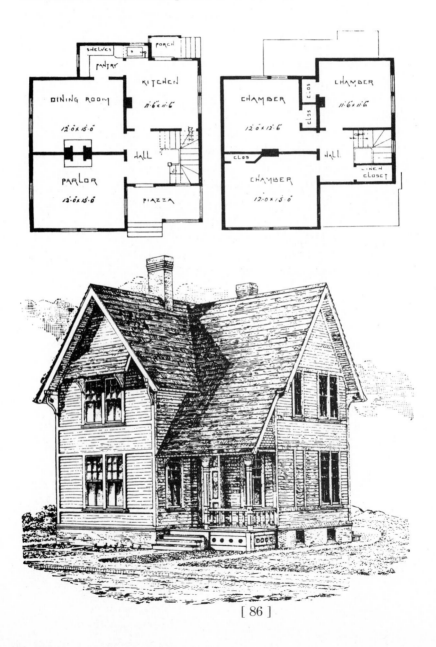

31. Residence of Rev. Dr. Marble, Newtown, Conn. (Cost $2,925).

This house commands a particularly fine view from both sides and the front, and is situated in one of the pleasantest country towns in New England, the hotels of this town being crowded during the summer months with people from the cities.

The exterior design is plain, yet picturesque, and at once gives one an idea of ease and comfort. The roofing over the Hall and Sitting-room is a particularly fine feature, and the elevation of the rear is very striking, the roof over porch being a part of the main roof.

The interior arrangements are very nice, the Hall being very spacious, and in it we have a very easy and handsome stair-case of plain design, constructed of Georgia pine; the newel extends up to ceiling of first floor, while the other two posts extend up to ceiling of second floor. In all country houses one of the first things to be aimed at is to secure ample stair-cases, and until a man can afford space for an easy ascent to a second floor he should stay below; and to-day we find in houses, where there is no necessity for it, stairs that are little better than step-ladders, making a pretence of breadth at the bottom with swelled steps, and winding the steps on approaching the floor above, thus making a trap for the old and for the children.

The corner fire-place between Parlor and Dining-room is a feature we indulge in to a great extent in these days of economy, sliding doors and fire-places, although we sometimes have clients who object to this, thinking it would not look as well as when placed in center of side wall; but when they are asked how this and that can be provided for with the best and most economical results, they readily give in.

There is no water-closet in the house, but an Earth-Closet is provided in the rear Hall, which is thoroughly ventilated.

The Dining-room is a very cheerful room and the Kitchen is reached through a passage also connecting with side veranda. The pantry is lighted with a window placed above press; each fire-place is furnished with a neat hard-wood mantel, and the Hall is finished in Georgia pine, the floor being laid with this material, and finished in natural color.

The exterior is painted as follows: Ground, light slate; trimmings, buff, and chamfers, black. Cost, $2,925.

The sight of this house in the locality in which it is built is very refreshing, and is greatly in advance of the old styles of rural box architecture to be found there. When people see beautiful things, they very naturally covet them, and they grow discontented in the possession of ugliness. Handsome houses, other things equal, are always the most valuable. They sell quickest and for the most money. Builders who feign a blindness to beauty must come to grief.

32. Floor Plan of a Clergyman's Residence.

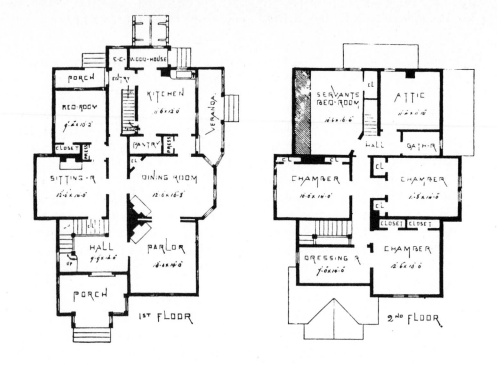

33. House Recently Erected in California (No Cost Given).

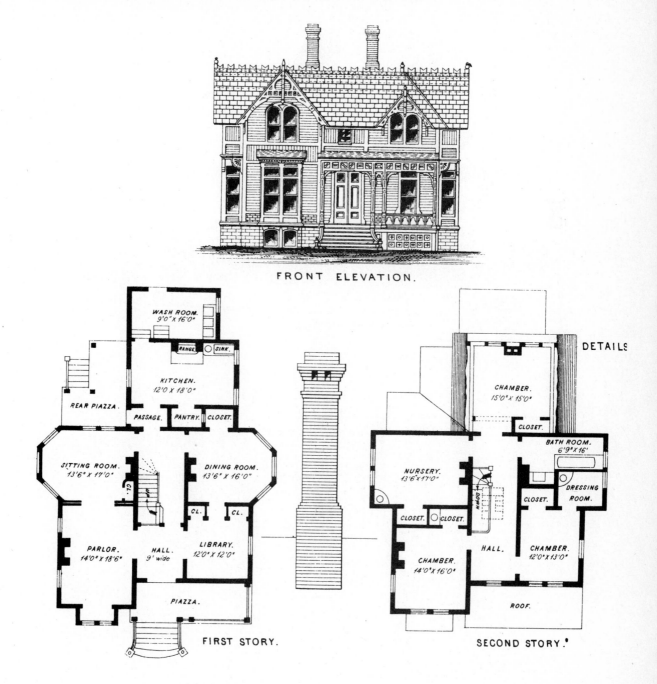

FRONT ELEVATION.

FIRST STORY.

SECOND STORY.

Source 34 from Shoppell's *Modern Houses*, 1900 (cost $3,600).

34. Perspective View and Floor Plans.

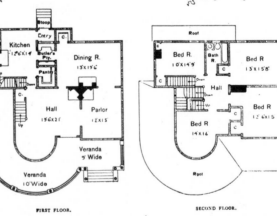

PERSPECTIVE.

DESCRIPTION.

For explanation of all symbols (* † etc.) see supplement page 120.

GENERAL DIMENSIONS: Width, including veranda, 43 ft.; depth, including veranda, 49 ft. 6 ins.

HEIGHTS OF STORIES: Cellar, 7 ft.; first story, 10 ft.; second story, 9 ft.; attic, 8 ft.

EXTERIOR MATERIALS: Foundation, brick; first story, clapboards; second story, gables, roofs and lower portion of veranda railing, shingles.

INTERIOR FINISH: Two coat plaster for papering; plaster, cornices and centers in hall, parlor and dining-room. Soft wood flooring and trim throughout. Main stairs, ash. Kitchen and bath-room, wainscoted. Chair-rail in dining-room. Picture molding in hall, parlor and dining-room. All interior woodwork grain filled and finished with hard oil.

COLORS: All clapboards, first story, Colonial yellow. Trim, including water-table, corner boards, casings, cornices, bands, veranda posts and rails, outside doors, conductors, etc., ivory white. Veranda floor and ceiling, oiled. Shingles on side walls and gables stained dark yellow. Roof shingles, dark red.

ACCOMMODATIONS: The principal rooms, and their sizes, closets, etc., are shown by the floor plans. Cellar under whole house with inside and outside entrances and concrete floor. One room finished in attic, remainder of attic floored for storage. Double folding doors between parlor and hall and parlor and dining-room. Direct communication from hall with dining-room, parlor and kitchen. Bathroom, with complete plumbing, in second story. Open fire-places in dining-room, parlor and hall. Wide veranda. Bay-window in hall and bedroom over. Two stationary wash-tubs in cellar under kitchen.

COST: $3,600, including mantels, range and heater. The estimate is based on † New York prices for labor and materials.

Price of working plans, specifications, detail drawings, etc., $35.
Price of †† bill of materials, ... 10.

FEASIBLE MODIFICATIONS: General dimensions, materials and colors may be changed. Cellar may be decreased in size or wholly omitted. Sliding doors may be used in place of folding doors. Portable range may be used instead of brick-set range. Servants' water-closet could be introduced in cellar. Fireplaces may be reduced in number.

The price of working plans, specifications, etc., for a modified design, varies according to the alterations required and will be made known upon application to the Architects.

Address, CO-OPERATIVE BUILDING PLAN ASSOCIATION, Architects, 203 Broadway and 164–6–8 Fulton Street, New York, N. Y.

35. Perspective View and Floor Plans.

PRICE
of Blue Prints,
together with a
complete set of
typewritten
specifications, is

$7.50

FIRST FLOOR PLAN

SECOND FLOOR PLAN

Design No. 15
Cost about $3,700

Size: width, 34 feet; length, 50 feet exclusive of porches. Blue prints consist of cellar and foundation plan; first and second floor plans; front, rear, two side elevations; wall sections and all necessary interior details.

QUESTIONS TO CONSIDER

For convenience, the evidence is divided into two sections. Sources 1 to 26 are advertisements from popular magazines and the 1897 and 1902 Sears Roebuck & Co. catalogues. The prices probably seem ridiculously low to you, but these items were reasonably priced and affordable (although not really cheap) for most middle-class Americans in cities, towns, and on the farms. Sources 27 to 36 are house plans readily available by mail and through pattern books. Again, the prices seem very low, but working-class family homes could be built for less than $1,000 (excluding the cost of the land) and middle-class comfortable homes for as little as $2,000 during this period.

You will find it helpful to jot down notes as you go through the advertisements. Ask yourself these questions about each advertisement: What emotion(s) does it appeal to? What fears? What hopes? Does it tell you anything about men's roles in society? About women's roles? About adults' concerns about young people? In other words, what messages are these advertisements sending?

Sources 27 and 28 are also advertisements. What do they tell you about people's needs and wants with regard to housing? The remaining evidence (Sources 29 to 35) consists of house plans from architectural pattern books, arranged chronologically (Palliser 1878, Comstock 1881, Shoppell 1900, Radford 1902). Look carefully at the exterior features of these houses, the interior rooms, and their comparative sizes. What use or uses would each room probably have? What similarities do you find in all the houses, from the mill hand's cottage ($1,200) to the suburban home ($3,700)? What differences are there? What impressions would a person walking by these houses receive? What about someone who visited the families living in these houses? What kinds of things do you think were important to the owners of these houses?

Finally, consider what you learned as a whole from the evidence in both sections. What do you know about the values, the hopes, and the fears of Americans around the turn of the century?

EPILOGUE

Of course, not all Americans could live like the middle-class families you just studied. The poor and the immigrants in the cities were crowded into windowless, airless tenement buildings that often covered an entire block.

Poor rural black and white sharecroppers in the South lived in one- or two-room shacks, and many farmers in the western plains and prairies could only afford to build sod houses for their families. During the Great Depression of the 1930s, many people, including middle-class families, lost their homes entirely through foreclosure, and the 1960s and 1970s saw the price of houses increase so rapidly that many families were priced out of the housing market. Even today, the problem of the homeless has not been solved.

The early twentieth century saw the captains of industry come under attack for what many came to believe were their excesses. Evidence of their disdain for and defiance of the public good as well as of their treatment of workers, their political influence, and their ruthless business practices came more and more to light, due to the efforts of reformers and muckraking journalists. The society that once had venerated the industrial barons began to worry that they had too much power and came to believe that such power should be restricted.

Architecture was also undergoing a rapid transformation. Neoclassical, Georgian, Colonial, and bungalow styles signaled a shift toward less ostentation and increased moderation in private dwellings. Perhaps the most striking work was done by Chicago architect Frank Lloyd Wright, who sought to give functional and social meaning to his designs and to make each structure blend into its unique landscape. According to Wright's concepts, there was no standard design for the "perfect house." Wright's ideas formed the basis for a series of movements that ultimately changed the perspective and direction of American architecture.

Progressive muckrakers also criticized advertising, particularly the claims of patent medicine advertisements. Such salesmanship, however, was described as "the brightest hope of America" by the 1920s. Bruce Barton, a talented salesman and founder of a huge advertising agency, even discovered "advertisements" in the Bible, which he described as the first "best seller." Although its image was slightly tarnished by the disillusionment accompanying the Great Depression, advertising helped "sell" World War II to the American public by encouraging conservation of scarce resources, and it emerged stronger and more persuasive than ever in the 1950s. Americans were starved for consumer goods after war-time rationing, and their rapid acceptance of a new form of media—television—greatly expanded advertising opportunities.

But advertising still had (and has) its critics. Writing in 1954, historian David Potter characterized advertising as the basic "institution of abundance." Advertising, he maintained, had become as powerful as religion or education had been in earlier eras—advertising, he said, now actually *created* the standards and values of our society. Because advertising lacked social goals or social responsibility, however, he believed that its power was dangerous. We must not forget, Potter warned, "that it ultimately regards man as a consumer and defines its own mission as one of stimulating him to consume."

CHAPTER FOUR

JUSTIFYING AMERICAN IMPERIALISM:
THE LOUISIANA PURCHASE
EXPOSITION, 1904

THE PROBLEM

From the formal end of Reconstruction in 1877 to the United States' entry into the First World War in 1917, Americans appeared to fall in love with world's fairs. Between 1876 and 1916, various United States cities hosted fourteen international expositions that were attended by nearly 100 million eager visitors.[1] Intended to stimulate economic development in the host cities as well as provide opportunities for manufacturers to show their newest products to millions of potential consumers, these expositions or world's fairs also acquainted provincial Americans with machines and technology (the Corliss engine, electric lights, the air brake, refrigeration, the dynamo, x-rays, the telephone, etc.), new delights (the Ferris wheel, ice cream cones, the hoochie-koochie dance, etc.), and spectacular architecture, art, and historical artifacts (the Liberty Bell was brought from Philadelphia to both the New Orleans and Atlanta expositions). As President William McKinley commented at the 1901 Pan-American Exposition in Buffalo (where he was soon after assassinated), "Expositions are the timekeepers of progress."

Visitors to the Louisiana Purchase Exposition in St. Louis in 1904[2] saw

1. The first international exposition was held in London's Crystal Palace in 1851. Between 1876 and 1916, American expositions were held in Philadelphia, New Orleans, Chicago, Atlanta, Nashville, Buffalo, Charleston, St. Louis, Jamestown, Portland, Seattle, San Francisco, and San Diego. Numerous regional expositions and fairs were also held.

2. The St. Louis Exposition commemorated the 100th anniversary of President Thomas Jefferson's acquisition of the Louisiana Territory from France in 1804.

all this, and more. More than 19 million people[3] attended the largest world's fair ever held (1,272 acres, 75 buildings, 70,000 exhibits).[4] Visitors could examine a display of 100 automobiles or watch demonstrations of totally electric cooking. But the highlight of the St. Louis Exposition was its Anthropology Department, headed by the preeminent Smithsonian Institution ethnologist W. J. McGee. The department brought to St. Louis representatives of "all the races of the world," who lived on the fairgrounds in villages designed to reproduce their "native habitats." For example, 1,200 people were brought from the Philippine Islands, an area acquired from Spain in the Spanish-American War of 1898 and where American soldiers recently (1902) had subdued a Filipino rebellion. On a 47-acre site, 6 villages were constructed for these people, where American visitors could observe them and their customs.

In this chapter you will be analyzing several photographs taken at the 1904 Louisiana Purchase Exposition in St. Louis. As noted earlier, in 1898 the United States had acquired a colonial empire from Spain as a result of the Spanish-American War. How did the exhibits at the 1904 St. Louis Exposition attempt to justify America's rise as an imperialist power? How do you think American visitors might have reacted to these exhibits?

BACKGROUND

Until the late nineteenth century, the United States' transoceanic foreign policy clearly had been of minor concern to the nation's citizens. Westward expansion and settlement, the slavery controversy and the Civil War, postwar reconstruction of the Republic, and industrialization and urbanization had alternately captured the attention of Americans and pushed foreign affairs into the background. But beginning in the latter part of the nineteenth century, several factors prompted Americans to look beyond their own shores, and by the end of the century, the United States had become a world power complete with a modest empire.

Initially, the American business community opposed this drift toward expansion and colonialism, believing that American industry would do well just meeting the needs of the rapidly growing population and fearing that a colonial empire would mean large armies and navies, increased government expenses, and the possibility of the nation's involvement in war. However, by

3. 19 million people (the official count; others were lower) represented 23.1 percent of the total U.S. population in 1904. Of course, not all visitors were Americans, and some people visited the exposition more than once and thus were counted more than once in the total figure.
4. In terms of acreage, the St. Louis Exposition remains the largest world's fair ever held. The 1939–1940 New York World's Fair covered 1,217 acres and the 1967 Montreal World's Fair 1,000 acres.

CHAPTER 4

JUSTIFYING
AMERICAN
IMPERIALISM:
THE LOUISIANA
PURCHASE
EXPOSITION,
1904

the mid-1890s, American business leaders were beginning to have second thoughts. The apparent cycle of economic depressions (1819, 1837, 1857, 1873, 1893) made some businessmen believe that American prosperity could be maintained only by selling surpluses of manufactured goods in foreign markets. Too, business leaders were constantly looking for areas in which to invest their surplus capital. Investments beyond the borders of the United States, they believed, would be more secure if the American government would act to stabilize the areas in which they invested. In 1895, the newly organized National Association of Manufacturers sounded both those chords at its convention, where the keynote speaker was soon-to-be-president William McKinley, an Ohio governor with decided expansionist leanings.

Yet it would be wrong to see American expansion and colonialism strictly as a scheme to better the nation's industrial and commercial interests. A number of other intellectual currents dovetailed with American commercial interests to create a powerful and popular urge toward imperialism. For example, those who advocated military growth (especially of a large, steam-powered navy) saw in American expansion a perfect justification for their position. Their interests were represented by increasingly influential lobbies in Washington. Especially important was Captain Alfred Thayer Mahan, whose book *The Influence of Sea Power Upon History* (published in 1890) argued persuasively that national self-preservation depended upon international trade protected by a large and powerful navy with worldwide

bases and refueling stations. Two of Mahan's disciples, Theodore Roosevelt and Henry Cabot Lodge, eventually achieved positions whereby they could put Mahan's philosophy to work.

Another current influencing American expansion was the dramatic increase in religious missionary zeal in the late nineteenth century. Working through both individual denominations and powerful congressional lobbies, missionaries argued that it was their duty to Christianize the world.[5] In the United States, Methodists, Baptists, Presbyterians, and Congregationalists were especially active, giving money and attention to their denominational missionary boards as well as to those who went out to convert the "heathen." In large part these missionaries were selfless, committed men and women. Some, however, attempted to westernize as well as Christianize their flocks, often denigrating or destroying indigenous cultures and traditions even as they brought modern health and educational institutions with them. All argued for the United States government to more actively protect the missionaries and open up other areas around the world to missionary work.

Accompanying this religious zeal was latent racism, a racism that in some ways differed little from white Americans' long-held attitudes about American Indians. Since the popularization of the work of Charles Darwin (*The Origin of Species,* 1859), a num-

---

5. Because the majority of Filipinos were Roman Catholics (making the Philippines the only Christian "nation" in Asia), obviously American missionaries to the Philippines after 1899 meant *Protestantize* when they said "Christianize."

ber of people had taken Darwin's ideas of "survival of the fittest" and "struggle for existence" and applied them to humans. Often the result was a notion of competition among races for world dominance. As Josiah Strong wrote in *Our Country: Its Possible Future and Its Present Crisis* (1885),

> this race of unequaled energy . . . will spread itself over the earth. If I read not amiss, this powerful race will move down upon Mexico, down upon Central and South America, out upon the islands of the sea, over upon Africa and beyond. And can anyone doubt that the result of this competition of races will be the "survival of the fittest"?

Clearly this idea of the racial superiority of Caucasians, together with other impulses, formed a powerful impetus to American expansion and colonization.

All these ideological impulses (economic, military, religious, racist) rested upon one common assumption: that the world was a great competitive battlefield and that those nations that did not grow and expand would wither and die. Indeed, this "growth mania," or fascination with growth and the measurement of growth, was perhaps the most powerful intellectual strain in all of American society. For those who accepted such an assumption, the world was a dangerous, competitive jungle in which individuals, races, religions, nations, corporations, and cities struggled for domination. Those that grew would continue to exist; those that did not grow would die.

The convergence of these intellectual strains in the late nineteenth century caused Americans to view the outside world as an area into which the United States' influence should expand. This expansionist strain was not an entirely new phenomenon; it had been an almost regular feature of American life almost from the time of the nation's beginning. Yet, except for the purchase of Alaska, this was the first time that large numbers of Americans seemed to favor the extension of United States influence into areas that would not be settled subsequently by Americans and would not eventually become states of the Union. In that sense, the American imperialism of the late nineteenth century was a new phenomenon, different from previous expansionist impulses. Instead, it more nearly resembled the "new" imperialism that engulfed European nations in the late nineteenth and early twentieth centuries, in which those nations rushed to carve out colonies or spheres of influence in Africa and Asia.

The Spanish-American War of 1898 caused the various impulses for United States expansion and colonization to converge. When Cubans began a revolt to secure their independence from Spain in 1895, most Americans were genuinely sympathetic toward the Cuban underdogs. Those genuine feelings were heightened by American newspaper reporters and editors, some of whom wrote lurid (and knowingly inaccurate) accounts of the Spanish "monsters" and the poor, downtrodden Cubans. President William McKinley tried to pressure Spain into making concessions and sent the American battleship *Maine* to Havana on a "courtesy call," an obvious move to underscore the United States'

CHAPTER 4

JUSTIFYING
AMERICAN
IMPERIALISM:
THE LOUISIANA
PURCHASE
EXPOSITION,
1904

position toward Spain. But on February 15, 1898, the *Maine* blew up in the Havana harbor. Although we now know (as a result of a 1976 study) that the explosion on the *Maine* was an internal one, almost surely the result of an accident, at the time many Americans, fired up by the press, were convinced that the Spanish had been responsible. Yet war with Spain did not come immediately and, in the opinion of some, was not inevitable, even after the *Maine* incident. However, on April 11, 1898, after two months of demands, negotiations, and arguments in which it sometimes appeared that war might be avoided, McKinley asked Congress for authorization to intervene in Cuba "in the name of humanity and civilization." On April 20, Congress granted authorization, and the Spanish-American War began.

If the Spanish-American War had not begun as an imperialistic venture, the convergence of the economic, military, religious, and racist impulses mentioned previously and the prostrate condition of Spain gave American leaders the opportunity to use the war and victory for expansionist purposes.

Once the United States had achieved a comparatively bloodless[6] victory against nearly impotent Spain, a general debate began over whether the United States should demand from Spain the surrender of its colonial em-

pire, the jewels of which were Cuba and the Philippine Islands. Although President McKinley admitted that he had to consult a globe to find out where the Philippine Islands were, he was never in doubt that they should become a part of a new American empire. McKinley thus pressured the Spanish to include the surrender of their empire in the peace treaty (signed in Paris on December 10, 1898) and submitted that treaty to the United States Senate on January 4, 1899. After a brisk debate in which opponents of acquisition charged that acquiring colonies went against America's history and morality, that acquiring the Philippines would embroil the United States in future wars, and that Filipinos would be able to migrate to the United States where they would compete with American labor, on February 6, 1899, the Senate ratified the treaty by a vote of 57-27, just one vote more than the two-thirds necessary for ratifying a treaty.[7] Learning of the vote, an exultant McKinley boasted that the Philippines would become

a land of plenty and increasing possibilities; a people redeemed from savage and indolent habits, devoted to the arts of peace, in touch with commerce and trade of all nations, enjoying the blessings of freedom, of civil and religious liberty, of education, and of homes, and whose children's children shall for ages hence bless the American republic because it emancipated

---

6. The Spanish-American War lasted less than 3 months. The United States suffered only 362 battle or battle-related deaths (an additional 5,100 died of either disease or food poisoning), and the war cost only $250 million.

7. Outside the Senate, opponents of imperialism included Carl Schurz, William James, Mark Twain, Andrew Carnegie, Charles Francis Adams, Jane Addams, and William Jennings Bryan.

their fatherland, and set them in the pathway of the world's best civilization.

The Senate vote, however, did not end the debate over whether the United States should become a colonial power. Two days before the Senate voted, fighting broke out between United States troops and Filipinos under Emilio Aguinaldo, who had helped American soldiers overthrow the Spanish and who expected the United States to grant the Philippines immediate independence. Before the United States broke Aguinaldo's insurrection, approximately 125,000 American troops served in the Philippines, 4,200 were killed in action, and 2,800 were wounded, but an alleged 220,000 Filipinos died in battle, from disease and famine, and through torture. Government censors kept war-related atrocities from the American people. By 1902, the Philippine insurrection had been broken.

In 1900, Democratic presidential nominee William Jennings Bryan campaigned against McKinley on an anti-imperialist platform. The incumbent won easily (probably because of the fairly widespread prosperity that American voters enjoyed in 1900), but Bryan carried 45.5 percent of the vote, a better showing for a loser in all but four presidential elections from 1900 to the present. Hence, although by the time the St. Louis Exposition opened in 1904 anti-imperialist rhetoric had lost much of its appeal, the issue was far from dead.

At the St. Louis Exposition, the "Philippine Reservation" was financially sponsored by the United States government, which contributed approximately one-third of the cost of the total exposition (an unprecedented act). How did the fair's various exhibits seek to justify American imperialism? How might American visitors have reacted to these exhibits, especially those in the Philippine Reservation? According to a 1904 *Harper's Magazine* article, the St. Louis Exposition "fills a visitor full of pictures . . . that keep coming up in his mind for years afterwards." What were those pictures?

THE METHOD

According to historian Robert W. Rydell, who wrote an excellent book about American international expositions in the late nineteenth and early twentieth centuries, expositions "propagated the ideas and values of the country's political, financial, corporate, and intellectual leaders and offered these ideas as the proper interpretation of social and political reality."[8] In other words, the millions of Americans who visited exhibits the Department of Anthropology created at the 1904 exposition saw what someone else wanted them to see.

8. Robert W. Rydell, *All the World's a Fair: Visions of Empire at American International Expositions, 1876–1916* (Chicago: University of Chicago Press, 1984), p. 3.

CHAPTER 4

JUSTIFYING
AMERICAN
IMPERIALISM:
THE LOUISIANA
PURCHASE
EXPOSITION,
1904

At the Philippine Reservation, visitors made their way through six Filipino villages erected by the United States government in which representatives of "all the races of the Philippine Islands" could be "studied" by scientists and where most Americans had their only opportunity to see Filipinos with their own eyes. This allowed the American government to use the Reservation to justify its imperialistic ventures in the Philippines and elsewhere. Through photographs taken by official exposition photographers, you will be able to see some of what the fair's visitors saw.

As you examine the photographs in this chapter's Evidence section, keep in mind that you are seeing what someone else wants you to see. The Philippine Islands in 1904 was a land that contained an enormous diversity of peoples, from the most "primitive" to the most technologically and culturally sophisticated. About seventy-five linguistic groups were represented, as well as a plethora of Western and non-Western religious (under Spanish rule, most Filipinos had become Roman Catholics) and social customs. Yet of the many peoples who inhabited the Philippine Islands, the United States government selected only six groups to inhabit the Reservation's villages. Five of the six groups are photographically depicted in the Evidence section.[9] Why do you think each group was selected to go to St. Louis? What impressions do you think each group left in the minds of American visitors?

9. Negro pygmies (or Negritos), Igorot, Tagalo, Bontoc, and Visayan. The sixth group was the Moros.

A second problem you will confront is the photographer's bias. As do journalists, photojournalists have a particular point of view or bias toward or against their subjects. These biases often affect the *way* subjects are presented to the viewers of the photographs. As you examine each photograph, think about the photographer's bias, including whether the subjects are presented in a favorable or unfavorable light.

Although you are not used to thinking of photographs as historical evidence, in fact photographs and other visual documents (drawings, paintings, movies) often can yield as much information as more traditional sources. As Charles F. Bryan, Jr. and Mark V. Wetherington noted,

> Through the eye of the camera, the researcher can examine people and places "frozen" in time. . . . Photographs can tell us much about the social preferences and pretensions of their subjects, and can catch people at work, at play, or at home. In fact, you can "read" a photograph in much the same manner as any other historical document. [10]

When a historian "reads" a photograph, it means that he or she will put the photograph into words, describing the photograph in terms of the photographer's intent, specific details about the photograph, and the overall impression the photograph makes.

10. Charles F. Bryan, Jr., and Mark V. Wetherington, *Finding Our Past: A Guidebook for Group Projects in Community History* (Knoxville: East Tennessee Historical Society, 1983), p. 26.

For you to read the photographs, you will have to subject each photograph to the following questions (take notes as you go):

1. What "message" is the photographer attempting to convey? How does the photographer convey that message (there may well be more than one way)?
2. Is the photographer biased in any way? How? What is the purpose of the photograph?
3. Are there buildings in the photograph? What impressions of these buildings does the photographer intend that viewers should get? How does the photograph seek to elicit those impressions?
4. Are there people in the photograph? Are they posed or "natural?" How has the photographer portrayed these people? What are the people doing (if anything)? What impressions of these people does the photographer intend that viewers of the photograph should retain?
5. Examine the people in more detail. What about their clothing? Their facial expressions? *Note:* Because exposures had to be lengthy, people often were forced to maintain long, fairly rigid poses.

After you have examined each photograph, look at all the photographs together. What "message" is the photographer (or photographers) intending to convey? Most professional photographers judge whether a photograph is good or poor by the responses it evokes in the viewer's minds. What is the relationship between the responses you imagine these photographs might have elicited with America's justification for imperialism?

CHAPTER 4

JUSTIFYING
AMERICAN
IMPERIALISM:
THE LOUISIANA
PURCHASE
EXPOSITION,
1904

THE EVIDENCE

Source 1 from Robert W. Rydell, *All the World's a Fair: Visions of Empire at American International Expositions, 1876–1916* (Chicago: University of Chicago Press, 1984), p. 158.

1. The Sunken Gardens.

Source 2 from J. W. Buel, ed., *Louisiana and the Fair: An Exposition of the World, Its People, and Their Achievements* (St. Louis: World's Progress Publishing Co., 1904), vol. 5, frontispiece.

2. Types and Development of Man.

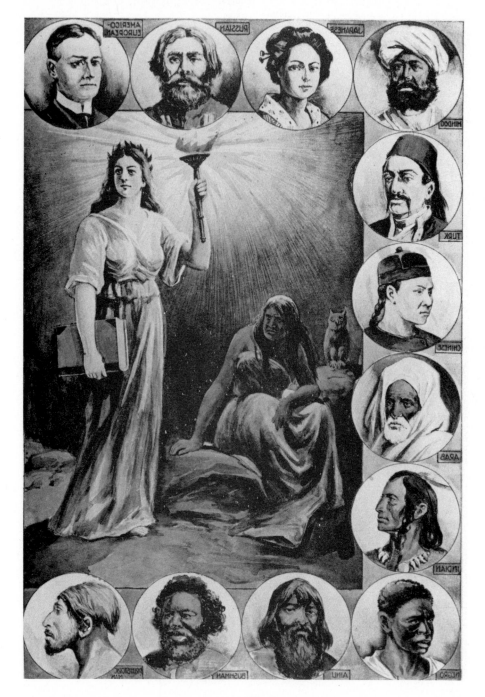

CHAPTER 4

JUSTIFYING
AMERICAN
IMPERIALISM:
THE LOUISIANA
PURCHASE
EXPOSITION
1904

Source 3 from Rydell, *All the World's a Fair,* p. 175.

3. Negrito Tribesman from the Philippines (Exposition Officials Named This Man "Missing Link").

Source 4 from *The World's Fair, Comprising the Official Photographic Views of the Universal Exposition Held in Saint Louis, 1904* (St. Louis: N. D. Thompson Publishing Co., 1903), p. 149.

4. Igorots from the Philippines.

Source 5 from Rydell, *All the World's a Fair*, p. 173.

5. Igorot Tribesmen and Visitors.

Source 6 from *The World's Fair, Comprising the Official Photographic Views*, p. 174.

6. Housekeeping in Igorot Village.

Sources 7 and 8 from Buel, *Louisiana and the Fair*, p. 1721.

7. Tagalo Women Washing.

8. Igorot Performing a Festival Dance.

Source 9 from Rydell, *All the World's a Fair*, p. 174.

9. Igorot Dance and Spectators.

Source 10 from Buel, *Louisiana and the Fair*, p. 1737.

10. Igorot Preparing a Feast of Dog.

Source 11 from *The World's Fair, Comprising the Official Photographic Views*, p. 169.

11. Bontoc Head Hunters, from the Philippines.

Sources 13 through 15 from *The World's Fair, Comprising the Official Photographic Views,* pp. 161; 163; 152–153.

13. Visayan Mothers with Their Children (Two of Whom Were Born at the Exposition).

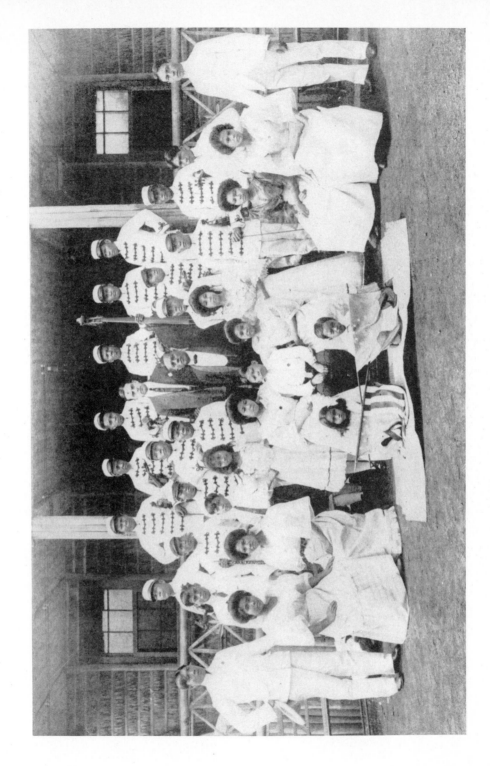

14. A Visayan Troupe of Singers, Dancers, and Orchestra.

15. Filipino Soldiers (with American Officers) Who Fought with the Americans During the Philippine Insurrection (1899–1902).

QUESTIONS TO CONSIDER

As you examine the fifteen photographs, first look for the photographer's intent and biases in each photograph. What "message" was the photographer trying to communicate? How might that message be used as a justification for American imperialism in the Philippines? For example, examine Source 1, which shows the impressive sunken gardens and surrounding buildings at the exposition. Who built these things? What impressions (amusement, awe, disgust, etc.) might viewers have of this scene? Now compare the structures in Source 1 to those in Sources 4 through 6 and 8. What "message" did photographers want viewers to receive?

The caption for Source 2 (from the official history of the Louisiana Purchase Exposition) reads in part, "The photogravure herewith is from an excellent specially prepared drawing which very accurately illustrates, as nearly as the science of ethnology is able to do, the characteristic types of mankind arranged in a progressive order of development from primitive or prehistoric man to the highest example of modern civilization." How does this photograph of a painting (which was on display at the exposition) help you assess the intent of all the photographers?

Sources 3 through 11 are of posed Philippine men and women from the Negrito, Igorot, Tagalo, and Bontoc tribes. These groups were among the most "primitive" of all Filipinos. Why did United States government officials select these people to appear at the St. Louis Exposition? How are these peoples portrayed by photographers? How are they dressed? What are they doing? What impressions might visitors or viewers of the photographs have of these peoples? When there are American visitors in the photographs (as in Sources 5, 9, and 12), what are they doing? Why did photographers place them in these pictures?

Source 12 is a photograph depicting a replica of an American school for Filipinos in the Philippines. What was the purpose of the photographer who took this picture? What is the photograph's message? What impressions would viewers have?

Sources 13 and 14 are photographs of Visayans, a people quite different from the Negritos, Igorot, Tagalo, and Bontocs. What was different about them? How might you account for these differences?[11] How might American visitors to the village and viewers of these photographs react to the Visayans as compared to other Filipino peoples at the exposition? What impressions would the Visayans make? How might the Visayans be used to justify American imperialism in the Philippines?

The last photograph, Source 15, is of a detachment of Filipino soldiers nicknamed the "Little Macs" who fought with the Americans during the Philippine Insurrection. How were these

11. *Note:* The Visayans were Roman Catholics, whereas all the other Filipinos brought to St. Louis practiced non-Western religions or held onto native Filipino religious customs. What does this tell you about the Visayans?

CHAPTER 4

JUSTIFYING
AMERICAN
IMPERIALISM:
THE LOUISIANA
PURCHASE
EXPOSITION,
1904

men depicted? Was the impression likely to be favorable or unfavorable? Do you think it is significant that the officers for this detachment were Americans? Why? How might the Little Macs be used to justify American imperialism in the Philippines?

Once you have examined the photographs individually, analyze them collectively. What was their collective message? How does that message relate to American actions in the Philippines from 1898 to the exposition in 1904? Could these photographs, or word descriptions of them, be used to justify American imperialism in the Philippines? How? Refer to specific photographs to prove your points.

EPILOGUE

At the Louisiana Purchase Exposition in 1904, American visitors saw countless exhibits that communicated very strong messages. Arranged and erected by the nation's corporate, intellectual, and political leaders, the exhibits nevertheless were what Americans wanted to see. These exhibits trumpeted America's own scientific, technological, and cultural prowess while at the same time offering living proof that it was the United States' economic, political, and moral duty to become a colonial power. In addition to Filipino villages, villages had been set up for American Indians and Alaskan Eskimo who, like the Filipinos, were wards of the United States. It was as powerful a visual justification for American imperialism as could possibly have been contrived.

Once the Philippine revolt was broken in 1902, the United States invested considerable time and energy trying to Americanize the Filipinos, largely through education and giving Filipinos an increasing voice in their own affairs. In 1913, President Woodrow Wilson appointed Francis B. Harrison Governor General of the Philippines, with the explicit instructions to prepare the Filipinos for their ultimate independence (a promise Congress gave its assent to in 1916, noting that independence would be granted "as soon as a stable government can be established"). Schools were set up throughout the islands, and by the 1930s, almost 50 percent of the population was literate. Gradually, American officials increased the percentage of Filipinos in the civil service, from 49 percent in 1903 to 94 percent in 1923. Elections were held for a Philippine legislature, although the real power remained in the hands of Americans.

In economic matters, however, the Americans' record in the Philippines was not so impressive. Economic power remained in the hands of a small, native Philippine landed elite who, with the cooperation of Americans, continued to dominate the Philippine economy. Between 1900 and 1935, poverty became more widespread, real wages actually declined, and sharecropping (like that in the American South) doubled. This was the situation when the Japanese attacked the Philippine Islands on December 8, 1941.

With the defeat of Japan in 1945, the United States moved quickly to grant independence to the Philippines (which occurred on July 4, 1946), although America's economic and military presence in the new nation remained strong. Favorable leases on military and naval bases were negotiated, and the Central Intelligence Agency closely monitored Philippine elections and on occasion secretly backed candidates for office.

In 1965, campaigning against widespread government corruption and favoritism to the landed elite, Ferdinand Marcos was elected president of the Philippines. A much-lauded war hero, Marcos entered politics in 1949, when he became the youngest person ever elected to the Philippine Congress. Once in power as president, however, Marcos increased the power of his office to virtual one-man rule, largely by hobbling or eradicating the other branches of government and by a brutal policy of political repression, with more than 50,000 political prisoners and numerous reported incidents of assassinations and torture. Even so, Marcos's rule was insecure. In the nation's economic expansion, profits went to a very few, usually Marcos's associates (in 1972, the poorest 20 percent of Filipinos received only 4.4 percent of the nation's income), and a population boom (2.5 percent per year) increased poverty and unemployment.

Things began coming apart for Marcos on August 21, 1983, when his principal political rival, Benigno Aquino, was shot and killed at the Manila airport as he was returning to the Philippines to lead an anti-Marcos political movement. Public opinion in both the Philippines and the United States believed that Marcos had been responsible for Aquino's death. By 1984, opinion polls in the Philippines showed a serious erosion of support for the Marcos government.

In 1986, Marcos was challenged for the presidency by Corazon Aquino, the widow of the killed opposition leader. The election results were clouded with charges of fraud, and both Marcos and Aquino claimed victory. By this time, the aging and ill Marcos had become increasingly isolated from the people, as he and his wife Imelda remained cloistered in the presidential palace. In February 1986, a general strike by Aquino supporters, the army turning against the government, and the increasing displeasure of the Reagan administration finally toppled Marcos, who fled the Philippines for American protection in Hawaii. Corazon Aquino became president, to face the nation's severe economic and political problems.

In one sense the Louisiana Purchase Exposition in St. Louis in 1904 marked the highpoint of Americans' interest in international expositions and world's fairs. As Americans became less provincial, especially after the introduction of modern communications media, attendance at such events declined. As a result, such expositions became smaller (as opposed to the St. Louis Exposition, which covered 1,272 acres, the Knoxville, Tennessee world's fair of 1982 was held on

CHAPTER 4

JUSTIFYING
AMERICAN
IMPERIALISM:
THE LOUISIANA
PURCHASE
EXPOSITION,
1904

less than 70 acres). Moreover, the purpose of American expositions changed. Rather than being celebrations of the nation's technological might or justifications for American imperialism, world's fairs were viewed by their backers as massive urban renewal projects, in which the city government would come into possession of valuable acreage to be used for economic development. Such was the goal of recent fairs in Portland, Knoxville, and New Orleans. Finally, increased cost and lowered attendance figures meant that such expositions could cost millions of dollars that never would be recouped. The New Orleans world's fair lost millions. As a result, Chicago, which had planned to host an international exposition in 1992, had second thoughts.

In 1904, however, millions of Americans came to St. Louis to visit the Louisiana Purchase Exposition, a massive reinforcement of their own ideas about American superiority and the rectitude of Euro-American world domination. An almost direct extension of the nineteenth-century concept of Manifest Destiny, United States imperialism cast Americans, still comparatively naive and provincial, into a world filled with opportunities and perils that their own ideology made them unprepared to understand.

HOMOGENIZING A PLURALISTIC CULTURE: PROPAGANDA DURING WORLD WAR I

One week after Congress approved the war declaration that brought the United States into World War I, President Woodrow Wilson signed Executive Order 2594, which created the Committee on Public Information, designed to mobilize public opinion behind the war effort. Apparently there was considerable worry in the Wilson administration that the American public, which had supported neutrality and noninvolvement, would not rally to the war effort.

Wilson selected forty-one-year-old journalist and political ally George Creel to head the Committee on Public Information. Creel rapidly established voluntary press censorship, which made the committee essentially the overseer of all war and war-related news. The committee also produced films, engaged some 75,000 lecturers (called "Four Minute Men") who delivered approximately 7.5 million talks, commissioned posters intended to stir up support for the war and sell war bonds (700 poster designs were submitted, and more than 9 million posters were printed in 1918 alone), and engaged in numerous other activities to blend this ethnically and ideologically diverse nation into a homogeneous nation in support of the country's war effort and to discredit any potential opposition to America's entry into the war.

In this chapter you will analyze the propaganda techniques of a modern nation at war. The evidence contains

CHAPTER 5

HOMOGENIZING
A PLURALISTIC
CULTURE:
PROPAGANDA
DURING WORLD
WAR I

material sponsored or commissioned by the Committee on Public Information (posters, newspaper advertisements, selections of speeches by Four Minute Men) as well as privately produced works (musical lyrics and commercial films) that tended to parallel the committee's efforts. Essentially, the question you are to answer is: how did the United States mobilize public opinion in support of the nation's participation in World War I? In addition, what were the consequences, positive and negative, of this mobilization of public opinion?

On a larger scale, you should be willing to ponder other questions as well, although they do not relate directly to the evidence you will examine. To begin with, is government-sponsored propaganda during wartime a good thing? When it comes into conflict with the First Amendment's guarantees of freedom of speech, which should prevail? Finally, is there a danger that government-sponsored propaganda can be carried too far? Do you think that was the case during World War I?

BACKGROUND

Although by the early twentieth century the United States had worldwide economic interests and even had acquired a modest colonial empire, many Americans wanted to believe that they were insulated from world affairs and impervious to world problems. Two great oceans seemed to protect the nation from overseas threats and problems, and the very enormity of the country and the comparative weakness of its neighbors appeared to secure it against all dangers. Let other nations waste their people and resources in petty wars over status and territory, Americans reasoned, but the United States should stand above such greed or insanity, and certainly should not wade in foreign mudpuddles.

To many Americans, European nations were especially suspect. For centuries, European nations had engaged in an almost ceaseless round of armed conflicts, wars for national unity or territory or even religion or empire. Moreover, in the eyes of many Americans, these bloody wars appeared to have solved little or nothing, and the end of one war seemed to be but a prelude to the next. Ambitious kings and their plotting ministers seemed to make Europe the scene of almost constant uproar, an uproar that many Americans saw as devoid of reason and morality. Nor did it appear that the United States, as powerful as it was, could have any effect on the unstable European situation.

For this reason most Americans greeted news of the outbreak of war in Europe in 1914 with equal measures of surprise and determination to not become involved. They applauded President Woodrow Wilson's August 4 proclamation of neutrality, his statement (issued two weeks later) urging Americans to be impartial in thought as well as in deed, and his insistence that the United States continue neutral commerce with all the belligerents. Few Americans protested German violation of Belgian neutrality. Indeed, most Americans (naively, as it turned out) believed that the United States both should and could remain aloof from the conflict in Europe.

But many factors pulled the United States into the conflict that later became known as World War I. America's economic prosperity to a large extent rested on commercial ties with Europe. United States trade with the Allies (England, France, Russia) exceeded $800 million in 1914, whereas trade with the Central Powers (Germany, Austria, Turkey) stood at approximately $170 million in that same year. Much of the trade with Great Britain and France was financed through loans from American banks, something President Wilson and Secretary of State William Jennings Bryan openly discouraged because both men believed that those economic interests might eventually draw the United States into the conflict. Indeed, Wilson and Bryan probably were correct. Nevertheless, American economic interests were closely tied to those of Great Britain and France. Thus a victory by the Central Powers might damage United States trade. As Wilson drifted to an acceptance of this fact, Bryan had to back down.

A second factor pulling the United States into the war was the deep-seated feelings of President Wilson himself. Formerly a constitutional historian (Wilson had been a college professor and university president before entering the political arena as a re-

form governor of New Jersey), Wilson had long admired the British people and their form of government. Although technically neutral, the president strongly, although privately, favored the Allies and viewed a German victory as unthinkable. Moreover, many of Wilson's key advisers and the people close to him were decidedly pro-British. Such was the opinion of the president's friend and closest adviser Colonel Edward House, as well as that of Robert Lansing (who replaced Bryan as secretary of state)[1] and Walter Hines Page (ambassador to England). These men and others helped strengthen Wilson's strong political opinions and influence the president's changing position toward the war in Europe. Hence, although Wilson asked Americans to be neutral in thought as well as in deed, in fact he and his principal advisers were neither. More than once, the President chose to ignore British violations of America's neutrality. Finally, when it appeared that the Central Powers might outlast their enemies, Wilson was determined to intercede.

A third factor affecting the United States' neutrality was the strong ethnic ties of many Americans to the Old World. Many Americans had been born in Europe, and an even larger number were the sons and daughters of European immigrants (Tables 1 and 2). Although these people considered

---

1. Bryan resigned in 1915, in protest over what he considered Wilson's too sharp note to Germany over the sinking of the passenger liner *Lusitania.* Wilson called the act "illegal and inhuman." Bryan sensed that the Wilson administration was tilting away from neutrality.

CHAPTER 5

HOMOGENIZING
A PLURALISTIC
CULTURE:
PROPAGANDA
DURING WORLD
WAR I

1. Foreign-Born Population, by Country of Birth*

Country of Birth	Total Foreign Born
England	813,853
Scotland	254,570
Ireland	1,037,234
Germany	1,686,108
Austria	575,627
Russia	1,400,495

*Both this and Table 2 were compiled from the United States census of 1920, the closest census to America's entrance into World War I (1917). The figures on Ireland include Northern Ireland, and the figures on Russia include the Baltic States.

2. Native-Born Population of Foreign or Mixed Parentage, by Country of Origin

Country of Origin of Parents	Total Native-Born Children
England and Wales	1,864,345
Scotland	514,436
Ireland	3,122,013
Germany	5,346,004
Austria	1,235,097
Russia	1,508,604

themselves to be, and were, Americans, some retained emotional ties to Europe that they sometimes carried into the political arena—ties that could influence America's foreign policy.

Finally, as the largest neutral commercial power in the world, the United States soon became caught in the middle of the commercial warfare of the belligerents. With the declaration of war, Great Britain and Germany both threw up naval blockades. Great Britain's blockade was designed to cut the Central Powers off from war material. American commercial vessels bound for Germany were stopped, searched, and often seized by the British navy. Wilson protested British policy many times, but to no effect. After all, the British navy was one of that nation's principal sources of military strength.

Germany's blockade was even more dangerous, partly because the vast majority of American trade was with England and France. In addition, however, Germany's chief method of blockading the Allies was the use of the submarine, a comparatively new weapon in 1914. Because of the nature of the submarine (lethal while underwater, not equal to other fighting vessels on the surface), it was difficult for the submarine to remain effective and at the same time adhere to international law, such as the requirement that sufficient warning be given before sinking an enemy ship. In 1915, hoping to terrorize the British into making peace, Germany unleashed its submarines in the Atlantic with orders to sink all ships flying Allied flags. In March, a German submarine sank the British passenger ship *Falaba*. Then on May 7, 1915, the British liner *Lusitania* was sunk with a loss of more than 1,000 lives, 128 of them American. Although Germany had published warnings in American newspapers specifically cautioning Americans not to travel on the *Lusitania* and although it was ultimately discovered that the *Lusitania* had gone down so fast (in only eighteen minutes) because the British were shipping ammunition in the hold of the passenger ship, Americans were shocked by the Germans' actions on the high seas. Most Americans, however, continued to believe that the United States should stay out of the war and approved of Wilson's statement, issued three days after the *Lusitania* went to the bottom, that "There is such a thing as a man being too proud to fight."

Yet a combination of economic interests, German submarine warfare, and other events gradually pushed the United States toward involvement. In early February 1917, Germany announced a policy of unrestricted submarine warfare against all ships—belligerent and neutral alike. Ships would be sunk without warning if found to be in what Germany designated forbidden waters. Later that month the British intercepted a secret telegram intended for the German minister in Mexico. In that telegram German foreign secretary Arthur Zimmermann offered Mexico a deal: Germany would help Mexico retrieve territory lost to the United States in the 1840s if Mexico would make a military alliance with Germany and would declare war on the United States in the event that the United States declared war on Germany. Knowing the impact such a telegram would make on American public opinion, the British quickly handed the telegram over to Wilson, who released it to the press. From that point, United States involvement in World War I was but a matter of time. On April 2, 1917, the president asked Congress for a declaration of war. On April 4, the Senate approved a war declaration (the vote was 82–6), and

the House of Representatives followed suit two days later (with a vote of 373–50).[2] And so Americans became embroiled in a war that for three years they had sought so strenuously to avoid.

At the outset of America's entry into the war, many governmental officials feared (incorrectly, as it turned out) that large blocs of Americans would not support the war effort. In 1917, the Bureau of the Census had estimated that approximately 4,662,000 people living in the United States had been born in Germany or one of the other Central Powers.[3] As Tables 1 and 2 show, the United States also contained a large number of Irish-Americans, many of whom were vehemently anti-British and hence emotionally sided with the Central Powers. Could this heterogeneous society be persuaded voluntarily to support the war effort? Could Americans of the same ethnic stock as the enemies be rallied to the cause?

Furthermore, there had been no decisive event to prompt the war declaration (some even thought the Zimmermann telegram was a British hoax). Would Americans support such a war

2. The fifty-six votes in the Senate and House against the declaration of war essentially came from three separate groups: senators and congressmen with strong German and Austrian constituencies, isolationists who believed the United States should not become involved on either side, and some Progressive reformers who maintained that the war would divert America's attention from political, economic, and social reforms. 3. No census had been taken since 1910, so this was a very rough guess. As shown in Table 1, it was much too high.

CHAPTER 5

HOMOGENIZING
A PLURALISTIC
CULTURE:
PROPAGANDA
DURING WORLD
WAR I

with sufficient unanimity? No firing on Fort Sumter or blowing up of the battleship *Maine* had forced America's entrance into World War I. The *Lusitania* sinking had occurred two years before the war declaration. Without the obvious threat of having been attacked, would the American people stand together to defeat the faraway enemy? Could American isolationist and noninterventionist opinion, very strong as late as the presidential election of 1916, be overcome? To solidify the nation behind the war, Wilson created the Committee on Public Information.

THE METHOD

For George Creel and the Committee on Public Information, the purposes of propaganda were very clear:

1. Unite a multiethnic, pluralistic society behind the war effort
2. Attract a sufficient number of men to the armed services and elicit universal civilian support for those men
3. Influence civilians to support the war effort by purchasing war bonds or by other actions (such as limiting personal consumption or rolling bandages)
4. Influence civilians to put pressure on other civilians to refrain from antiwar comments, strikes, antidraft activities, unwitting dispersal of information to spies, and other public acts that could hurt the war effort

To achieve these ends, propaganda techniques had to be employed with extreme care. For propaganda to be effective, it would have to contain one or more of the following features:

1. Portrayal of American and Allied servicemen in the best possible light
2. Portrayal of the enemy in the worst possible light
3. Portrayal of the American and Allied cause as just and the enemy's cause as unjust
4. Message to civilians that they were being involved in the war effort in important ways
5. Communication of a sense of urgency to civilians

In this chapter you are given the following six types of World War I propaganda to analyze, some of it produced directly by the Committee on Public Information and some produced privately but examined by the committee:

1. Popular songs performed in music halls or vaudeville houses. Although the Committee on Public Information did not produce this material, it could have discouraged performances of "unpatriotic" material.
2. Newspaper and magazine advertisements produced directly by the Committee on Public Information.
3. Posters, approved by the committee and used for recruiting, liberty loans, and other purposes.

4. An editorial cartoon, produced privately but generally approved by the committee.

5. A selection of speeches by Four Minute Men, volunteers engaged by the committee to speak in theaters, churches, and other gatherings. Their speeches were not to exceed four minutes in length—hence, their name. The committee published a newsletter that offered suggestions and material for speaking topics.

6. A review of the documentary film *Pershing's Crusaders,* 1918, and some advertising suggestions to theater owners concerning the film *Kultur.* The film industry was largely self-censored, but the committee could—and did—stop the distribution of films that, in its opinion, hurt the war effort. *Pershing's Crusaders* was a committee-produced film, whereas *Kultur* was a commercial production.

As you examine the evidence, you will see that effective propaganda operates on two levels. On the surface there is the logical appeal for support to help win the war. On another level, however, certain images and themes are employed to excite the emotions of the people for whom the propaganda is designed. As you examine the evidence, ask yourself the following questions:

1. For whom is this piece of propaganda designed?
2. What is this piece of propaganda trying to get people to think? To do?
3. What logical appeal is being made?
4. What emotional appeals are being made?
5. What might be the results, positive and negative, of these kinds of appeals?

In songs, speeches, advertisements, and film reviews, are there key words, important images? Where there are illustrations (advertisements, posters, cartoons), what facial expressions and images are used? Finally, are there any common logical and emotional themes running through American propaganda during World War I? How did the United States use propaganda to mobilize public opinion during World War I? What were some of the consequences, positive and negative, of this type of propaganda?

CHAPTER 5

HOMOGENIZING
A PLURALISTIC
CULTURE:
PROPAGANDA
DURING WORLD
WAR I

THE EVIDENCE

Source 1: Popular song by George M. Cohan, 1917.

1. "Over There."

Johnnie, get your gun,
Get your gun, get your gun,
Take it on the run,
On the run, on the run.
Hear them calling you and me,
Every son of liberty.
Hurry right away,
No delay, no delay,.
Make your daddy glad
To have had such a lad.
Tell your sweetheart not to pine,
To be proud her boy's in line.

Chorus (repeat chorus twice)
Over there, over there,
Send the word, send the word over there—
That the Yanks are coming,
The Yanks are coming,
The drums rum-tumming
Ev'rywhere.
So prepare, say a pray'r,
Send the word, send the word to beware.
We'll be over, we're coming over,
And we won't come back till it's over
Over there.

Source 2: Popular song, from Alfred E. Cornbise, *War as Advertised: The Four Minute Men and America's Crusade, 1917–1918* (Philadelphia: American Philosophical Society, 1984), p. 70.

2. Untitled. *(To be sung to a variation of "My Country Tis of Thee")*

Come, freemen of the land,
Come meet the great demand,
True heart and open hand,
    Take the loan!

For the hopes that prophets saw,
For the swords your brothers draw,
For liberty and law
    Take the loan!

Sources 3 through 5: Advertisements from James R. Mock and Cedric Larson, *Words That Won the War: The Story of the Committee on Public Information* (Princeton: Princeton University Press, © 1939), pp. 64; 169; 98.

3. Urging Americans to Report the Enemy.

Spies *and* Lies

German agents are everywhere, eager to gather scraps of news about our men, our ships, our munitions. It is still possible to get such information through to Germany, where thousands of these fragments—often individually harmless—are patiently pieced together into a whole which spells death to American soldiers and danger to American homes.

But while the enemy is most industrious in trying to collect information, and his systems elaborate, he is *not* superhuman—indeed he is often very stupid, and would fail to get what he wants were it not deliberately handed to him by the carelessness of loyal Americans.

Do not discuss in public, or with strangers, any news of troop and transport movements, or bits of gossip as to our military preparations, which come into your possession.

Do not permit your friends in service to tell you—or write you—"inside" facts about where they are, what they are doing and seeing.

Do not become a tool of the Hun by passing on the malicious, disheartening rumors which he so eagerly sows. Remember he asks no better service than to have you spread his lies of disasters to our soldiers and sailors, gross scandals in the Red Cross, cruelties, neglect and wholesale executions in our camps, drunkenness and vice in the Expeditionary Force, and other tales certain to disturb American patriots and to bring anxiety and grief to American parents.

And do not wait until you catch someone putting a bomb under a factory. Report the man who spreads pessimistic stories, divulges—or seeks—confidential military information, cries for peace, or belittles our efforts to win the war.

Send the names of such persons, even if they are in uniform, to the Department of Justice, Washington. Give all the details you can, with names of witnesses if possible—show the Hun that we can beat him at his own game of collecting scattered information and putting it to work. The fact that you made the report will not become public.

You are in contact with the enemy today, just as truly as if you faced him across No Man's Land. In your hands are two powerful weapons with which to meet him—discretion and vigilance. *Use them.*

COMMITTEE ON PUBLIC INFORMATION
8 JACKSON PLACE, WASHINGTON, D. C.

George Creel, Chairman
The Secretary of State
The Secretary of War
The Secretary of the Navy

Contributed through Division of Advertising

United States Gov't Comm. on Public Information

CHAPTER 5

HOMOGENIZING
A PLURALISTIC
CULTURE:
PROPAGANDA
DURING WORLD
WAR I

4. Fighting the Enemy by Buying Liberty Bonds.

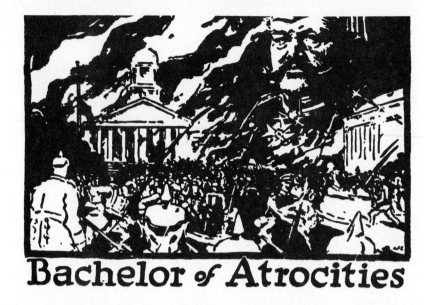

Bachelor *of* Atrocities

IN the vicious guttural language of Kultur, the degree A. B. means Bachelor of Atrocities. Are you going to let the Prussian Python strike at your Alma Mater, as it struck at the University of Louvain?[4]

The Hohenzollern[5] fang strikes at every element of decency and culture and taste that your college stands for. It leaves a track so terrible that only whispered fragments may be recounted. It has ripped all the world-old romance out of war, and reduced it to the dead, black depths of muck, and hate, and bitterness.

You may soon be called to fight. But you are called upon right now to buy Liberty Bonds. You are called upon to economize in every way. It is sometimes harder to live nobly than to die nobly. The supreme sacrifice of life may come easier than the petty sacrifices of comforts and luxuries. You are called to exercise stern self-discipline. Upon this the Allied Success depends.

Set aside every possible dollar for the purchase of Liberty Bonds. Do it relentlessly. Kill every wasteful impulse, that America may live. Every bond you buy fires point-blank at Prussian Terrorism.

BUY U. S. GOVERNMENT BONDS FOURTH LIBERTY LOAN

Contributed through Division of Advertising

United States Gov't Comm. on Public Information

This space contributed for the Winning of the War by
A. T SKERRY, '84, and CYRILLE CARREAU, '04.

4. The University of Louvain, in Belgium, was pillaged and partially destroyed by German troops. Some professors were beaten and others killed, and the library (containing 250,000 books and manuscripts, some irreplaceable) was totally destroyed. The students themselves were home for summer vacation.

5. Hohenzollern was the name of the German royal family since the nation's founding in 1871. It had been the Prussian royal family since 1525.

5. Contrasting the American Idea with the German Idea.

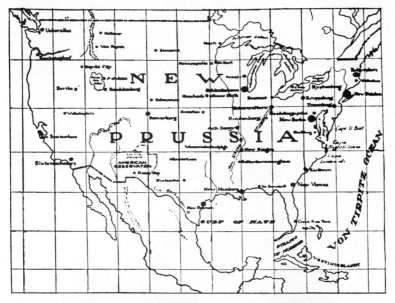

THE GERMAN IDEA

SHALL this war make Germany's word the highest law in the world? Read what she expects. Here are the words of her own spokesmen. Then ask yourself where Germany would have the United States stand after the war.

Shall we bow to Germany's wishes––assist German ambition?

No. The German idea must be so completely crushed that it will never again rear its venomous head.

It's a fight, as the President said, "to the last dollar, the last drop of blood."

THE AMERICAN IDEA

The President's Flag Day Speech, With Evidence of Germany's plans. 32 pages.
The War Message and the Facts Behind It. 32 pages.
The Nation in Arms. 16 pages.
Why We Fight Germany.
War, Labor and Peace.

THE GERMAN IDEA

Conquest and Kultur. 160 pages.
German War Practices. 96 pages.
Treatment of German Militarism and German Critics.
The German War Code.

COMMITTEE ON PUBLIC INFORMATION
8 JACKSON PLACE, WASHINGTON, D. C.

Contributed through Division of Advertising, United States Govern'mt Committee on Public Information

George Creel, Chairman
The Secretary of State
The Secretary of War
The Secretary of the Navy

This space contributed for the Winning of the War by

The Publisher of *Publisher*

CHAPTER 5

HOMOGENIZING
A PLURALISTIC
CULTURE:
PROPAGANDA
DURING WORLD
WAR I

Source 6: Poster from *The James Montgomery Flagg Poster Book,* introduction by Susan E. Meyer (New York: Watson-Guptill Publications, © 1975). Courtesy of the Library of Congress.

6. The Famous Uncle Sam Poster.

Source 7: Poster from Peter Stanley, *What Did You Do in the War, Daddy?*
(Melbourne: Oxford University Press, © 1983), p. 55.

7. Germany Portrayed as a Raging Beast.

8. **Recruiting Poster.**

9. **Recruiting Poster.**

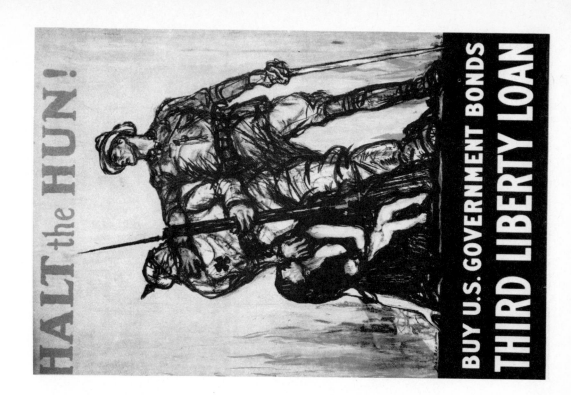

11. Urging Americans to Buy Liberty Bonds.

10. Poster Depicting Our Relationship with Our Ally, England.

CHAPTER 5

HOMOGENIZING
A PLURALISTIC
CULTURE:
PROPAGANDA
DURING WORLD
WAR I

Source 12: Poster from Peter Stanley, *What Did You Do in the War, Daddy?*, p. 65.

12. Fourth Liberty Bond Campaign.

13. Boy Scout Motto and Liberty Bonds.

Source 15: Poster from Darracott, *The First World War in Posters*, p. 30.

15. Promotional Poster for Red Cross.

The GREATEST MOTHER in the WORLD

Red Cross
Christmas
Roll Call
Dec. 16-23rd

Source 14: Poster from *The James Montgomery Flagg Poster Book*.

14. Actresses Promote Liberty Bonds.

STAGE WOMEN'S WAR RELIEF

Source 17: Poster from Darracott, *The First World War in Posters*, p. 40.

17. Liberty Bond Campaign.

Source 16: Poster from Anthony Crawford, *Posters in the George C. Marshall Research Foundation* (Charlottesville: University of Virginia Press, © 1939), p. 30.

16. Poster Targeting the American Women.

CHAPTER 5

HOMOGENIZING
A PLURALISTIC
CULTURE:
PROPAGANDA
DURING WORLD
WAR I

Source 18: Editorial cartoon from John Higham, *Strangers in the Land: Patterns of American Nativism,* 1860–1925 (New Brunswick, N.J.: Rutgers University Press, 1955), p. 210.

18. German-American Dr. Karl Muck, Conductor of the Boston Symphony Orchestra, Needed a Police Escort When He Conducted a Concert in March 1918 in New York City.

Sources 19 through 22 from a selection of speeches by Four Minute Men, from Alfred E. Cornbise, *War As Advertised: The Four Minute Men and America's Crusade, 1917–1918* (Philadelphia: American Philosophical Society, 1984), pp. 72–73; 122; 60; 27.

19. Speech by a Four Minute Man.

Ladies and Gentlemen:

I have just received the information that there is a German spy among us—a German spy watching *us*.

He is around, here somewhere, reporting upon you and me—sending reports about us to Berlin and telling the Germans just what we are doing with the Liberty Loan. From every section of the country these spies have been getting reports over to Potsdam[6]—not general reports but details—where the loan is going well and where its success seems weak, and what people are saying in each community.

For the German Government is worried about our great loan. Those Junkers[7] fear its effect upon the German *morale*. They're raising a loan this month, too.

If the American people lend their billions now, one and all with a hip-hip-hurrah, it means that America is united and strong. While, if we lend our money half-heartedly, America seems weak and autocracy remains strong.

Money means everything now; it means quicker victory and therefore less bloodshed. We are *in* the war, and now Americans can have but *one* opinion, only *one* wish in the Liberty Loan.

Well, I hope these spies are getting their messages straight, letting Potsdam know that America *is hurling back* to the autocrats these answers:

For treachery here, attempted treachery in Mexico, treachery everywhere—*one billion*.

For murder of American women and children—*one billion more*.

For broken faith and promise to murder more Americans—*billions and billions more*.

And then we will add:

In the world fight for Liberty, our share—*billions and billions and billions and endless billions*.

Do not let the German spy hear and report that *you* are a slacker.

6. Potsdam (a suburb of Berlin) was where the Kaiser lived.
7. Junkers were the Prussian nobility.

CHAPTER 5

HOMOGENIZING
A PLURALISTIC
CULTURE:
PROPAGANDA
DURING WORLD
WAR I

20. Part of a Speech by a Four Minute Man.

German agents are telling the people of this . . . race[8] through the South
that if they will not oppose the German Government, or help our Government, they will be rewarded with Ford automobiles when Germany is in
control here. They are told that 10 negroes are being conscripted to 1 white
man in order that the Negro race may be killed off; and that the reason
Germany went into Belgium was to punish the people of that country for
the cruel treatment of the negroes in the Congo.

21. Poem Read by Four Minute Men: "It's Duty Boy."

My boy must never bring disgrace to his immortal sires—
At Valley Forge and Lexington they kindled freedom's fires,
John's father died at Gettysburg, mine fell at Chancellorsville;
While John himself was with the boys who charged up San Juan Hill.
And John, if he was living now, would surely say with me,
"No son of ours shall e'er disgrace our grand old family tree
By turning out a slacker when his country needs his aid."
It is not of such timber that America was made.
I'd rather you had died at birth or not been born at all,
Than know that I had raised a son who cannot hear the call
That freedom has sent round the world, its precious rights to save—
This call is meant for you, my boy, and I would have you brave;
And though my heart is breaking, boy, I bid you do your part,
And show the world no son of mine is cursed with craven heart;
And if, perchance, you ne'er return, my later days to cheer,
And I have only memories of my brave boy, so dear,
I'd rather have it so, my boy, and know you bravely died
Than have a living coward sit supinely by my side.
To save the world from sin, my boy, God gave his only son—
He's asking for MY boy, to-day, and may His will be done.

8. At the front lines in France, Germans barraged America's African American soldiers with
leaflets urging them to desert (none did). One of those propaganda leaflets said, in part,
"Do you enjoy the same rights as the white people do in America . . . or are you rather not
treated over there as second-class citizens?" As to the charge of discrimination against African Americans by draft boards, there were numerous complaints that African Americans
found it almost impossible to get exemptions from military service. In the end, about 31
percent of the African Americans who registered were called into service, as opposed to 26
percent of the registered whites. To counteract German propaganda, prominent African
American persons were sent to France to lecture to the African American troops.

22. Poem Read by Four Minute Men.

Attention, Mr. Farmer Man, and listen now to me,
and I will try and show to you what I can plainly see.
Your Uncle Sam, the dear old man who's been so good to you,
is needing help and watching now to see what you will do.
Your Uncle's in the great world war and since he's entered in
it's up to every one of us to see that he shall win.
He's trying hard to "speed things up" and do it with a dash,
and so just now he's asking you to aid him with your cash.
Remember, all he asks of you is but a simple loan,
and every patriot comes across without a single moan.
Should Uncle Sammy once get mad (he will if you get lax),
he then will exercise his right, and make you pay a tax.
Should Kaiser Bill and all his hordes, once get across the Pond,
d'ye think he'll waste his time on you, and coax to take a bond?
Why no, siree. He'd grab and hold most everything he saw.
He'd take your farm, your stock and lands, your wife and babies all.
He'd make you work, he'd make you sweat, he'd squeeze you till you'd
groan.
So be a man, and come across. Let Uncle have that loan.

Source 23: Film review of *Pershing's Crusaders* from *Literary Digest*, June 8, 1918.

23. Seeing Our Boys "Over There."

Multiform are the war-activities of Uncle Sam. Whoever would have thought
of him a year ago as an *impresario* in moving pictures? In a small way this
has been one of his war-activities, but now he boldly challenges competition
with the biggest and launches his "Pershing's Crusaders" for the benefit of
the American Army, the American Navy, and the Allied War-Relief. The initial performance at the Lyric Theater, New York, brought out an audience
that might have swelled to the dimensions of a Metropolitan Opera crowd if
capacity had permitted. Mr. E. H. Sothern and our former Ambassador to
Germany, Mr. James W. Gerard, were present to speak, but the pictures of
the boys at the front were the thing, and the country will eagerly await the
sight of her sons in their present environment here and "over there." As
described by the *New York Tribune*, we learn that—

> Whoever took the pictures have not depended on the popularity of the subject
> alone, for they show a fine attention to detail that is most satisfying, when
> everything connected with the boys at the front is of vital interest.

[141]

CHAPTER 5

HOMOGENIZING
A PLURALISTIC
CULTURE:
PROPAGANDA
DURING WORLD
WAR I

The pictures show "the mailed fist of the world," and altho this is merely symbolic, it is such a telling hit that it is impossible not to mention it. Germany and France are shown as tho modeled in clay, and then slowly, out of the center of Germany, rises a volcano, and a huge mailed fist appears scattering mud and sand and lava over France.

The first part of the picture shows how plots, fires, strikes, etc., were fomented by German agents in America; how America is putting her hand to the plow to feed the Allies; the huge cantonments which have sprung up to house the Army; cutting the khaki clothes by machinery. Other subjects are: What American women are doing; how the army shoes are made; feeding America's Army; mighty ships in the building; supremacy in the air will strike down the German vultures; our Navy; camouflage of the sea; our own submarines; in the aviation camps; baptizing the boys ordered to the front; tenderness and skill at the dressing-stations; the sniper's job; the victor of yesterday and the victor of to-morrow, and Pershing's crusaders and their Allies, who will get the Kaiser.

Source 24 from *The Moving Picture World,* September 28, 1918.

24. Promotional Tips to Theater Managers.

ADVERTISING AIDS FOR BUSY MANAGERS

"KULTUR."

William Fox Presents Gladys Brockwell in a Typical Example of the Brutality of the Wilhelmstrasse to Its Spy-slaves.

Cast.

Countess Griselda Von Arenburg,
　　　　　　　　　　　　Gladys Brockwell
Eliska ....Georgia Woodthorpe
René de Bornay................William Scott
Baron von Zeller ....Willard Louis
Archduke Franz Ferdinand ....Charles Clary
Danilo ....Nigel de Brullier
The Kaiser ....William Burress
Emperor Franz Josef.........Alfred Fremont

Directed by Edward J. Le Saint.

The Story: The Kaiser decides that the time is ripe for a declaration of war, and sends word to his vassal monarch of Austria. René de Bornay is sent by France to discover what is being planned. He meets the Countess, who falls in love with him. She sickens of the spy system and declares that she is done with it, but is warned that she cannot withdraw. She is told to secure René's undoing, but instead procures his escape and in her own boudoir is stood against the wall and shot for saving the man whom she loves better than her life.

Feature Gladys Brockwell as Countess Griselda Von Arenburg and William Scott as René de Bornay.

Program and Advertising Phrases: Gladys Brockwell, Star of Latest Picture, Exposing Hun Brutality and Satanic Intrigue.
How An Austrian Countess Gave Her All for Democracy.
She Was an Emperor's Favorite Yet She Died for World Freedom.
Story of an Emperor's Mistress and a Crime That Rocked the World.
Daring Exposure of Scandals and Crimes in Hun Court Circles.
Astonishing Revelations of Hun Plots to Rape Democracy.

Advertising Angles: Do not offer this as a propaganda story, but tell that it is one of the angles of the merciless Prussian spy system about which has been woven a real romance. Play up the spy angle heavily both in your newspaper work and through window cards with such lines as "even the spies themselves hate their degradation." Miss Brockwell wears some stunning and daring gowns in this play, and with these special appeal can be made to the women.

Sources 1 and 2 are songs that were popular during World War I. Each song should be analyzed for its message. What was "Over There" urging young men to do? How would that song appeal to the home front? What emotions were the lyrics trying to arouse? The untitled song was intended exclusively for the home front. What sacrifices were expected of Americans who did not go to war? How did the song appeal to these people?

The next evidence consists of three advertisements (Sources 3 to 5) produced by the Committee on Public Information. How were the Germans portrayed in "Spies and Lies?" In "Bachelor of Atrocities?" In "The German Idea?" How could Americans counteract Germans and their actions? Were there any dangers inherent in the kinds of activities the CPI was urging on patriotic Americans?

In some ways, poster art, which follows in the evidence, is similar to editorial cartoons, principally because the artist has only one canvas or frame on which to tell his or her story. Yet the poster must be more arresting than the cartoon, must convey its message rapidly, and must avoid ambiguities or confusion. Posters were an extremely popular form of propaganda during World War I. Indeed, so popular were the posters of James Montgomery Flagg (1877–1960) that, along with other artists and entertainers, Flagg helped sell $1,000 Liberty Bonds by performing (in his case, painting posters) in front of the New York Public Library. The well-known "Tell That to the Marines" was created there.

As you examine the four posters[9] in Sources 6 through 9, determine their intended audience. What emotional appeal did each poster make? What feelings did each poster seek to elicit? The poster in Source 10 ("Side by Side") is quite different from its predecessors in this exercise. How is it different? What appeal was it making? The next two posters, Sources 11 and 12, ("Halt the Hun" and "Remember Belgium") were intended to encourage American civilians to buy Liberty Bonds. What logical and emotional appeals were being made? How are the two posters similar? How did they use innuendos to make their point? See also the last poster presented in the evidence (Source 17, "The Hun—his Mark"). How is that poster similar to Sources 11 and 12?

The four posters in Sources 13 through 16 were each intended to elicit a different reaction from those who saw it. Yet they are remarkably similar in their logical and emotional appeals. What do these posters have in common? How are women portrayed in Sources 14 through 16?

The editorial cartoon from the *New York Herald* (Source 18) is self-explanatory. What emotions do the cartoon elicit? What actions, intended or unintended, might result from those emotions?

9. The first poster ("I Want YOU for the U.S. Army") by Flagg is the most famous American poster ever created. The idea was taken from a British poster by Alfred Leete, and Flagg drew himself as Uncle Sam. The poster is still used by the United States Army.

CHAPTER 5

HOMOGENIZING
A PLURALISTIC
CULTURE:
PROPAGANDA
DURING WORLD
WAR I

Sources 19 through 22, by the Four Minute Men, are from the Committee on Public Information's *Bulletin,* which was distributed to all volunteer speakers (they also received a letter of commendation and a certificate from President Wilson after the war). What logical and emotional appeals were made in each selection?

No sound films were produced in the United States before 1927. Until that time a small orchestra or (more prevalent) a piano accompanied a film's showing. What dialogue there was— and there was not much—was done in subtitles. Therefore, the best means we have to learn about these films, short of actually viewing them, is to analyze movie reviews. The review presented in Source 23 is of the film *Pershing's Crusaders,* a documentary produced by the Committee on Public Information in 1918.[10] Can you tell from the review what logical and emotional appeals were made in the film?

The advertising aids for the film *Kultur* (Source 24) suggest a number of phrases and angles designed to attract audiences. What are the strongest emotional appeals that were suggested to theater owners? Do those same appeals also appear in the other evidence?

You must now summarize your findings and return to the central questions: How did the United States use propaganda to mobilize public opinion in support of our participation in World War I? What were the consequences, positive and negative, of the mobilization of public opinion?

EPILOGUE

The creation of the Committee on Public Information and its subsequent work shows that the Wilson administration had serious doubts concerning whether the American people, multiethnic and pluralistic as they were, would support the war effort with unanimity. And, to be sure, there was opposition to American involvement in the war, not only from socialist Eugene Debs and the left but also from reformers Robert LaFollette, Jane Addams, and others. As it turned out, however, the Wilson administration's worst fears proved groundless. Americans of all ethnic backgrounds overwhelmingly supported the war effort, sometimes rivaling each other in patriotic ardor. How much of this unanimity can be attributed to patriotism and how much to the propaganda efforts of the Committee on Public Information will never really be known. Yet, for whatever reason, it can be said that the war had a kind of unifying effect on the American people. Women sold Liberty Bonds, worked for such agencies as the Red Cross, rolled bandages, and cooperated in the government's efforts to conserve food and fuel. Indeed, even African Americans

10. *Pershing's Crusaders* is in the National Archives in Washington, D.C.

sprang to the colors, reasoning, as did the president of Howard University, that service in the war might help them achieve long-withheld civil and political rights.

However, this homogenization was not without its price. Propaganda was so effective that it created a kind of national hysteria, sometimes with terrible results. Vigilante-type groups often shamefully persecuted German-Americans, lynching one German-American man of draft age for not having been in uniform (the man was physically ineligible, having only one eye) and badgering German-American children in and out of school. Many states forbade the teaching of German in schools, and a host of German words were purged from the language (sauerkraut became liberty cabbage, German measles became liberty measles, hamburgers became liberty steaks, frankfurters became hot dogs). The city of Cincinnati even banned pretzels from saloons. In such an atmosphere, many Americans lived in genuine fear of being accused of spying or of becoming victims of intimidation or violence. In a society intent upon homogenization, being different could be dangerous.

During such hysteria, one would expect the federal government in general and the Committee on Public Information in particular to have attempted to dampen the more extreme forms of vigilantism. However, it seemed as if the government had become the victim of its own propaganda. The Postmaster General (Albert Burleson), empowered to censor the mail, looking for examples of treason, insurrection, or forcible resistance to laws, used his power to suppress all socialist publications, all anti-British and pro-Irish mail, and anything that he believed threatened the war effort. One movie producer, Robert Goldstein, was sentenced to ten years in prison for releasing his film *The Spirit of '76* (about the American Revolution) because it portrayed the British in an unfavorable light.[11] Socialist party leader Eugene Debs was given a similar sentence for criticizing the war in a speech in Canton, Ohio. The left-wing union, Industrial Workers of the World (IWW), was broken. Freedom of speech, press, and assembly were violated countless times, and numerous lynchings, whippings, and tar and featherings occurred. Excesses by both government and private individuals were as effective in *forcing* homogeneity as were the voluntary efforts of American people of all backgrounds.

Once the hysteria had begun, it is doubtful whether even President Wilson could have stopped it. Yet Wilson showed no inclination to do so, even stating that dissent was not appreciated by the government. Without the president to reverse the process, the hysteria continued unabated.

Before the outbreak of World War I, anti-immigrant sentiment had been growing, although most Americans seem to have believed that the solution was to Americanize the immigrants rather than to restrict their entrance. But the drive toward homogenization that accompanied America's war hysteria acted to increase cries for re-

11. This gave rise to a court case with the improbable title *United States v. The Spirit of '76.*

CHAPTER 5

HOMOGENIZING
A PLURALISTIC
CULTURE:
PROPAGANDA
DURING WORLD
WAR I

stricting further immigration and to weaken champions of the "melting pot." As restriction advocate Madison Grant wrote in 1922, "The world has seen many such [racial] mixtures and the character of a mongrel race is only just beginning to be understood at its true value. . . . Whether we like to admit it or not, the result of the mixture of two races . . . gives us a race reverting to the more ancient, generalized and lower type." Labor leaders, journalists, and politicians called for immigration restrictions, and a general immigration restriction (called the National Origins Act) became law in 1924.

This insistence on homogenization also resulted in the Red Scare of 1919, during which Attorney General A. Mitchell Palmer violated civil liberties in a series of raids, arrests, and deportations directed largely against recent immigrants. As seen, the efforts to homogenize a pluralistic nation could have its ugly side as well.

As Americans approached the Second World War, some called for a revival of the Committee on Public Information. Yet President Franklin Roosevelt rejected this sweeping approach. The Office of War Information was created, but its role was a restricted one. Even so, Japanese-Americans were subjected to relocation and humiliation in one of the more shameful episodes of recent American history. And although propaganda techniques were considerably more subtle, they nevertheless displayed features that would cause Americans to hate their enemies and want to destroy them. Japanese especially were portrayed as barbaric. In general, however, a different spirit pervaded the United States during World War II, a spirit generally more tolerant of American pluralism and less willing to stir Americans into an emotional frenzy.

And yet, the possibility that propaganda will create mass hysteria and thus endanger the civil rights of some Americans is present in every national crisis, especially in wartime. In the "total wars" of the twentieth century, in which civilians played as crucial a role as fighting men (in factories, in training facilities for soldiers, and in shipping soldiers and material to the front), the mobilization of the home front was a necessity. But could that kind of mobilization be carried too far?

CHAPTER SIX

PERSUASION AND THE PROGRESSIVES: REGULATING CHILD LABOR

THE PROBLEM

"Brilliant men, beautiful jazz babies, champagne baths, midnight revels, petting parties in the purple dawn, all ending in one terrific smashing climax that makes you gasp,"[1] one movie advertisement promised in the 1920s. And all over the country, short-haired flappers wearing makeup and skirts above their knees were dancing to the latest jazz music with their dates. The men had their hair slicked back, doused themselves with aftershave colognes, and wore baggy trousers like the enormously popular movie star, Rudolph Valentino. College men and women smoked in public, drank illegal liquor from hip flasks, and seemed to be engaged in endless partying. On one level at least, the 1920s could be

1. Frederick Lewis Allen, *Only Yesterday* (New York: Harper & Row, 1957; originally published 1931), p. 101.

characterized by some carefree young people having a very good time.

But there was another, more serious, side to the 1920s. More than a million young children from ten to fifteen were working sixty or more hours a week for pitifully low wages. In this chapter you will be examining the efforts of Progressive reformers to inform the public about the plight of working children and to pass laws to prohibit child labor. You will also be analyzing excerpts from two important U.S. Supreme Court decisions that declared these federal child labor laws unconstitutional.

The central questions you will be answering are: how did the Progressives persuade the public to support federal legislation regulating child labor? Why did the Supreme Court strike down these laws?

CHAPTER 6

PERSUASION
AND THE
PROGRESSIVES:
REGULATING
CHILD LABOR

BACKGROUND

In the last decades of the nineteenth century, a spirit of reform called progressivism swept through the United States. Progressivism affected both major political parties and inspired the formation of countless new organizations dedicated to change. Some people still clung to the rather fatalistic attitude that one version of social Darwinism reinforced: the fittest would survive, and one should not interfere with the natural processes. Progressives, however, were much more optimistic and believed that although America was basically a sound country, it could be even better and fairer. Progressives thought that economic, political, and social problems could be solved by right-minded citizens, usually by legislation and sometimes by constitutional amendment. According to the Progressives, experts such as statisticians, social scientists, and field investigators should first accumulate as much data as possible and then pass on this information to the public through books, magazine articles, lectures, and displays. Once the public was informed of the scope and nature of the problem, public opinion would provide support for whatever laws were necessary.

The Progressives themselves generally were educated women and men. Most had grown up in small towns but lived their adult lives in cities. As historian Paul Boyer noted, Progressives often attempted to impose their own values and a kind of "village order" on those whom they wished to help. Nevertheless, social workers, teachers, lawyers, doctors, ministers,

editors, writers, and business people worked actively and tirelessly to improve (as they believed) various aspects of American life. Political reformers campaigned for women's suffrage, the direct popular election of U.S. senators, the city manager or commission form of municipal government, and so forth. Economic reformers supported such goals as a graduated income tax, a lower tariff, the regulation of big businesses, and better wages and working conditions for labor. Finally, many Progressive reformers dedicated their lives to questions of social justice. For example, settlement house workers concentrated their efforts on their immigrant neighbors, and the Women's Trade Union League worked for laws protecting women workers. The National Association of Colored Women and, later, the National Association for the Advancement of Colored People (NAACP) both worked to improve conditions for African Americans, and the Taylorites[2] devoted their energies to increasing efficiency and productivity in the workplace.

Progressivism then was not really *one* single reform movement but a series of reform movements. The Progressive era is often associated with the presidencies of Theodore Roosevelt and Woodrow Wilson and the general time period between 1900 and 1914. But progressivism actually began in the 1880s and continued (with dimin-

2. Followers of Frederick Taylor, an engineer who used time-and-motion studies to develop efficient ways of performing various jobs.

ished force) through the 1920s. During this later period, after World War I, was when the attempts to eliminate the abuses involved in child labor culminated—and ultimately failed.

Progressives often noted that children had always worked. But this earlier work, they insisted, had been healthy work on the family farm or at home or in an apprenticeship learning a useful trade. Nineteenth-century urbanization and industrialization had changed all that, and as early as 1853, a young man named Charles Loring Brace had founded a Children's Aid Society in New York City. Brace was concerned about the children of the urban poor, often called "street arabs," who sold newspapers, shined shoes and boots, or peddled matches. Children's Aid Societies rapidly spread to the larger cities, where they established children's lodging houses, offered minimal instruction in skilled trades, and by the 1890s placed thousands of boys with families in the West, where the boys would work on farms in return for their room, board, and clothing.

By the 1890s, however, the problem had become far too great to be alleviated by programs such as those of the Children's Aid Societies. Massive immigration from southern and eastern Europe, the rapidly accelerating pace of industrialization, the increasing urbanization, and even the economic goals of New South advocates combined to create a huge demand for the labor of young children. From the employers' point of view, children worked for very little money; they were small, quick, and energetic; and they could be disciplined easily by an adult overseer. From many parents'

point of view, formal education was relatively worthless for those who had to make a living at semiskilled or unskilled work. Furthermore, even though working children made very small wages, the wages could be added to the family's income. As one woman told a social worker, her ten-year-old son only made about thirty-five cents a day in the factory, but it was enough money to provide supper for their family of seven every night.

The census figures tell part of the story—in 1890, more than 1.5 million children between the ages of ten and fifteen were employed, almost one out of every five children in that age range! In 1900, there were 1.7 million gainfully employed children, in 1910, 2 million, and in 1920, slightly more than 1 million. The census, however, did not really provide an accurate count of working children. Employed children younger than ten years—and there were many—were not reported, nor were children who labored in tenement apartments with their parents on "homework" (such as making artificial flowers) or who worked in the street trades (for example, messenger boys). Moreover, the 1920 census was taken in the winter rather than the spring and thus did not count the thousands of children who worked in seasonal agricultural or cannery jobs.

What kinds of jobs did these young children do? Boys worked in the coal mines at various tasks: picking slate out of coal, opening and closing the underground ventilating trap doors, and sorting and sizing coal. Thousands of boys also worked in glass factories, usually in the furnace room assisting the glass blowers. Young girls and boys worked in the textile mills,

CHAPTER 6

PERSUASION
AND THE
PROGRESSIVES:
REGULATING
CHILD LABOR

particularly in the South. They also shucked oysters, peeled shrimp, and prepared vegetables for the canneries. Both boys and girls, including very young children aged three or four, helped in tenement homework. Besides making artificial flowers and feather plumes for women's hats, such work included shelling nuts, sorting coffee beans, making lace, stuffing dolls, and making decorative boxes. In the garment trade, a great deal of sewing was "put out" to families, and both boys and girls helped with this chore.

The conditions under which these children worked were appalling. Breaker boys who removed the waste materials from coal sat in a dust-filled room for ten to eleven hours a day on boards balanced over the coal chute. Glass blowers' assistants worked from 5:00 P.M. to 3:00 A.M. in the stiflingly hot furnace room, and then walked home in the cold night air. In the textile mills, the windows were kept closed to insure high humidity (which kept the cotton from breaking apart) and the children worked eleven or twelve hours a day, five and a half days a week. Even worse were the hours at canneries where many children as young as four or five years old worked alongside their parents or siblings. Cannery work began at 3:00 A.M. or 4:00 A.M. and continued until the harvest or catch of the day was processed—in peak seasons, as long as eighteen hours a day.

Not surprisingly, child laborers were generally anemic, underweight, and shorter than nonworking children their age. They frequently suffered from curvature of the spine and other physical growth-related abnor-

malities. Children who inhaled coal dust or lint suffered respiratory illnesses such as chronic bronchitis, pneumonia, and tuberculosis, while those who worked in hot, damp, and humid conditions were often victims of heat prostration, skin problems, or rheumatism. Child workers also had a higher accident rate than adult workers—serious cuts, burns, and broken (or amputated) hands, arms, feet, and legs were the most common injuries. Many child laborers smoked cigars or cigarettes, drank alcohol, swore, and gambled; in other words, they had what the Progressives would have called "vicious habits."

Child workers and adult women workers were concentrated in low paying industries, and despite working long hours they earned very little money. Wages varied by geographic area and by occupation, but even so, adult male workers were always paid the most money, women earned approximately half of what men earned, and child workers were paid slightly less than women. In a 1908 study of wages in Massachusetts' five largest industries, progressive economist Scott Nearing found that most adult males earned between nine and twenty dollars a week, although 30 percent of the adult male workers earned less than nine dollars a week. Eighty percent of the adult women workers, however, earned between five and ten dollars a week, and 50 percent of the child workers earned less than six dollars a week. In Kansas, only 12 percent of adult male workers earned less than nine dollars a week, 61 percent of female workers earned less than seven dollars a week, and 58 percent of child workers earned less than five dollars a week. In New Jersey, 85 percent of child workers received weekly wages under five dollars!

Progressive reformers and educators became increasingly worried about the numbers of young children who were working and the effects of such work on children's physical, moral, and intellectual well-being. In 1902, a group of these reformers formed the New York Child Labor Committee, and two years later, the National Child Labor Committee (NCLC) was organized. From the beginning, the NCLC attracted prominent supporters, possessed capable and respected leaders, and included members from both the North and the South. The NCLC's goals were to gather information, educate the public about the problem, work for laws to regulate child labor, and provide minimum standards for the employment of children.

The NCLC hired field investigators and published the findings in their own journal, the *Child Labor Bulletin*, as well as in middle-class mass circulation magazines such as *Arena* and *McClure's*. Impressed by the effectiveness of Jacob Riis's books, *How the Other Half Lives* (1890) and *The Battle with the Slum* (1902), exposés illustrated with photographs, the NCLC hired Lewis Hine as a field investigator/photographer. Hine was from Wisconsin and had gone to work in a furniture factory when he was fifteen. Eventually, with some assistance, he was able to get an education and became a schoolteacher in New York City. An enthusiastic amateur photographer, he quit teaching to work full time for the NCLC when he was thirty-four years old.

For the next ten years, Lewis Hine traveled throughout the country, photographing child laborers in the cotton and tobacco fields of the South and in the textile mills, shrimp, and oyster canneries. In the Midwest and border states he investigated glass factories and coal mines. He also took pictures of newsboys, messenger boys, and children working in New York City tenements and sweatshops. The result was thousands of photographs that the NCLC used in displays, magazine articles and books, and even at congressional hearings.

By 1916, Progressive reformers, along with labor unions and an aroused public opinion, had spurred the passage of the Keating-Owen Act. This federal law basically prohibited products made by children younger than sixteen (in mines or quarries) and younger than fourteen (in other manufacturing) from being shipped across state lines. It also set the work standards for children between the ages of fourteen and sixteen: they could work no more than eight hours a day, only between 6:00 A.M. and 7:00 P.M., six days a week. Finally, the law provided a system of federal inspection and monetary fines for employers who violated the law. In *Hammer v. Dagenhart* (1919), the U.S. Supreme Court, in a five to four decision, declared this law unconstitutional.

Progressives were surprised and shocked by the decision and moved quickly to obtain another child labor law. This time, Congress passed an amendment to a tax revenue act to regulate child labor. This amendment had all the major provisions of the Keating-Owen Act, except that instead of prohibiting the products of child

CHAPTER 6

PERSUASION
AND THE
PROGRESSIVES:
REGULATING
CHILD LABOR

labor from interstate commerce, it placed a very heavy tax on them. Once again, in *Bailey v. Drexel Furniture* (1922), the Supreme Court, this time by an eight to one decision, declared the federal child labor law unconstitutional.

After this second defeat, many Progressive reformers in the NCLC and their allies, such as the U.S. Children's Bureau, decided that there was no choice except to work for a child labor amendment to the U.S. Constitution. The congressional debates were lengthy and heated, but by 1924, both houses of Congress had approved the amendment by more than the necessary two-thirds vote. Congress was given the power to regulate the labor of young people up to age eighteen.

The general climate of opinion in the 1920s, however, was much different from the reform spirit of the pre–World War I era. A postwar Red Scare made many people hostile to change because they feared communistic influences on the reformers, and most Americans merely wanted to return to what President Harding called "normalcy" after the war. In the 1920s, Americans admired successful businessmen, and labor unions repre-

sented by the American Federation of Labor were quiescent, not wanting to alienate public opinion. The economy, although actually unstable, seemed to be booming, with more and more consumer goods available for almost everyone.

As the amendment went to the states for ratification in 1924, the opposition immediately organized a campaign against it. The major arguments were that the amendment would take rights away from parents, would take rights away from the states, would bankrupt many businesses, and was communistic. Although three states (Arkansas, Arizona, and California) ratified the amendment, in a widely publicized public referendum, Massachusetts voters rejected it by a three to one margin. State after state also rejected the amendment during the 1920s, and by the time of the 1929 stock market crash, all hope of ratification had been lost.

First, study the photographs. Why were they so effective in convincing people to oppose child labor? Then analyze the excerpts from the two Supreme Court decisions. Why did the majority of the court believe that these laws were unconstitutional?

THE METHOD

Technological advances by the end of the nineteenth century had made using cameras and developing photographs easier, but both the equipment and methods were still cumbersome and primitive by today's standards.

Nevertheless, people were fascinated by photography, and many talented amateurs, such as E. Alice Austen, spent hours taking pictures of their families, friends, and homes. Indeed, these photographs are an important source of evidence for social historians trying to reconstruct how Americans lived in the past.

Jacob Riis and Lewis Hine, however, thought of themselves as documentary photographers—that is, their pictures would be used to document conditions as they saw them. Riis even occasionally rearranged his subjects so as to show the worst sides of life in the slums, although there is no evidence that Hine did the same. Nevertheless, Hine was a committed reformer opposed to child labor and carefully chose the circumstances under which he would take his photographs and exactly what he would include in each picture.

These documentary photographs, then, are not intended to present a balanced or unbiased view of working children. They are intended to appeal to the viewers' emotions and motivate the viewers to work for change. As a student looking at these photographs, you will have to be specific about *what* you feel and then try to determine *why* the photograph makes you feel that way.

Although documentary photographs are visual evidence that appeal to the emotions, the Supreme Court decisions are a more familiar kind of evidence—written evidence that you must read carefully for the reasoning it contains.

The nine justices of the U.S. Supreme Court are appointed by the president of the United States with the approval of the Senate, and serve for the remainder of their lifetimes unless they resign or are removed. Most presidents try to appoint justices whose outlooks and opinions are simi-lar to their own, and generally, although not always, who belong to the same political party as the president. Once appointed, however, Supreme Court justices are completely independent and sometimes change their position—a justice who was supposed to be liberal may turn out to be conservative and vice versa. Justices are, of course, supposed to be neutral and decide each case on its own merits, but courts do tend to take on political "personalities": some Supreme Courts are liberal and others are conservative.

The Supreme Court that decided the Hammer case (1918) was a relatively conservative court. One member had been appointed by President Grover Cleveland in 1894, one by President William McKinley (1898), two by President Theodore Roosevelt (1902 and 1903), two by President William Howard Taft (1911 and 1912), and three by President Woodrow Wilson (1914 and 1916). There were only two changes in the personnel of the court that decided the Bailey case: former President Taft became chief justice, replacing President Cleveland's appointee who had died, and George Sutherland took the place of one of President Wilson's appointees who had resigned. There were six Republicans and three Democrats on the court that decided the Hammer case; there were eight Republicans and one Democrat on the court for the Bailey case.

In this period, however, both political parties were sympathetic to efforts to regulate child labor. Why, then, did the Court declare both these federal child labor laws unconstitutional? In answering this question, it will help to refer to the Constitution itself (there is

CHAPTER 6

PERSUASION
AND THE
PROGRESSIVES:
REGULATING
CHILD LABOR

usually a copy in the appendix of your history textbook). Remember that the Supreme Court justices also read what the Constitution says and then try to decide what it means. For help, they often rely on precedents, that is, similar cases already decided by previous Supreme Court decisions. But their reasoning should be clearly reflected in their decisions, both the majority and the minority opinions in the first case (no minority opinion was written in the *Bailey* case). Your task is to describe and explain the reasoning in both Supreme Court cases.

THE EVIDENCE

Source 1 from John R. Kemp, ed., *Lewis Hine: Photographs of Child Labor in the New South* (Jackson: University Press of Mississippi, 1986), p. 6.

1. Boys Working in a Cigar Plant.

Sources 2 and 3 from Verna Posever Curtis and Stanley Mallach, *Photography and Reform: Lewis Hine & The National Labor Committee* (Milwaukee: Milwaukee Art Museum, 1984), pp. 18; opposite the title page.

2. Exhibition Panel (no. 57) Appealing to the Public by Comparing Child Labor Conditions in Massachusetts and Georgia.

3. National Child Labor Committee Display.

Source 4 from Alexander Alland Sr., *Jacob A. Riis: Photographer and Citizen* (Aperture, 1974), p. 147.

4. Street Arabs.

Source 5 from Judith M. Gutman, *Lewis Hine and The American Social Conscience* (New York: Walker, 1967), p. 77.

5. View of the Pennsylvania Breaker. The Dust was so Dense at Times as to Obscure the View. South Pittston, Pennsylvania. January 1911.

Source 6 from Kemp, *Lewis Hine: Photographs of Child Labor*, p. 87.

6. "Carrying-in" Boy in Alexandria Glass Factory, Alexandria, Va. Works on Day Shift One Week and Night Shift Next Week. June 1911.

CHAPTER 6

PERSUASION
AND THE
PROGRESSIVES:
REGULATING
CHILD LABOR

Sources 7 and 8 from Gutman, *Lewis Hine and The American Social Conscience,* pp. 99; 91.

7. Glass Work Boy, Night Shift. Indiana. August 1908.

8. **Shuckers in the Varn and Platt Canning Company. Yonges Island. 1913.**

CHAPTER 6

PERSUASION
AND THE
PROGRESSIVES:
REGULATING
CHILD LABOR

Sources 9 and 10 from Kemp, *Lewis Hine: Photographs of Child Labor,* pp. 73; 55.

9. In Dunbar, Louisiana, Group of Oyster Shuckers Working in Canning Factory of Dunbar, Lopez, Dukate Co. All but the Very Smallest Babies Work. All Began at 3:30 A.M., Expected to Work Until 5 P.M. The Little Girl in Center Is Working; Her Mother Says She is a Real Help to Her. March 1911.

10. Two of the Tiny Workers, a Raveler and a Looper, in Loudon
Hoisery Mills. Loudon, Tennessee. December 1910.

Sources 11 and 12 from Curtis and Mallach, *Photography and Reform,* pp. 85; 76.

11. Ten-Year-Old Picker on Gildersleeve Tobacco Farm. Gildersleeve, Connecticut. August 6, 1917.

12. Horman Hall, 210 Park Street. Lindale, Georgia. April 1913. Went to Work Over a Year ago in Massachusetts Mills When 10½ years old. Family Record says Born Oct. 26, 1901. Doffing.[3] No Real Reason for His Work as Father and Several Others Are Working.

3. A doffer replaced empty machine bobbins with reels filled with thread.

Source 13 from Gutman, *Lewis Hine and The American Social Conscience*, p. 81.

13. Newsies at Skeeter Branch. St. Louis, Missouri. 11:00 A.M., May 9, 1910.

Sources 14 and 15 from Allon Schoener, *Portal to America: The Lower East Side, 1870-1925* (New York: Holt Rinehart and Winston, 1967), pp. 176; 182.

14. Boy with Bundle of Homework.

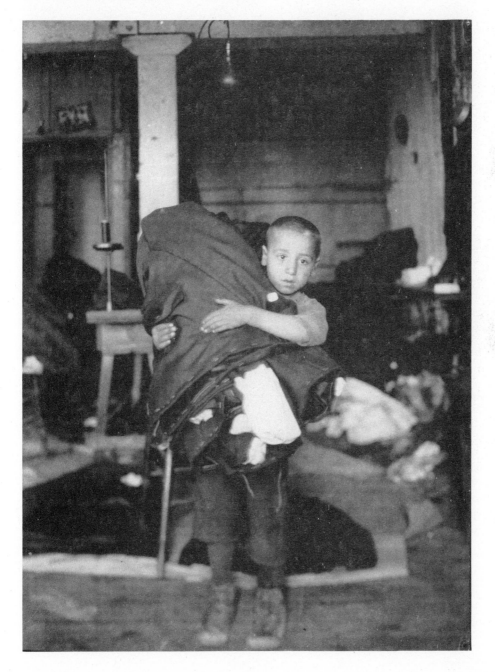

15. Children Working on Clothing Homework.

Source 16 from *Hammer v. Dagenhart,* 247 U.S. 251, 38 S.Ct. 529, 62 L.Ed. 1101 (1918). Source for both court cases: Mason, Alpheus Thomas, and William M. Beaney, *American Constitutional Law: Introductory Essays and Selected Cases,* 5th ed. Englewood Cliffs, N.J.: Prentice-Hall, 1972, pp. 233–236, 279–281.

16. An Act of Congress of 1916 forbade the shipment in interstate commerce of products of child labor. A father of two children who worked in a North Carolina cotton mill sought and obtained an injunction against enforcement of the Act, on the ground that it was unconstitutional. The Government appealed.

MR. JUSTICE DAY delivered the opinion of the Court. . . .

The controlling question for decision is: Is it within the authority of Congress in regulating commerce among the States to prohibit the transportation in interstate commerce of manufactured goods, the product of a factory in which, within thirty days prior to their removal therefrom, children under the age of fourteen have been employed or permitted to work, or children between the ages of fourteen and sixteen years have been employed or permitted to work more than eight hours in any day, or more than six days in any week, or after the hour of 7 o'clock P.M. or before the hour of 6 o'clock A.M.?

The power essential to the passage of this act, the Government contends, is found in the commerce clause of the Constitution which authorizes Congress to regulate commerce with foreign nations and among the States.

In *Gibbons* v. *Ogden* . . . Chief Justice Marshall, speaking for this court, and defining the extent and nature of the commerce power, said, "It is the power to regulate, that is, to prescribe the rule by which commerce is to be governed." In other words, the power is one to control the means by which commerce is carried on, which is directly the contrary of the assumed right to forbid commerce from moving and thus destroy it as to particular commodities. But it is insisted that adjudged cases in this court establish the doctrine that the power to regulate given to Congress incidentally includes the authority to prohibit the movement of ordinary commodities and therefore that the subject is not open for discussion. The cases demonstrate the contrary. They rest upon the character of the particular subjects dealt with and the fact that the scope of governmental authority, state or national, possessed over them is such that the authority to prohibit is as to them but the exertion of the power to regulate.

The first of these cases is *Champion* v. *Ames,* . . . the so-called Lottery Case, in which it was held that Congress might pass a law having the effect to keep the channels of commerce free from use in the transportation of tickets used in the promotion of lottery schemes. In *Hipolite Egg Co.* v. *United States,* 220 U.S. 45, this court sustained the power of Congress to pass the Pure Food and Drug Act, which prohibited the introduction into the States by means of interstate commerce of impure foods and drugs. . . .

In *Caminetti* v. *United States,* 242 U.S. 470, we held that Congress might prohibit the transportation of women in interstate commerce for the purpose of debauchery and kindred purposes. In *Clark Distilling Co.* v. *Western Maryland Railway Co.,* 242 U.S. 311 . . . concluding the discussion which sustained the authority of the government to prohibit the transportation of liquor in interstate commerce, the court said: "The exceptional nature of the subject here regulated is the basis upon which the exceptional power exerted must rest and affords no ground for any fear that such power may be constitutionally extended to things which it may not, consistently with the guaranties of the Constitution, embrace."

CHAPTER 6

PERSUASION
AND THE
PROGRESSIVES:
REGULATING
CHILD LABOR

In each of these instances the use of interstate transportation was necessary to the accomplishment of harmful results. In other words, although the power over interstate transportation was to regulate, that could only be accomplished by prohibiting the use of the facilities of interstate commerce to effect the evil intended.

This element is wanting in the present case. The thing intended to be accomplished by this statute is the denial of the facilities of interstate commerce to those manufacturers in the States who employ children within the prohibited ages. The act in its effect does not regulate transportation among the States, but aims to standardize the ages at which children may be employed in mining and manufacturing within the States. The goods shipped are of themselves harmless. The act permits them to be freely shipped after thirty days from the time of their removal from the factory. When offered for shipment, and before transportation begins, the labor of their production is over, and the mere fact that they were intended for interstate commerce transportation does not make their production subject to federal control under the commerce power.

Commerce "consists of intercourse and traffic . . . and includes the transportation of persons and property, as well as the purchase, sale and exchange of commodities." The making of goods and the mining of coal are not commerce, nor does the fact that these things are to be afterwards shipped or used in interstate commerce, make their production a part thereof. *Delaware, Lackawanna & Western R. R. Co.* v. *Yurkonis*, 238 U.S. 439. . . .

The grant of power to Congress over the subject of interstate commerce was to enable it to regulate such commerce, and not to give it authority to control the States in the exercise of the police power over local trade and manufacture.

The grant of authority over a purely federal matter was not intended to destroy the local power always existing and carefully reserved to the States in the Tenth Amendment to the Constitution. . . .

That there should be limitations upon the right to employ children in mines and factories in the interest of their own and the public welfare, all will admit. That such employment is generally deemed to require regulation is shown by the fact that the brief of counsel states that every State in the Union has a law upon the subject, limiting the right to thus employ children. In North Carolina, the State wherein is located the factory in which the employment was had in the present case, no child under twelve years of age is permitted to work.

It may be desirable that such laws be uniform, but our Federal Government is one of enumerated powers; "this principle," declared Chief Justice Marshall in *McCulloch* v. *Maryland* . . . "is universally admitted." . . .

In interpreting the Constitution it must never be forgotten that the nation is made up of States to which are entrusted the powers of local government. And to them and to the people the powers not expressly [sic] delegated to the national government are reserved. . . . To sustain this statute would not be in our judgment a recognition of the lawful exertion of congressional authority over interstate commerce, but would sanction an invasion by the federal power of the control of a matter purely local in its character, and over which no authority has been delegated to Congress in conferring the power to regulate commerce among the States.

We have neither authority nor disposition to question the motives of Congress in enacting this legislation. The purposes intended must be attained consistently with constitutional limitations and not by an invasion of the powers of the States. This court has no more important function than that which devolves upon it the obligation to preserve inviolate the constitutional limitations upon the exercise of authority, federal and state, to the end that each may continue to discharge, harmoniously with the other, the duties entrusted to it by the Constitution.

In our view the necessary effect of this act is, by means of a prohibition against the movement in interstate commerce of ordinary commercial commodities, to regulate the hours of labor of children in factories and mines within the States, a purely state authority. Thus the act in a twofold sense is repugnant to the Constitution. It not only transcends the authority delegated to Congress over commerce but also exerts a power as to a purely local matter to which the federal authority does not extend. The far-reaching result of upholding the act cannot be more plainly indicated than by pointing out that if Congress can thus regulate matters entrusted to local authority by prohibition of the movement of commodities in interstate commerce, all freedom of commerce will be at an end, and the power of the State over local matters may be eliminated, and thus our system of government be practically destroyed.

For these reasons we hold that this law exceeds the constitutional authority of Congress. It follows that the decree of the District Court must be

Affirmed.

MR. JUSTICE HOLMES, dissenting. . . .

The first step in my argument is to make plain what no one is likely to dispute—that the statute in question is within the power expressly given to Congress if considered only as to its immediate effects and that if invalid it is so only upon some collateral ground. The statute confines itself to prohibiting the carriage of certain goods in interstate or foreign commerce. Congress is given power to regulate such commerce in unqualified terms. It would not be argued today that the power to regulate does not include the

CHAPTER 6

PERSUASION
AND THE
PROGRESSIVES:
REGULATING
CHILD LABOR

power to prohibit. Regulation means the prohibition of something, and when interstate commerce is the matter to be regulated I cannot doubt that the regulation may prohibit any part of such commerce that Congress sees fit to forbid. At all events it is established by the Lottery Case and others that have followed it that a law is not beyond the regulative power of Congress merely because it prohibits certain transportation out and out. . . . So I repeat that this statute in its immediate operation is clearly within the Congress' constitutional power.

The question then is narrowed to whether the exercise of its otherwise constitutional power by Congress can be pronounced unconstitutional because of its possible reaction upon the conduct of the States in a matter upon which I have admitted that they are free from direct control. I should have thought that that matter had been disposed of so fully as to leave no room for doubt. I should have thought that the most conspicuous decisions of this Court had made it clear that the power to regulate commerce and other constitutional powers could not be cut down or qualified by the fact that it might interfere with the carrying out of the domestic policy of any State. . . .

The notion that prohibition is any less prohibition when applied to things now thought evil I do not understand. But if there is any matter upon which civilized countries have agreed—far more unanimously than they have with regard to intoxicants and some other matters over which this country is now emotionally aroused—it is the evil of premature and excessive child labor. I should have thought that if we were to introduce our own moral conceptions where in my opinion they do not belong, this was preeminently a case for upholding the exercise of all its powers by the United States.

But I had thought that the propriety of the exercise of a power admitted to exist in some cases was for the consideration of Congress alone and that this Court always had disavowed the right to intrude its judgment upon questions of policy or morals. It is not for this Court to pronounce when prohibition is necessary to regulation if it ever may be necessary—to say that it is permissible as against strong drink but not as against the product of ruined lives.

The act does not meddle with anything belonging to the States. They may regulate their internal affairs and their domestic commerce as they like. But when they seek to send their products across the state line they are no longer within their rights. If there were no Constitution and no Congress their power to cross the line would depend upon their neighbors. Under the Constitution such commerce belongs not to the States but to Congress to regulate. It may carry out its views of public policy whatever indirect effect they may have upon the activities of the States. Instead of being encountered by a prohibitive tariff at her boundaries the State encounters the public policy of the United States which it is for Congress to express. The public policy of the United States is shaped with a view to the benefit of the nation as a whole. If, as has been the case within the memory of men still living, a State should take a different view of the propriety of sustaining a lottery from that which generally prevails, I cannot believe that the fact would require a different decision from that reached in *Champion* v. *Ames*. Yet in that case it would be said with quite as much force as in this that Congress was attempting to intermeddle with the State's domestic affairs. The national welfare as understood by Congress may require a different attitude within its sphere from that of some self-seeking State. It seems to me entirely constitutional for Congress to enforce its understanding by all the means at its command.

MR. JUSTICE MCKENNA, MR. JUSTICE BRANDEIS and MR. JUSTICE CLARKE concur in this opinion.

Source 17 from *Bailey v. Drexel Furniture Company* (Child Labor Tax Case), 259 U.S. 20, 42 S.Ct. 449, 66 L.Ed. 817 (1922).

17. In the Revenue Act of 1919, Congress imposed a tax on mine and quarry employers of children under sixteen and mill and factory owners who employed children under fourteen or who permitted children between fourteen and sixteen to work more than an eight-hour day and a six-day week. The tax was levied on net profits. The Drexel Furniture Company, which had employed a boy under fourteen paid the tax under protest and then sued to recover the amount paid. The District Court sustained the company, and the collector obtained a writ of error.

MR. CHIEF JUSTICE TAFT delivered the opinion of the court.

This case presents the question of the constitutional validity of the Child Labor Tax Law. . . .

The law is attacked on the ground that it is a regulation of the employment of child labor in the States—an exclusively state function under the Federal Constitution and within the reservations of the Tenth Amendment. It is defended on the ground that it is a mere excise tax levied by the Congress of the United States under its broad power of taxation conferred by § 8, Article I, of the Federal Constitution. We must construe the law and interpret the intent and meaning of Congress from the language of the act. The words are to be given their ordinary meaning unless the context shows that they are differently used. Does this law impose a tax with only that

CHAPTER 6

PERSUASION
AND THE
PROGRESSIVES:
REGULATING
CHILD LABOR

incidental restraint and regulation which a tax must inevitably involve? Or does it regulate by the use of the so-called tax as a penalty? If a tax, it is clearly an excise. If it were an excise on a commodity or other thing of value we might not be permitted under previous decisions of this court to infer solely from its heavy burden that the act intends a prohibition instead of a tax. But this act is more. It provides a heavy exaction for a departure from a detailed and specified course of conduct in business. That course of business is that employers shall employ in mines and quarries, children of an age greater than sixteen years; in mills and factories, children of an age greater than fourteen years, and shall prevent children of less than sixteen years in mills and factories from working more than eight hours a day or six days in the week. If an employer departs from this prescribed course of business, he is to pay the Government one-tenth of his entire net income in the business for a full year. The amount is not to be proportioned in any degree to the extent or frequency of the departures, but is to be paid by the employer in full measure whether he employs five hundred children for a year, or employs only one for a day. Moreover, if he does not know the child is within the named age limit, he is not to pay; that is to say, it is only where he knowingly departs from the prescribed course that payment is to be exacted. Scienter is associated with penalties not with taxes. The employer's factory is to be subject to inspection at any time not only by the taxing officers of the Treasury, the Department normally charged with the collection of taxes, but also by the Secretary of Labor and his subordinates whose normal function is the advancement and protection of the welfare of the workers. In the light of these features of the act, a court must be blind not to see that the so-called tax is imposed to stop the employment of children within the age limits prescribed. Its prohibitory and regulatory effect and purpose are palpable. All others can see and understand this. How can we properly shut our minds to it?

It is the high duty and function of this court in cases regularly brought to its bar to decline to recognize or enforce seeming laws of Congress, dealing with subjects not entrusted to Congress but left or committed by the supreme law of the land to the control of the States. We can not avoid the duty even though it require us to refuse to give effect to legislation designed to promote the highest good. The good sought in unconstitutional legislation is an insidious feature because it leads citizens and legislators of good purpose to promote it without thought of the serious breach it will make in the ark of our covenant or the harm which will come from breaking down recognized standards. In the maintenance of local self-government, on the one hand, and the national power, on the other, our country has been able to endure and prosper for near a century and a half.

Out of a proper respect for the acts of a coordinate branch of the Government, this court has gone far to sustain taxing acts as such, even though there has been ground for suspecting from the weight of the tax it was intended to destroy its subject. But, in the act before us, the presumption of validity cannot prevail, because the proof of the contrary is found on the very face of its provisions. Grant the validity of this law, and all that Congress would need to do, hereafter, in seeking to take over to its control any one of the great number of subjects of public interest, jurisdiction of which the States have never parted with, and which are reserved to them by the Tenth Amendment, would be to enact a detailed measure of complete regulation of the subject and enforce it by so-called tax upon departures from it. To give such magic to the word "tax" would be to break down all constitutional limitation of the powers of Congress and completely wipe out the sovereignty of the States.

The difference between a tax and a penalty is sometimes difficult to define and yet the consequences of the distinction in the required method of their collection often are important. Where the sovereign enacting the law has power to impose both tax and penalty the difference between revenue production and mere regulation may be immaterial, but not so when one sovereign can impose a tax only, and the power of regulation rests in another. Taxes are occasionally imposed in the discretion of the legislature on proper subjects with the primary motive of obtaining revenue from them and with the incidental motive of discouraging them by making their continuance onerous. They do not lose their character as taxes because of the incidental motive. But there comes a time in the extension of the penalizing features of the so-called tax when it loses its character as such and becomes a mere penalty with the characteristics of regulation and punishment. Such is the case in the law before us. Although Congress does not invalidate the contract of employment or expressly declare that the employment within the mentioned ages is illegal, it does exhibit its intent practically to achieve the latter result by adopting the criteria of wrong-doing and imposing its principal consequence on those who transgress its standard.

The case before us can not be distinguished from that of *Hammer v. Dagenhart*. . . . Congress there enacted a law to prohibit transportation in interstate commerce of goods made at a factory in which there was employment of children with the same ages and for the same number of hours a day and days in a week as are penalized by the act in this case. This court held the law in that case to be void. It said:

In our view the necessary effect of this act is, by means of prohibition against the movement in interstate commerce of ordinary commercial commodities, to

CHAPTER 6

PERSUASION
AND THE
PROGRESSIVES:
REGULATING
CHILD LABOR

regulate hours of labor of children in factories and mines within the States, a purely state authority.

In the case at the bar, Congress in the name of a tax which on the face of the act is a penalty seeks to do the same thing, and the effort must be equally futile. . . .

But it is pressed upon us that this court has gone so far in sustaining taxing measures the effect or tendency of which was to accomplish purposes not directly within congressional power that we are bound by authority to maintain this law.

The first of these is *Veazie Bank v. Fenno,* 8 Wall. 533. . . .

The next case is that of *McCray v. United States.* . . . In neither of these cases did the law objected to show on its face as does the law before us the detailed specifications of a regulation of a state concern and business with a heavy exaction to promote the efficacy of such regulation. . . .

. . . *United States v. Doremus,* 249 U.S. 86 . . . involved the validity of the Narcotic Drug Act, 38 Stat. 785, which imposed a special tax on the manufacture, importation and sale or gift of opium or coca leaves or their compounds or derivatives. . . .

The court said that the act could not be declared invalid just because another motive than taxation, not shown on the face of the act, might have contributed to its passage. This case does not militate against the conclusion we have reached in respect of the law now before us. The court, there, made manifest its view that the provisions of the so-called taxing act must be naturally and reasonably adapted to the collection of the tax and not solely to the achievement of some other purpose plainly within state power. . . .

For the reasons given, we must hold the Child Labor Tax Law invalid and the judgment of the District Court is

Affirmed.

MR. JUSTICE CLARKE dissents.

Sources 1 to 3 show the ways reformers used Lewis Hine's photographs. How, and on what bases, were the reformers trying to persuade people to support reform? Source 4 is a Riis photograph of street arabs. What would be the middle-class reaction to it? Why? The remaining photographs (Sources 5 through 15) were taken by Hine. Look at the children carefully. How would you describe them to someone who had not seen these pictures? What do you especially notice about the children? Which picture do you think is the most effective in appealing to your emotions? Why is it effective?

Now look at the Hammer case (Source 16). On what part of the Constitution is the argument based? How do the majority of the justices read and interpret that part? Why did four of the nine justices disagree? What is the basis of their disagreement? What is Holmes arguing should be the proper interpretation of that part of the Constitution? The dissenting justice in the Bailey case (Source 17) did not explain his vote. What are the main argu-

ments of the majority? What is the relationship of this case to the Hammer case? On what part of the Constitution did the justices base their decision that this second child labor law was unconstitutional?

It is clear that many Americans—probably even a majority—favored some kind of legislation to regulate child labor. Much of this public opinion was greatly influenced by documentary photographers who illustrated the worst aspects of the employment of young children. In your opinion, is it ethically defensible to use photographs to spur reform efforts? Or is it possible for photographers to be more objective when examining a subject?

Furthermore, what of the roles of the Supreme Court with respect to issues involving social change or reform? Should the Court be more responsive to public opinion? If both houses of our elected Congress have passed a law, should the Supreme Court be able to strike it down as unconstitutional? Why or why not?

Ironically, interest in the child labor amendment revived during the severe depression of the 1930s. With millions of adults unemployed, employment and exploitation of child laborers seemed intolerable. In fact, during the first six months of 1933, nine

more states ratified the amendment. The National Industrial Recovery Act (NIRA), a New Deal measure to regulate production and labor, also regulated child labor, but it was declared unconstitutional in 1935 (*Schechter Poultry Company v. U.S.*). President

CHAPTER 6

PERSUASION
AND THE
PROGRESSIVES:
REGULATING
CHILD LABOR

Roosevelt was so upset by the way the Supreme Court was striking down New Deal legislation (often by 5–4 decisions) that he tried to "pack" the Court by increasing the number of justices. Both parties and public opinion strongly opposed this plan, but before the bill came to a final vote, two of the previously anti–New Deal justices had shifted to uphold important New Deal measures. And as the older justices resigned within the next few years, Roosevelt was able to appoint men of his own choice to the Court anyway.

In the meantime, organized opposition to the child labor amendment increased again. While the NIRA was in force, the number of employed children had decreased dramatically, but after the Supreme Court decision, the number of working children rose once more. Clearly, state law could not effectively deal with the problem, and a Gallup poll in 1936 showed that 61 percent of the American public supported the child labor amendment. However, the amendment never became part of the Constitution. Instead,

the Fair Labor Standards Act (1938) regulated the employment of children younger than sixteen years (eighteen-year-olds in dangerous work) and was upheld by the Supreme Court in *United States v. Darby* (1941). The opinion was unanimous and noted that *Hammer v. Dagenhart* "should be and now is overruled."

Of course, there are still young working children who are not completely protected by the law. Many of these children deliver newspapers, cut lawns, babysit, collect scrap metal, and work in such family owned businesses as restaurants. Perhaps the largest group of unprotected children are those of migrant workers who follow the crops from state to state, live in substandard housing, and receive inadequate medical care. But the combination of state and federal employment laws, along with higher standards of school attendance, protects most children today from the abuses of early twentieth-century child labor practices.

SURVIVING THE GREAT DEPRESSION

THE PROBLEM

"Hard times," one historian called it— an experience that left an invisible scar on a generation of Americans, according to another. Both historians were referring to the Great Depression, which persisted through nearly the entire decade of the 1930s, leaving millions of Americans jobless, hungry, and homeless. Estimates of the number of unemployed during those years vary (even today, young people entering the work force for the first time, women reentering the job market, and blacks seeking jobs are often underreported in the unemployment statistics). Nevertheless, between one-fourth and one-third of all American workers were unable to find jobs in 1932, and there is no doubt that by that year the depression was deep, severe, and worldwide.

In the United States, the difference between the economic indicators in 1929 and 1932 was startling: $8.7 billion in profits became a $5.6 billion deficit, the gross national product was cut in half, exports fell nearly 80 percent, and farm income was down 63 percent. By 1932, 4,377 banks had failed.

How did average people react to the depression? What did they think about what was happening? Were their lives changed by the depression? If so, how did they cope with these changes? In this chapter you will be studying how to use the technique of oral history for interviewing Americans who were children or young people during the 1930s about their experiences in the depression.

BACKGROUND

The newly elected Herbert Hoover was at first bewildered and somewhat defensive about the rapid downward spiral of the nation's economy. As did many Americans, Hoover believed in the basic soundness of capitalism, advocated the values of an older individualism, and maintained that the role of the federal government in the economy should be quite limited. Nevertheless, Hoover was a compassionate man, unlike some of the members of his cabinet. As private relief sources dried up, the president authorized public-works projects and some institutional loans, at the same time vetoing other relief bills and trying to convince the nation that prosperity would return soon. Americans turned out at the polls in record numbers for the election of 1932—and voted for the Democratic candidate Franklin D. Roosevelt in equally record numbers.

We know how the government reacted to the spreading economic calamities after March 1933—Congress rapidly passed an assortment of programs collectively known as the New Deal. Calling together a group of experts (mainly professors and lawyers) to form a "brain trust," the newly elected president acted quickly to try to restore the confidence of the nation. In his fireside radio chats as well as in his other speeches, Roosevelt consistently reassured the American public that the country's economic institutions were sound. In the meantime, Congress met in an emergency session to begin the difficult process of providing immediate relief for the needy and legislation for longer-term recovery. The First and Second Agricultural Adjustment Acts were intended to aid farmers by discouraging overproduction; the National Recovery Act was part of a wide-ranging effort to provide

public-works projects for the unemployed and establish fair practice codes for business and industry. Young people were the subject of special attention—the National Youth Administration helped finance the educations of many students, and the Civilian Conservation Corps provided work camps for thousands of unemployed young men.

Eleanor Roosevelt was equally active in her efforts to mitigate the effects of the depression. With boundless energy, she traveled throughout the country, observing conditions firsthand and reporting to her husband. Three groups—blacks, young people, and women—were the primary focus of her concern. Eleanor Roosevelt was one of the few New Dealers deeply committed to black civil rights; she championed both individuals and the movement whenever she could. Young people had easy access to Mrs. Roosevelt, and women found her sympathetic to their pleas for inclusion in work relief projects. Her nontraditional behavior as First Lady was controversial and inspired many unflattering jokes and cartoons, but for millions of Americans, Eleanor Roosevelt was the heart of the New Deal efforts to overcome the depression.

Aimed at relief, recovery, and (sometimes) reform of the American economy, New Deal programs alleviated but did not solve the problems that had spread across the nation with the depression.

In this chapter, you will be given proper interview techniques and then will be expected to interview a person who actually lived through the great

Depression. Then you will be examining several interviews Studs Terkel conducted for his book about the depression. Finally, you will be analyzing an interview a student conducted. Studying these interviews will help you sharpen your analytical skills before you conduct your own interview. Finally, you will be actually interviewing a person who was a child or a young adult during the 1930s. Try to find out what that person's experiences were, and then analyze the degree to which that person's account supports or contradicts what historians believe were the major effects of the Great Depression upon the lives of "ordinary" Americans.

THE METHOD

Historians often wish they could ask specific questions of the participants in a historical event—questions that are not answered in surviving diaries, letters, and other documents. Furthermore, many people, especially the poor, uneducated, and members of minority groups, did not leave written records and thus often are overlooked by historians.

But when historians are dealing with the comparatively recent past, they do have an opportunity to ask questions by using a technique called oral history. Oral history—interviewing famous and not-so-famous people about their lives and the events they observed or participated in—can greatly enrich knowledge of the past. It can help the historian capture the "spirit of an age" as seen through the eyes of average citizens, and it often bridges the gap between impersonal forces (wars, epidemics, depressions) and the personal and individual responses to them. Furthermore, oral history allows the unique to emerge from the total picture: the conscientious objector who would not serve in the army, the woman who did not marry and devote herself to raising a family, and so forth.

Oral history is both fascinating and challenging. It seems easy to do, but it is really rather difficult to do well. There is always the danger that the student may "lead" the interview by imposing his or her ideas on the subject. Equally possible is that the student may be led away from the subject by the person being interviewed.

Still other problems sometimes arise: the student may miss the subtleties in what is being said or may assume that an exceptional person is representative of many people. Some older people like to tell only the "smiling side" of their personal history—that is, they prefer to talk about the good things that happened to them, not the bad things. Others actually forget what happened or are influenced by reading or television. Some older people cannot resist sending a message to younger people by recounting how hard it was in the past, how few luxuries they had when they were young, how far they had to walk to school, and so forth. Yet oral history, when used carefully and judiciously along with other sources, is an invaluable tool that helps one re-create a sense of our past.

Recently much attention has been paid—and rightly so—to protecting the rights and privacy of human subjects. For this reason, the federal government requires that the interviewee consent to the interview and be fully aware of how the interview is to be used. The interviewer must explain the purpose of the interview, and the person being interviewed must sign a release form (for samples, see Sources 1 to 3). Although these requirements are intended to apply mostly to psychologists and sociologists, historians who use oral history are included as well.

The Great Depression of the 1930s presents an almost matchless opportunity for the oral historian. Most Americans past the age of sixty-five (11.3 percent of the total population in 1980) even today have vivid memories of the depression. Of course, those memories vary, depending on the individual's age, socioeconomic status, race, sex, and region. But together the recollections of a number of people should present an accurate picture of the depression and how the people responded to it. Not only will this approach to the past bring your reading about the depression to life, it may also present a few surprises not contained in what you have read.

THE EVIDENCE

Sources 1 and 2 from Collum Davis, Kathryn Back, and Kay MacLean, *Oral History: From Tape to Type* (Chicago: American Library Assn., © 1977), pp. 14 and 15).

1. Sample Unconditional Release.

Tri-County Historical Society

For and in consideration of the participation by   Tri-County Historical Society   in any programs involving the dissemination of tape-recorded memories and oral history material for publication, copyright, and other uses, I hereby release all right, title, or interest in and to all of my tape-recorded memoirs to   Tri-County Historical Society   and declare that they may be used without any restriction whatsoever and may be copyrighted and published by the said   Society,   which may also assign said copyright and publication rights to serious research scholars.

In addition to the rights and authority given to you under the preceding paragraph, I hereby authorize you to edit, publish, sell and/or license the use of my oral history memoir in any other manner which the ___Society___ considers to be desirable and I waive any claim to any payments which may be received as a consequence thereof by the ___Society.___

PLACE   Indianapolis, Indiana

DATE   July 14, 1975

_____
Harold S. Johnson
(Interviewee)

_____
Jane Rogers
(for   Tri-County Historical Society   )

2. Sample Conditional Release.

Tri-County Historical Society

I hereby release all right, title, or interest in and to all or any part of my tape-recorded memoirs to ___Tri-County Historical Society,___ subject to the following stipulations:

That my memoirs are to be *closed* until five years following my death.

PLACE   Indianapolis,

Indiana

DATE   July 14, 1975

_____
Harold S. Johnson
(Interviewee)

_____
Jane Rogers
(for   Tri-County Historical Society   )

Source 3 from the University of Tennessee.

3. Form Developed by a Large U.S. History Survey Class at the University of Tennessee, Knoxville, 1984.

This form is to state that I have been interviewed by _____ on
                                                        (Interviewer)
_____ on my recollections of the Great Depression and life in
       (date)
the 1930's. I understand that this interview will be used in a class project

at the University of Tennessee, and that the results will be saved for

future historians.

_____
                    Signature

_____
                    Date

4. Instructions for Interviewers.

1. Establish the date, time, and place of the interview well in advance. You may wish to call and remind the interviewee a few days before your appointment.
2. Clearly state the purpose of the interview *at the beginning*. In other words, explain why the class is doing this project.
3. Prepare for the interview by carefully reading background information about the depression and by writing down and arranging the questions you will be asking to guide the interview.
4. It is usually a good idea to keep most of your major questions broad and general so the interviewee will not simply answer with a word or two ("How did you spend your leisure time?"). Specific questions such as "How much did it cost to go to the movies?" are useful for obtaining more details.
5. Avoid loaded questions such as "Everybody liked Eleanor Roosevelt, didn't they?" Instead, keep your questions neutral—"What did you think about Eleanor Roosevelt and the things she did?"

6. If any of your questions involve controversial matters, it is better to ask them toward the end of the interview, when the interviewee is more comfortable with you.

7. Always be courteous, and be sure to give the person enough time to think, remember, and answer. Never argue, even if he or she says something with which you strongly disagree. Remember that the purpose of the interview is to find out what *that person* thinks, not what you think.

8. Always take notes, even if you are tape-recording the interview. Notes will help clarify unclear portions of the tape and will be essential if the recorder malfunctions or the tape is accidentally erased.

9. Many who use oral history believe that the release forms should be signed at the beginning of the interview; others insist that this often inhibits the person who is to be interviewed and therefore should not be done until the end of the session. Although students who are only using the material for a class exercise are not always held strictly to the federal requirements, it is still better to obtain a signed release. Without such a release, the tape cannot be heard and used by anyone else (or deposited in an oral history collection), and the information the tape contains cannot be published or made known outside the classroom.

10. Try to write up the results of your interview as soon as possible after completing the interview. Even in rough form, these notes will help you capture the sense of what was said as well as the actual information that was presented.

5. A Suggested Interview Plan.

Remember that the person you have chosen to interview is a *person,* with feelings, sensitivities, and emotions. If you intend to tape-record the interview, ask permission first. If you believe that a tape recorder will inhibit the person you have selected, then leave it at home and rely on your ability to take notes.

The following suggestions may help you get started. People usually remember the personal aspects of their lives more vividly than they remember national or international events. That is a great advantage in this exercise because what you are attempting to find out is how this person lived during the depression. Begin by getting the following important data on the interviewee:

1. Name
2. Age in 1930
3. Race, sex

4. Where the person lived in the 1930s and what that area was like then
5. Family background (what the interviewee's parents did for a living; number of brothers, sisters; whether interviewee considered himself or herself rich, middle class, poor)
6. Educational background

Then move to the aspects of the person's life that will flesh out your picture of the 1930s.

1. What did this person do for a living?
2. Was the person ever unemployed during the depression? What did she or he do?
3. If the interviewee was young during the depression, what about her or his parents?
4. How did the person spend leisure time? If single, what were the dating and courtship practices like?
5. How important was the family? The church? The school? Other institutions?

These questions will give you a fairly good idea of how the person lived during the 1930s. You should supplement these with questions of your own, formed to help clarify the points above. For example,

1. Did the person know other people worse off than she or he? Did the person help them? If so, in what ways?
2. Was the person's life in the 1920s altered by the depression? How?
3. Did the person go to the movies often? What did the person see? What about the radio and radio programs? How much did it cost to see a movie in the 1930s? How much was a coke or a soda?

Finally, review some of the basic legislation of the New Deal and the significant events of the era. Then, as a class or in small groups, develop some questions about these programs and events. For example,

1. Did the person ever get employment through programs like the WPA or CCC? If not, did the interviewee know others who did?
2. Does the person remember any new unions or efforts to unionize local industries during the 1930s? Were there any major strikes?

Such questions might well be tailored to different geographic and economic locations—farming, mining, urban, small town, South, West, Midwest, Northeast.

Sources 6 through 11: Interviews from Studs Terkel, *Hard Times* (New York: Pocket Books, 1978), pp. 139–142, 123–124, 104–105, 445–449, 62–63, and 148–150, respectively.

6. Hank Oettinger, Linotype Operator.

I came from a very small town in northern Wisconsin. It had been ravaged by the lumber barons. It was cut-over land, a term you hear very often up there. It was a one industry town: tourist business. During the winter, there was nothing.

A lot of people who suffered from the Depression—it was new to them. It wasn't new to me. I was number ten in a family of eleven. My father, who had one leg, worked in a lumber mill for a while. Lost it, held a political job for a while, Registrar of Deeds. Lost it. Ninety-two percent of the people in the country were on welfare in the early years of the Depression.

We could have gone on relief, but my father refused. Foolish pride. He would not accept medical care, even. I had, oh God, a beautiful set of teeth. To have one filled was $2 at the time, I think. Oh, my gosh, my teeth just went. Eventually, I got to work and saved most of them. But the fact that he wouldn't even accept medical relief—stubborn Dutchman! . . .

I remember seeing a hunger march to City Hall. It was a very cold, bitter day. My boss was looking out of the window with me. I didn't know what the hell it was. He says, "They ought to lock the bastards up." I thought to myself: Lock them up for what? All of a sudden, the printing business like everything else went kerplop. I was laid off in '31. I was out of work for over two years. I'd get up at six o'clock every morning and make the rounds. I'd go around looking for work until about eight thirty. The library would open at nine. I'd spend maybe five hours in the library.

The feeling among people was beautiful. Supposing some guy was a hunter. He'd go out and get a hold of some ducks or some game, they'd have their friends over and share it. . . .

I had it drilled in me: there are no such things as classes in America. I awoke one day. I was, by this time, working for a newspaper in Waukesha. They had a picture of this farm woman, standing in the window of her home and the dust had completely covered everything, and there was a dead cow. And here, at the bottom of the same page, they had a picture of Bernard Baruch. He had made some big deal in the stock market and was on somebody's yacht. I looked at one picture and then the other. No classes in America.

I was making sixty-seven cents an hour as a linotype operator. At about $27 a week, I was a big shot. I was rolling. And gradually got involved in the union movement. The printers played a big role in the early days of the CIO.[1] This may seem unusual, a high class craft union went along with John L. Lewis against the old aristocracy of labor.

The union man today under forty knows absolutely nothing about the struggles. They don't want to upset the wonderful applecart they have. We used to sing, in the organizing days of the CIO, "Solidarity Forever." The Communists were active in it. Hell, we'd even sing "The Internationale"[2] on occasion. Could I get a young printer today, who drives a big Buick, who has a home in the suburbs—could I get him to sing "Arise, ye prisoners of starvation"?

7. Dorothe Bernstein, Waitress.

I went into an orphan home in 1933. I was about ten. I had clean clothes all the time, and we had plenty to eat. We'd go through the park when we walked to school. Railroad tracks came somewhere. The picture's like it was yesterday.

The men there waited for us to go through and hand them our lunches. If we had something the dietitian at the home would prepare that we didn't like. We'd give them the little brown paper bags.

Today I tell my daughters: be careful of people, especially a certain type that look a certain way. Then we didn't have any fear. You'd never think that if you walked by people, even strangers: gee, that person I got to be careful of. Nobody was really your enemy. These were guys who didn't have work. Who'd probably work if there was work. I don't know how they got where they were going or where they ended up. They were nice men. You would never think they would do you bodily harm. They weren't bums. These were hard luck guys.

On Fridays, we used to give 'em our lunch, all of us. They might be 125 of us going to school, carrying the same brown paper bag, with mashed sardine sandwiches and mayonnaise on it. This was thirty some years ago. I still don't eat a sardine. (Laughs.) . . .

People talk about the good old times. These can't be the good old times when men wanted to work and couldn't work. When your kids wanted milk and you had to go scratch for it. I remember one girl friend I went to store with. She was real ashamed because they had food stamps. I remember how apologetic she was to me. It kind of embarrassed her. She said, "You want to wait outside?"

1. Congress of Industrial Organizations, a labor organization founded by John L. Lewis in 1935.
2. A revolutionary song of Communists and workers.

Louise was a Bohemian girl. Her mother had a grocery store that they lived behind. Louise used to do the books, and there was always owing. You never said to the people: "Do you have the money to pay me?" They would say, "Write it in the book." And you wrote it in the book, because this was their family food, and they had to have it. It wasn't that you were giving it away. Eventually, you'd be paid.

I never knew any real millionaires who were diving out of windows. I would read it like it was fiction. Who had that kind of fantastic money? They would kill themselves because of loss of it? To me, it's easier and nicer to scratch a little bit and get up.

You know, when you get down so low that you can't get any lower, there's no place else to go but up. You do either one of two things: you either lay down and die, or you pull yourself up by your bootstraps and you start over.

8. Clifford Burke, Retired Man Who Does Volunteer Work in a Black Neighborhood.

The negro was born in depression. It didn't mean too much to him, The Great American Depression, as you call it. There was no such thing. The best he could be is a janitor or a porter or shoeshine boy. It only became official when it hit the white man. If you can tell me the difference between the depression today and the Depression of 1932 for a black man, I'd like to know it. Now, it's worse, because of the prices. Know the rents they're payin' out here? I hate to tell ya.

We had one big advantage. Our wives,they could go to the store and get a bag of beans or a sack of flour and a piece of fat meat, and they could cook this. And we could eat it. Steak? A steak would kick in my stomach like a mule in a tin stable. Now you take the white fella, he couldn't do this. His wife would tell him: Look, if you can't do any better than this, I'm gonna leave you. I seen it happen. He couldn't stand bringing home beans instead of steak and capon. And he couldn't stand the idea of going on relief like a Negro. . . .

I never applied for PWA or WPA, 'cause as long as I could hustle, there was no point in beating the other fellow out of a job, cuttin' some other guy out. . . .

9. Elsa Ponselle, Elementary School Principal.

I began to teach in December, 1930, and I was paid until June, 1931. When we came back, the city had gone broke. We kept on teaching, of course. I didn't go hungry and had a place to live. My father provided me with enough money to get by. But it was another thing for the men who were married and had children.

They began to pay us with warrants, which carried six percent interest. A marvelous investment. But not for the teachers who had to take them for pay. They had to peddle those warrants for what they could get. It was a promise to pay when the city got some money. We didn't think we'd ever get paid, but the businessmen knew better. . . .

The Depression hit other members of my family. My brother, a tailor, like my father, was working one day every three months. He had a wife and two children. We were able to help him out. My sister-in-law came to me one day and said: "You want to hear something really funny? Johnny came home and said he had to bring some canned goods to school for the poor children. Where the hell is he gonna find kids poorer than we are?" We protected the kids from any idea that they were deprived. . . .

Do you realize how many people in my generation are not married? Young teachers today, they just naturally get married. All the young men are around. There were young men around when we were young. But they were supporting mothers.

It wasn't that we didn't have a chance. I was going with someone when the Depression hit. We probably would have gotten married. He was a commercial artist and had been doing very well. I remember the night he said, "They just laid off quite a few of the boys." It never occurred to him that he would be next. He was older than most of the others and very sure of himself. This was not the sort of thing that was going to happen to *him*. Suddenly he was laid off. It hit him like a ton of bricks. And he just disappeared. . . .

. . . The rich, then, had an instinct for self-preservation. They didn't flaunt their money, if you remember. They didn't have fancy debutante parties, because it was not the thing to do. They were so God-damned scared they'd have a revolution. They damn near did, too, didn't they? Oooohhh, were they scared! What's more scared than a million dollars?

The Depression was a way of life for me, from the time I was twenty to the time I was thirty. I thought it was going to be forever and ever and ever. That people would always live in fear of losing their jobs. You know, *fear.* And, yet, we had, in a way, a wonderful time. We were young. . . .

How can you talk about the Depression without talking about F.D.R.? I remember when he was at the Chicago Stadium and all of us ran from school to get there. He came in on his son's arm. We didn't realize that he was really and truly crippled until we saw the braces. He got up there and the place just absolutely went up in smoke. What was tremendous about him was—

with all the adoration—his sense of humor. He acted as though he didn't take himself seriously.

And Eleanor. Eleanor. I think she's the greatest thing that ever happened to anybody. I think of the way they talked about her, about her looks, about her voice. I used to get so rabid. Why I didn't have high blood pressure, I don't know.

10. Mary Owsley, Farm Woman Who Was Born in Kentucky and Moved to Oklahoma in 1929.

There was thousands of people out of work in Oklahoma City. They set up a soup line, and the food was clean and it was delicious. Many, many people, colored and white, I didn't see any difference, 'cause there was just as many white people out of work than were colored. Lost everything they had accumulated from their young days. And these are facts. I remember several families had to leave in covered wagons. To Californy, I guess.

See, the oil boom come in '29. People come from every direction in there. A coupla years later, they was livin' in everything from pup tents, houses built out of cardboard boxes and old pieces of metal that they'd pick up—anything that they could find to put somethin' together to put a wall around 'em to protect 'em from the public.

I knew one family there in Oklahoma City, a man and a women and seven children lived in a hole in the ground. You'd be surprised how nice it was, how nice they kept it. They had chairs and tables,and beds back in that hole. And they had the dirt all braced up there, just like a cave.

Oh, the dust storms, they were terrible. You could wash and hang clothes on a line, and if you happened to be away from the house and couldn't get those clothes in before that storm got there, you'd never wash that out. . . . These storms, when they would hit, you had to clean house from the attic to ground. Everything was covered in sand. Red sand, just full of oil.

The majority of people were hit and hit hard. They were mentally disturbed you're bound to know, 'cause they didn't know when the end of all this was comin'. There was a lot of suicides that I know of. From nothin' else but just they couldn't see any hope for a better tomorrow. I absolutely know some who did. Part of 'em were farmers and part of 'em were businessmen, even. They went flat broke and they committed suicide on the strength of it, nothing else.

A lot of times one family would have some food. They would divide. And everyone would share. Even the people that were quite well to do, they was ashamed. 'Cause they were eatin,' and other people wasn't.

My husband was very bitter. That's just puttin' it mild. He was an intelligent man. He couldn't see why as wealthy a country as this is, that there was any sense in so many people starving to death. . . .

11. Joe Morrison, Coal Miner.

Once I counted the people that I gave a lift to from Detroit to southern Indiana. It was fourteen people that I give a lift to that day. One was a woman with three children. Detroit was a one-industry town. When auto went down, everything went down. If there was a job in the auto plant, there'd be two hundred men for that job. (Laughs.)

In '30 and '31 you'd see freight trains, you'd see hundreds of kids, young kids, lots of 'em, just wandering all over the country. Looking for jobs, looking for excitement. . . . The one thing that was unique was to see women riding freight trains. That was unheard of, never had been thought of before. But it happened during the Depression. Women gettin' places by ridin' freight trains. Dressed in slacks or dressed like men, you could hardly tell 'em. Sometimes some man and his wife would get on, no money for fare.

You'd find political discussions going on in a boxcar. Ridin' a hundred miles or so, guys were all strangers, maybe two or three knew each other, pairs. There might be twenty men involved. They would discuss politics, what was happening. What should be done about this, that and so forth.

Source 12 from an interview in Tennessee, Fall 1987.

12. Ryan and his Grandparents.

Ryan is the student interviewer, Lorene is his grandmother, Clyde is his grandfather.

RYAN. I'd like to ask you a few basic questions about your background and early memories, beginning around 1925. When were you married, and what do you remember of your home in your youth?

LORENE. I was born in nineteen and eight, so I was twenty-two in nineteen and thirty, wouldn't that be right?

RYAN. I think so. Where did you both go to school?

LORENE. We both went to school in K *[a very small town in Tennessee].*

RYAN. Where did you live when you were first married?

LORENE. The first few years we lived with papa C and mama J. *[Clyde's parents.]* Then we bought forty acres off of papa C's section and lived in that little log house, across the field from them, on another road. We lived there until the depression hit so hard, and he went to *[the nearest big city in Tennessee]* and got a job in a foundry.

RYAN. What was your life like on the farm, and what did you do to make the cash you needed?

LORENE. We milked cows and sold milk. We had a lot of cows and hogs, a team of mules and a team of mares, and we had a wagon and we had a buggy (laughter) and all of that, and we raised all that we ate, we had our own milk and our own butter and our own chickens and our own hogs, and we plenty to eat, and we had a big garden . . .

CLYDE. and little to wear.

LORENE. had little to wear, but we had plenty to eat and a place to stay. He dug a cellar in the back yard, by the well, and I had five hundred cans of fruit in that cellar. We had everything we needed to eat; all we had to buy, see, he carried our corn to the mill and we had our meal ground. We had to buy flour and sugar and coffee,

CLYDE. and salt and soda.

LORENE. Yes, and that's all that we had to buy, because we had everything, more than we have now, we had eggs and chickens and big old hams in the smokehouse (laughter).

RYAN. Just running over, huh? When did you first hear of the depression? When did you first hear of bank collapses or sense that everything was going up in smoke?

CLYDE. Well, when the banks closed down . . . well, a truck would come by pickin' up our milk every day, and when the banks closed down the truck stopped . . . pickin' our milk up.

LORENE. And that was the first thing that hit us. And we'd bought these cows at a good price, and when the milk route stopped, they didn't then, because people didn't need 'em. Didn't have a route for the milk. And we had some pretty cows, and some that you'd paid about a hundred dollars for, wasn't it?

CLYDE. Yeah.

LORENE. and sold 'em for ten–fifteen dollars.

RYAN. So what was next? Did you lose your money in the bank?

LORENE. We didn't have any money to lose. We had our home, and it paid for, and our stock . . . and you had a big load of lambs, didn't we, you had somebody come and take a truckload of lambs to *[the nearest big city]* to sell, and he went with them. And when they had 'em sold, and the haul bill was paid, how much was it you had left?

CLYDE. I had twelve dollars, I think, left after I paid the truck bill to *[the nearest big city]*.

LORENE. And you think about that . . . a truckload! Of lambs!

CLYDE. Top lambs.

LORENE. And the man came back that afternoon and he blowed the horn out front, and I went to the door, and he said, "*[Clyde]* didn't come back. He said tell you he'd see you Saturday night. He says he's got him a job in *[the nearest big city]* and he's stayin' to work." So I was there by myself, and we lacked a little bit havin' the crop finished and had everything done but havin' the hay sowed. Anyway, I stayed there until, I reckon August, and then we moved to *[the nearest big city]*.

RYAN. What year would that have been?

LORENE. 1937.

RYAN. 1937? Didn't you feel anything back in 1929 to 1930, or did you know that there was a depression that early?

CLYDE. (Laughter) yeah, I knew all about it.

LORENE. Oh, it was hard, honey, it was hard.

RYAN. But didn't you feel it back then, or did it take seven years to reach you?

LORENE. Well, we just didn't have anything. We didn't lose anything, only we didn't have anything, couldn't find any work to do. He'd work all day for fifty cents and take his lunch, just anything he could do. And then when they got to building the roads, he took his wagon and team and hauled gravel, and that was the next best thing that happened, about your money, I guess, because we got a little money then.

RYAN. Did you know people who did lose their savings in a bank?

LORENE. Why yes. You remember your aunt G, her first husband had just made a delivery of his trees that he'd worked all summer and sold, and put the money in the bank, and the bank closed and got every bit of it. And he didn't have a penny left to pay his wholesale bill, or to live on or anything, and he just cried like a baby. It was terrible.

RYAN. Did people get broken up when they tried to find work, or were communities disrupted?

LORENE. No, I don't think so. I think people all stuck together very well. All that I knew.

RYAN. What did you have to do without?

LORENE. Clothes. No cash to buy clothes. I remember one time L *[her brother]* was goin' to *[the nearest big city]* and invited me to go along, and your granddaddy had one dollar, and he gave it to me to carry with me on the trip. . . . One dollar. And we'd take chickens to the store and sell, to get the things we needed, and eggs, we'd take eggs by the case, take thirty dozen at a time.

CLYDE. I guess we had around a hundred hens. Get eight cents a dozen for the eggs.

RYAN. Was there anything such as leisure time?

LORENE. Yes, there was more leisure time, really, you wouldn't think there was because we didn't have any washing machine, we didn't have any refrigerators, we didn't have any electric stoves, we had to carry in our wood and make our fires in our fireplace, and our cookstove, and draw water out of our well and clean our lamps to fill them up with oil, but it seemed like we had more time to visit people,

CLYDE. Get a gallon of kerosene for about eight cents, that'd burn us two or three weeks in our lamps.

RYAN. So what did you do in your leisure time?

LORENE. We visited our families, we'd spend the night with *[Ryan's aunt and uncle]*, we'd go to papa T's and mama O's *[her parents]* and spend the weekend; we just got by. And we always went to church.

RYAN. You went to *[the nearest big city]* in '37; when did you come back?

LORENE. No, we went there in . . . '36, and came back in '37, and your mother was born in '38.

CLYDE. Uh, the foundry shut down, and I worked a little carpentry work, the fellah laid me off from that and I came home the next day.

LORENE. (Laughter) I guess he had a good reason to do that, didn't he?

RYAN. You didn't make a carpenter, huh?

CLYDE. No, he just didn't have much to do.

LORENE. We left in August of '36, I believe, and came back . . . let me see, in April of '37.

CLYDE. And I sold trees that summer.

LORENE. Then we moved to K *[the small town where they had gone to school]*, didn't we? Yes, we got enough money, you sold trees that year, and we got enough money to buy us a house and lot in K. That was in the latter part of '37.

RYAN. So you never planned on being a farmer again?

LORENE. No, he said then he's through.

CLYDE. No, I quit. I kept a team a year or two after that, and hired a boy to help, I hired a boy to help me for eight dollars a month . . .

LORENE. To make a crop.

CLYDE. And he done as much work as anybody'd do.

RYAN. What was your knowledge of politics at the time? (Mutual laughter) What'd you think about Hoover?

LORENE. Aw . . . he thought. . . .

CLYDE. I thought he oughta been shot or hung.

RYAN. What did he do wrong?

CLYDE. Everything. People lost their jobs and homes and killed theirselves, and terrible times.

RYAN. What about Roosevelt?

LORENE. He was great.

CLYDE. Well, he got things straightened out.

RYAN. Have either one of you heard about Roosevelt's New Deal?

LORENE. No. . . .

RYAN. What did that mean to you?

CLYDE. I wouldn't know.

RYAN. Were there any kind of government work programs to get people back to work?

CLYDE. Yeah, they had the WPA.

RYAN. Did you ever get into that?

CLYDE. No, I never got on that.

LORENE. That was kinda like . . . welfare.

RYAN. Really? Did people look down on that?

LORENE. Yes, I think they did. Cause they'd say, "What do they do?" and you'd say, "Oh, he's on WPA."

RYAN. What kind of work was that?

LORENE. They did everything. They'd work on the roads, and they'd go around to places and build people's outdoor toilets and everything. There's a lot of people had their outdoor toilets built that didn't have them until the WPA come along. Just anything to make 'em a job.

RYAN. Tell me about when you went to work on the roads.

CLYDE. Well, I went to work on the road for the state, now, hauling gravel, and they'd pay me seventy cents a yard. I made, a lot of times fifty dollars a day.

RYAN. That must have been a fortune.

LORENE. It was. That was great then. He was young and strong, he'd go into work early and come home late. . . .

RYAN. What caused you to move off your forty acres in K?

LORENE. Well, we just weren't making what we really wanted to make, and he decided he didn't want to farm any more, and he wanted to go into the nursery business and sell nursery stock 'cause we could make more money at that. . . .

RYAN. So what I understand from you is that there wasn't a crash.

LORENE. There was a crash for people that had money, but for people that didn't have money . . . it was just that times was hard and hard and harder.

RYAN. More of a gradual thing?

LORENE. Yes, that's right. You just can't imagine. You have no idea. I've never known what it was to be hungry, and a lot of people have known

that . . . because we raised our own food, aw . . . we had gobs of food. I
remember the year we married, he put out a big patch of sweet potatoes,
and when we dug those we had a wagon, a big wagon . . .

CLYDE. . . . With sideboards on it.

LORENE. Of sweet potatoes! And you couldn't sell them! We thought we
weren't poor like some, even though we didn't have cash. But we needed
very little other than what we had, and that's not poor.

QUESTIONS TO CONSIDER

Sources 1 through 3 are sample release forms. Why might some people want to close their memoirs until after their deaths? What value might it be to a neighborhood, town, or state to accumulate an oral history collection?

If no one in your family is past sixty-five, how will you go about finding someone to interview for this project? If you do have older relatives, what would be the special advantages of interviewing them? Would there be any disadvantages? Which do you think might be the most difficult part(s) of the interview you will be conducting? Why?

There is a great deal of literature about conducting oral history interviews, and the Instructions for Interviewers (Source 4) lists some of the most helpful hints from the literature. It is particularly important to prepare interview questions in advance and to avoid leading your interviewee by asking loaded questions. The interview plan presented in the evidence (Source 5) is in the form of suggestions—something to get you started. How can you learn more about the New Deal programs and their impact? About what your interviewee thought about the Roosevelts?

Sources 6 through 11 are brief excerpts from the book *Hard Times: An Oral History of the Depression*. The author, Studs Terkel, was a young law school student at the beginning of the Great Depression. He lived with his parents in Chicago until the mid-1930s, when he gave up the idea of being a lawyer, became a radio script writer, and worked odd jobs. Eventually he turned to journalism, interviewing ordinary people about their experiences. The excerpts included in the evidence are from interviews with a variety of people who lived in different parts of the country. As you study each excerpt, note the specific points emphasized by the person being interviewed. Then try to find patterns in their experience as a whole—what do these patterns tell you about people's feelings, perceptions, and reactions to the depression?

For example, try to identify the socioeconomic class (upper, middle, lower) to which these people belonged at the time of the depression. (The occupations, such as waitress, coal miner, and teacher, listed after their names indicate the occupations the people had at the time they were interviewed.) Some of the interviewees, like Hank Oettinger, Clifford Burke, and Elsa Ponselle, tell you directly, but others, like Dorothe Bernstein, Mary Owsley, and Joe Morrison, give you only indirect clues to their backgrounds.

At least four of the six people mention specific personal effects the depression had on them. What were those effects? Furthermore, Morrison, Owsley, and Oettinger came from regions that were especially hard hit by the depression. Why were their regions hit so hard? Is there anything in the evidence to indicate how the depression affected women and blacks? How did those interviewed react to other people and their hardships? How did their communities react? Finally, several of the people interviewed compared conditions during the depression with conditions at the present time. What conclusions did they reach?

Source 12 is Ryan's interview with his grandparents in Tennessee. What were the most significant things that he found out? Are there any questions or further information you would have liked him to ask or determine? Are there any messages in what his grandparents are telling him?

EPILOGUE

"When did you notice that times were getting better, that maybe the depression was letting up?", Ryan asked his grandparents. His grandmother replied that it was not until after Pearl Harbor, when she, her husband, and their young daughter (Ryan's mother) went to Detroit to work in the World War II defense plants. After the war they returned to Tennessee, where they still live today.

"People talk about the good old times," Dorothe Bernstein told Studs Terkel. "These can't be the good old times when men wanted to work and couldn't work." In spite of her conclusion, however, the popularity of sentimental television shows like "The Waltons" and 1930s collectible items like Depression glass and Shirley Temple dolls indicate that many Americans may well be nostalgic for the "good old days."

Yet for Americans who lived through the depression, the fear of a recurring depression lingered even after World War II. After the war, women and blacks were relegated to low-level jobs and marginal positions in both educational institutions and the work place as returning veterans and other middle-class white men concentrated on climbing the professional and corporate ladders. The 1950s American

[198]

dream centered on the traditional nuclear family, inhabiting a ranch-style suburban house fully equipped with a modern kitchen, a television set, and two cars. The cold war added a new fear—atomic warfare—to the old economic anxieties, and the conservative swing in national politics was matched by the conservative mood in high schools and on college campuses across the nation.

It would not be until the 1960s, when a new generation came of age, that Americans (especially women, blacks, and young people) would begin to raise real questions about our country and its postdepression values.

THE BURDENS OF POWER:
THE DECISION TO
DROP THE ATOMIC BOMB, 1945

At 2:45 A.M. on August 6, 1945, three B-29 bombers took off from an American airbase in the Marianas, bound for Japan. Two of the airplanes carried cameras and scientific instruments; the third carried an atomic bomb, a new type of weapon with the destructive power of 20,000 tons of TNT.

In the Japanese city of Hiroshima, residents were so undisturbed by the sight of so few enemy planes that most did not bother to go to air raid shelters. When the bomb exploded 2,000 feet above the city, 80,000 people were killed instantly, and at least that many died soon afterward of radiation poisoning.[1] More than 80 percent of Hiroshima's buildings were destroyed, and the flash of light was so intense that shadowlike "silhouettes" of people who had disappeared had been "photographed" onto the walls of buildings and rubble.

The decision to drop the atomic bomb on Hiroshima ultimately rested with President Harry S Truman, who had been in office only 116 days when the bomb was dropped and, indeed, had known of its existence only since April 25. The war in Europe ended with the surrender of Nazi Germany in early May of 1945. But Japan was still to be conquered, and there was enormous hostility against the Japanese in the United States. Truman's

---

1. The actual number of bomb-related deaths at Hiroshima has been the subject of much dispute. The U.S. Strategic Bombing Survey estimated the number of people who were killed instantly at 80,000. An August 1946 survey placed the total number killed (instantly and soon after, from radiation poisoning) at more than 122,000. A 1961 Japa- nese study contended that the true figure was about 166,000. In the late 1970s, a careful estimate by Japanese officials placed the total bomb-related deaths (as of November 1945) at 130,000. The total population of Hiroshima at the time the bomb was dropped was 300,000.

military advisers told him that an invasion of the Japanese mainland could cost the United States between 500,000 and 1,000,000 casualties. At the same time, however, the situation in Europe was grave, as it became increasingly clear that the wartime alliance between the United States and the Soviet Union was rapidly deteriorating. As for President Truman, he had been suspicious of the Russians since 1941, and the eroding alliance only confirmed his worst fears. To what extent might the dropping of the atomic bomb on Hiroshima be used to threaten the Soviets with American military prowess in the postwar years? Moreover, at the Yalta conference, Soviet Premier Josef Stalin promised to enter the war against Japan approximately three months after the fall of Germany. To what extent was the atomic bomb used to end the war in the Pacific before the Russians could become involved and thus increase the Soviet Union's power in Asia?

In this chapter you will be analyzing the evidence to answer four major questions. (1) Why did President Truman decide to drop the atomic bomb on Hiroshima? (2) What principal factors went into that decision? (3) Were there any alternatives to using the atomic bomb? If so, why did President Truman not choose one of the alternatives? (4) Who were the key figures who helped President Truman make up his mind? Why did he heed the words of some advisers but not others?

Even though you will have to go beyond the evidence provided here, you should also be willing to ponder the important question of whether President Truman's decision to use the atomic bomb on Hiroshima was the proper one. To answer that question (a controversial one even today), you will have to combine the evidence with material in the Background section of this chapter and with other reading.

BACKGROUND

In 1918, New Zealand physicist Ernest Rutherford was criticized for his failure to attend a meeting of a British committee of scientists trying to create a defense against German submarines during World War I. Rutherford's excuse for his absence shocked his fellow scientists: "Talk softly, please, I have been engaged in experiments which suggest that the atom can be artificially disintegrated. If it is true, it is of far greater importance than a war."

By the 1920s, separate research centers investigating the splitting of the atom had been established at Göttingen (Germany), Cambridge (England), and Copenhagen (Denmark). Physicists and chemists from all over the Western world came to these centers to study and perform research, encouraging each other and sharing their ideas in what was, briefly, a true international community of scientists. Experiments were carried out using

CHAPTER 8

THE BURDENS
OF POWER: THE
DECISION TO
DROP THE
ATOMIC BOMB,
1945

comparatively crude equipment as scientists groped in the dark for the essence of matter itself and how that matter could be transformed. Some researchers had used alpha particles[2] to bombard atoms of nitrogen, thereby rearranging nitrogen atoms and changing them into oxygen and hydrogen. When others asked the scientists the practical usefulness of their work, most of the scientists simply shrugged; they did not know. Yet they felt that they were on the brink of an important scientific breakthrough in unlocking the riddles of the universe itself.

In 1932, scientists at Cambridge discovered the neutron,[3] a subatomic particle that could be used to bombard and split atoms. That important discovery speeded up atomic research considerably. Neutrons were used to split atoms in Paris, Cambridge, Rome, Zurich, and Berlin. Building on those experiments, in 1934, scientists in Rome created the first chain reaction, in which the split atoms themselves released neutrons, which in turn split other atoms. In late 1938, two German physicists at Berlin's Kaiser Wilhelm Institute used neutrons to successfully split atoms of uranium. That type of uranium (U-235) was a highly unstable element that, when split by neutrons, created significant amounts of radioactivity.

At this point, politics entered the realm of science. In early 1933, Adolph Hitler came to power in Germany as an avowed nationalist, expansionist, and anti-Semite. Czechoslovakia, occupied by Germany in 1938, was the only place in Europe that held large stocks of high-grade uranium. Although Hitler himself always was cool toward atomic research, officers in the German War Department recognized that a chain reaction of uranium could produce an extremely powerful weapon and urged scientists in Berlin to push forward. Interestingly, those scientists purposely slowed down their work, fearing the uses Hitler might make of such an atomic device. Scientists working in Germany who were unsympathetic to or fearful of Hitler fled the country, principally to England and the United States. One such person was Leo Szilard, a Hungarian who recognized that a possible race over the production of atomic weapons might develop between Germany and other nations. At Columbia University in New York, Szilard urged upon his fellow émigrés a self-imposed moratorium on publishing the results of their atomic research in scientific journals. At the same time, in October 1939, Szilard was instrumental in getting world-famous mathematician and scientist Albert Einstein to write a letter to President Roosevelt proposing a speed-up of American atomic research. Roosevelt gave his vague go-ahead, although funds were not made available to the scientists, most of whom were centered at Columbia University, until December 6, 1941 (ironically, one day before the Japanese attacked Pearl Harbor).

Once the United States was officially in World War II, President Roosevelt gave his full support to the top-secret project to develop atomic

2. Alpha particles are positively charged composite particles consisting of two protons and two neutrons that are indistinguishable from the nucleus of a helium atom.
3. Rutherford predicted the existence of the neutron in 1915. Fittingly, it was his laboratory that proved his theoretical hunch correct.

weaponry, a project that in the end cost more than $2 billion (carefully hidden from Congress). In 1942, British and United States scientists merged their efforts to create the Manhattan Project, the code name for the building of an atomic bomb.

To direct the Manhattan Project, Roosevelt chose General Leslie Groves, forty-eight years old in 1942 and a career military officer well-known for his skill in administration. An FBI investigation of Groves showed only that he had an incredible weakness for chocolate (he stored his private supply of chocolate in the same safe that contained some of the world's most vital nuclear secrets). He often called the scientists "my crackpots" but was an able administrator who provided his "crackpots" with everything they desired. Ultimately, the Manhattan Project employed more than 150,000 people (only a dozen or so of whom knew of the whole operation) who worked at the University of Chicago, Oak Ridge (Tennessee), Hanford (Washington), and Los Alamos (New Mexico).[4]

The Manhattan Project was given its urgency by the fear that Hitler would have his hands on an atomic bomb before the Allies. As noted, what the scientists of the West did not know was that German physicists, because they hated Hitler and feared nuclear weaponry, had purposely slowed down their efforts. In 1944, soldiers of American General George Patton's advancing armies captured the papers of one of the German scientists engaged in nuclear research; the papers showed that Germany was at least two years behind the West in the development of atomic weapons.

This fact presented American scientists with a real dilemma. The entire goal of the Manhattan Project was to beat Hitler to the atomic bomb, but now it was clear that nuclear research, purposely retarded by German physicists, was years away from building a successful nuclear device for the Third Reich. As Albert Einstein said, "If I had known that the Germans would not succeed in constructing the atomic bomb, I would never have lifted a finger." Several other scientists agreed with Einstein and hoped that, even if the bomb was developed, it would never be used.

Yet, as seen above, political and military considerations rarely were far from nuclear research. Even with Nazi Germany close to defeat, President Truman, who assumed the presidency upon Roosevelt's death on April 12, 1945, looked upon a world filled with dangers. Japan remained unconquered, and Truman's military advisers predicted a fearful toll if the Japanese mainland was invaded. Too, relations with the Soviet Union, an ally in the war against Germany, were deteriorating rapidly. To what extent might Truman see the atomic bomb as the military and political solution to both these problems?

---

4. Columbia University scientists were transferred to the University of Chicago, away from the coast, where they continued their experiments and calculations. Oak Ridge was a city built by the Manhattan Project in an isolated area of East Tennessee; there U-235 was extracted from the more passive U-238. Hanford was where plutonium (used in the bomb dropped on Nagasaki) was produced, a new element that Chicago scientists discovered by using neutrons to bombard U-238. Los Alamos was where the bombs were assembled and tested.

CHAPTER 8

THE BURDENS
OF POWER: THE
DECISION TO
DROP THE
ATOMIC BOMB,
1945

It is important to note that what eventually became the cold war between the Soviet Union and the West actually had its origins in World War II itself, long before it was known that the atomic bomb would work. In many ways, the only factor that brought the Soviet Union and the West together as allies was their mutual enemy, Hitler's Germany. Soviet Premier Josef Stalin, whose nation had been invaded twice by Germany in the twentieth century, viewed the West as a constant threat. To Stalin, the Soviet Union had carried the burden of the fight against Hitler since 1941 (until the 1944 Allied landing at Normandy, in France, to create a "second front" against Germany), had suffered staggering casualties, and had seen whole areas of the Soviet Union utterly devastated.[5] To guard against another such invasion, Stalin believed that the Soviet Union must dominate the nations of eastern Europe and not let a strong Germany emerge from World War II. Increasingly suspicious of Great Britain and the United States, Stalin believed that he needed to keep those nations as unaware as possible of his country's economic and military vulnerability, a belief that resulted in a policy of secrecy toward the West.

Many policymakers in Great Britain and the United States were as suspi-

cious of the Soviet Union as Stalin was of them. Britain's Prime Minister Winston Churchill had distrusted the Russians since the Bolshevik Revolution of 1917, believed that Russian communists had a master plan for world domination, and urged that a hard line be taken against Stalin. On the other hand, President Franklin Roosevelt, although harboring few illusions about the Soviet Union, hoped that by making some concessions he could lessen Stalin's fears and gain the Soviet premier's cooperation in the postwar world and in forming the United Nations. At the Yalta Conference in February 1945, Roosevelt, Churchill, and Stalin agreed that the postwar governments of eastern Europe would be freely elected but pro-Russian. The three powers also agreed on the temporary partition of Germany into three zones of occupation to be governed cooperatively by the three victorious powers, who eventually would merge these zones into one reconstructed and reformed German state. The city of Berlin, well within the projected Soviet zone, likewise would be divided into three administrative sectors. In addition, the Soviet Union was given the right to exact heavy reparations from a defeated Germany, which ultimately amounted to the dismantling of German industry within the Russian zone for shipment to the Soviet Union. Stalin agreed to enter the war against Japan three months after the fall of Germany and also promised to conclude a treaty with China's Chiang Kai-shek, the person the United States hoped would lead China after the defeat of Japan. Even amid these joint declarations of unity at Yalta, however, considerable distrust remained.

5. Russian military deaths are estimated to have exceeded 7 million. In contrast, Germany suffered approximately 3.5 million military deaths, China 2.2 million, Japan 1.3 million, Great Britain and the Commonwealth 500,000, and the United States 350,000. Indeed, when civilian deaths are added to military deaths, the Soviet Union lost a total of 40 percent of all people killed in World War II, or approximately 20 of 50 million.

Roosevelt's death brought Truman to the presidency. Truman's views of the Soviet Union were closer to those of Churchill than to Roosevelt's. Although Truman honored agreements (or reparations, the partitioning of Germany and Berlin, and the return of Russian "traitors" to the Soviet government) and ordered the United States Army (which had advanced beyond the line Roosevelt, Churchill, and Stalin earlier had agreed on) to draw back, in other ways he made it clear that his policy toward the Soviet Union would be different from that of Roosevelt's. Immediately after the surrender of Germany, Truman cut off aid to the Soviet Union, reasoning that the war in Europe had ended and that further assistance was unnecessary. Stalin was outraged. Furthermore, at the Potsdam Conference, Truman demanded that free elections be held immediately in eastern Europe, a demand that Stalin unhesitatingly rejected. Also at Potsdam, Truman informed Stalin that the United States had developed a new weapon of enormous destructive power, a fact Stalin probably already knew through espionage.

Thus it is evident that, even before the end of World War II, the alliance between the Soviet Union and the West had eroded badly. Deep suspicions and distrust on both sides caused leaders of the United States and the Soviet Union to view the other as a dangerous threat to peace and stability. As Truman confronted his first days in office and considered whether to use the atomic bomb against Japan, he faced other difficult decisions with regard to the Soviet Union. Should the bomb be used on Japan to save American lives? Could the bomb's secrets be used as a "bargaining chip" with the Soviet Union?

THE METHOD

Although they are sometimes written several years after a particular event has occurred, nevertheless personal memoirs are treated by historians as *primary sources* (evidence that is contemporary to the event being analyzed), principally because the authors of these memoirs were present when that event was taking place. Indeed, as seen in this chapter, some of those people were more than mere eyewitnesses—some were key figures in the event itself. Therefore, personal memoirs can be invaluable tools for those seeking to understand the past, a particular decision people made in the past, and the factors that went into the making of that decision.

Yet one always must be cautious when using personal diaries, memoirs, or reminiscences. The historian must keep in mind that each memoir is only one person's view or perspective of the event or decision. Was the author in a good position to see how a particular event unfolded or how a particular decision was made? Was the author aware of all the factors and people involved? Generally, the further away from the event or decision the author

CHAPTER 8

THE BURDENS
OF POWER: THE
DECISION TO
DROP THE
ATOMIC BOMB,
1945

was, the less reliable that author's memories are considered to be. Therefore, as you examine each piece of evidence, ask yourself this question: Was the person in a good position to see what she or he is reporting?

The next thing you must look for is the author's *intent* in writing down recollections in the first place. Does the author of the memoir have a bias? If so, what is it? Is the author seeking to justify, defend, attack, or exonerate? Does the author magnify or minimize his or her role in the decision? Why?

Be alert for the author's intent, stated or hidden, and possible biases.

Sometimes authors of memoirs either accidentally or purposely omit vital information or distort the facts. Have any of the authors of the memoirs in this chapter done so? How can you tell? Aside from simple forgetfulness or having a poor vantage point, can you think of any other reasons why this was done?

As you read each selection carefully, keep the following chart to help you recall the above points:

Author	Position	What Author Should Be Expected To Know	Biases?	Agreement or Disagreement with Other Memoirs (Omissions?)

And as you examine each piece of evidence, keep the central questions you are to answer firmly in mind:

1. Why did President Truman decide to drop the atomic bomb on Hiroshima?
2. What principal factors went into that decision?
3. Were there any alternatives to using the atomic bomb? If so, why didn't

President Truman choose one of them?
4. Who were the key figures who helped Truman with his decision? Why did he heed the words of some advisers but not those of others?
5. Do you think the decision President Truman made to drop the atomic bomb on Hiroshima, was the proper one?

Source 1 from Harry S Truman, *Memoirs: Year of Decisions* (Garden City, N.Y.: Doubleday and Company, 1955), pp. 10–11, 416–423.

1. Harry S Truman (President of the United States, April 12, 1945–January 1953).[6]

My own knowledge of these developments had come about only after I became President, when Secretary Stimson had given me the full story. He had told me at that time that the project was nearing completion and that a bomb could be expected within another four months. It was at his suggestion, too, that I had then set up a committee of top men and had asked them to study with great care the implications the new weapon might have for us.[7]

Secretary Stimson headed this group as chairman, and the other members were George L. Harrison, president of the New York Life Insurance Company, who was then serving as a special assistant to the Secretary of War; James F. Byrnes, as my personal representative; Ralph A. Bard, Under Secretary of the Navy; Assistant Secretary William L. Clayton for the State Department; and three of our most renowned scientists—Dr. Vannevar Bush, president of the Carnegie Institution of Washington and Director of the Office of Scientific Research and Development; Dr. Karl T. Compton, president of the Massachusetts Institute of Technology and Chief of Field Service in the Office of Scientific Research and Development; and Dr. James B. Conant, president of Harvard University and chairman of the National Defense Research Committee.

This committee was assisted by a group of scientists, of whom those most prominently connected with the development of the atomic bomb were Dr. Oppenheimer,[8] Dr. Arthur H. Compton, Dr. E. O. Lawrence, and the Italian-born Dr. Enrico Fermi. The conclusions reached by these men, both in the advisory committee of scientists and in the larger committee, were brought to me by Secretary Stimson on June 1.

It was their recommendation that the bomb be used against the enemy as soon as it could be done. They recommended further that it should be used

6. We have rearranged Truman's recollections in order to put events closer to chronological order.
7. This was the Interim Committee, referred to in other memoirs.
8. J. Robert Oppenheimer (1904–1967) directed the Los Alamos part of the Manhattan Project and was a key figure in America's nuclear research.

CHAPTER 8

THE BURDENS
OF POWER: THE
DECISION TO
DROP THE
ATOMIC BOMB,
1945

without specific warning and against a target that would clearly show its devastating strength. I had realized, of course, that an atomic bomb explosion would inflict damage and casualties beyond imagination. On the other hand, the scientific advisers of the committee reported, "We can propose no technical demonstration likely to bring an end to the war; we see no acceptable alternative to direct military use." It was their conclusion that no technical demonstration they might propose, such as over a deserted island, would be likely to bring the war to an end. It had to be used against an enemy target.

The final decision of where and when to use the atomic bomb was up to me. Let there be no mistake about it. I regarded the bomb as a military weapon and never had any doubt that it should be used. The top military advisers to the President recommended its use, and when I talked to Churchill he unhesitatingly told me that he favored the use of the atomic bomb if it might aid to end the war.

In deciding to use this bomb I wanted to make sure that it would be used as a weapon of war in the manner prescribed by the laws of war. That meant that I wanted it dropped on a military target. I had told Stimson that the bomb should be dropped as nearly as possibly upon a war production center of prime military importance.

Stimson's staff had prepared a list of cities in Japan that might serve as targets. Kyoto, though favored by General Arnold[9] as a center of military activity, was eliminated when Secretary Stimson[10] pointed out that it was a cultural and religious shrine of the Japanese.

Four cities were finally recommended as targets: Hiroshima, Kokura, Niigata, and Nagasaki. They were listed in that order as targets for the first attack. The order of selection was in accordance with the military importance of these cities, but allowance would be given for weather conditions at the time of the bombing. Before the selected targets were approved as proper for military purposes, I personally went over them in detail with Stimson, Marshall,[11] and Arnold, and we discussed the matter of timing and the final choice of the first target.

General Spaatz, who commanded the Strategic Air Forces, which would deliver the bomb on the target, was given some latitude as to when and on which of the four targets the bomb would be dropped. That was necessary because of weather and other operational considerations. In order to get

9. General Henry Harley "Hap" Arnold (1886–1950) was commanding general of the U.S. Army Air Forces.
10. Henry L. Stimson (1867–1950) was Secretary of War.
11. General George Catlett Marshall (1880–1959) was Chief of Staff of the U.S. Army.

preparations under way, the War Department was given orders to instruct General Spaatz that the first bomb would be dropped as soon after August 3 as weather would permit. . . .

A month before the test explosion of the atomic bomb the service Secretaries and the Joint Chiefs of Staff had laid their detailed plans for the defeat of Japan before me for approval. There had apparently been some differences of opinion as to the best route to be followed, but these had evidently been reconciled, for when General Marshall had presented his plan for a two-phase invasion of Japan, Admiral King[12] and General Arnold had supported the proposal heartily.

The Army plan envisaged an amphibious landing in the fall of 1945 on the island of Kyushu, the southernmost of the Japanese home islands. This would be accomplished by our Sixth Army, under the command of General Walter Krueger. The first landing would then be followed approximately four months later by a second great invasion, which would be carried out by our Eighth and Tenth Armies, followed by the First Army transferred from Europe, all of which would go ashore in the Kanto plains area near Tokyo. In all, it had been estimated that it would require until the late fall of 1946 to bring Japan to her knees.

This was a formidable conception, and all of us realized fully that the fighting would be fierce and the losses heavy. But it was hoped that some of Japan's forces would continue to be preoccupied in China and others would be prevented from reinforcing the home islands if Russia were to enter the war.

There was, of course, always the possibility that the Japanese might choose to surrender sooner. Our air and fleet units had begun to inflict heavy damage on industrial and urban sites in Japan proper. Except in China, the armies of the Mikado had been pushed back everywhere in relentless successions of defeats.

Acting Secretary of State Grew had spoken to me in late May[13] about issuing a proclamation that would urge the Japanese to surrender but would assure them that we would permit the Emperor to remain as head of the state. Grew backed this with arguments taken from his ten years' experience as our Ambassador in Japan, and I told him that I had already given thought to this matter myself and that it seemed to me a sound idea. Grew had a draft of a proclamation with him, and I instructed him to send it by

12. Admiral Ernest J. King (1878–1956) was Chief of Naval Operations. He favored using the bomb on Hiroshima.
13. This was the important May 28 meeting. See Joseph C. Grew, *Turbulent Era: A Diplomatic Record of Forty Years, 1904–1945*, ed. Walter Johnson (Boston: Houghton Mifflin Company, 1952), Vol. 2, pp. 1421–1428.

CHAPTER 8

THE BURDENS
OF POWER: THE
DECISION TO
DROP THE
ATOMIC BOMB,
1945

the customary channels to the Joint Chiefs and the State-War-Navy Co-ordinating Committee in order that we might get the opinions of all concerned before I made my decision.

On June 18 Grew reported that the proposal had met with the approval of his Cabinet colleagues and of the Joint Chiefs. The military leaders also discussed the subject with me when they reported the same day. Grew, however, favored issuing the proclamation at once, to coincide with the closing of the campaign on Okinawa, while the service chiefs were of the opinion that we should wait until we were ready to follow a Japanese refusal with the actual assault of our invasion forces.

It was my decision then that the proclamation to Japan should be issued from the forthcoming conference at Potsdam. This, I believed, would clearly demonstrate to Japan and to the world that the Allies were united in their purpose. By that time, also, we might know more about two matters of significance for our future effort: the participation of the Soviet Union and the atomic bomb. We knew that the bomb would receive its first test in mid-July. If the test of the bomb was successful, I wanted to afford Japan a clear chance to end the fighting before we made use of this newly gained power. If the test should fail, then it would be even more important to us to bring about a surrender before we had to make a physical conquest of Japan. General Marshall told me that it might cost half a million American lives to force the enemy's surrender of his home grounds. . . .

At Potsdam, as elsewhere, the secret of the atomic bomb was kept closely guarded. We did not extend the very small circle of Americans who knew about it. Churchill naturally knew about the atomic bomb project from its very beginning, because it had involved the pooling of British and American technical skill.

On July 24 I casually mentioned to Stalin that we had a new weapon of unusual destructive force. The Russian Premier showed no special interest. All he said was that he was glad to hear it and hoped we would make "good use of it against the Japanese." . . .

On July 28 Radio Tokyo announced that the Japanese government would continue to fight. There was no formal reply to the joint ultimatum of the United States, the United Kingdom, and China. There was no alternative now. The bomb was scheduled to be dropped after August 3 unless Japan surrendered before that day.

On August 6, the fourth day of the journey home from Potsdam, came the historic news that shook the world. I was eating lunch with members of the *Augusta's* crew when Captain Frank Graham, White House Map Room watch officer, handed me the following message:

TO THE PRESIDENT

FROM THE SECRETARY OF WAR

Big bomb dropped on Hiroshima August 5 at 7:15 P.M. Washington time. First reports indicate complete success which was even more conspicuous than earlier test.

I was greatly moved. I telephoned Byrnes aboard ship to give him the news and then said to the group of sailors around me, "This is the greatest thing in history. It's time for us to get home.". . .

Source 2 from Henry L. Stimson and McGeorge Bundy, *On Active Service in Peace and War* (New York: Harper and Brothers, 1948), pp. 613–633.

2. Henry L. Stimson (Secretary of War, 1941–1945).[14]

The policy adopted and steadily pursued by President Roosevelt and his advisers was a simple one. It was to spare no effort in securing the earliest possible successful development of an atomic weapon. The reasons for this policy were equally simple. The original experimental achievement of atomic fission had occurred in Germany in 1938, and it was known that the Germans had continued their experiments. In 1941 and 1942 they were believed to be ahead of us, and it was vital that they should not be the first to bring atomic weapons into the field of battle. Furthermore, if we should be the first to develop the weapon, we should have a great new instrument for shortening the war and minimizing destruction. At no time, from 1941 to 1945, did I ever hear it suggested by the President, or by any other responsible member of the government, that atomic energy should not be used in the war. All of us of course understood the terrible responsibility involved in our attempt to unlock the doors to such a devastating weapon; President Roosevelt particularly spoke to me many times of his own awareness of the catastrophic potentialities of our work. But we were at war, and the work must be done. I therefore emphasize that it was our common objective, throughout the war, to be the first to produce an atomic weapon and use it. The possible atomic weapon was considered to be a new and tremendously powerful explosive, as legitimate as any other of the deadly explosive weapons of modern war. The entire purpose was the production of a military

14. Parts of this chapter had appeared earlier as "The Decision to Use the Atomic Bomb" in the February 1947 number of *Harper's Magazine*.

CHAPTER 8

THE BURDENS
OF POWER: THE
DECISION TO
DROP THE
ATOMIC BOMB,
1945

weapon; on no other ground could the wartime expenditure of so much time and money have been justified. The exact circumstances in which that weapon might be used were unknown to any of us until the middle of 1945, and when that time came, as we shall presently see, the military use of atomic energy was connected with larger questions of national policy. . . .

As time went on it became clear that the weapon would not be available in time for use in the European theater, and the war against Germany was successfully ended by the use of what are now called conventional means. But in the spring of 1945 it became evident that the climax of our prolonged atomic effort was at hand. By the nature of atomic chain reactions, it was impossible to state with certainty that we had succeeded until a bomb had actually exploded in a full-scale experiment; nevertheless it was considered exceedingly probable that we should by midsummer have successfully detonated the first atomic bomb. This was to be done at the Alamogordo Reservation in New Mexico. It was thus time for detailed consideration of our future plans. What had begun as a well-founded hope was now developing into a reality.

On March 15, 1945 I had my last talk with President Roosevelt. . . .

I did not see Franklin Roosevelt again. The next time I went to the White House to discuss atomic energy was April 25, 1945, and I went to explain the nature of the problem to a man whose only previous knowledge of our activities was that of a Senator who had loyally accepted our assurance that the matter must be kept a secret from him. Now he was President and Commander-in-Chief, and the final responsibility in this as in so many other matters must be his. President Truman accepted this responsibility with the same fine spirit that Senator Truman had shown before in accepting our refusal to inform him.

I discussed with him the whole history of the project. We had with us General Groves, who explained in detail the progress which had been made and the probable future course of the work. I also discussed with President Truman the broader aspects of the subject, and the memorandum which I used in this discussion is again a fair sample of the state of our thinking at the time.

[Here Stimson reproduced his nine-point memorandum, which emphasized his concerns that the scientific and technological process of making an atomic bomb would not remain the monopoly of the United States for very long; that the proliferation of atomic devices in the hands of numerous nations would constitute a serious threat to civilization; that no international weapons controls had worked in the past; that the United States should think very seriously before deciding to share the bomb with

anyone; that the bomb, if used properly, might ensure world peace; and that a select committee should be appointed to study and make recommendations on short- and long-range atomic policy.]

The next step in our preparations was the appointment of the committee. This committee, which was known as the Interim Committee, was charged with the function of advising the President on the various questions raised by our apparently imminent success in developing an atomic weapon. I was its chairman, but the principal labor of guiding its extended deliberations fell to George L. Harrison, who acted as chairman in my absence. . . .

The discussions of the committee ranged over the whole field of atomic energy, in its political, military, and scientific aspects. That part of its work which particularly concerns us here relates to its recommendations for the use of atomic energy against Japan, but it should be borne in mind that these recommendations were not made in a vacuum. The committee's work included the drafting of the statements which were published immediately after the first bombs were dropped, the drafting of a bill for the domestic control of atomic energy, and recommendations looking toward the international control of atomic energy. . . .

[Here Stimson summarized the Interim Committee's recommendations to President Truman, which agree with Truman's recollections on p. 207.]

In reaching these conclusions the Interim Committee carefully considered such alternatives as a detailed advance warning or a demonstration in some uninhabited area. Both of these suggestions were discarded as impractical. They were not regarded as likely to be effective in compelling a surrender of Japan, and both of them involved serious risks. Even the New Mexico test would not give final proof that any given bomb was certain to explode when dropped from an airplane. Quite apart from the generally unfamiliar nature of atomic explosives, there was the whole problem of exploding a bomb at a predetermined height in the air by a complicated mechanism which could not be tested in the static test of New Mexico. Nothing would have been more damaging to our effort to obtain surrender than a warning or a demonstration followed by a dud—and this was a real possibility. Furthermore, we had no bombs to waste. It was vital that a sufficient effect be quickly obtained with the few we had. . . .

The principal political, social, and military objective of the United States in the summer of 1945 was the prompt and complete surrender of Japan. Only the complete destruction of her military power could open the way to lasting peace.

CHAPTER 8

THE BURDENS
OF POWER: THE
DECISION TO
DROP THE
ATOMIC BOMB,
1945

Japan, in July, 1945, had been seriously weakened by our increasingly violent attacks. It was known to us that she had gone so far as to make tentative proposals to the Soviet Government, hoping to use the Russians as mediators in a negotiated peace. These vague proposals contemplated the retention by Japan of important conquered areas and were therefore not considered seriously. There was as yet no indication of any weakening in the Japanese determination to fight rather than accept unconditional surrender. If she should persist in her fight to the end, she had still a great military force. . . .

[Here Stimson summarized the military strength of the Japanese.]

As we understood it in July, there was a very strong possibility that the Japanese Government might determine upon resistance to the end, in all the areas of the Far East under its control. In such an event the Allies would be faced with the enormous task of destroying an armed force of five million men and five thousand suicide aircraft, belonging to a race which had already amply demonstrated its ability to fight literally to the death.

The strategic plans of our armed forces for the defeat of Japan, as they stood in July, had been prepared without reliance upon the atomic bomb, which had not yet been tested in New Mexico. We were planning an intensified sea and air blockade, and greatly intensified strategic air bombing, through the summer and early fall, to be followed on November 1 by an invasion of the southern island of Kyushu. This would be followed in turn by an invasion of the main island of Honshu in the spring of 1946. The total U.S. military and naval force involved in this grand design was of the order of 5,000,000 men; if all those indirectly concerned are included, it was larger still.

We estimated that if we should be forced to carry this plan to its conclusion, the major fighting would not end until the latter part of 1946, at the earliest. I was informed that such operations might be expected to cost over a million casualties, to American forces alone. Additional large losses might be expected among our allies and, of course, if our campaign were successful and if we could judge by previous experience, enemy casualties would be much larger than our own.

It was already clear in July that even before the invasion we should be able to inflict enormously severe damage on the Japanese homeland by the combined application of 'conventional' sea and air power. The critical question was whether this kind of action would induce surrender. It therefore became necessary to consider very carefully the probable state of mind of the enemy, and to assess with accuracy the line of conduct which might end his will to resist.

With these considerations in mind, I wrote a memorandum for the President, on July 2, which I believe fairly represents the thinking of the American Government as it finally took shape in action. This memorandum was prepared after discussion and general agreement with Joseph C. Grew, acting Secretary of State, and Secretary of the Navy Forrestal, and when I discussed it with the President, he expressed his general approval. . . .

[Stimson's memorandum to President Truman of July 2, 1945, summed up the thinking of military and civilian advisers on the situation with regard to Japan. In the memorandum, Stimson reported that he and others had concluded that an invasion of the Japanese mainland would be costly; that Japan was very close to surrender; that a properly worded call on Japan to surrender (coupled with a threat of total destruction if Japan refused) might induce Japan to capitulate, thus making an invasion of the Japanese mainland unnecessary. Obviously, the existence of the as yet untested atomic bomb was not mentioned in the memorandum, for security purposes.]

The adoption of the policy outlined in the memorandum of July 2 was a decision of high politics; once it was accepted by the President, the position of the atomic bomb in our planning became quite clear. I find that I stated in my diary, as early as June 19, that 'the last chance warning . . . must be given before an actual landing of the ground forces in Japan, and fortunately the plans provide for enough time to bring in the sanctions to our warning in the shape of heavy ordinary bombing attack and an attack of S-1.' S-1 was a code name for the atomic bomb.

There was much discussion in Washington about the timing of the warning to Japan. The controlling factor in the end was the date already set for the Potsdam meeting of the Big Three. It was President Truman's decision that such a warning should be solemnly issued by the U.S. and the U.K. from this meeting, with the concurrence of the head of the Chinese Government, so that it would be plain that *all* of Japan's principal enemies were in entire unity. This was done, in the Potsdam ultimatum of July 26, which very closely followed the above memorandum of July 2, with the exception that it made no mention of the Japanese Emperor.

On July 28 the Premier of Japan, Suzuki, rejected the Potsdam ultimatum by announcing that it was 'unworthy of public notice.' In the face of this rejection we could only proceed to demonstrate that the ultimatum had meant exactly what it said when it stated that if the Japanese continued the war, 'the full application of our military power, backed by our resolve, will mean the inevitable and complete destruction of the Japanese armed

CHAPTER 8

THE BURDENS
OF POWER: THE
DECISION TO
DROP THE
ATOMIC BOMB,
1945

forces and just as inevitably the utter devastation of the Japanese home-land.' . . .

As I read over what I have written, I am aware that much of it, in this year of peace, may have a harsh and unfeeling sound. It would perhaps be possible to say the same things and say them more gently. But I do not think it would be wise. As I look back over the five years of my service as Secretary of War, I see too many stern and heartrending decisions to be willing to pretend that war is anything else than what it is. The face of war is the face of death; death is an inevitable part of every order that a wartime leader gives. The decision to use the atomic bomb was a decision that brought death to over a hundred thousand Japanese. No explanation can change that fact and I do not wish to gloss it over. But this deliberate, premeditated destruction was our least abhorrent choice. The destruction of Hiroshima and Nagasaki put an end to the Japanese war. It stopped the fire raids, and the strangling blockade; it ended the ghastly specter of a clash of great land armies. . . .

Source 3 from Dwight D. Eisenhower, *The White House Years: Mandate for Change, 1953–1956* (Garden City, N.Y.: Doubleday and Company, 1963), pp. 312–313.

3. General Dwight D. Eisenhower (Supreme Commander, Allied Military Forces in Europe).[15]

. . . The incident took place in 1945 when Secretary of War Stimson, visiting my headquarters in Germany, informed me that our government was preparing to drop an atomic bomb on Japan. I was one of those who felt that there were a number of cogent reasons to question the wisdom of such an act. I was not, of course, called upon, officially, for any advice or counsel concerning the matter, because the European theater, of which I was the commanding general, was not involved, the forces of Hitler having already been defeated. But the Secretary, upon giving me the news of the successful bomb test in New Mexico, and of the plan for using it, asked for my reaction, apparently expecting a vigorous assent.

During his recitation of the relevant facts, I had been conscious of a feeling of depression and so I voiced to him my grave misgivings, first on the basis of my belief that Japan was already defeated and that dropping the

15. Eisenhower was commander of the Allied military forces in Europe.

bomb was completely unnecessary, and secondly because I thought that our country should avoid shocking world opinion by the use of a weapon whose employment was, I thought, no longer mandatory as a measure to save American lives. It was my belief that Japan was, at that very moment, seeking some way to surrender with a minimum loss of "face." The Secretary was deeply perturbed by my attitude, almost angrily refuting the reasons I gave for my quick conclusions. . . .

Source 4 from William D. Leahy, *I Was There* (New York: Whittlesey House, 1950), pp. 440–442.

4. Admiral William D. Leahy (Chief of Staff to Presidents Roosevelt and Truman).

In the spring of 1945 President Truman directed Mr. Byrnes to make a special study of the status and prospects of the new atomic explosive on which two billion dollars already had been spent. Byrnes came to my home on the evening of June 4 to discuss his findings. He was more favorably impressed than I had been up to that time with the prospects of success in the final development and use of this new weapon.

Once it had been tested, President Truman faced the decision as to whether to use it. He did not like the idea, but was persuaded that it would shorten the war against Japan and save American lives. It is my opinion that the use of this barbarous weapon at Hiroshima and Nagasaki was of no material assistance in our war against Japan. The Japanese were already defeated and ready to surrender because of the effective sea blockade and the successful bombing with conventional weapons.

It was my reaction that the scientists and others wanted to make this test because of the vast sums that had been spent on the project. Truman knew that, and so did the other people involved. However, the Chief Executive made a decision to use the bomb on two cities in Japan. We had only produced two bombs at that time. We did not know which cities would be the targets, but the President specified that the bombs should be used against military facilities. . . .

One of the professors associated with the Manhattan Project told me that he had hoped the bomb wouldn't work. I wish that he had been right. . . .

CHAPTER 8

THE BURDENS
OF POWER: THE
DECISION TO
DROP THE
ATOMIC BOMB,
1945

Source 5 from Joseph C. Grew, *Turbulent Era: A Diplomatic Record of Forty Years, 1904–1945,* ed. Walter Johnson (Boston: Houghton Mifflin Company, 1952), Vol. 2, pp. 1421–1428.

5. Joseph C. Grew (Former Ambassador to Japan and in 1945 Under Secretary of State and briefly Acting Secretary of State).

For a long time I had held the belief, based on my intimate experience with Japanese thinking and psychology over an extensive period, that the surrender of the Japanese would be highly unlikely, regardless of military defeat, in the absence of a public undertaking by the President that unconditional surrender would not mean the elimination of the present dynasty if the Japanese people desired its retention. I furthermore believed that if such a statement could be formulated and issued shortly after the great devastation of Tokyo by our B-29 attacks on or about May 26, 1945, the hands of the Emperor and his peace-minded advisers would be greatly strengthened in the face of the intransigent militarists and that the process leading to an early surrender might even then be set in motion by such a statement. Soviet Russia had not then entered the war against Japan, and since the United States had carried the major burden of the war in the Pacific, and since the President had already publicly declared that unconditional surrender would mean neither annihilation nor enslavement, I felt that the President would be fully justified in amplifying his previous statement as suggested. My belief in the potential effect of such a statement at that particular juncture was fully shared and supported by those officers in the Department of State who knew Japan and the Japanese well, . . .

In my own talk with the President on May 28, he immediately said that his own thinking ran along the same lines as mine, but he asked me to discuss the proposal with the Secretaries of War and Navy and the Chiefs of Staff and then to report to him the consensus of that group. A conference was therefore called and was held in the office of the Secretary of War in the Pentagon Building on May 29, 1945, and the issue was discussed for an hour. According to my memorandum of that meeting it became clear in the course of the discussion that Mr. Stimson, Mr. Forrestal, and General Marshall (Admiral King was absent) were all in accord with the principle of the proposal but that for certain military reasons, not then divulged, it was considered inadvisable for the President to make such a statement at that juncture. It later appeared that the fighting on Okinawa was still going on, and it was felt that such a declaration as I proposed would be interpreted by the Japanese as a confession of weakness. The question of timing was the nub of the whole matter, according to the views expressed. I duly reported this to the President, and the proposal for action was, for the time being, dropped.

When Mr. Byrnes became Secretary of State over a month later, I endeavored to interest him in the importance and urgency of a public statement along the lines proposed, but during those few days he was intensely occupied in preparing for the Potsdam Conference, and it was only on the morning of his departure for Potsdam that I was able to hand him a draft on which a declaration might be based. This was the draft I had shown to the President. Mr. Byrnes was already on his way out of his office to drive to the airport, and his last action before leaving was to place our draft in his pocket. Mr. Stimson was then already in Europe and I urged Jack McCloy, Assistant Secretary of War, when he met him over there, to tell Mr. Stimson how strongly I felt about the matter.

Mr. Stimson did take energetic steps at Potsdam to secure the decision by the President and Mr. Churchill to issue the proclamation. In fact, the opinion was expressed to me by one American already in Potsdam, that if it had not been for Mr. Stimson's wholehearted initiative, the Potsdam Conference would have ended without any proclamation to Japan being issued at all. But even Mr. Stimson was unable to have included in the proclamation a categorical undertaking that unconditional surrender would not mean the elimination of the dynasty if the Japanese people desired its retention.

The main point at issue historically is whether, if immediately following the terrific devastation of Tokyo by our B-29s in May, 1945,[16] "the President had made a public categorical statement that surrender would not mean the elimination of the present dynasty if the Japanese people desired its retention, the surrender of Japan could have been hastened.

"That question can probably never be definitively answered but a good deal of evidence is available to shed light on it. From statements made by a number of the moderate former Japanese leaders to responsible Americans after the American occupation, it is quite clear that the civilian advisers to the Emperor were working toward surrender long before the Potsdam Proclamation, even indeed before my talk with the President on May 28, for they knew then that Japan was a defeated nation. The stumbling block that they had to overcome was the complete dominance of the Japanese Army over the Government, and even when the moderates finally succeeded in getting a decision by the controlling element of the Government to accept the Potsdam terms, efforts were made by the unreconciled elements in the Japanese Army to bring about nullification of that decision. The Emperor

---

16. The following quotation is taken from a letter from Grew to Stimson, February 12, 1947.

CHAPTER 8

THE BURDENS
OF POWER: THE
DECISION TO
DROP THE
ATOMIC BOMB,
1945

needed all the support he could get, and in the light of available evidence I myself and others felt and still feel that if such a categorical statement about the dynasty had been issued in May, 1945, the surrender-minded elements in the Government might well have been afforded by such a statement a valid reason and the necessary strength to come to an early clear-cut decision.

"If surrender could have been brought about in May, 1945, or even in June or July, before the entrance of Soviet Russia into the war and the use of the atomic bomb, the world would have been the gainer.

"The action of Prime Minister Suzuki in rejecting the Potsdam ultimatum by announcing on July 28, 1945, that it was 'unworthy of public notice' was a most unfortunate if not an utterly stupid step.[17] Suzuki, who was severely wounded and very nearly assassinated as a moderate by the military extremists in 1936, I believe from the evidence which has reached me was surrender-minded even before May, 1945, if only it were made clear that surrender would not involve the downfall of the dynasty. That point was clearly *implied* in Article 12 of the Potsdam Proclamation that 'The occupying forces of the Allies shall be withdrawn from Japan as soon as . . . there has been established in accordance with the freely expressed will of the Japanese people a peacefully inclined and responsible government.' This however was not, at least from the Japanese point of view, a categorical undertaking regarding the dynasty, nor did it comply with your [Henry L. Stimson's] suggestion that it would substantially add to the chances of acceptance if the ultimatum should contain a statement that we would not exclude a constitutional monarchy under the present dynasty. Suzuki's reply was typical of oriental methods in retaining his supposed bargaining position until he knew precisely what the Potsdam Proclamation meant in that respect. The Asiatic concern over the loss of assumed bargaining power that might arise from exhibiting what might be interpreted as a sign of weakness is always uppermost in Japanese mental processes. He can seldom be made to realize that the time for compromise has passed if it ever existed. This explains but certainly does not excuse Suzuki's reply, and the result of his reply was to release the atom bomb to fulfill its appointed purpose. Yet I and a good many others will always feel that had the President issued as far back as May, 1945, the recommended categorical statement that the Japanese dynasty would be retained if the Japanese people freely desired its retention, the atom bomb might never have had to be used at all. . . ."

17. See Truman memoirs, p. 210, and Stimson memoirs, p. 215.

Source 6 from John L. McCloy, *The Challenge to American Foreign Policy*
(Cambridge, MA: Harvard University Press, 1953), pp. 40–44.

6. John L. McCloy (Assistant Secretary of War, 1941–1945).

The habit of confining large questions on the conduct of the war to purely
military considerations, which President Roosevelt instituted and which
was almost unconsciously carried on by his successor, was strikingly exem-
plified by a conference which took place in the White House in June, 1945.

After the surrender of the German forces, but before Potsdam and before
the Japanese surrender, President Truman, at the instigation of the Joint
Chiefs of Staff, called a meeting to consider the type of operations our future
campaign against Japan should take. The particular question posed was
whether an attack should be launched on the main islands of Japan, and if
so, which ones. But the general question presented related to the whole
course of future operations necessary to bring about a Japanese surrender.

The Joint Chiefs were present. The Secretary of War was present for at
least a part of the time and one of his representatives. Neither the Secretary
of State nor any of his representatives attended.

After putting the question to the President, the Joint Chiefs proposed an
early attack on Kyushu, presenting an estimate of the time necessary to
mount the attack, the likely casualties, and the probable results. It was
suggested that this attack should be followed up by a much heavier one on
Honshu and across the Tokyo plain. Together the plans amounted to a major
operation.

The prospect of an attack on the main Japanese islands, even at that late
date, was not too attractive. Memories of the beaches and uplands of Tara-
wa, Iwo Jima and Okinawa were in everyone's minds, yet no alternative to
this course was proposed. The Chiefs of Staff of the respective services were
unanimous as to the necessity of the operation.

The President, conscious of his heavy responsibility, individually polled
all the Chiefs present and then rendered his decision: attack Kyushu; plan
for Honshu, but return for further instructions before the preparations arrived at a point beyond which there would not be further opportunity for a
free choice on the part of the President.

It is necessary for a full understanding of this incident to recall for a moment the background of the conference. The greatest enemy military force
in Europe had recently surrendered without condition. Great Britain and
the United States possessed between them what was incomparably the
greatest naval force the world had ever seen. We possessed an air superiority over Japan so overwhelming as to be almost fantastic.

CHAPTER 8

THE BURDENS
OF POWER: THE
DECISION TO
DROP THE
ATOMIC BOMB,
1945

We had an impregnable moral position before Japan and the world. We had advanced across the Pacific to the main islands after an act of outrageous aggression on the part of Japan. On top of it all, we possessed the secret of the atom bomb. All present in the room knew that the scientists and engineers working on that project had given definite assurances that within a very short period of time an atomic explosion embodying military consequences of great significance would occur. Other points of superiority could be recounted.

After the President's decision had been made and the conference was breaking up, an official, not theretofore participating,[18] suggested that serious attention should be given to a political attempt to end the war. The meeting fell into a tailspin, but after control was recovered, the idea appealed to several present. It appealed particularly to the President, and to one member of the Joint Chiefs of Staff, who, by the way, was the one member of that body who had no responsibility to a particular service.

It was also at this meeting that the suggestion was first broached that warning be given the Japanese of our possession of the bomb before we dropped it. Although all present were "cleared," the uninhibited mention of the "best-kept secret of the war" caused a sense of shock, even among that select group.

Now this incident indicates that at that time everyone was so intent on winning the war by military means that the introduction of political considerations was almost accidental. It cannot be charged against the military that they did not initially put forward the suggestion of political action. It was not their job to do so. Nor did any one of them oppose the thought of political action, though several of the Chiefs were not too happy about it. Not one of the Chiefs nor the Secretary thought well of a bomb warning, an effective argument being that no one could be certain, in spite of the assurances of the scientists, that the "thing would go off." At that time, we had not yet had the benefit of the Alamogordo test.

As a result of the meeting, a rather hastily composed paper was drawn up. It embodied the idea which later formed the basis of the appeal to the Japanese to surrender. That proposal, it will be recalled, was refused brusquely by the Japanese Government. Yet, as we now know, it did provoke considerable discussion and divergence of opinion among the Japanese military leaders and politicians. It is interesting to speculate whether, better prepared, this proposal might not have included statements of the policy which we put into effect in Japan almost immediately after the war ended. Such a proposal might well have induced surrender without the use of the

18. As it turns out, "an official" was McCloy himself. See Forrestal memoirs, p. 229.

bomb. What effect that might have had on postwar developments is a subject worthy of conjecture.

Although no one from the State Department was present at the conference
which has been described, Mr. Joseph Grew for some time had been most
energetically urging a political approach to the Japanese, but his thoughts
never seemed effectively to have gotten to the White House, at least prior
to the June meeting. . . .

Source 7 from James F. Byrnes, *All in One Lifetime* (New York: Harper and
Brothers, 1958), pp. 282–287, 290–291, 300–301.

7. James F. Byrnes (Secretary of State, 1945–1947).

Then, on April 25, Secretary Stimson gave him a memorandum, the opening
paragraphs of which contained the fateful prophecy, "Within four months
we shall in all probability have completed the most terrible weapon ever
known in human history, one bomb of which could destroy a whole city.". . .

*[Here Byrnes discussed the formation and composition of the Interim Committee (see
Truman's memoirs, p. 207.]*

As I heard these scientists and industrialists predict the destructive
power of the weapon, I was thoroughly frightened. I had sufficient imagination to visualize the danger to our country when some other country possessed such a weapon. Thinking of the country most likely to become unfriendly to us, I asked General Marshall and some of the others at the
meeting how long it would take the Soviets to develop such a bomb. The
consensus was that they would have the secret in two or three years, but
could not actually produce a bomb in less than six or seven years. One or
two expressed the opinion that Soviet progress would depend upon whether
or not they had taken German scientists and production experts as prisoners of war for the purpose of having them work on such weapons. No one
seemed too alarmed at the prospect because it appeared that in seven years
we should be far ahead of the Soviets in this field; and, of course, in 1945
we could not believe that after their terrible sacrifices, the Russians would
think of making war for many years to come.

A few days after the committee was appointed, President Truman referred
to me a letter addressed to President Roosevelt by Dr. Albert Einstein, dated
March 25, which was in President Roosevelt's office at the time of his death
at Warm Springs. In it Dr. Einstein requested the President to receive Dr.

CHAPTER 8

THE BURDENS
OF POWER: THE
DECISION TO
DROP THE
ATOMIC BOMB,
1945

L. Szilard,[19] "who proposes to submit to you certain considerations and recommendations." After citing Dr. Szilard's reputation in the scientific field, Dr. Einstein went on to say that Dr. Szilard was concerned about the lack of adequate contact between the atomic scientists and the Cabinet members who were responsible for determining policy. Dr. Einstein concluded with the hope that the President would give his personal attention to what Dr. Szilard had to say.

President Truman asked me to see Szilard, who came down to Spartanburg, bringing with him Dr. H. C. Urey and another scientist. As the Einstein letter had indicated he would, Szilard complained that he and some of his associates did not know enough about the policy of the government with regard to the use of the bomb. He felt that scientists, including himself, should discuss the matter with the Cabinet, which I did not feel desirable. His general demeanor and his desire to participate in policy making made an unfavorable impression on me, but his associates were neither as aggressive nor apparently as dissatisfied.

In response to his statement that the younger scientists were very critical of Doctors Bush, Compton and Conant,[20] I asked him his opinion of Oppenheimer. He quickly expressed enthusiastic admiration. I told him then that he should feel better because the following week, upon the suggestion of the three scientists about whom he complained, Dr. Oppenheimer would meet with the Interim Committee. This pleased Szilard and his companions, and the conversation passed to a more general discussion of atomic matters. What they told me did not decrease my fears of the terrible weapon they had assisted in creating.

These oppressive thoughts, and the burden of security, made themselves felt in meetings of the Interim Committee. A few days later, when I mentioned to General Groves the scientists' visit to Spartanburg, he told me that he already knew of it; that one of his intelligence agents had been following the three gentlemen, as they followed others connected with the project. The diligence of Groves impressed me then as it had done before. . . .

On June 1, 1945, our Interim Committee unanimously recommended to President Truman that the bomb should be used without specific warning and as soon as practicable against a military installation or a war plant in the Japanese islands. It had been suggested that it first be used against an

19. For Szilard, see pp. 232–235. In 1945, Szilard was working on the Manhattan Project at the University of Chicago.
20. On Bush, Compton, and Conant, see Truman memoirs, p. 207. Some scientists at the Manhattan Project believed that the Interim Committee did not include people who represented their views. See Szilard memoirs, p. 232.

isolated island with representatives of Japan and other nations invited to observe the test. This alternative was rejected. There was also the question of giving the Japanese fair warning about the time and place of the explosion; but because we felt that American prisoners of war would be brought into the designated area, this idea was not adopted. We were also told by the experts that whatever the success of the test bomb, they would not guarantee that another would explode when dropped. Further, if we gave the Japanese advance notice and then the bomb failed to explode, our optimism would have only played into the hands of the Japanese militarists.

Meanwhile, arrangements for the test firing at Alamogordo went on. People who lived in the area had to be moved away. The task of writing news releases that would tend to allay public fears after the explosion and at the same time guard the secret from the enemy was placed in the skilled hands of William H. Laurence of *The New York Times*. The degree of uncertainty about what power the bomb would actually develop is evidenced by a story he wrote for the *Times* on June 29, 1951. He related that on the day preceding the test, a hundred scientists were invited to participate in a pool, each guessing at the bomb's power in terms of TNT. It had been designed to produce an explosive force equal to 20,000 tons. Dr. Oppenheimer, the director of the Los Alamos laboratory where it had been constructed, guessed 300 tons and most of the others less than 500. Of the participants in the pool at a dollar a chance, Professor I. I. Rabi of Columbia University, who arrived late and found the low numbers taken, won with his estimate of 18,000 tons.

Though it is sometimes said that for many months the success of the bomb was assured, another indication to the contrary is the fact that though we had but three bombs, and could not hope to possess another for many months, our scientific advisers felt it essential to devote one to a test firing.

The awesome responsibility for accepting the committee's recommendations rested, of course, with President Truman. Inasmuch as I represented him, I felt a measure of this responsibility. However, I knew that the Joint Chiefs planned to invade Japan about November first. In our successful efforts to penetrate the perimeter of Japanese defenses in the Pacific, we had suffered approximately 300,000 casualties. Though the Japanese Navy was nearly destroyed, the imperial armies remained intact, and were estimated by our General Staff to number over five million effective troops. At least that number of United States soldiers, sailors and airmen would be involved in the attack on the Japanese homeland, and a fifth of these, it was thought, would be casualties. Under these circumstances, it was certainly essential to end the war as soon as possible and avoid the invasion. The day the committee reached agreement, I communicated its decision to President

CHAPTER 8

THE BURDENS
OF POWER: THE
DECISION TO
DROP THE
ATOMIC BOMB,
1945

Truman. He said he had been giving thought to the problem and, while reluctant to use this weapon, saw no way of avoiding it. Thereafter, Secretary Stimson formally presented him a written statement, setting forth our recommendations in his lucid and convincing style. . . .[21]

On our arrival[22] we were informed that Stalin, who traveled by train for health reasons, would be delayed for a day. However, the Prime Minister was already in residence; his quarters, about a mile away, he had designated as "10 Downing Street, Potsdam," this address appearing on the dinner menus when he entertained. Stalin's quarters were more remote, located in the vast wooded park surrounding Cecilienhof Palace, where the meetings were to be held. Though we received official invitations to visit his quarters on several occasions, it was obvious that their location was a well-guarded secret to the Conference personnel generally.

We spent a morning with our military advisers, and in the afternoon the President, Admiral Leahy, and I drove into Berlin. Here we saw what remained of the German Chancellery and other relics of the broken regime. But our small party had no monopoly on sightseeing. On our return I heard from Will Clayton and Ed Pauley (our representative on the Reparations Committee) that they had seen machinery from a manufacturing plant which had been moved from the U.S. zone of Germany into the Soviets' shortly before our arrival. It was now standing in an open field. They also had heard stories of all kinds of materials and even herds of cattle being taken to Russia. We knew that in our quarters the original bath fixtures had vanished, others having been hurriedly substituted for our use, and there was plain evidence that the Soviets were unilaterally awarding themselves reparations, both in large and small quantities.

About noon the next day, July 17, Stalin called on the President. It was, of course, their first meeting. Molotov accompanied him and from that moment things began to happen. For more than an hour the four of us remained in conference, Chip Bohlen and Pavlov doing the interpreting. After an exchange of greetings, and some remarks on his long and tiresome train journey, Stalin launched into a discussion of Russia's entry into the Japanese war. He reported that the Japanese had already made overtures to him to act as mediator, to which he had given no definite reply since they did not provide for an unconditional surrender. But he left me with the distinct impression that he was not anxious to see an end to the fighting until Soviet entry into the war could help secure the concessions he expected of China. He said he had not yet reached an agreement with the Chinese Premier, T.

21. This was Stimson's July 2 memorandum. See Stimson memoirs, p. 215.
22. At the Potsdam Conference, July 1945.

V. Soong, on certain matters, and that this was necessary before he could declare war. Negotiations had been halted until after the Potsdam meeting, he said, and mentioned, among other unsettled questions, arrangements for the Port of Dairen. The President commented that the United States wanted to be certain that Dairen was maintained as an open port, and Stalin said that would be its status, should the Soviets obtain control of it.

Not having been at Yalta on the day the so-called secret agreement was arrived at, and having been out of government service for three months, I could make no statement of my own knowledge, but having heard a few days before that there had been an understanding between President Roosevelt and Stalin that Dairen should be an open port, I supported the President's statement in a general way, saying that our people understood that at Yalta President Roosevelt had taken the same position. Stalin merely repeated that that would be its status under Soviet control. Nevertheless, I was disturbed about what kind of bargain he might coerce China into making, for the very fact that they had not reached agreement made me suspect that Stalin was increasing his demands. The President told Stimson that night that "he had clinched the Open Door in Manchuria." I was encouraged but not quite that confident. However, the President and I felt that, without appearing to encourage Chiang to disregard any pledges made by Roosevelt at Yalta, we should let him know that the United States did not want him to make additional concessions to the Soviets. Then the President received from Chiang a cable stating that China had gone the limit to fulfill the Yalta agreement. I prepared a message which the President approved and on the 23rd sent to Chiang Kai-shek: "I asked that you carry out the Yalta agreements, but I have not asked that you make any concessions in excess of that agreement. If you and Generalissimo Stalin differ as to the correct interpretation of the Yalta agreement, I hope you will arrange for Soong to return to Moscow and continue your efforts to reach complete understanding."

Our purpose was stated in the first sentence. The second sentence was to encourage the Chinese to continue negotiations after the adjournment of the Potsdam Conference. I had some fear that if they did not, Stalin might immediately enter the war, knowing full well that he could take not only what Roosevelt and Churchill, and subsequently Chiang, had agreed to at Yalta, but—with China divided and Chiang seeking Soviet support against Chinese Communists—whatever else he wanted. On the other hand, if Stalin and Chiang were still negotiating, it might delay Soviet entrance and the Japanese might surrender. The President was in accord with that view. . . .

The President and I discussed whether or not we were obligated to inform Stalin that we had succeeded in developing a powerful weapon and shortly

CHAPTER 8

THE BURDENS
OF POWER: THE
DECISION TO
DROP THE
ATOMIC BOMB,
1945

would drop a bomb in Japan. Though there was an understanding that the Soviets would enter the war with Japan three months after Germany surrendered, which would make their entrance about the middle of August, with knowledge of the Japanese peace feeler and the successful bomb test in New Mexico, the President and I hoped that Japan would surrender before then. However, at luncheon we agreed that because it was uncertain, and because the Soviets might soon be our allies in that war, the President should inform Stalin of our intention, but do so in a casual way.

He then informed the British of our plan, in which they concurred. Upon the adjournment of the afternoon session, when we arose from the table, the President, accompanied by our interpreter, Bohlen, walked around to Stalin's chair and said, substantially, "You may be interested to know that we have developed a new and powerful weapon and within a few days intend to use it against Japan." I watched Stalin's expression as this was being interpreted, and was surprised that he smiled blandly and said only a few words. When the President and I reached our car, he said that the Generalissimo had replied only, "That's fine. I hope you make good use of it against the Japanese."

I did not believe Stalin grasped the full import of the President's statement, and thought that on the next day there would be some inquiry about this "new and powerful weapon," but I was mistaken. I thought then and even now believe that Stalin did not appreciate the importance of the information that had been given him; but there are others who believe that in the light of later information about the Soviets' intelligence service in this country, he was already aware of the New Mexico test, and that this accounted for his apparent indifference. . . .

Source 8 from James Forrestal, *The Forrestal Diaries,* ed. Walter Millis and E. S. Duffield (New York, Viking Press, 1951), pp. 55, 70–71, 74–78, 80–81.

8. James Forrestal (Secretary of the Navy).

11 May 1945
I had a meeting in my office this morning with Ambassador Harriman,[23] Admiral Edwards,[24] Vice Admiral Cooke.[25]
Harriman said he thought it was time to come to a conclusion about the

23. Averill Harriman, Ambassador to Moscow.
24. Vice Admiral Richard S. Edwards, Deputy Chief of Naval Operations.
25. Vice Admiral Charles M. Cooke, Jr., Chief of Staff to King.

necessity for the early entrance of Russia into the Japanese war. He said he was satisfied they were determined to come in it because of their requirements in the Far East. [He described the territorial concessions made at Yalta.] He said the Russians, he believed, much more greatly feared a separate peace by ourselves with Japan than any fear of ourselves about their concluding such an arrangement. He said he thought it was important that we determine our policy as to a strong or weak China, that if China continued weak Russian influence would move in quickly and toward ultimate domination. He said that there could be no illusion about anything such as a "free China" once the Russians got in, that the two or three hundred millions in that country would march when the Kremlin ordered.

Vice Admiral Cooke said he thought the necessity for Russia's early participation was very much lessened as a result of recent events, although the Army he didn't think shared that view.

Admiral Edwards: The best thing for us would be if the Japanese would agree to a basis of unconditional surrender which still left them in their own minds some face and honor.

8 March 1947   *Meeting with McCloy*

... McCloy recalled the meeting with President Truman at the White House at which the decision was taken to proceed with the invasion of Kyushu. He said this for him illustrated most vividly the necessity for the civilian voice in military decisions even in time of war. He said that what he had to say was pertinent not merely to the question of the invasion of the Japanese mainland but also to the question of whether we needed to get Russia in to help us defeat Japan. At this particular meeting, which occurred in the summer of 1945, before the President went to Potsdam, where, under the pressure of Secretary Byrnes, he stated his principal mission would be to get the Russians into the war against the Japs, the President made the rounds of his military advisers and asked them to tell him whether the Japanese mainland invasion was necessary. They all agreed it was. He finally left it that they would proceed with the plannings for the invasion of Kyushu but that they were to raise the question with him again before its execution and he would reserve decision on whether or not the attack should be carried into the Tokyo plan [plain?].

As the meeting broke up, McCloy said he had not been asked but wanted to state his views.[26] (Neither Stimson nor I was at this meeting.) He said that he thought before the final decision to invade Japan was taken or it was decided to use the atomic bomb political measures should be taken; the

26. See McCloy memoirs, p. 222.

CHAPTER 8

THE BURDENS
OF POWER: THE
DECISION TO
DROP THE
ATOMIC BOMB,
1945

Japanese should be told of what had happened to Germany, particularly in view of the fact that some of their people who had been in Germany were back in Japan and would be able to report on the destruction and devastation which they had witnessed; that the Japs should be told, furthermore, that we had another and terrifyingly destructive weapon which we would have to use if they did not surrender; that they would be permitted to retain the Emperor and a form of government of their own choosing. He said the military leaders were somewhat annoyed at his interference but that the President welcomed it and at the conclusion of McCloy's observations ordered such a political offensive to be set in motion.

13 July 1945   *Japanese Peace Feeler*

The first real evidence of a Japanese desire to get out of the war came today through intercepted messages from Togo, Foreign Minister, to Sato, Jap Ambassador in Moscow, instructing the latter to see Molotov if possible before his departure for the Big Three meeting [the Potsdam Conference], and if not then, immediately afterward, to lay before him the Emperor's strong desire to secure a termination of the war. This he said arose not only out of the Emperor's interest in the welfare of his own subjects but out of his interest toward mankind in general. He was anxious, he said, to see cessation of bloodshed on both sides. Togo said to convey to the Russians the fact that they wanted to remain at peace with Russia, that the Japanese did not desire permanent annexation of any of the territories they had conquered in Manchuria. Togo said further that the unconditional surrender terms of the Allies was about the only thing in the way of termination of the war and he said that if this were insisted upon, of course the Japanese would have to continue the fight.

Sato's response . . . was to protest that the proposals were quite unrealistic; looked at objectively it was clear that there was no chance now of dividing Russia from the other Allies.

15 July 1945   *Japanese Peace Feeler*

Messages today on Japanese-Russian conversations. Togo, Foreign Minister, insisted that Sato present to Molotov the request of the Emperor himself. Sato's replies insistently pointed out the lack of reality in Togo's apparent belief that there is a chance of persuading Russia to take independent action on the Eastern war. He stated very bluntly and without any coating how fantastic is the hope that Russia would be impressed by Japanese willingness to give up territory which she had already lost. . . . Throughout Sato's message ran a note of cold and realistic evaluation of Japan's position;

and he said that the situation was rapidly passing beyond the point of Japan's and Russia's cooperating in the security of Asia but [that the question was] rather whether there would be any Manchukuo or even Japan itself left as entities. The gist of his final message was that it was clear that Japan was thoroughly and completely defeated and that the only course open was quick and definite action recognizing such fact. . . .

It is significant that these conversations began before there could have been much effect from the thousand-plane raids of the Third Fleet and several days before the naval bombardment of Kamaishi.

24 July 1945   *Japanese Peace Feeler*
. . . Finally, on the first of July, Sato sent a long message outlining what he conceived to be Japan's position, which was in brief that she was now entirely alone and friendless and could look for succor from no one. . . . He strongly advised accepting any terms, including unconditional surrender, on the basis that this was the only way of preserving the entity of the Emperor and the state itself. . . .

The response to his message was that the Cabinet in council had weighed all the considerations which he had raised and that their final judgment and decision was that the war must be fought with all the vigor and bitterness of which the nation was capable so long as the only alternative was the unconditional surrender.

28 July 1945
. . . Talked with Byrnes [now at Potsdam as American Secretary of State, having succeeded Mr. Stettinius on the conclusion of the San Francisco Conference]. . . . Byrnes said he was most anxious to get the Japanese affair over with before the Russians got in, with particular reference to Dairen and Port Arthur. Once in there, he felt, it would not be easy to get them out. . . .

29 July 1945
. . . On the way back to our headquarters we passed the equipment of an American armored division drawn up alongside the road. It included tanks and light armored vehicles and must have extended for about three miles. Commodore Schade said the Russians were much impressed by it. There came back to my mind the President's remark about Stalin's observation about the Pope: When Churchill suggested that the Pope would still be a substantial influence in Europe, Stalin snorted and said, "How many divisions has the Pope got?" . . .

CHAPTER 8

THE BURDENS
OF POWER: THE
DECISION TO
DROP THE
ATOMIC BOMB,
1945

Source 9 from Leo Szilard, "Reminiscences," in *The Intellectual Migration: Europe and America, 1930–1960,* ed. Donald Fleming and Bernard Bailyn (Cambridge, Mass.: Harvard University Press, 1969), pp. 122–133.

9. Dr. Leo Szilard (Physicist, Manhattan Project).

In the spring of '45 it was clear that the war against Germany would soon end, and so I began to ask myself, "What is the purpose of continuing the development of the bomb, and how would the bomb be used if the war with Japan has not ended by the time we have the first bomb?"

Initially we were strongly motivated to produce the bomb because we feared the Germans would get ahead of us, and the only way to prevent them from dropping bombs on us was to have bombs in readiness ourselves. But now, with the war won, it was not clear what we were working for. . . .

[Distrusting scientists on the Interim Committee, Szilard drafted a memorandum to President Roosevelt on how nuclear scientists should be consulted in the decision to drop the bomb. Roosevelt died (with the memorandum on his desk), and Szilard then secured an appointment with Matt Connelly, Truman's appointment secretary.]

He read the memorandum carefully from beginning to end, and then he said, "I see now this is a serious matter. At first I was a little suspicious, because this appointment came through Kansas City." Then he said, "The President thought that your concern would be about this matter, and he has asked me to make an appointment with you with James Byrnes, if you are willing to go down to see him in Spartanburg, South Carolina." We said that we would be happy to go anywhere that the President directed us, and he picked up the phone and made an appointment with Byrnes for us. I asked whether I might bring Dr. H. C. Urey along, and Connelly said I could bring along anyone whom I wanted. So I phoned Chicago and asked Urey to join us in Washington, and together we went down the next day to Spartanburg, taking an overnight train from Washington.

We were concerned about two things: we were concerned first about the role which the bomb would play in the world after the war, and how America's position would be affected if the bomb were actually used in the war; we were also concerned about the future of atomic energy, and about the lack of planning as to how this research might be continued after the war. It was clear that the project set up during the war would not be continued but would have to be reorganized. But the valuable thing was not the big projects; the valuable things were the numerous teams, which somehow crystallized during the war, of men who had different abilities and who liked to work with each other. We thought that these teams ought to be preserved even though the projects might be dissolved.

We did not quite understand why we had been sent by the President to see James Byrnes. He had previously occupied a high position in the government, but was now out of the government and was living as a private citizen in Spartanburg. Clearly the President must have had in mind appointing him to a government position, but what position? Was he to be the man in charge of the uranium work after the war, or what? We did not know.

Finally we arrived in Spartanburg, and I gave Byrnes Einstein's letter to read and the memorandum which I had written.[27] Byrnes read the memorandum, and then we started to discuss the problem. When I spoke of my concern that Russia might become an atomic power—and might become an atomic power soon, if we were to demonstrate the power of the bomb and use it against Japan—his reply was, "General Groves tells me there is no uranium in Russia."

I told Byrnes that there was certainly a limited amount of rich uranium ore in Czechoslovakia to which Russia had access; but apart from this, it was very unlikely that in the vast territory of Russia there should be no low-grade uranium ores. High-grade uranium ore is, of course, another matter: high-grade deposits are rare, and it is not at all sure whether new high-grade deposits can be found. In the past, only the high-grade deposits were of interest because the main purpose of mining uranium ores was to produce radium, and the price of radium was such that working low-grade uranium ores would not have been profitable. But when you are dealing with atomic energy you are not limited to high-grade ores; you can use low-grade ones, and I doubted very much that anyone in America would be able to say, in a responsible way, that there were no major low-grade uranium deposits in Russia.

I thought it would be a mistake to disclose the existence of the bomb to the world before the government had made up its mind how to handle the situation after the war. Using the bomb certainly would disclose that the bomb exists. As a matter of fact, even testing the bomb would disclose that the bomb exists. Once the bomb has been tested and shown to go off, it would not be possible to keep it a secret.

Byrnes agreed that if we refrained from testing the bomb, people would conclude that its development did not succeed. However, he said that we had spent two billion dollars on developing the bomb, and Congress would

---

27. See Byrnes's memoirs, p. 223. Einstein's letter, addressed to President Roosevelt, was a letter of introduction for Szilard.

CHAPTER 8

THE BURDENS
OF POWER: THE
DECISION TO
DROP THE
ATOMIC BOMB,
1945

want to know what we got for the money spent. "How would you get Congress to appropriate money for atomic energy research if you do not show results for the money which has been spent already?"

I saw his point at that time, and in retrospect I see even more clearly that it would not have served any useful purpose to keep the bomb secret, waiting for the government to understand the problem and to formulate a policy; for the government will not formulate a policy unless it is under pressure to do so, and if the bomb had been kept secret there would have been no pressure for the government to do anything in this direction.

Byrnes thought that the war would be over in about six months, and this proved to be a fairly accurate estimate. He was concerned about Russia's postwar behavior. Russian troops had moved into Hungary and Rumania; Byrnes thought it would be very difficult to persuade Russia to withdraw her troops from these countries, and that Russia might be more manageable if impressed by American military might. I shared Byrnes's concern about Russia's throwing around her weight in the postwar period, but I was completely flabbergasted by the assumption that rattling the bomb might make Russia more manageable.

I began to doubt that there was any way for me to communicate with Byrnes in this matter, and my doubt became certainty when he turned to me and said, "Well, you come from Hungary—you would not want Russia to stay in Hungary indefinitely." I certainly didn't want Russia to stay in Hungary indefinitely, but what Byrnes said offended my sense of proportion. I was concerned at this point that by demonstrating the bomb and using it in the war against Japan, we might start an atomic arms race between America and Russia which might end with the destruction of both countries. I was *not* disposed at this point to worry about what would happen to Hungary.

After all was said that could be said on this topic, the conversation turned to the future of the uranium project. To our astonishment, Byrnes showed complete indifference. This is easy to understand in retrospect because, contrary to what we had suspected, he was not slated to be director of the uranium project but he was slated to be secretary of state.

I was rarely as depressed as when we left Byrnes's house and walked toward the station. I thought to myself how much better off the world might be had I been born in America and become influential in American politics, and had Byrnes been born in Hungary and studied physics. In all probability there would have been no atomic bomb, and no danger of an arms race between America and Russia. . . .

The time approached when the bomb would be tested. The date was never communicated to us in Chicago, nor did we ever receive any official indication of what was afoot. However, I concluded that the bomb was about to be tested when I was told that we were no longer permitted to call Los Alamos over the telephone. This could mean only one thing: Los Alamos must get ready to test the bomb, and the Army tried by this ingenious method to keep the news from the Chicago project.

[Szilard returned to Chicago, where he circulated a petition against the use of the bomb on Japan. The petition, signed by several scientists at the University of Chicago, was never presented to Truman. Similarly, a report authored by Dr. James Franck, which urged international control of nuclear energy, was ignored. For that document, see Robert Jungk, Brighter Than a Thousand Suns: A Personal History of the Atomic Scientists, *trans. James Cleugh (New York: Harcourt, Brace, and Company, 1958), pp. 348–360.]*

Source 10 from Leslie R. Groves, *Now It Can Be Told: The Story of the Manhattan Project* (New York: Harper and Brothers, 1962), pp. 324, 412–415.

10. General Leslie R. Groves (Director, Manhattan Project).

I was waiting when the General arrived, and immediately handed him the written report, which was about two pages long.[28] Within a minute or two we were joined by General Arnold, and then by Harrison. After a brief discussion, General Marshall called the Secretary of War on the telephone. Mr. Stimson was then at Highhold, his house on Long Island, for he had come back from Europe quite worn-out, and had gone home for a day or two of rest. The telephone circuit over which we talked was specially designed to be secure. After receiving the facts, he extended his very warm congratulations for me to convey to all concerned.

General Marshall expressed his feeling that we should guard against too much gratification over our success, because it undoubtedly involved a large number of Japanese casualties. I replied that I was not thinking so much about those casualties as I was about the men who had made the Bataan death march.[29] When we got into the hall, Arnold slapped me on the back and said, "I am glad you said that—it's just the way I feel." I have always

---

28. The message was that the bomb had been dropped on Hiroshima, with devastating effects.

29. On April 9, 1942, the 35,000 half–starved American and Filipino troops on Bataan (in the Philippines) surrendered to the Japanese. The Japanese promptly marched their captives sixty miles without food or water in brutal heat, committing numerous atrocities along the way. Approximately one-third of the captives died. The incident became known as the "Bataan Death March."

CHAPTER 8

THE BURDENS
OF POWER: THE
DECISION TO
DROP THE
ATOMIC BOMB,
1945

thought that this was the real feeling of every experienced officer, particularly those who occupied positions of great responsibility, including General Marshall himself. . . .

QUESTIONS TO CONSIDER

The selections begin with the memoirs of President Harry S Truman because it was he who ultimately had to make the decision to drop the atomic bomb on Hiroshima. According to Truman, what figures were most influential in his thinking? What alternatives did Truman himself think he had?

Truman's July 26 proclamation calling on the Japanese to surrender is a crucial piece of evidence. According to Truman (based on his conversations with Acting Secretary of State Joseph Grew), what was the nature of the proclamation to be? Did Truman offer any more details about that proclamation? Keep these points in mind because they are of some importance later.

Secretary of War Henry Stimson was one of Truman's key advisers. How did Stimson enhance Truman's memories with regard to the April 25 meeting (where the President received his first full briefing on the bomb)? Did Stimson add important information about the Interim Committee?

Stimson's recollections of the July 26 proclamation to Japan (he called it the Potsdam Ultimatum) adds one vital piece of information Truman did not mention. What was it? How important was this piece of information? How important was its omission by Truman?

The memoirs of Eisenhower and Leahy were included to give you the views of two military men concerning the detonation of the atomic bomb. Both men seem to have been opposed. Why? According to Eisenhower, what was Stimson's reaction? Why? According to Leahy, who was "pushing" the bomb? Why?

Joseph Grew probably knew the Japanese thinking better than anyone in Truman's inner circle, having been ambassador to Japan for several years. According to Grew, what was the situation in Japan in early July 1945? In his view, would Japan have surrendered if the atomic bomb had *not* been dropped? What did Grew think of the July 26 Potsdam Ultimatum (it was, after all, his idea)?

According to John McCloy, how did the Potsdam Ultimatum originate? McCloy called the document a "rather hastily composed paper." Why? Did McCloy see any alternatives? More important, how influential did McCloy think Grew was in Truman's "inner circle"? Why? In a larger sense, what point was McCloy trying to make?

James Byrnes was Truman's personal observer on the Interim Committee and soon after his Secretary of State. What apparently was one of Byrnes's important concerns with regard to the dropping of the bomb? How influential would you say this view was?

Byrnes's meeting with scientists Leo Szilard and H. C. Urey apparently went badly, a fact corroborated by Szilard's reminiscences. Why? What does this tell you about Byrnes?

According to Byrnes, what were the United States' alternatives in July 1945? Reporting on the Potsdam Conference, how did Byrnes portray Stalin? Furthermore, Byrnes raised a key point with regard to the Soviet Union's entrance into the war against Japan. It had been agreed earlier that the Soviets would reach an agreement with the Chinese *before* entering the war. How did Byrnes view these negotiations? Why did he hope the Soviets and the Chinese would take a long time in reaching an agreement? What does this tell you about Byrnes's thinking? His biases? How does Forrestal's diary help us understand Byrnes's thinking? How did Forrestal clarify the situation in Japan? Did he offer any clues as to how United States officials believed the Soviet Union should be dealt with?

Leo Szilard was a native Hungarian who fled Hitler's Germany for the United States. What was the nature of his concerns about the bomb that he had helped develop? How did he describe the meeting with Byrnes? What did Szilard believe was Byrnes's chief concern?

What did Szilard think of the Interim Committee? What did that opinion prompt him to do? What were the results? How does the Franck "Report" add to our understanding of the opinions of many scientists at the University of Chicago with regard to the bomb?

General Leslie Groves was the military director of the Manhattan Project. In what ways did he justify the dropping of the bomb on Hiroshima?

Now return to the central questions. Why did President Truman decide to drop the atomic bomb on Hiroshima? What factors went into his decision? Were there any alternatives to dropping the bomb? If so, why did Truman not pursue them? What advisers were and were not influential with Truman? Finally, do you think Truman's decision was the proper one?

EPILOGUE

Two days after the United States dropped the uranium atomic bomb on Hiroshima, the Soviet Union declared war on Japan and invaded Manchuria. Meanwhile, Japanese scientists, realizing the magnitude of what had happened at Hiroshima, begged their government to surrender. Japanese military leaders stubbornly refused.

Therefore, the next day (August 9), the United States dropped a second atomic bomb (this one using plutonium instead of uranium) on Nagasaki, with equally devastating results. On August 10, the Japanese emperor asserted himself against the military and agreed to surrender on the terms announced in the Potsdam Ultimatum

CHAPTER 8

THE BURDENS
OF POWER: THE
DECISION TO
DROP THE
ATOMIC BOMB,
1945

of July 26. On September 2, the formal surrender took place, and the Second World War had come to an end, with a total loss of life of approximately 50 million military personnel and civilians.

The scientists who worked on the Manhattan Project were of two minds concerning Hiroshima and Nagasaki. American physicist Robert Brode probably spoke for the majority when he said, "But if I am to tell the whole truth I must confess that our relief was really greater than our horror," principally because the war at last was over. Yet American electronics specialist William Higinbotham spoke for others when he wrote to his mother, "I am not a bit proud of the job we have done . . . perhaps this is so devastating that man will be forced to be peaceful." As for Robert Oppenheimer, the director of the Los Alamos operations and popularly known as the "father of the bomb," he feared that Hiroshima and Nagasaki were only the beginning and that a nuclear arms race between the United States and the Soviet Union was almost inevitable.

Most other Americans were also of two minds about the bomb. Even as they enthusiastically celebrated the end of the war, at the same time the specter of the atomic bomb frightened them and made their collective future insecure. A few years later, when *Time* magazine asked an eight-year-old boy what he wanted to be when he grew up, the boy replied "Alive!"

Some Americans criticized Truman's decision to drop atomic bombs on Hiroshima and Nagasaki. Several African American newspaper editors were especially critical, claiming that no such horrible device would ever have been dropped on "white" Germans and that Japanese were victims because they were not Caucasians. For the most part, however, Americans rejoiced at the war's end, even though they feared the weapon that had ended it.

Oppenheimer was prophetic that the postwar years would witness a nuclear arms race between the United States and the Soviet Union. Both nations had scooped up as many German scientists as they could to supplement their own atomic weapons research. Moreover, the Soviet Union tried to pierce American atomic secrecy through espionage. Neither side seems to have been fully committed to international control (through the United Nations) of atomic research. The Soviets rejected such a plan in 1946,[30] and in 1947, President Truman issued his "loyalty order," which placed government employees, including nuclear scientists, under rigid scrutiny.

In August 1949, a United States Air Force "flying laboratory" picked up traces of radioactive particles in the atmosphere in East Asia, a clear indication that the Soviet Union had detonated an atomic device. In January 1950, Truman gave orders for the United States to proceed with the development of a hydrogen bomb, nicknamed "Super" by some scientists. That bomb was tested on November 1, 1952. By 1953, however, the Soviet Union announced that it too possessed such a bomb. The nuclear arms race

30. The plan, conceived by the United States, forbid the Soviet Union from developing its own atomic weapon and would have created an international agency to control nuclear raw materials.

was well underway, given even more urgency by the cold war mentality that gripped both superpowers in the late 1940s and 1950s.[31]

By the 1980s, several other nations possessed atomic devices, thus increasing world tensions. Yet the two superpowers appeared to be acting more responsibly, gradually moving toward arms limitation treaties and agreements providing for the elimination of certain types of nuclear armaments. In December 1987, President Ronald Reagan and Soviet Premier Mikhail Gorbachev signed a historic treaty that eliminated enough medium-and short-range nuclear arms to have destroyed Hiroshima 32,000 times. The threat of a nuclear holocaust had been lessened; however, it had not been eliminated.

Thus President Truman's decision to drop an atomic bomb on Hiroshima was one that was to have far-reaching consequences for all peoples who inhabited the earth during the second half of the twentieth century, and very likely far beyond that. What factors went into that momentous decision? What alternatives, if any, did Truman have? Was the atomic bomb a blessing or a nightmare?

31. Oppenheimer had opposed the development of the hydrogen bomb. In late 1953, he was accused of having had "associations" with Communists and with disloyalty. A closed-door hearing (April 12–May 6, 1954) ended with Oppenheimer's security clearance being removed.

CHAPTER NINE

THE SECOND RED SCARE:
HUAC vs HOLLYWOOD (1947)

THE PROBLEM

On October 20, 1947, congressman J. Parnell Thomas, chairman of the House Committee on Un-American Activities (HUAC), called to order what perhaps were the most sensational hearings in the committee's long and checkered history. Since 1945, the committee had promised to investigate communist infiltration into the American film industry, largely centered in Hollywood, California. At that time, congressman John E. Rankin (D, Miss.), a committee member, promised that HUAC would uncover in Hollywood "one of the most dangerous plots ever instigated for the overthrow of the government." When open hearings finally were convened in October 1947, popular and press interest was fanned by a series of famous witnesses (including Walt Disney, Robert Taylor, Gary Cooper, and Ronald Reagan) as well as by the number of Hollywood personal-

ities who either attended one session of the hearings or who spoke vigorously against them (Lauren Bacall, Humphrey Bogart, Gene Kelly, Jane Wyatt, Danny Kaye, Judy Garland, Frank Sinatra, Henry Fonda, John Houseman, Gregory Peck, and many others).

The HUAC investigations of Hollywood took place in an atmosphere of considerable fear and anxiety. The wartime alliance of the United States and the Soviet Union had completely deteriorated and was replaced by what many referred to as the cold war between the two postwar superpowers. Each side regarded the other as a potential threat against which constant vigilance must be maintained. In such an atmosphere, many Americans became convinced that Soviet spies and agents had infiltrated the federal government as well as many American institutions. Hence, as HUAC began its investigations of alleged communist infiltration of the film industry, some people, caught up in the suspicion and distrust that marked the cold war, were willing to believe that Communists were using moving pictures to disseminate anti-American propaganda.

In this chapter you will be reading and analyzing selections from those October 1947 hearings and then answering the following four questions:

1. Based on the evidence at your disposal, to what extent did Communists in Hollywood constitute (in the words of Congressman Rankin) "the greatest hotbed of subversive activities in the United States?" In other words, based on the evidence in this chapter, was the communist threat to America's film industry a genuine one?

2. Based on excerpts from the hearings, how much hard evidence was there that supported charges of communist infiltration of Holly-

wood? What was the nature of the evidence presented?

3. What effects did the October 1947 HUAC hearings have on the Hollywood film community?

4. What does the evidence in this chapter tell you about the nature and character of the second red scare of the late 1940s and 1950s?

Finally, you should be willing to go beyond the evidence provided to answer the following two questions:

5. In your opinion, did the members of the House Committee on Un-American Activities act responsibly in their investigations of communist infiltration of the film industry? What evidence would you use to prove your point?

6. Should the constitutional rights of Americans who are Communists be protected and ensured the same ways as are the rights of Americans who are not Communists? Why or why not?

BACKGROUND

The years immediately following the end of the First World War in 1918 were filled with tension and anxiety for the American people. More than 112,000 American soldiers, sailors, and marines had died to (in President Woodrow Wilson's words) "make the world safe for democracy."[1] Yet the

treaties that formally brought the war to an end were harsh, a far cry from the idealism Wilson had whipped up among the American people. The result was a cynical aftertaste, a spirit that dominated much of American life in the 1920s.

At the same time, many in the West viewed the Bolshevik Revolution of 1917 in Russia and the call by the

1. The United States suffered approximately 49,000 battle-related deaths. The remainder of the troop deaths were due to disease, primarily the Spanish influenza epidemic of

1918–1919, which killed roughly 25 million people worldwide.

CHAPTER 9

THE SECOND
RED SCARE:
HUAC VS
HOLLYWOOD
(1947)

Communist International (Comintern) for a worldwide Bolshevik revolution as a direct threat to their governments and way of life. In response, several nations—including the United States—sent troops to Russia in an attempt to support the Russian enemies of Bolshevism. The United States contributed approximately five thousand soldiers to this effort, but foreign intervention in the Russian civil war ultimately was unsuccessful. Western European nations and the United States feared the spread of Bolshevism. Thus World War I ended not with solutions to international problems but with more problems.

At home, conversion to a peacetime economy resulted in high unemployment rates and inflation of prices. A wave of postwar strikes—3,600 in 1919 alone—idled more than 4 million workers, including shipyard and steelworkers and the Boston police force. Violence against African Americans in the South increased dramatically, with 78 recorded lynchings in 1919 alone. Yet African Americans who had abandoned the South for opportunities in northern cities also faced antiblack violence. In Chicago in July 1919, the killing of an African American youth who was swimming in an area of Lake Michigan traditionally reserved for whites touched off five days of rioting in which 38 people lost their lives. More than two dozen other cities experienced racial violence in that year as well. Simultaneously, the end of the war brought a resumption in the wave of immigrants, mostly from southern and eastern Europe, who arrived on American shores. To many Americans, inflation, unemployment, strikes, racial violence, and the resumption of

immigration were threats to their hopes of returning to their safe and ordered prewar world, a world that in fact no longer existed.

The Bolshevik Revolution gave many Americans a convenient scapegoat for their postwar troubles. A few Americans were involved in radical activities, as evidenced by the discovery of numerous mail bombs intended for thirty-six prominent government leaders. Americans, however, identified communist conspirators as the cause of all their postwar difficulties. The result was the first Red Scare, fueled by the politically ambitious Attorney General A. Mitchell Palmer. Under Palmer's direction, raids were staged against radical organizations. Thousands were arrested and denied their civil liberties, and some three hundred were deported. At the same time, a revived Ku Klux Klan gained enormous popularity in the South and Midwest, principally by emphasizing their nativist, anti-immigrant and anti-African American dogmas. The first Red Scare ended sometime in the early 1920s, when the Palmer-incited hysteria and the strength of the Ku Klux Klan began declining.

In many ways, the period following the end of World War II in 1945 was similar to the years after World War I. The return of approximately sixteen million servicemen to civilian life (more than 10 percent of the nation's total population) was accomplished more smoothly than after World War I, principally because pent-up consumer demand for housing, automobiles, and other products stimulated the national economy. Nevertheless, a large portion of the six million women who had entered the labor force during the war were expected to turn over their jobs to the returning servicemen, whether or not they wanted to. Similar to the post–World War I period, consumer demand produced a rapid inflation rate, which was not brought under control until the early 1950s. Also, labor unrest was widespread as unions pushed for wage increases they had not demanded during the wartime emergency. By the end of 1946, roughly five million workers had gone on strike. In response, President Harry Truman threatened to draft striking railroad workers into the army and briefly seized control of the nation's coal mines when the United Mine Workers went on strike.

For African Americans, the years after the World War II were ones of opportunity and challenge. Almost 900,000 African Americans, both men and women, had served in the armed forces, and more than 1 million blacks migrated from the South to take industrial jobs in other sections of the nation. By 1945, roughly one-third of the nation's African American population lived outside the South,[2] were voting for the first time, and were beginning to push for political and social rights to complement their economic gains.

Probably the greatest similarity to the post–World War I epoch, however, was the advent of another Red Scare. The United States had emerged from the war as the world's industrial and military leader, and many Americans were anxious that the country not retreat into isolationism but use its

power to build a better postwar world. As President Franklin Roosevelt's close adviser Harry Hopkins remembered, "We really believed in our hearts that this was the dawn of the new day we had all been praying for and talking about for so many years."

This optimism, however, was soon tempered by the realities of the postwar world. Two major superpowers emerged from World War II: the United States and the Soviet Union. The total defeat of the Axis Powers (Germany, Italy, and Japan) and the wartime devastation of much of Western Europe created power vacuums in Western and Central Europe and parts of Asia. In time, each postwar superpower came to believe that the other was trying to take advantage of that unstable situation for its own purposes. Soviet Premier Josef Stalin feared that the West would learn how economically and militarily vulnerable the Soviet Union actually was and quickly move into those power vacuums. To counter this potential threat, Stalin was determined to dominate the nations of Eastern Europe, especially Poland, and to make Soviet influence felt in Central Europe as well, especially in Germany. At the same time, many Americans, including the new President Harry Truman, believed that Russian Communists were dedicated to the overthrow of capitalism and democracy and intent on world domination. As a result, the American government became increasingly committed to propping up the pro-American governments of Western Europe and Asia, determined that the Soviets would not swoop into these power vacuums. And as both the Soviet Union and the United States became more suspicious

2. In 1940, five years earlier, the percentage of African Americans living outside the South was 23 percent.

CHAPTER 9

THE SECOND
RED SCARE:
HUAC VS
HOLLYWOOD
(1947)

and secretive in their dealings with one another, both powers resorted to widespread espionage activities.

The year 1947 witnessed an increase in international tensions and a heightening of cold war hysteria. In February 1947, a financially desperate Great Britain informed the United States that it was unable to maintain support to the government of Greece, itself beset with economic problems and besieged by communist guerrillas.[3] Truman responded almost immediately with the Truman Doctrine, which promised United States support to "free peoples who are resisting attempted subjugation by armed minorities or outside pressures." In May, a bipartisan Congress backed Truman with a $400 million aid package to Greece and Turkey. The United States had issued a challenge to Stalin. The world waited nervously for the next events of the cold war.

Meanwhile, Americans were becoming increasingly convinced of the danger of Soviet spies and agents in the United States. On March 22, 1947, Truman issued an executive order (known as the Loyalty Order) that required investigations of federal employees in the executive branch. This hunt for "subversives" was put into effect in August.

On June 5, in his commencement address to graduates of Harvard University, Secretary of State George Marshall unveiled what became known as the Marshall Plan. The plan was to provide American funds for the eco-

nomic recovery of European countries whose postwar economic problems made them vulnerable to communism. The Soviet Union denounced the Marshall Plan and accused the United States of warmongering.

Thus by the time the HUAC investigations of Hollywood convened in Washington in October 1947, the world was filled with cold war tensions and the United States had entered into the second Red Scare.

The second Red Scare affected almost every aspect of Americans' behavior and collective thought. Most states joined the federal government in requiring loyalty oaths and establishing loyalty review boards, many of which flagrantly disregarded the constitutional safeguards of those under suspicion. Worse, a growing number of private individuals (some historians have called them "loyalty sleuths") added to the alarm by hunting subversives on their own. Almost anyone was a potential target.[4]

What caused someone to be accused of subversion? In 1947, United States Attorney General Tom C. Clark issued a list of "subversive organizations" thought to be dominated by or sympathetic to Communists. Although most of the listed organizations conformed to neither criterion (several were leftist but not communist), membership or former membership in any of them could be the basis for suspicion. For example, both the Southern Conference

3. Contrary to American beliefs, Stalin was not supporting the communist guerrillas in Greece, and even disapproved of their actions.

4. Young screen actress Nancy Davis was rumored to be the subject of such an investigation. She appealed for help to Screen Actors Guild president Ronald Reagan, claiming that there was no truth to the accusations against her. Reagan offered her the assistance of his office. Later, Nancy Davis became Mrs. Ronald Reagan.

for Human Welfare and the High-lander Center (in East Tennessee), advocates of civil rights for African Americans, were labelled as subversive and subjected to investigations and its members harassed—in spite of the fact that one leader of the Southern Conference for Human Welfare was Dr. Frank P. Graham, the widely respected president of the University of North Carolina.

In the 1930s, during the depths of the depression and the rise of fascism in Europe, many Americans, many of them idealistic college students, joined leftist organizations. During World War II, when the American government purposely was cultivating sentiment for its Russian allies against Hitler (amid much publicity, First Lady Eleanor Roosevelt cut the cake at a birthday party honoring the Red Army), these men and women rarely made a secret of these affiliations. Most abandoned those organizations after World War II, when many came to believe that Stalin was not fulfilling their idealistic hopes. Former memberships, however, often returned to haunt people during the second Red Scare. People having friends or associates who had been accused of subversion and people who obstructed, criticized, or refused to cooperate with anticommunist investigations also came under suspicion. In short, a person could be accused on the most trivial and insubstantial "evidence"; many were.

In such an atmosphere, when accusations could cost people their jobs, ruin careers, or alienate friends, it is not surprising that people generally embraced extreme patriotism, conformity, and a collective mentality that strongly encouraged a "don't be differ-ent, don't make waves" approach to living. A few people resisted, but the majority went along, afraid of either a communist menace or being destroyed by someone's accusation against them, no matter how groundless. Government employees and teachers were but two groups under continual investigation. Everyone—from businesspeople to actors, actresses, and writers—were deeply affected and afraid. And because both Republicans and Democrats participated in this hysteria, there was little political objection to its excesses.

The period of the second Red Scare was a confusing one for the American film industry, largely centered in Hollywood, California. On one hand, film makers had traditionally opposed censorship from outside the industry, preferring instead to let Hollywood police itself as to language, sexual material, and sociopolitical opinions. On the other hand, many people in the film community felt strongly that leftists within that community were such a threat to the United States and the independence of the film industry that these people must be rooted out by any means possible. Therefore, when the House Committee on Un-American Activities in 1947 undertook an investigation of communism in Hollywood, the film community was deeply divided. Some members of that community resented what they considered political intrusion into the creative arts, but others cooperated with the committee, offering examples of leftist activity in the film industry and names of men and women thought to have communist affiliations.

The House Committee on Un-American Activities, formed in 1938 as a

CHAPTER 9
THE SECOND
RED SCARE:
HUAC VS
HOLLYWOOD
(1947)

temporary committee to investigate fascist and communist activities in the United States, had long been eager, according to one member, "to track down the footprints of Karl Marx in movieland." Republican victories in the 1946 congressional elections gave Republicans control of both the House of Representatives and the Senate and, as a result, the chairs of all congressional committees. The chairmanship of HUAC fell to J. Parnell Thomas of New Jersey, a man determined to purge Hollywood of all communist and leftist influence. Under Thomas, the committee held closed hearings in Los Angeles in May 1947, and, amid much ballyhoo, open hearings in Washington in October.

The evidence in this chapter is taken from those October hearings. Read the evidence carefully, and answer the questions posed at the beginning of the chapter.

THE METHOD

The exclusive purpose of hearings by congressional committees or subcommittees is to gather information to use in drafting legislation. Occasionally, however, congressional committees and subcommittees stray from that purpose. As you examine the evidence, ask yourself whether HUAC's investigation of Hollywood strayed from the purpose of hearings. In other words, why do you think the hearings were held in the first place? Note that a good deal of HUAC's attention focused on the federal government's wartime role in Hollywood. Does this concern give you a clue as to one reason why HUAC conducted these hearings?

Almost immediately, you will recognize two things about these HUAC hearings. First, the witnesses can be divided into two categories: "friendly" (that is, those willing to cooperate with HUAC) and "unfriendly." It helps to divide the witnesses into these two groups. Does the committee treat the two groups differently? If so, in what ways?

Second, although congressional hearings are not trials, the two events share certain traits. Committee members try to build a case, much like trial attorneys, by arranging evidence and witnesses to suit their aims. Too, like attorneys, congressional committee members sometimes try to get both friendly and unfriendly witnesses to say things that the witnesses do not want to say. Can you see the similarities in the October 1947 hearings? More important, do you think the case HUAC built is convincing? Why or why not? In other words, did Communists in Hollywood constitute a serious threat to the film industry? How much hard evidence was there in the hearings that proved such a threat existed? As you come across what you consider to be such evidence, be sure to note it for later use.

To answer questions 3 and 4, you will have to exercise some historical imagination. As in any community, the film community was made up of people who held all sorts of opinions but who were required to work together to produce the product. And as in other communities, people in the film community were not merely coworkers but neighbors who socialized with one another and whose children often went to school and played together. They attended churches and synagogues together, served on local charitable groups and PTAs, and dined at each other's homes. As you read the evidence, imagine what effects the HUAC hearings might have had on the film community.

Finally, you can gain a great deal of understanding about the *style* and *nature* of the second Red Scare by examining the evidence. As you read the selections from the hearings, can you think of some adjectives to describe the second Red Scare? How would you go about proving that those adjectives were accurate?

Questions 5 and 6 require that you combine material from the Evidence and Background sections of this chapter with your other reading. The answers to these questions will be statements of your opinion. Even so, you must be able to support your opinions with evidence. Be careful of people who support their opinions with *apparent* pieces of evidence but that in fact are other statements of opinion. For example, someone might argue that accused Communists in Hollywood should have been jailed, citing as evidence that "they constituted a threat to America." The latter statement, as you can see, is not evidence but another statement of opinion, one that in itself to be proved requires evidence. As you answer all the questions in this chapter, including the last two, be sure to draw a fine line between *real* and *pseudo*evidence.

THE EVIDENCE

Sources 1 through 16 from House of Representatives, Committee on Un-American Activities, *Hearings Regarding the Communist Infiltration of the Motion Picture Industry,* October 20–30, 1947 (Washington: Government Printing Office, 1947), pp. 1–3, 10–12, 17, 38–39, 55, 58–59, 70–76, 82–88, 92–94, 100, 103–104, 106–107, 109–112, 128–130, 138, 165–169, 171–175, 198, 214, 217, 219–224, 231, 233, 282–284, 289–295, 306–309, 522.

COMMITTEE ON UN-AMERICAN ACTIVITIES

J. PARNELL THOMAS, New Jersey, *Chairman*

KARL E. MUNDT, South Dakota

JOHN MCDOWELL, Pennsylvania

RICHARD M. NIXON, California

RICHARD B. VAIL, Illinois

JOHN S. WOOD, Georgia

JOHN E. RANKIN, Mississippi

J. HARDIN PETERSON, Florida

HERBERT C. BONNER, North Carolina

ROBERT E. STRIPLING, *Chief Investigator*

BENJAMIN MANDEL, *Director of Research*

CHAPTER 9
THE SECOND
RED SCARE:
HUAC VS
HOLLYWOOD
(1947)

1. J. Parnell Thomas, Chairman (Opening Remarks).

. . . The committee is well aware of the magnitude of the subject which it is investigating. The motion-picture business represents an investment of billions of dollars. It represents employment for thousands of workers, ranging from unskilled laborers to high-salaried actors and executives. And even more important, the motion-picture industry represents what is probably the largest single vehicle of entertainment for the American public—over 85,000,000 persons attend the movies each week.

However, it is the very magnitude of the scope of the motion-picture industry which makes this investigation so necessary. We all recognize, certainly, the tremendous effect which moving pictures have on their mass audiences, far removed from the Hollywood sets. We all recognize that what the citizen sees and hears in his neighborhood movie house carries a powerful impact on his thoughts and behavior.

With such vast influence over the lives of American citizens as the motion-picture industry exerts, it is not unnatural—in fact, it is very logical—that subversive and undemocratic forces should attempt to use this medium for un-American purposes.

I want to emphasize at the outset of these hearings that the fact that the Committee on Un-American Activities is investigating alleged Communist influence and infiltration in the motion-picture industry must not be considered or interpreted as an attack on the majority of persons associated with this great industry. I have every confidence that the vast majority of movie workers are patriotic and loyal Americans.

This committee, under its mandate from the House of Representatives, has the responsibility of exposing and spotlighting subversive elements wherever they may exist. As I have already pointed out, it is only to be expected that such elements would strive desperately to gain entry to the motion-picture industry, simply because the industry offers such a tremendous weapon for education and propaganda. That Communists have made such an attempt in Hollywood and with considerable success is already evident to this committee from its preliminary investigative work. . . .

I cannot emphasize too strongly the seriousness of Communist infiltration, which we have found to be a mutual problem for many, many different fields of endeavor in the United States. Communists for years have been conducting an unrelentless "boring from within" campaign against America's democratic institutions. While never possessing a large numerical strength, the Communists nevertheless have found that they could dominate the activities of unions or other mass enterprises in this country by capturing a few strategic positions of leadership. . . .

There is no question that there are Communists in Hollywood. We cannot minimize their importance there, and that their influence has already made itself felt has been evidenced by internal turmoil in the industry over the Communist issue. Prominent figures in the motion-picture business have been engaged in a sort of running battle over Communist infiltration for the last 4 or 5 years and a number of anti-Communist organizations have been set up within the industry in an attempt to combat this menace.

The question before this committee, therefore, and the scope of its present inquiry, will be to determine the extent of Communist infiltration in the Hollywood motion-picture industry. We want to know what strategic positions in the industry have been captured by these elements, whose loyalty is pledged in word and deed to the interests of a foreign power.

The committee is determined that the hearings shall be fair and impartial. We have subpoenaed witnesses representing both sides of the question. All we are after are the facts.

Now, I want to make it clear to the witnesses, the audience, the members of the press, and other guests here today that this hearing is going to be conducted in an orderly and dignified manner at all times. But if there is anyone here today or at any of the future sessions of this hearing who entertains any hopes or plans for disrupting the proceedings, he may as well dismiss it from his mind.

2. Jack L. Warner, Vice President, Warner Bros. Studios.

. . . Ideological termites have burrowed into many American industries, organizations, and societies. Wherever they may be, I say let us dig them out and get rid of them. My brothers and I will be happy to subscribe generously to a pest-removal fund. We are willing to establish such a fund to ship to Russia the people who don't like our American system of government and prefer the communistic system to ours.

That's how strongly we feel about the subversives who want to overthrow our free American system.

If there are Communists in our industry, or any other industry, organization, or society who seek to undermine our free institutions, let's find out about it and know who they are. Let the record be spread clear, for all to read and judge. The public is entitled to know the facts. And the motion-picture industry is entitled to have the public know the facts.

Our company is keenly aware of its responsibilities to keep its product free from subversive poisons. With all the vision at my command, I scrutinize the planning and production of our motion pictures. It is my firm belief

CHAPTER 9

THE SECOND
RED SCARE:
HUAC VS
HOLLYWOOD
(1947)

that there is not a Warner Bros. picture that can fairly be judged to be hostile to our country, or communistic in tone or purpose.

Many charges, including the fantasy of "White House pressure" have been leveled at our wartime production Mission to Moscow.[5] In my previous appearance before members of this committee, I explained the origin and purposes of Mission to Moscow.

That picture was made when our country was fighting for its existence, with Russia as one of our allies. It was made to fulfill the same wartime purpose for which we made such other pictures as Air Force, This Is the Army, Objective Burma, Destination Tokyo, Action in the North Atlantic, and a great many more.

If making Mission to Moscow in 1942 was a subversive activity, then the American Liberty ships which carried food and guns to Russian allies and the American naval vessels which convoyed them were likewise engaged in subversive activities. The picture was made only to help a desperate war effort and not for posterity.

The Warner Bros. interest in the preservation of the American way of life is no new thing with our company. Ever since we began making motion pictures we have fostered American ideals and done what we could to protect them.

Not content with merely warning against dangers to our free system, Warner Bros. has practiced a policy of positive Americanism. We have gone, and will continue to go, to all possible lengths to iterate and reiterate the realities and advantages of America.

Good American common sense is the determining factor in judging motion-picture scripts before they are put in production and motion-picture scenes after they are photographed. We rely upon a deep-rooted, pervading respect for our country's principles.

One of those American principles is the right to gripe and criticize in an effort to improve. That right to gripe is not enjoyed under communistic dictatorships. To surrender that privilege under pressure would betray our American standards.

Freedom of expression, however, does not, under our Constitution and laws, include a license to destroy. . . .

[In response to questions from Stripling and Thomas, Warner admitted that he had discovered that some of his script writers had tried to insert "un-American" lines in

---

5. *Mission to Moscow* was the film adaptation of the best-selling memoirs of former U.S. Ambassador to the Soviet Union (1936–1938) Joseph E. Davies. Davies was an admirer of Stalin, and the memoirs showed the Soviet Union in a highly favorable light.

Warner films, and that those writers were not rehired. In the closed hearings in Hollywood, Warner supplied the committee with the names of those writers.]

MR. STRIPLING. Well, is it your opinion now, Mr. Warner, that Mission to Moscow was a factually correct picture, and you made it as such?

MR. WARNER. I can't remember.

MR. STRIPLING. Would you consider it a propaganda picture?

MR. WARNER. A propaganda picture——

MR. STRIPLING. Yes.

MR. WARNER. In what sense?

MR. STRIPLING. In the sense that it portrayed Russia and communism in an entirely different light from what it actually was?

MR. WARNER. I am on record about 40 times or more that I have never been in Russia. I don't know what Russia was like in 1937 or 1944 or 1947, so how can I tell you if it was right or wrong?

MR. STRIPLING. Don't you think you were on dangerous ground to produce as a factually correct picture one which portrayed Russia——

MR. WARNER. No; we were not on dangerous ground in 1942, when we produced it. There was a war on. The world was at stake.

MR. STRIPLING. In other words——

MR. WARNER. We made the film to aid in the war effort, which I believe I have already stated.

MR. STRIPLING. Whether it was true or not?

MR. WARNER. As far as I was concerned, I considered it true to the extent as written in Mr. Davies' book.

MR. STRIPLING. Well, do you suppose that your picture influenced the people who saw it in this country, the millions of people who saw it in this country?

MR. WARNER. In my opinion, I can't see how it would influence anyone. We were in war and when you are in a fight you don't ask who the fellow is who is helping you.

MR. STRIPLING. Well, due to the present conditions in the international situation, don't you think it was rather dangerous to write about such a disillusionment as was sought in that picture?

MR. WARNER. I can't understand why you ask me that question, as to the present conditions. How did I, you, or anyone else know in 1942 what the conditions were going to be in 1947. I stated in my testimony our reason for making the picture, which was to aid the war effort—anticipating what would happen.

MR. STRIPLING. I don't see that this is aiding the war effort, Mr. Warner—with the cooperation of Mr. Davies or with the approval of the Government—to make a picture which is a fraud in fact.

CHAPTER 9

THE SECOND
RED SCARE:
HUAC VS
HOLLYWOOD
(1947)

MR. WARNER. I want to correct you, very vehemently. There was no cooperation of the Government.

MR. STRIPLING. You stated there was.

MR. WARNER. I never stated the Government cooperated in the making of it. If I did, I stand corrected. And I know I didn't.

MR. STRIPLING. Do you want me to read that part, Mr. Chairman?

THE CHAIRMAN. No; I think we have gone into this Mission to Moscow at some length. . . .

3. Samuel G. Wood, Producer and Director.

. . . MR. STRIPLING. Will you tell the committee of the efforts that you are aware of on the part of the Communists to infiltrate the Screen Directors Guild?

MR. WOOD. There is a constant effort to get control of the guild. In fact, there is an effort to get control of all unions and guilds in Hollywood. I think our most serious time was when George Stevens was president; he went in the service and another gentleman took his place, who died, and it was turned over to John Cromwell. Cromwell, with the assistance of three or four others, tried hard to steer us into the Red river, but we had a little too much weight for that.

MR. STRIPLING. Will you name the others?

MR. WOOD. Irving Pichel, Edward Dmytryk, Frank Tuttle, and—I am sorry, there is another name there. I forget.

MR. STRIPLING. If you think of it, will you give it for the record?

MR. WOOD. Yes. . . .

MR. STRIPLING. Is it your opinion that there are Communist writers in the motion-picture industry?

MR. WOOD. Oh, yes. It is not my opinion, I know positively there are.

MR. STRIPLING. Would you care to name any that you know yourself to be Communists?

MR. WOOD. Well, I don't think there is any question about Dalton Trumbo; any question about Donald Ogden Stewart. The reporter asked the question of a great many writers, "Are you a member of the Communist Party," or "Are you a Communist?"

MR. STRIPLING. Did they deny it?

MR. WOOD. They didn't answer it.

MR. STRIPLING. Was John Howard Lawson one of those persons?

MR. WOOD. Oh, yes; he is active in every piece of Communist work going on.

MR. STRIPLING. Is there any question in your mind that John Howard Lawson is a Communist?

MR. WOOD. If there is, then I haven't any mind. I suppose there are 19 gentlemen back there that say I haven't.

MR. STRIPLING. When did you first notice this effort on the part of the Communists to enter Hollywood or to exert influence in the motion-picture industry?

MR. WOOD. Well, I think they really started working around 1930, some, I forget the exact time. I think we were very conscious of it, had been for some time, but like everyone else we probably hadn't done anything, because it is quite an effort and you get quite smeared, and a lot of people would like to duck that. It is fun to play bridge, for instance, rather than to check on something like that. We felt it more, I think, just previously [sic] to our organization in 1944.

MR. STRIPLING. That was the reason, in other words, that you formed your organization, was to combat the increased activity on the part of the Communists in the industry?

MR. WOOD. Yes, sir; we felt there was a great danger, and it was in the interest of self-defense on our business, because we felt a normal responsibility for our business. It has been very kind to a lot of us, and we want to protect it.

MR. STRIPLING. Now, Mr. Wood, would you give the committee some of these examples in which the Communists have exerted influence in the motion-picture industry? In other words, how do they go about it, what is the mechanics of it?

MR. WOOD. There are a number of ways. I think the thing that is very important, and the thing I was most anxious about, is the pride of Americans in working. They are pretty subtle. For instance, a man gets a key position in the studio and has charge of the writers. When you, as a director or a producer, are ready for a writer you ask for a list and this man shows you a list. Well, if he is following the party line his pets are on top or the other people aren't on at all. If there is a particular man in there that has been opposing them they will leave his name off the list. Then if that man isn't employed for about 2 months they go to the head of the studio and say, "Nobody wants this man." The head is perfectly honest about it and says, "Nobody wants to use him, let him go." So a good American is let out. But it doesn't stop there. They point that out as an example and say, "You better fall in line, play ball, or else." And they go down the line on it.

MR. STRIPLING. That is true in the case of writers. Would you say it is true in any other branch of the industry?

CHAPTER 9

THE SECOND
RED SCARE:
HUAC VS
HOLLYWOOD
(1947)

MR. WOOD. I don't think in any part of the business, they will use a party who is opposed to their ideas, if they can avoid it, and they can usually avoid it.

MR. STRIPLING. They operate as cliques, in other words?

MR. WOOD. Oh, yes; they have their meetings every night. They are together; they work for one purpose.

MR. STRIPLING. What is that purpose, Mr. Wood?

MR. WOOD. Well, I think they are agents of a foreign country myself.

MR. STRIPLING. I see. . . .

4. Louis B. Mayer, Head, Metro-Goldwyn-Mayer Studios.

. . . During my 25 years in the motion-picture industry I have always sought to maintain the screen as a force for public good.

The motion-picture industry employs many thousands of people. As is the case with the newspaper, radio, publishing, and theater businesses, we cannot be responsible for the political views of each individual employee. It is, however, our complete responsibility to determine what appears on the motion-picture screen.

It is my earnest hope that this committee will perform a public service by recommending to the Congress legislation establishing a national policy regulating employment of Communists in private industry. It is my belief they should be denied the sanctuary of the freedom they seek to destroy.

Communism is based upon a doctrine inconsistent with American liberty. It advocates destruction of the system of free enterprise under which our industry has achieved popularity among the freedom-loving peoples of the world.

Our hatred of communism is returned in full measure. The Communists attack our screen as an instrument of capitalism. Few, if any, of our films ever reach Russia. It hates us because it fears us. We show too much of the American way of life, of human dignity, of the opportunity and the happiness to be enjoyed in a democracy.

More than any other country in the world, we have enjoyed the fullest freedom of speech in all means of communication. It is this freedom that has enabled the motion picture to carry the message to the world of our democratic way of life.

The primary function of motion pictures is to bring entertainment to the screen. But, like all other industries, we were lending every support to our Government in the war effort, and whenever a subject could be presented as entertaining, we tried, insofar as possible, to cooperate in building morale. . . .

There were a number of representatives of the Government who made periodical visits to the studios during the war. They discussed with us from time to time the types of pictures which they felt might assist the war effort. They were coordinators and at no time did they attempt to tell us what we should or should not do. We made our own decisions on production. We are proud of our war efforts and the results speak for themselves.

Mention has been made of the picture Song of Russia, as being friendly to Russia at the time it was made. Of course it was. It was made to be friendly. In 1938 we made Ninotchka, and shortly thereafter Comrade X, with Clark Gable and Hedy Lamarr—both of these films kidded Russia.

It was in April of 1942 that the story for Song of Russia came to our attention. It seemed a good medium of entertainment and at the same time offered an opportunity for a pat on the back for our then ally, Russia. It also offered an opportunity to use the music of Tschaikovsky. We mentioned this to the Government coordinators and they agreed with us that it would be a good idea to make the picture.

According to research I have made, our newspapers were headlining the desperate situation of the Russians at Stalingrad at that time. Admiral Standley, American Ambassador to the Soviet Union, made a vigorous plea for all-out aid. He pleaded for assistance second only to the supplies being provided the United States Fleet, and emphasized that the best way to win the war was to keep the Russians killing the Germans, and that the most effective way was to give them all the help they needed.

The United States Army Signal Corps made The Battle of Stalingrad, released in 1943, with a prolog expressing high tribute from President Roosevelt, our Secretaries of State, War, and Navy, and from Generals Marshall and MacArthur.

The final script of Song of Russia was little more than a pleasant musical romance—the story of a boy and girl that, except for the music of Tschaikovsky, might just as well have taken place in Switzerland or England or any other country on the earth.

I thought Robert Taylor ideal for the leading male role in Song of Russia, but he did not like the story. This was not unusual as actors and actresses many times do not care for stories suggested to them.

At the time, Taylor mentioned his pending commission in the Navy, so I telephoned the Secretary of the Navy, Frank Knox, and told him of the situation, recalling the good that had been accomplished with Mrs. Miniver and other pictures released during the war period. The Secretary called back

CHAPTER 9
THE SECOND
RED SCARE:
HUAC VS
HOLLYWOOD
(1947)

and said he thought Taylor could be given time to make the film before being called to the service. Accordingly, Taylor made the picture.

Since 1942 when the picture was planned, our relationship with Russia has changed. But viewed in the light of the war emergency at the time, it is my opinion that it could not be construed as anything other than for the entertainment purpose intended and a pat on the back for our then ally, Russia. . . .

MR. SMITH. Are there any Communists, to your knowledge, in Metro-Goldwyn-Mayer?

[Responding to questions, Mayer testified that he had been told that Dalton Trumbo and Lester Cole were Communists. Mayer also stated that his attorneys advised him that he should not fire a person who had been accused of being a Communist, fearing a lawsuit for damages, but that he would dismiss such a person if there was sufficient proof of communist activities.]

MR. SMITH. Going back to the picture Song of Russia, I notice in your statement, Mr. Mayer, you state:

The final script of Song of Russia was little more than a pleasant musical romance—the story of a boy and girl that, except for the music of Tschaikovsky, might just as well have taken place in Switzerland or England or any other country on the earth.

Is that your definite opinion on that particular picture?

MR. MAYER. Basically, yes.

MR. SMITH. Don't you feel the picture had scene after scene that grossly misrepresented Russia as it is today, or as it was at that time?

MR. MAYER. I never was in Russia, but you tell me how you would make a picture laid in Russia that would do any different than what we did there?

MR. SMITH. Don't you feel from what you have read, and from what you have heard from other people, that the scenes just did not depict Russia in one iota?

MR. MAYER. We did not attempt to depict Russia; we attempted to show a Russian girl entreating this American conductor to conduct a concert in her village where they have a musical festival every year and as it inevitably happens this girl fell in love with the conductor, and he with her. Then we showed the attack of the Germans on the Russians and the war disrupted this union.

MR. SMITH. The original story was written by whom, Mr. Mayer!

MR. MAYER. I don't recall now. . . .

MR. SMITH. Did you read the first script, Mr. Mayer?

MR. MAYER. Yes, sir.

MR. SMITH. What was your opinion at that time?

MR. MAYER. They had farm collectivism in it and I threw it out and said, "This will not be made until they give me the story they told me originally when I approved the making of it."

MR. SMITH. In other words, the first script, in your opinion, was not producible?

MR. MAYER. Not the first.

MR. SMITH. Why not?

MR. MAYER. Because I will not preach any ideology except American, and I don't even treat that. I let that take its own course and speak for itself.

MR. SMITH. That showed an ideology or condition, so far as Russia is concerned, that you did not approve of?

MR. MAYER. I wouldn't have it.

MR. SMITH. As to the last script then, was the script, in your opinion, satisfactorily cleaned up?

MR. MAYER. I think so; yes, sir.

MR. SMITH. Who was responsible, if you know, for taking the collectivism and other things out of the script?

MR. MAYER. I ordered it out, and the producer said it would all be rewritten, and it was. That is why Taylor was delayed getting into the service.

THE CHAIRMAN. May I ask a question right there?

MR. SMITH. Yes, sir.

THE CHAIRMAN. Mr. Mayer, you say the main reason why Taylor was delayed getting into the service was because the first script had these foreign ideologies in it and was not acceptable to you, so there was this delay?

MR. MAYER. Yes, sir.

MR. SMITH. Did a Government representative ever come to you, Mr. Mayer, about that picture, as to the making of it?

MR. MAYER. I don't recall anybody coming about the making of it. I think I told them about it or discussed it with them. So much happened in that period, coming and going. They had an office out there—War Information, I think they called themselves.

MR. SMITH. Have you seen the picture recently, Mr. Mayer?

MR. MAYER. Yes, sir.

MR. SMITH. What are your feelings about the picture, as to the damage it might cause to the people in the United States, that is, misleading them as to conditions in Russia?

MR. MAYER. What scenes are you referring to?

MR. SMITH. Do you recall scenes in there at the night club when everybody was drinking?

MR. MAYER. They do in Moscow.

CHAPTER 9

THE SECOND
RED SCARE:
HUAC VS
HOLLYWOOD
(1947)

MR. SMITH. Do you feel that that represents Russia as it is today?

MR. MAYER. I didn't make it as it is today, I made it when they were our ally in 1943. . . .

5. Ayn Rand, Novelist and Screenwriter.[6]

. . . MR. STRIPLING. Now, Miss Rand, you have heard the testimony of Mr. Mayer?

MISS RAND. Yes. . . .

MR. STRIPLING. Which says that the picture Song of Russia has no political implications?

MISS RAND. Yes.

MR. STRIPLING. Did you at the request of Mr. Smith, the investigator for this committee, view the picture Song of Russia?

MISS RAND. Yes.

MR. STRIPLING. Within the past 2 weeks?

MISS RAND. Yes; on October 13 to be exact.

MR. STRIPLING. In Hollywood?

MISS RAND. Yes.

MR. STRIPLING. Would you give the committee a break-down of your summary of the picture relating to either propaganda or an untruthful account or distorted account of conditions in Russia?

MISS RAND. Yes. . . .

[Rand proceeded to give an almost scene-by-scene critique of the film Song of Russia, pointing out how inaccurate, in her opinion, the living conditions in Russia were portrayed. She added that she believed that a comparison between Russians fighting against invading Germans and the men on the village green at Lexington was blasphemy and that other parts of the film "made me sick."]

My whole point about the picture is this: I fully believe Mr. Mayer when he says that he did not make a Communist picture. To do him justice, I can tell you I noticed, by watching the picture, where there was an effort to cut propaganda out. I believe he tried to cut propaganda out of the picture, but the terrible thing is the carelessness with ideas, not realizing that the mere presentation of that kind of happy existence in a country of slavery and horror is terrible because it is propaganda. You are telling people that it is all right to live in a totalitarian state.

6. Rand, author of the best-selling novel *The Fountainhead* (1943) was born in St. Petersburg, Russia, emigrated in 1926, and was a fierce and well-known critic of communism.

Now, I would like to say that nothing on earth will justify slavery. In war or peace or at any time you cannot justify slavery. You cannot tell people that it is all right to live under it and that everybody there is happy. . . .

6. Adolph Menjou, Screen Actor.

. . . MR. STRIPLING. Have you observed any Communist propaganda in pictures, or un-American propaganda in pictures which were produced in Hollywood?

MR. MENJOU. I have seen no communistic propaganda in pictures—if you mean "vote for Stalin," or that type of communistic propaganda. I don't think that the Communists are stupid enough to try it that way. I have seen in certain pictures things I didn't think should have been in the pictures.

MR. STRIPLING. Could you tell the committee whether or not there has been an effort on the part of any particular group in the motion-picture industry to inject Communist propaganda into pictures or to leave out scenes or parts of stories which would serve the Communist Party line?

MR. MENJOU. I don't like that term "Communist propaganda," because I have seen no such thing as Communist propaganda, such as waving the hammer and sickle in motion pictures. I have seen things that I thought were against what I considered good Americanism, in my feeling. I have seen pictures I thought shouldn't have been made—shouldn't have been made, let me put it that way. . . .

MR. STRIPLING. Mr. Menjou, do you have any particular pictures in mind—

MR. MENJOU. Well——

MR. STRIPLING. When you make that statement? . . .

MR. MENJOU. Will you repeat the question, please?

MR. STRIPLING. Yes. Well, we will approach it this way. We have had testimony here to the effect that writers who were members of the Screen Writers Guild have attempted to inject un-American propaganda into motion pictures. Are you aware that that is the case, or has been the case, in Hollywood at any time?

MR. MENJOU. I don't think that I am competent to answer that question. I am a member of the Screen Actors Guild, and I think a member of the Screen Writers Guild would be far more competent to answer that. If you want to ask me if I know of any un-American propaganda in any pictures that I appeared, I will be glad to give you my thoughts.

MR. STRIPLING. Will you give an example?

CHAPTER 9

THE SECOND
RED SCARE:
HUAC VS
HOLLYWOOD
(1947)

MR. MENJOU. I don't think the picture Mission to Moscow should have been made. It was a perfectly completely dishonest picture. . . .

I also do not think that the picture North Star was a true picture, from what I have been able to learn after reading over 150 books on the subject. This was a picture showing the German attack on the Russians and certain parts of it were not true. It has been quite some time ago since I saw the picture. I thought that picture would have been better unmade. Fortunately, those pictures were unsuccessful.

MR. STRIPLING. As a generality, would you say that the more entertaining the picture is, the better opportunity there might be to put across propaganda?

MR. MENJOU. Yes. The better the entertainment the more dangerous the propaganda becomes, once it is injected into the picture. . . .

MR. STRIPLING. Do you consider that the Communist Party members in this country are engaged in treasonable activities?

MR. MENJOU. Definitely.

MR. STRIPLING. Mr. Menjou, this committee also has a legislative function as well as an investigative function. During this session there were two bills introduced which sought to outlaw the Communist Party. Do you think that the Communist Party should be outlawed by legislation?

MR. MENJOU. I believe that the Communist Party in the United States should be outlawed by the Congress of the United States. It is not a political party. It is a conspiracy to take over our Government by force, which would enslave the American people, as the Soviet Government— 14 members of the Politburo—hold the Russian people in abject slavery. Any one of a dozen books will prove it. This is not hearsay. Dozens of other testimony will prove what horrors are going on in Russia today, so horrible that you cannot read them without becoming ill.

Now, we don't want that here.

MR. STRIPLING. Now, Mr. Menjou, there has been quite a bit said and written in the Communist publications and certain left-wing organizations have circulated pamphlets to the effect that this committee is trying to bring about thought control.

MR. MENJOU. Well, I also have heard many other words—"witch-hunting." I am a witch-hunter if the witches are Communists. I am a Red-baiter. I make no bones about it whatsoever. I would like to see them all back in Russia. I think a taste of Russia would cure many of them. . . .

MR. VAIL. Mr. Menjou, do you think there is justification for the action of this committee in its instituting an investigation of Communist activities in Hollywood?

MR. MENJOU. Do I think so? Certainly.

MR. VAIL. In the daily papers in the past few days I noticed a statement that was signed by a number of prominent Hollywood actors and actresses deploring the investigation and describing it as a smear. What is your impression of the people who were signatory to that statement?

MR. MENJOU. I am just as shocked and amazed—which I believe were their words—as they said they were shocked and amazed. I don't believe any of them has ever made a serious study of the subject. I believe they are innocent dupes; that is my impression of them, innocent dupes.

I guarantee not one of them could name four men on the Politburo; I guarantee not one of them could name a date or an action against Russia or a violation of the antiaggression pacts which Mr. Stalin violated. If these people will only read and read and read and read, they will wake up. I have all the sympathy in the world for them; I am sorry for them.

MR. VAIL. I have no more questions.

THE CHAIRMAN. Mr. Nixon.

MR. NIXON. Mr. Menjou, from what you have said to charge a person with being a Communist is a very serious thing?

MR. MENJOU. Yes, sir.

MR. NIXON. You would not want that charge made?

MR. MENJOU. Without substantiation, that is right. That is playing right into the Communists' hands.

MR. NIXON. In answer to a question by Mr. Stripling you indicated that although you might now know whether a certain person was a Communist, I think you said he certainly acted like a Communist.

MR. MENJOU. If you belong to a Communist-front organization and you take no action against the Communists, you do not resign from the organization when you still know the organization is dominated by Communists, I consider that a very, very dangerous thing.

MR. NIXON. Have you any other tests which you would apply which would indicate to you that people acted like Communists?

MR. MENJOU. Well, I think attending any meetings at which Mr. Paul Robeson appeared and applauding or listening to his Communist songs in America, I would be ashamed to be seen in an audience doing a thing of that kind. . . .

THE CHAIRMAN. It has been said in the press by certain individuals in the United States that these hearings now being held by the Un-American Activities Committee are a censorship of the screen. What have you to say about that?

MR. MENJOU. I think that is juvenile.

THE CHAIRMAN. So anybody that would make such a statement would be considered as such?

[261]

CHAPTER 9

THE SECOND
RED SCARE:
HUAC VS
HOLLYWOOD
(1947)

MR. MENJOU. It is perfectly infantile to say this committee is trying to control the industry. How could they possibly control the industry! They wouldn't know anything about it. You wouldn't know how to make a picture or anything else. I don't see how that could be said by any man with the intelligence of a louse. . . .

I would move to the State of Texas if it [Communism] ever came here because I think the Texans would kill them on sight. . . .

7. John Charles Moffitt, Film critic for *Esquire* magazine, Former Screenwriter.

. . . MR. STRIPLING. Did you ever join any organizations while you were in Hollywood in connection with being a writer for the motion-picture industry?

MR. MOFFITT. Yes, sir; I did. In 1937, shocked by the conduct of the Fascists in Spain, I joined an organization known as the Hollywood Anti-Nazi League. Both my wife and I became members of that organization. We contributed considerable sums of money—for us—to what we supposed was the buying of ambulances and medical supplies for the assistance of the Loyalists in Spain.

After we had been in that organization some months we were invited to what turned out to be a more or less star chamber meeting, an inner corps meeting. It took place in the home of Mr. Frank Tuttle, a director. Mr. Herbert Biberman, who had been responsible for my being in the Anti-Nazi League, was there, as was his wife, Miss Gail Sondergaard, an actress. Donald Ogden Stewart was also one of those present.

[Moffitt then related that he and his wife were shocked to learn at that meeting that the leaders of the Anti-Nazi League were Communists. In addition to Biberman and Stewart, Moffitt named John Howard Lawson as one of the league's leaders.]

MR. STRIPLING. We will go back to your activities in the Anti-Nazi League.

MR. MOFFITT. During the period I referred to, the period between the time I discovered that this was a Communist front organization and the period some 6 weeks later, when I resigned, I had several conversations with Mr. Biberman, Mr. Lawson, and others of that organization.

During the course of it Mr. Lawson made this significant statement: He said:

As a writer do not try to write an entire Communist picture.

He said:

The producers will quickly identify it and it will be killed by the front office.

He said:

As a writer try to get 5 minutes of the Communist doctrine, 5 minutes of the party line in every script that you write.

He said:

Get that into an expensive scene, a scene involving expensive stars, large sets or many extras, because—

He said:

then even if it is discovered by the front office the business manager of the unit, the very watchdog of the treasury, the very servant of capitalism, in order to keep the budget from going too high, will resist the elimination of that scene. If you can make the message come from the mouth of Gary Cooper or some other important star who is unaware of what he is saying, by the time it is discovered he is in New York and a great deal of expense will be involved to bring him back and reshoot the scene.

If you get the message into a scene employing many extras it will be very expensive to reshoot that scene because of the number of extras involved or the amount of labor that would be necessary to light and reconstruct a large set.

That was the nucleus of what he said at that time.

I later heard another statement by Mr. Lawson. That was made in the summer of 1941 when some young friends of mine who were attending what was purported to be a school for actors in Hollywood—I think it was on Labrea Boulevard—asked me to go over and hear one of the lectures, instructions on acting.

I went over on this night and Mr. Lawson was the lecturer. During the course of the evening Mr. Lawson said this—and I think I quote it practically verbatim—Mr. Lawson said to these young men and women who were training for a career of acting, he said:

It is your duty to further the class struggle by your performance.

He said—

If you are nothing more than an extra wearing white flannels on a country club veranda do your best to appear decadent, do your best to appear to be a snob; do your best to create class antagonism.

He said—

If you are an extra on a tenement street do your best to look downtrodden, do your best to look a victim of existing society. . . .

CHAPTER 9

THE SECOND
RED SCARE:
HUAC VS
HOLLYWOOD
(1947)

8. Ruppert Hughes, Screenwriter.

[Hughes testified that John Howard Lawson and others had made the Screen Writers Guild "an instrument of communist power." In response, Hughes and others founded the Screen Playwrights, in 1935 or 1936. Under attack from the Screen Writers Guild as Fascists and a company union, the Screen Playwriters were forced to disband. Hughes then testified how Biberman and others had refused to attack Hitler when Germany was allied with the Soviet Union.]

That is the way I tell a Communist, a man who never says a word against the bloodiest butcher in history, Stalin, and who says violent words against the most modest American. That is my test.

MR. STRIPLING. Mr. Hughes, do you consider the Screen Writers Guild to be under Communist domination at the present time?

MR. HUGHES. Weakeningly so. It was absolutely under Communist domination when the authority was put to use. It was voted for something like 310 to 7 and the poor 7 were hissed and booed. It was revived, then the last vote was something like 225 to 125. The anti-Communists are trying to take it back and I have some hopes they will succeed. It has been, up to the present, strongly dominated by Communists.

MR. STRIPLING. Do you think the Communists in Hollywood at the present time are on the defensive or the offensive?

MR. HUGHES. I think they are on the defensive now because they are losing a great many of those fashion followers who thought it was smart to be Communists and who now find it is unpopular and are deserting them. . . .

THE CHAIRMAN. The Chair would like to say . . . this committee has made a very thorough investigation of Communist personnel in Hollywood. We have a very complete record on at least 79 persons active out in Hollywood. The time will come in these hearings when this documented evidence will be presented, so I just want to let you know now you cannot make the kind of investigation we can, but we have made a very thorough investigation, and that material will be presented at this public hearing either some time this week or some time next week. . . .

9. Robert Taylor, Film Actor.

. . . MR. STRIPLING. During the time you have been in Hollywood has there been any period during which you considered that the Communist Party or the fellow travelers of the Communist Party were exerting any influence in the motion-picture industry?

MR. TAYLOR. Well, of course, I have been looking for communism for a long time. I have been so strongly opposed to it for so many years; I think in the past 4 or 5 years, specifically, I have seen more indications which seemed to me to be signs of communistic activity in Hollywood and the motion-picture industry.

MR. STRIPLING. In any particular field?

MR. TAYLOR. No, sir. I suppose the most readily determined field in which it could be cited would be in the preparation of scripts—specifically, in the writing of those scripts. I have seen things from time to time which appeared to me to be slightly on the pink side, shall we say; at least, that was my personal opinion.

MR. STRIPLING. Could we have a little better order?

THE CHAIRMAN (pounding gavel). Please come to order.

MR. STRIPLING. Mr. Taylor, in referring to the writers, do you mean writers who are members of the Screen Writers Guild?

MR. TAYLOR. I assume that they are writers of the Screen Writers Guild. There seem to be many different factions in skills in Hollywood. I don't know just who belongs to what sometimes, but I assume they are members of the guild.

MR. STRIPLING. Are you a member of any guild?

MR. TAYLOR. I am a member of the Screen Actors Guild; yes, sir.

MR. STRIPLING. Have you ever noticed any elements within the Screen Actors Guild that you would consider to be following the Communist Party line?

MR. TAYLOR. Well, yes, sir; I must confess that I have. I am a member of the board of directors of the Screen Actors Guild. Quite recently I have been very active as a director of that board. It seems to me that at meetings, especially meetings of the general membership of the guild, there is always a certain group of actors and actresses whose every action would indicate to me that if they are not Communists they are working awfully hard to be Communists. I don't know. Their tactics and their philosophies seem to me to be pretty much party-line stuff. . . .

MR. STRIPLING. Mr. Taylor, these people in the Screen Actors Guild who, in your opinion follow the Communist Party line, are they a disrupting influence within the organization?

MR. TAYLOR. It seems so to me. In the meetings which I have attended, at least on issues in which apparently there is considerable unanimity of opinion, it always occurs that someone is not quite able to understand what the issue is and the meeting, instead of being over at 10 o'clock or 10:30 when it logically should be over, probably winds up running until

CHAPTER 9
THE SECOND
RED SCARE:
HUAC VS
HOLLYWOOD
(1947)

1 or 2 o'clock in the morning on such issues as points of order, and so on.

[In response to questions, Taylor named Howard DaSilva and Karen Morley as "disruptive" but refused to call them Communists.]

MR. STRIPLING. Mr. Taylor, have you ever participated in any picture as an actor which you considered contained Communist propaganda?

MR. TAYLOR. I assume we are now referring to Song of Russia. I must confess that I objected strenuously to doing Song of Russia at the time it was made. I felt that it, to my way of thinking at least, did contain Communist propaganda. However, that was my personal opinion. A lot of my friends and people whose opinions I respect did not agree with me.

When the script was first given me I felt it definitely contained Communist propaganda and objected to it upon that basis. I was assured by the studio that if there was Communist propaganda in that script it would be eliminated. I must admit that a great deal of the things to which I objected were eliminated.

Another thing which determined my attitude toward Song of Russia was the fact that I had recently been commissioned in the Navy and was awaiting orders. I wanted to go ahead and get in the Navy. However, it seems at the time there were many pictures being made to more or less strengthen the feeling of the American people toward Russia.

I did Song of Russia. I don't think it should have been made. I don't think it would be made today.

MR. STRIPLING. Mr. Taylor, in connection with the production of Song of Russia, do you know whether or not it was made at the suggestion of a representative of the Government?

MR. TAYLOR. I do not believe that it was made at the suggestion of a Government representative; no, sir. I think the script was written and prepared long before any representative of the Government became involved in it in any way.

MR. STRIPLING. Were you ever present at any meeting at which a representative of the Government was present and this picture was discussed?

MR. TAYLOR. Yes, sir; in Mr. L. B. Mayer's office. One day I was called to meet Mr. Mellett whom I met in the company of Mr. Mayer and, as I recall, the Song of Russia was discussed briefly. I don't think we were together more than 5 minutes.

It was disclosed at that time that the Government was interested in the picture being made and also pictures of that nature being made by other studios as well. As I say, it was to strengthen the feeling of the American people toward the Russian people at that time.

MR. STRIPLING. The Mellet you referred to is Mr. Lowell Mellett?

MR. TAYLOR. Yes, sir.

MR. STRIPLING. He was the Chief of the Bureau of Motion Pictures of the Office of War Information?

MR. TAYLOR. That is right. However, may I clarify something?

MR. STRIPLING. Yes; go right ahead.

MR. TAYLOR. If I ever gave the impression in anything that appeared previously that I was forced into making Song of Russia, I would like to say in my own defense, lest I look a little silly by saying I was ever forced to do the picture, I was not forced because nobody can force you to make any picture.

I objected to it but in deference to the situation as it then existed I did the picture. . . .

[Taylor then testified that he had seen scripts with communist material and had objected. He then named Lester Cole as a person who was "reputedly a Communist" and added that he would refuse to act in a film with a person he knew to be a Communist.]

MR. STRIPLING. You definitely consider them to be a bad influence upon the industry?

MR. TAYLOR. I certainly do; yes, sir.

MR. STRIPLING. They are a rotten apple in the barrel?

MR. TAYLOR. To me they are and I further believe 99.9 percent of the people in the motion-picture industry feel exactly as I do.

MR. STRIPLING. What do you think would be the best way to approach the problem of ridding the industry of the Communists who are now entrenched therein?

[Taylor's reply, a lengthy one, was that he would discharge all Communists from the motion picture industry. He said he believed most producers would do the same if they were protected by legislation.]

MR. STRIPLING. Mr. Taylor, do you consider that the motion picture primarily is a vehicle of entertainment and not of propaganda?

MR. TAYLOR. I certainly do. I think it is the primary job of the motion-picture industry to entertain; nothing more, nothing less.

MR. STRIPLING. Do you think the industry would be in a better position if it stuck strictly to entertainment without permitting political films to be made, without being so labeled?

CHAPTER 9

THE SECOND
RED SCARE:
HUAC VS
HOLLYWOOD
(1947)

MR. TAYLOR. I certainly do. Moreover, I feel that largely the picture business does stick to entertainment. I do not think they let themselves be side-tracked too much with propaganda films and things of that sort. Every once in a while things do sneak in that nobody catches. If the Communists are not working in the picture business there is no motive for their sneaking things in.

MR. STRIPLING. Mr. Taylor, returning to the picture Song of Russia for a moment, Miss Ayn Rand gave the committee a review of the picture several days ago. In the picture there were several scenes, particularly a wedding scene at which a priest officiated; also several other scenes at which the clergy was present. When you were making this picture were you under the impression that freedom of religion was enjoyed in Russia?

MR. TAYLOR. No sir; I never was under the impression that freedom of religion was enjoyed in Russia. However, I must confess when it got down to that part of the picture the picture was about two-thirds gone and it didn't actually occur to me until you mentioned it just a minute ago. . . .

10. Howard Rushmore, Journalist, Former Member (1936–1939) of the Communist Party.

. . . MR. STRIPLING. Did you ever hold any position in the Communist Party?

MR. RUSHMORE. I did.

MR. STRIPLING. Will you enumerate to the committee the positions you held in the party?

MR. RUSHMORE. Chiefly film critic for the Daily Worker. I was also on the Daily Worker as managing editor of their Sunday magazine, as city editor on Sunday, and had a few jobs like that, but chiefly as film critic.

MR. STRIPLING. Why did you break with the party?

MR. RUSHMORE. Largely over the review of Gone With the Wind, which I criticized for its defects, calling it a magnificent bore, but parts here and there I thought praiseworthy. For a period of a year the party had been insisting movies be handled in a much more tough fashion, shall I say, and I thought that to ask for a boycott of Gone With the Wind was a little strong. There developed quite an argument over that and I resigned and left the party December 27, 1939. . . .

MR. STRIPLING. Who was the commissar of the motion-picture industry when you were in the Communist Party?

MR. RUSHMORE. At the time I was there the person in charge of party activities in Hollywood was John Howard Lawson.

MR. STRIPLING. Mr. Chairman, John Howard Lawson is a writer——

MR. RUSHMORE. He is a writer.

MR. STRIPLING. And one of those who has been subpoenaed before the committee.

Did you ever meet John Howard Lawson?

MR. RUSHMORE. I did.

MR. STRIPLING. Where did you meet him?

MR. RUSHMORE. The date would be late 1937 or early 1938, on the ninth floor of the Communist Party headquarters, 35 East Twelfth Street.

MR. STRIPLING. The ninth floor. Is there any particular significance to the ninth floor?

MR. RUSHMORE. That is the inner sanctum, the place where the national officers of the Community Party have their headquarters. . . .

11. Ronald Reagan, Actor, President of the Screen Actor's Guild.

. . . MR. STRIPLING. As a member of the board of directors, as president of the Screen Actors Guild, and as an active member, have you at any time observed or noted within the organization a clique of either Communists or Fascists who were attempting to exert influence or pressure on the guild?

MR. REAGAN. . . . There has been a small group within the Screen Actors Guild which has consistently opposed the policy of the guild board and officers of the guild, as evidenced by the vote on various issues. That small clique referred to has been suspected of more or less following the tactics that we associate with the Communist Party.

MR. STRIPLING. Would you refer to them as a disruptive influence within the guild?

MR. REAGAN. I would say that at times they have attempted to be a disruptive influence.

MR. STRIPLING. You have no knowledge yourself as to whether or not any of them are members of the Communist Party?

MR. REAGAN. No, sir; I have no investigative force, or anything, and I do not know.

MR. STRIPLING. Has it ever been reported to you that certain members of the guild were Communists?

MR. REAGAN. Yes, sir; I have heard different discussions and some of them tagged as Communists. . . .

Whether the party should be outlawed, I agree with the gentlemen that preceded me that that is a matter for the Government to decide. As a citizen I would hesitate, or not like, to see any political party outlawed on the basis of its political ideology. We have spent 170 years in

CHAPTER 9

THE SECOND
RED SCARE:
HUAC VS
HOLLYWOOD
(1947)

this country on the basis that democracy is strong enough to stand up and fight against the inroads of any ideology. However, if it is proven that an organization is an agent of a power, a foreign power, or in any way not a legitimate political party, and I think the Government is capable of proving that, if the proof is there, then that is another matter. . . .

12. Gary Cooper, Film Actor.

. . . MR. SMITH. Are you a member of the Screen Actors Guild?

MR. COOPER. Yes; I have been a member since the guild was organized.

MR. SMITH. During the time that you have been in Hollywood, have you ever observed any communistic influence in Hollywood or in the motion-picture industry?

MR. COOPER. I believe I have noticed some.

MR. SMITH. What do you believe the principal medium is that they use Hollywood or the industry to inject propaganda?

MR. COOPER. Well, I believe it is done through word of mouth——

THE CHAIRMAN. Will you speak louder, please, Mr. Cooper?

MR. COOPER. I believe it is done through word of mouth and through the medium of pamphleting—and writers, I suppose.

MR. SMITH. By word of mouth, what do you mean, Mr. Cooper?

MR. COOPER. Well, I mean sort of social gatherings.

MR. SMITH. That has been your observation?

MR. COOPER. That has been my only observation; yes.

MR. SMITH. Can you tell us some of the statements that you may have heard at these gatherings that you believe are communistic?

MR. COOPER. Well, I have heard quite a few, I think, from time to time over the years. Well, I have heard tossed around such statements as, "Don't you think the Constitution of the United States is about 150 years out of date?" and—oh, I don't know—I have heard people mention that, well, "Perhaps this would be a more efficient Government without a Congress"—which statements I think are very un-American.

[Cooper then stated that he had turned down "quite a few scripts" because they contained communist ideas, but he could not recall the titles. He added that he turned down one script because it was about a man organizing an army "who would never fight to defend their country."]

MR. SMITH. Mr. Cooper, have you ever had any personal experience where you feel the Communist Party may have attempted to use you?

MR. COOPER. They haven't attempted to use me, I don't think, because, apparently, they know that I am not very sympathetic to communism. Several years ago, when communism was more of a social chit-chatter in parties for offices, and so on, when communism didn't have the implications that it has now, discussion of communism was more open and I remember hearing statements from some folks to the effect that the communistic system had a great many features that were desirable, one of which would be desirable to us in the motion-picture business in that it offered the actors and artists—in other words, the creative people—a special place in Government where we would be somewhat immune from the ordinary leveling of income. And as I remember, some actor's name was mentioned to me who had a house in Moscow which was very large—he had three cars, and stuff, with his house being quite a bit larger than my house in Beverly Hills at the time—and it looked to me like a pretty phony come-on to us in the picture business. From that time on, I could never take any of this pinko mouthing very seriously, because I didn't feel it was on the level.

[Evidence was then introduced that Communists in Italy had claimed that Cooper was sympathetic to communism and had advocated communism before an audience of 90,000 in Philadelphia. Cooper replied that he had never been to Philadelphia and understood that "you would have a hard time getting 90,000 people out in Philadelphia for anything."]

THE CHAIRMAN. Do you believe as a prominent person in your field that it would be wise for us, the Congress, to pass legislation to outlaw the Communist Party in the United States?

MR. COOPER. I think it would be a good idea, although I have never read Karl Marx and I don't know the basis of communism, beyond what I have picked up from hearsay. From what I hear, I don't like it because it isn't on the level. So I couldn't possibly answer that question. . . .

13. Lela E. Rogers, Mother and Manager of Ginger Rogers, Film Actress.

. . . THE CHAIRMAN. Mrs. Rogers, you stated that you had heard that Clifford Odets was a Communist. What do you base that upon?

MRS. ROGERS. I have here a column of Mr. O. O. McIntyre, date lined January 8, 1936, in which Mr. McIntyre says Mr. Clifford Odets, play writer, is a member of the Communist Party. I never saw that denied. . . .

[271]

CHAPTER 9

THE SECOND
RED SCARE:
HUAC VS
HOLLYWOOD
(1947)

MR. STRIPLING. Mrs. Rogers, Mr. Robert Taylor, and Mr. Robert Montgomery, among others, have testified that they would not act in a cast or picture in which Communists were in the cast, or in which Communist lines were written into the script. As your daughter's manager, so to speak, have you and your daughter ever objected to or turned down scripts because you felt that there were lines in there for her to speak which you felt were un-American or Communist propaganda?

MRS. ROGERS. Many times.

MR. STRIPLING. You have turned down many scripts for these reasons?

MRS. ROGERS. Yes, sir. We turned down Sister Carrie, by Theodore Dreiser, because it was just as open propaganda as None But the Lonely Heart. . . .

14. Walt Disney, Head, Walt Disney Studios.

. . . MR. SMITH. Have you had at any time, in your opinion, in the past, have you at any time in the past had any Communists employed at your studio?

MR. DISNEY. Yes; in the past I had some people that I definitely feel were Communists.

MR. SMITH. As a matter of fact, Mr. Disney, you experienced a strike at your studio, did you not?

MR. DISNEY. Yes.

MR. SMITH. And is it your opinion that that strike was instituted by members of the Communist Party to serve their purposes?

MR. DISNEY. Well, it proved itself so with time, and I definitely feel it was a Communist group trying to take over my artists and they did take them over.

THE CHAIRMAN. Do you say they did take them over?

MR. DISNEY. They did take them over.

MR. SMITH. Will you explain that to the committee, please?

[Disney related the story of the attempt by Herbert Sorrell, who Disney called a Communist, to shift his employees to another union. Disney demanded an election, and Sorrell countered with a strike. Disney then said he was smeared by "commie front organizations" and publications, which he proceeded to name. In that group he included the League of Women Voters but later apologized, saying his naming of that organization had been an error.]

15. John Howard Lawson, Screenwriter.

Mr. Stripling, the first witness.

MR. CRUM.[7] Mr. Chairman——

MR. STRIPLING. Mr. John Howard Lawson.

MR. CRUM. Mr. Chairman——

THE CHAIRMAN. I am sorry——

MR. CRUM. May I request the right of cross-examination? I ask you to bring back and permit us to cross-examine the witnesses, Adolph Menjou, Fred Niblo, John Charles Moffitt, Richard Macauley, Rupert Hughes, Sam Wood, Ayn Rand, James McGuinness——

THE CHAIRMAN. The request——

MR. CRUM. Howard Rushmore——

(The chairman pounding gavel.)

MR. CRUM. Morrie Ryskind, Oliver Carlson——

THE CHAIRMAN. The request is denied.

MR. CRUM. In order to show that these witnesses lied.

THE CHAIRMAN. That request is denied. Mr. Stripling, the first witness.

MR. STRIPLING. John Howard Lawson.

(John Howard Lawson, accompanied by Robert W. Kenny and Bartley Crum take places at witness table.)

THE CHAIRMAN. Stand and please raise your right hand. Do you solemnly swear the testimony you are about to give is the truth, the whole truth, and nothing but the truth, so help you God?

MR. LAWSON. I do.

THE CHAIRMAN. Sit down, please.

MR. LAWSON. Mr. Chairman, I have a statement here which I wish to make——

THE CHAIRMAN. Well, all right; let me see your statement.

(Statement handed to the chairman.)

MR. STRIPLING. Do you have a copy of that?

MR. CRUM. We can get you copies.

THE CHAIRMAN. I don't care to read any more of the statement. The statement will not be read. I read the first line.

MR. LAWSON. You have spent 1 week vilifying me before the American public——

THE CHAIRMAN. Just a minute——

7. Crum was an attorney representing the nineteen Hollywood figures who had been named as Communists.

CHAPTER 9

THE SECOND
RED SCARE:
HUAC VS
HOLLYWOOD
(1947)

MR. LAWSON. And you refuse to allow me to make a statement on my rights as an American citizen.

THE CHAIRMAN. I refuse you to make the statement, because of the first sentence in your statement. That statement is not pertinent to the inquiry.

Now, this is a congressional committee—a congressional committee set up by law. We must have orderly procedure, and we are going to have orderly procedure.

Mr. Stripling, identify the witness.

MR. LAWSON. The rights of American citizens are important in this room here, and I intend to stand up for those rights, Congressman Thomas.

MR. STRIPLING. Mr. Lawson, will you state your full name, please!

MR. LAWSON. I wish to protest against the unwillingness of this committee to read a statement, when you permitted Mr. Warner, Mr. Mayer, and others to read statements in this room.

My name is John Howard Lawson.

MR. STRIPLING. What is your present address?

MR. LAWSON. 9354 Burnett Avenue, San Fernando, Calif.

MR. STRIPLING. When and where were you born?

MR. LAWSON. New York City.

MR. STRIPLING. What year?

MR. LAWSON. 1984.

MR. STRIPLING. Give us the exact date.

MR. LAWSON. September 25.

MR. STRIPLING. Mr. Lawson, you are here in response to a subpena which was served upon you on September 19, 1947; is that true?

MR. LAWSON. That is correct. . . .

MR. STRIPLING. What is your occupation, Mr. Lawson?

MR. LAWSON. I am a writer.

MR. STRIPLING. How long have you been a writer?

MR. LAWSON. All my life—at least 35 years—my adult life.

MR. STRIPLING. Are you a member of the Screen Writers Guild?

MR. LAWSON. The raising of any question here in regard to membership, political beliefs,or affiliation——

MR. STRIPLING. Mr. Chairman——

MR. LAWSON. Is absolutely beyond the powers of this committee.

MR. STRIPLING. Mr. Chairman——

MR. LAWSON. But——

(The chairman pounding gavel.)

MR. LAWSON. It is a matter of public record that I am a member of the Screen Writers Guild.

MR. STRIPLING. I ask——

[Applause.]

THE CHAIRMAN. I want to caution the people in the audience: You are the guests of this committee and you will have to maintain order at all times. I do not care for any applause or any demonstrations of one kind or another.

MR. STRIPLING. Now, Mr. Chairman, I am also going to request that you instruct the witness to be responsive to the questions.

THE CHAIRMAN. I think the witness will be more responsive to the questions.

MR. LAWSON. Mr. Chairman, you permitted——

THE CHAIRMAN (pounding gavel). Never mind——

MR. LAWSON (continuing). Witnesses in this room to make answers of three or five hundred words to questions here.

THE CHAIRMAN. Mr. Lawson, you will please be responsive to these questions and not continue to try to disrupt these hearings.

MR. LAWSON. I am not on trial here, Mr. Chairman. This committee is on trial here before the American people. Let us get that straight.

THE CHAIRMAN. We don't want you to be on trial.

MR. STRIPLING. Mr. Lawson, how long have you been a member of the Screen Writers Guild?

MR. LAWSON. Since it was founded in its present form, in 1933.

MR. STRIPLING. Have you ever held any office in the guild?

MR. LAWSON. The question of whether I have held office is also a question which is beyond the purview of this committee.

(The chairman pounding gavel.)

MR. LAWSON. It is an invasion of the right of association under the Bill of Rights of this country.

THE CHAIRMAN. Please be responsive to the question.

MR. LAWSON. It is also a matter——

(The chairman pounding gavel.)

MR. LAWSON. Of public record——

THE CHAIRMAN. You asked to be heard. Through your attorney, you asked to be heard. And we want you to be heard. And if you don't care to be heard, then we will excuse you and we will put the record in without your answers.

MR. LAWSON. I wish to frame my own answers to your questions, Mr. Chairman, and I intend to do so.

THE CHAIRMAN. And you will be responsive to the questions or you will be excused from the witness stand.

MR. LAWSON. I will frame my own answers, Mr. Chairman.

THE CHAIRMAN. Go ahead, Mr. Stripling.

CHAPTER 9

THE SECOND
RED SCARE:
HUAC VS
HOLLYWOOD
(1947)

MR. STRIPLING. I repeat the question, Mr. Lawson: Have you ever held any position in the Screen Writers Guild?

MR. LAWSON. I stated that it is outside the purview of the rights of this committee to inquire into any form of association——

THE CHAIRMAN. The Chair will determine what is in the purview of this committee.

MR. LAWSON. My rights as an American citizen are no less than the responsibilities of this committee of Congress.

THE CHAIRMAN. Now you are just making a big scene for yourself and getting all "het up." [Laughter.]

Be responsive to the questioning, just the same as all the witnesses have. You are no different from the rest.

Go ahead, Mr. Stripling.

MR. LAWSON. I am being treated differently from the rest.

THE CHAIRMAN. You are not being treated differently.

MR. LAWSON. Other witnesses have made statements, which included quotations from books, references to material which had no connection whatsoever with the interest of this committee.

THE CHAIRMAN. We will determine whether it has connection.

Now, you go ahead——

MR. LAWSON. It is absolutely beyond the power of this committee to inquire into my association in any organization.

THE CHAIRMAN. Mr. Lawson, you will have to stop or you will leave the witness stand. And you will leave the witness stand because you are in contempt. That is why you will leave the witness stand. And if you are just trying to force me to put you in contempt, you won't have to try much harder. You know what has happened to a lot of people that have been in contempt of this committee this year, don't you?

MR. LAWSON. I am glad you have made it perfectly clear that you are going to threaten and intimidate the witnesses, Mr. Chairman.

(The chairman pounding gavel.)

MR. LAWSON. I am an American and I am not at all easy to intimidate, and don't think I am.

(The chairman pounding gavel.)

MR. STRIPLING. Mr. Lawson, I repeat the question. Have you ever held any position in the Screen Writers Guild?

MR. LAWSON. I have stated that the question is illegal. But it is a matter of public record that I have held many offices in the Screen Writers Guild. I was its first president, in 1933, and I have held office on the board of directors of the Screen Writers Guild at other times.

MR. STRIPLING. You have been employed in the motion-picture industry; have you not?

MR. LAWSON. I have.

MR. STRIPLING. Would you state some of the studios where you have been employed?

MR. LAWSON. Practically all of the studios, all the major studios.

MR. STRIPLING. As a screen writer?

MR. LAWSON. That is correct.

MR. STRIPLING. Would you list some of the pictures which you have written the script for?

MR. LAWSON. I must state again that you are now inquiring into the freedom of press and communications, over which you have no control whatsoever. You don't have to bring me here 3,000 miles to find out what pictures I have written. The pictures that I have written are very well known. They are such pictures as Action in the North Atlantic, Sahara——

MR. STRIPLING. Mr. Lawson——

MR. LAWSON. Such pictures as Blockade, of which I am very proud and in which I introduced the danger that this democracy faced from the attempt to destroy democracy in Spain in 1937. These matters are all matters of public record.

MR. STRIPLING. Mr. Lawson, would you object if I read a list of the pictures, and then you can either state whether or not you did write the scripts?

MR. LAWSON. I have no objection at all.

MR. STRIPLING. Did you write Dynamite, by M-G-M?

MR. LAWSON. I preface my answer, again, by saying that it is outside the province of this committee, but it is well known that I did.

MR. STRIPLING. The Sea Bat, by M-G-M?

MR. LAWSON. It is well known that I did.

MR. STRIPLING. Success at Any Price, RKO?

MR. LAWSON. Yes; that is from a play of mine, Success Story.

MR. STRIPLING. Party Wire, Columbia?

MR. LAWSON. Yes; I did.

MR. STRIPLING. Blockade, United Artists, Wanger?

MR. LAWSON. That is correct.

MR. STRIPLING. Algiers, United Artists, Wanger?

MR. LAWSON. Correct.

MR. STRIPLING. Earth Bound, Twentieth Century Fox.

MR. LAWSON. Correct.

MR. STRIPLING. Counterattack, Columbia.

CHAPTER 9

THE SECOND
RED SCARE:
HUAC VS
HOLLYWOOD
(1947)

MR. LAWSON. Correct.

MR. STRIPLING. You have probably written others; have you not, Mr. Lawson?

MR. LAWSON. Many others. You have missed a lot of them.

MR. STRIPLING. You don't care to furnish them to the committee, do you?

MR. LAWSON. Not in the least interested.

MR. STRIPLING. Mr. Lawson, are you now, or have you ever been a member of the Communist Party of the United States?

MR. LAWSON. In framing my answer to that question I must emphasize the points that I have raised before. The question of communism is in no way related to this inquiry, which is an attempt to get control of the screen and to invade the basic rights of American citizens in all fields.

MR. MCDOWELL. Now, I must object——

MR. STRIPLING. Mr. Chairman——

(The chairman pounding gavel.)

MR. LAWSON. The question here relates not only to the question of my membership in any political organization, but this committee is attempting to establish the right——

(The chairman pounding gavel.)

MR. LAWSON (continuing). Which has been historically denied to any committee of this sort, to invade the rights and privileges and immunity of American citizens, whether they be Protestant, Methodist, Jewish, or Catholic, whether they be Republican or Democrats or anything else.

THE CHAIRMAN (pounding gavel). Mr. Lawson, just quiet down again.

Mr. Lawson, the most pertinent question that we can ask is whether or not you have ever been a member of the Communist Party. Now, do you care to answer that question?

MR. LAWSON. You are using the old technique, which was used in Hitler Germany in order to create a scare here——

THE CHAIRMAN (pounding gavel). Oh——

MR. LAWSON. In order to create an entirely false atmosphere in which this hearing is conducted——

(The chairman pounding gavel.)

MR. LAWSON. In order that you can then smear the motion-picture industry, and you can proceed to the press, to any form of communication in this country.

THE CHAIRMAN. You have learned——

MR. LAWSON. The Bill of Rights was established precisely to prevent the operation of any committee which could invade the basic rights of Americans.

Now, if you want to know——

MR. STRIPLING. Mr. Chairman, the witness is not answering the question.

MR. LAWSON. If you want to know——

(The chairman pounding gavel.)

MR. LAWSON. About the perjury that has been committed here and the perjury that is planned.

THE CHAIRMAN. Mr. Lawson——

MR. LAWSON. You permit me and my attorneys to bring in here the witnesses that testified last week and you permit us to cross-examine these witnesses, and we will show up the whole tissue of lie——

THE CHAIRMAN (pounding gavel). We are going to get the answer to that question if we have to stay here for a week.

Are you a member of the Communist Party, or have you ever been a member of the Communist Party?

MR. LAWSON. It is unfortunate and tragic that I have to teach this committee the basic principles of American——

THE CHAIRMAN (pounding gavel). That is not the question. That is not the question. The question is: Have you ever been a member of the Communist Party?

MR. LAWSON. I am framing my answer in the only way in which any American citizen can frame his answer to a question which absolutely invades his rights.

THE CHAIRMAN. Then you refuse to answer that question; is that correct?

MR. LAWSON. I have told you that I will offer my beliefs, affiliations, and everything else to the American public, and they will know where I stand.

THE CHAIRMAN (pounding gavel). Excuse the witness——

MR. LAWSON. As they do from what I have written.

THE CHAIRMAN (pounding gavel). Stand away from the stand——

MR. LAWSON. I have written Americanism for many years, and I shall continue to fight for the Bill of Rights, which you are trying to destroy.

THE CHAIRMAN. Officers, take this man away from the stand——[8]

[Applause and boos.]

THE CHAIRMAN (pounding gavel). There will be no demonstrations. No demonstrations, for or against. Everyone will please be seated. . . .

8. After Lawson had been led from the stand, the committee's investigator produced what he said was Lawson's Communist Party membership card.

CHAPTER 9

THE SECOND
RED SCARE:
HUAC VS
HOLLYWOOD
(1947)

16. Eric Johnston, Motion Picture Executive, President of the Motion Picture Association of America.

I'm not here to try to whitewash Hollywood, and I'm not here to help sling a tar brush at it, either.

I want to stick to the facts as I see them.

There are several points I'd like to make to this committee.

The first one is this: A damaging impression of Hollywood has spread all over the country as a result of last week's hearings. You have a lot of sensational testimony about Hollywood. From some of it the public will get the idea that Hollywood is running over with Communists and communism.

I believe the impression which has gone out is the sort of scare-head stuff which is grossly unfair to a great American industry. It must be a great satisfaction to the Communist leadership in this country to have people believe that Hollywood Communists are astronomical in number and almost irresistible in power.

Now, what are the facts? Not everybody in Hollywood is a Communist. I have said before that undoubtedly there are Communists in Hollywood, but in my opinion the percentage is extremely small.

I have had a number of close looks at Hollywood in the last 2 years, and I have looked at it through the eyes of an average businessman. I recognize that as the world's capital of show business, there is bound to be a lot of show business in Hollywood. There is no business, Mr. Chairman, like show business. But underneath there is the solid foundation of patriotic, hardworking, decent citizens. Making motion pictures is hard work. You just don't dash off a motion picture between social engagements.

The great bulk of Hollywood people put their jobs first. But I can assure you you won't find a community in the country where hearts are any bigger or the purses more open when it comes to helping out worthy endeavors. Take any national campaign for the public good, and you'll find Hollywood people contributing their time and their money.

Every other country in the world is trying to build up its motion-picture industry, and I can verify that, having just traveled in 12 countries in Europe where they are all trying to build up their motion-picture industry. These governments are trying to do it through government subsidies and devices of all kinds. The American motion-picture industry grew by its own efforts. It has rejected subsidies and Government assistance. It wants no hand-out from Government. All it asks is a fair shake and a chance to live and to grow and to serve its country without being unfairly condemned and crucified.

I wind up my first point with a request of this committee. The damaging impression about Hollywood should be corrected. I urge your committee to do so in these public hearings.

There is another damaging impression which should be corrected. The report of the subcommittee said that some of the most flagrant Communist propaganda films were produced as the result of White House pressure. This charge has been completely refuted by the testimony before you.

My second point includes another request of the committee.

The report of your subcomittee stated that you had a list of all pictures produced in Hollywood in the last 8 years which contained Communist propaganda. Your committee has not made this list public. Until the list is made public the industry stands condemned by unsupported generalizations, and we are denied the opportunity to refute these charges publicly.

Again, I remind the committee that we have offered to put on a special showing of any or all of the pictures which stand accused so that you can see for yourselves what's in them. The contents of the pictures constitute the only proof.

Unless this evidence is presented and we are given the chance to refute it in these public hearings, it is the obligation of the committee to absolve the industry from the charges against it.

Now, I come to my third point—a vitally important one to every American and to the system under which we live.

It is free speech.

Now, I've been advised by some persons to lay off it. I've been told that if I mentioned it I'd be playing into the hands of Communists. But nobody has a monopoly on the issue of free speech in this country. I'm not afraid of being right, even if that puts me in with the wrong company. I've been for free speech ever since I first read the lives of great men of the past who fought and died for this principle—and that was in grade school.

There is nothing I can add to what every great American has said on the subject since the founding of the Republic. Our freedoms would become empty and meaningless without the keystone of our freedom arch—freedom of speech—freedom to speak, to hear, and to see.

When I talk about freedom of speech in connection with this hearing, I mean just this: You don't need to pass a law to choke off free speech or seriously curtail it. Intimidation or coercion will do it just as well. You can't make good and honest motion pictures in an atmosphere of fear.

I intend to use every influence at my command to keep the screen free. I don't propose that Government shall tell the motion-picture industry, directly or by coercion, what kind of pictures it ought to make. I am as whole-

CHAPTER 9
THE SECOND
RED SCARE:
HUAC VS
HOLLYWOOD
(1947)

souledly against that as I would be against dictating to the press or the radio, to the book publishers or to the magazines.

One of the most amazing paradoxes has grown out of this hearing. At one point we were accused of making Communist propaganda by not making pictures which show the advantages of our system. In other words, we were accused of putting propaganda on the screen by keeping it out.

That sort of reasoning is a little staggering, especially when you know the story of American pictures in some foreign countries. We are accused of Communist propaganda at home, but in Communist-dominated countries in Europe our motion-picture films are banned because they contain propaganda for capitalism.

We can't be communistic and capitalistic at one and the same time. I've said it before, but I'd like to repeat it. There is nothing more feared or hated in Communist countries than the American motion picture.

To sum up this point: We insist on our rights to decide what will or will not go in our pictures. We are deeply conscious of the responsibility this freedom involves, but we have no intention to violate this trust by permitting subversive propaganda in our films.

Now, my next point is this:

When I was before this committee last March, I said that I wanted to see Communists exposed. I still do. I'm heart and soul for it. An exposed Communist is an unarmed Communist. Expose them, but expose them in the traditional American manner.

But I believe that when this committee or any other agency undertakes to expose communism it must be scrupulous to avoid tying a red tag on innocent people by indiscriminate labeling.

It seems to me it is getting dangerously easy to call a man a Communist without proof or even reasonable suspicion. When a distinguished leader of the Republican Party in the United States Senate is accused of following the Communist Party line for introducing a housing bill, it is time, gentlemen, to give a little serious thought to the dangers of thoughtless smearing by gossip and hearsay.

Senator Robert Taft isn't going to worry about being called a Communist. But not every American is a Senator Taft who can properly ignore such an accusation. Most of us in America are just little people, and loose charges can hurt little people. They take away everything a man has—his livelihood, his reputation, and his personal dignity.

When just one man is falsely damned as a Communist in an hour like this when the Red issue is at white heat, no one of us is safe.

Gentlemen, I maintain that preservation of the rights of the individual is a proper duty for this Committee on Un-American Activities. This country's entire tradition is based on the principle that the individual is a higher power than the state; that the state owes its authority to the individual, and must treat him accordingly.

Expose communism, but don't put any American who isn't a Communist in a concentration camp of suspicion. We are not willing to give up our freedoms to save our freedoms.

I now come to my final point:

What are we going to do positively and constructively about combating communism? It isn't enough to be anti-Communist any more than it is to be antismallpox. You can still die from smallpox if you haven't used a serum against it. A positive program is the best antitoxin of the plague of communism.

Communism must have breeding grounds. Men and women who have a reasonable measure of opportunity aren't taken in by the prattle of Communists. Revolutions plotted by frustrated intellectuals at cocktail parties won't get anywhere if we wipe out the potential causes of communism. The most effective way is to make democracy work for greater opportunity, for greater participation, for greater security for all our people.

The real breeding ground of communism is in the slums. It is everywhere where people haven't enough to eat or enough to wear through no fault of their own. Communism hunts misery, feeds on misery, and profits by it.

Freedoms walk hand-in-hand with abundance. That has been the history of America. It has been the American story. It turned the eyes of the world to America, because America gave reality to freedom, plus abundance when it was still an idle daydream in the rest of the world.

We have been the greatest exporter of freedom, and the world is hungry for it. Today it needs our wheat and our fuel to stave off hunger and fight off cold, but hungry and cold as they may be, men always hunger for freedom.

We want to continue to practice and to export freedom.

If we fortify our democracy to lick want, we will lick communism—here and abroad. Communists can hang all the iron curtains they like, but they'll never be able to shut out the story of a land where freemen walk without fear and live with abundance.

[Applause.]

(The chairman pounding gavel.) . . .

[Following Johnston's testimony, nine of the unfriendly witnesses were called: Dalton Trumbo, Alvin Maltz, Alvah Bessie, Samuel Ornitz, Herbert Biberman, Edward Dmytryk, Adrian Scott, Ring Lardner, Jr., and Lester Cole. With the exception of Maltz, none was allowed to make a statement, each was forced from the witness chair,

CHAPTER 9
THE SECOND
RED SCARE:
HUAC VS
HOLLYWOOD
(1947)

and then was identified by the committee's investigator as having been a card-carry-ing member of the Communist Party. Only later was the authenticity of those cards ever challenged.]

THE CHAIRMAN. The Chair would like to make this statement.

The hearings today conclude the first phase of the committee's investigation of communism in the motion-picture industry. While we have heard 39 witnesses, there are many more to be heard. The Chair stated earlier in the hearing he would present the records of 79 prominent people associated with the motion-picture industry who were members of the Communist Party or who had records of Communist affiliations. We have had before us 11 of these individuals. There are 68 to go. This hearing has concerned itself principally with spotlighting Communist personnel in the industry.

There is, however, an equally dangerous phase of this inquiry which deals with Communist propaganda in various motion pictures and the techniques employed. At the present time the committee has a special staff making an extensive study of this phase of the committee's inquiry. Either the full committee or a subcommittee will resume hearings on this matter in the near future, either in Washington or in Los Angeles, at which time those persons whose Communist records the committee has will be given an opportunity to appear before the committee to confirm or deny those affiliations. We will also have a number of witnesses who will deal with propaganda in the films and the techniques employed.

I want to emphasize that the committee is not adjourning sine die, but will resume hearings as soon as possible. The committee hearings for the past 2 weeks have clearly shown the need for this investigation. Ten prominent figures in Hollywood whom the committee had evidence were members of the Communist Party were brought before us and refused to deny that they were Communists. It is not necessary for the Chair to emphasize the harm which the motion-picture industry suffers from the presence within its ranks of known Communists who do not have the best interests of the United States at heart. The industry should set about immediately to clean its own house and not wait for public opinion to force it to do so.

The hearings are adjourned.

(Whereupon, at 3 p.m., the committee adjourned.)

QUESTIONS TO CONSIDER

Those who attended the first day of the HUAC hearings should have had a good indication of what was to follow. How did HUAC chairman J. Parnell Thomas set the tone for the hearings in his opening remarks? Toward the end of his opening remarks, Thomas said, "All we are after are the facts." Do you think that statement was true?

Jack L. Warner's testimony is typical of that given by friendly witnesses at the hearings. In what way was it typical? How did his opening statement attempt to satisfy the committee while at the same time defend his studio? Was the committee satisfied? What did it attempt to get Warner to say? Was Samuel Wood more cooperative?

Before the hearings began, Thomas claimed on the floor of Congress that HUAC had a complete list of Hollywood-made films that contained communist propaganda. During the hearings, the committee focused its attention on two films: *Mission to Moscow* and *Song of Russia*. By looking at the testimonies of Jack Warner, Louis Mayer, Ayn Rand, and Robert Taylor, what was the committee trying to get the witnesses to say? To what extent do you think *Mission to Moscow* and *Song of Russia* were pieces of communist propaganda? Use the evidence to bolster your case. To what extent do you think the federal government encouraged the making of these pictures (HUAC spent a good deal of time on this question)? If the government did so, why? On the other hand, what was the committee apparently trying to establish?

One of the important things a historian must do is evaluate the validity of testimony. A good question to ask is: was an individual who gave testimony in a position to know about those things she or he claimed to have known? Using that criterion, how would you evaluate the validity of the testimonies of Menjou, Moffitt, Hughes, Rushmore, and Reagan? Which ones were in the best positions to know the facts? How does Reagan's testimony "fit" with the others? How does Warner's testimony fit with the others? To what extent does this testimony expose the threat of communist infiltration into the film industry?

Gary Cooper, Lela Rogers, and Walt Disney were extremely well-known figures in Hollywood and in the nation in general. What did their testimony add to the proceedings? Did they add any hard evidence to support HUAC's investigation?

John Howard Lawson was the first unfriendly witness to be called. As you already know, he had been identified previously by a number of witnesses as a Communist. Do you think he was a Communist? Do you think he posed a significant threat to the United States? To the film industry? Did the committee treat Lawson differently than earlier witnesses? On another note, why do you think Lawson (and others) refused to answer when asked if they were Communists? Do you think this tactic was a wise one?

Eric Johnston's statement to the committee is an important part of the hearings. What were its principal points?

CHAPTER 9

THE SECOND
RED SCARE:
HUAC VS
HOLLYWOOD
(1947)

What do you think of those points? Would you call Johnston a friendly or an unfriendly witness, or neither? For example, do you think Johnston viewed HUAC's investigation of Hollywood as beneficial or detrimental to the nation's interests? Use his testimony to prove your point.

J. Parnell Thomas's closing remarks offered a broad hint to motion picture executives who wanted the hearings stopped because of possible unfriendly publicity. What hint did Thomas give? What do you think of the process he suggested?

EPILOGUE

Two days after the HUAC hearings adjourned, the New York *Herald Tribune* commented that they had produced "a good deal of nonsense and very little else." Although at least some of the unfriendly witnesses undoubtedly were Communists, the committee failed to uncover any effective conspiracy to mold American public opinion through the movies. Nevertheless, an aroused public and nervous New York financial interests upon which Hollywood relied demanded that film executives take steps to bar "suspicious" people from the film industry. In November 1947, fifty motion picture executives held a two-day meeting at the Waldorf-Astoria Hotel in New York, at which they established an informal but highly effective blacklist that prevented suspicious people from finding jobs in films. No studio would hire a blacklisted writer, director, producer, actor, or actress, nor would any film in which a blacklisted person had taken part be distributed. Some careers were permanently ruined; other men and women were unable to find work in films for years; still others, like screenwriter Carl Foreman, were forced to leave the

United States to continue their film work. As actor and strong anti-Communist John Wayne said, "I'll never regret having helped run [Carl] Foreman out of the country."[9] Also in November 1947, the House of Representatives voted that the ten unfriendly witnesses (by this time dubbed the "Hollywood Ten") were in contempt of Congress, and they were sentenced to prison and fines. After their appeals were exhausted, the ten began serving their prison terms in 1950.

By then, cold war tensions had increased markedly. In 1948, former Communist Whittaker Chambers accused Alger Hiss, once a well-placed figure in the State Department, of being a Communist. Although the case is still a fairly controversial one, Hiss's later conviction for perjury seemed to give weight to Chambers's charges. Moreover, in 1948 to 1949, the crisis in

9. Before Foreman was blacklisted and forced to leave Hollywood, he and Stanley Kramer collaborated on the film *High Noon,* considered by many to be a film classic and the first adult western. The film was released early in 1952 and won the New York Film Critics' award for best picture of 1952.

Berlin reached its height when the Soviets blockaded Berlin and the United States and its allies airlifted food and supplies to the city. Then, in 1949, the American-backed Nationalist government in China fell to the Communists, led by Mao Zedong. Nearly hysterical, Americans asked themselves how this tragedy had occurred.

In February 1950, then little-known junior senator from Wisconsin Joseph McCarthy provided what for many Americans was an "answer" to that question. China had fallen and communism was growing stronger, McCarthy asserted, because the government was riddled with Communists who, he charged, had burrowed their way into the State Department, the Voice of America, and even the United States Army. In a series of highly publicized investigations, in the end McCarthy actually proved little or nothing. Yet his charges, many of them without any foundation, made Americans even more nervous. The federal government revived the Smith Act (1940) and used the recently enacted McCarren Internal Securities Act to investigate and remove suspicious persons from government service. The careers of several innocent people were permanently damaged.

In June 1950, the cold war suddenly became very hot. On June 25, troops from communist North Korea invaded United States-supported South Korea. Truman responded immediately, sending United States troops to help the beleaguered South Koreans. These forces had turned the tide of battle when Mao Zedong sent Chinese troops into battle on the side of North Korea.

As in the 1920s, however, the red scare of the late 1940s and 1950s gradually abated. Senator Joseph McCarthy had been discredited in the 1954 Army hearings, was censured by the United States Senate in that same year, and died in 1957. Many believe that the televising of the 1954 Army-McCarthy hearings proved the Senator's undoing, a blow from which he never recovered. Gradually, Americans came to believe that it was better to try to negotiate with Communists in the Soviet Union, China, and elsewhere than to try to eradicate them. Indeed, even Ronald Reagan, who was a "cold warrior" and who once referred to the Soviet Union as the "evil empire," as president was willing to negotiate with the Soviets on cutbacks in nuclear weapons.

Those who had been blacklisted in Hollywood gradually drifted back into the industry, a few even recapturing their former prominence. Dalton Trumbo and Ring Lardner, Jr., both members of the Hollywood Ten, actually increased in prestige, Trumbo as the screenwriter for *Spartacus* (1960) and Lardner for his work on *The Cincinnati Kid* (1965) and *M*A*S*H* (1970). Carl Foreman, who wrote the script for *High Noon,* remained in England, where he wrote or cowrote the screenplays for *The Bridge on the River Kwai, The Mouse That Roared, The Guns of Navaronne,* and *The Victors.* In certain cases, however, his work was uncredited because some major studios still feared repercussions if they openly re-employed blacklisted artists. Hollywood Ten member Herbert Biberman formed a company of blacklisted artists that made the 1954 film *Salt of the Earth,* a powerful and

CHAPTER 9

THE SECOND
RED SCARE:
HUAC VS
HOLLYWOOD
(1947)

moving picture about a miners' strike in New Mexico. But that film itself was blacklisted and was not generally released until the 1960s. It is now available on videocassette and, because of its history, has become something of a cult classic.

For its part, HUAC never gave Congress a formal report of its findings from the 1947 hearings on communism in Hollywood, probably because, as you have seen, there was little evidence to support its sensational charges. In 1951, HUAC turned its attention once again to Hollywood, with equally inconclusive results, although more unfriendly witnesses were blacklisted.

Throughout the 1950s, HUAC continued its sensational and well-publicized investigations of communism in the United States, most of which uncovered little or nothing. In the 1960s, the committee (in 1969 renamed the House Committee on Internal Security) conducted a series of outlandish investigations of civil rights groups and Vietnam War protesters. In January 1975, the committee was permanently disbanded. By that time, however, it had accumulated information on more than 750,000 Americans, the vast majority of whom had had no affiliation with communism.

In Hollywood itself, the investigations left a residue of bitterness, anger, suspicion, and loss of community cohesion. In that sense, the Hollywood community was a microcosm of America itself during its second Red Scare.

CHAPTER TEN

A GENERATION IN WAR
AND TURMOIL:
THE AGONY OF VIETNAM

Time magazine called it "history's largest happening" when 400,000 young people—most between the ages of sixteen and thirty—gathered together on an August weekend in 1969 for a rock concert. The Woodstock Music and Art Fair, held on a six hundred-acre farm in upstate New York, featured such well-established stars as Jimi Hendrix, Janis Joplin, and Jefferson Airplane along with a host of relative newcomers such as Joe Cocker and the group Crosby, Stills, and Nash. Inadequate sanitation facilities, a shortage of food, and pouring rain did not hamper the harmony and community spirit of the crowd. Although police estimated that almost 90 percent of the concert goers were smoking marijuana, there were no reported rapes, fights, or robberies and very few arrests. "People are finally getting together," one young man told a reporter.

He could not have been more wrong. Thousands of miles away, on the other side of the world, other young Americans were fighting a desperate war in Southeast Asia. And even at Woodstock, people were singing along with Country Joe McDonald in his popular, satirical antiwar song:

> And it's 1,2,3,
> What are we fighting for?
> Don't ask me I don't give a damn
> Next stop is Vietnam

Many people, of course, did care very much, and Americans were bitterly divided over the question of our participation in the war in Vietnam. In this chapter, you will be analyzing the experiences of several members of the baby boom generation so as to understand these differences in public opinion. Why did some people disagree so strongly about the war?

CHAPTER 10

A GENERATION
IN WAR AND
TURMOIL: THE
AGONY OF
VIETNAM

BACKGROUND

Not quite one year after Woodstock, on May 4, 1970, a group of students at Kent State University in Ohio were protesting against the United States' military activities in Vietnam. Such protests had been spreading across college campuses since President Nixon had announced an "incursion"[1] into Cambodia in a television speech four days earlier. In response to the protests, the Ohio National Guard was called out to keep order. While a large crowd gathered, some protesting students gave flowers to the guardsmen, many of whom were about the same age as the students, and urged them to "make love, not war." But others threw stones at the guardsmen and taunted them. Tensions rose until shots rang out—the guardsmen had fired into a crowd of students. Four students were killed, and eleven were wounded.

Shock spread across the nation. Many college students went on strike, disrupting or shutting down more than 250 college campuses. Increasing numbers of antiwar protesters went to Washington, D.C., to demonstrate against the widening war in Southeast Asia.

Not all Americans, however, were outraged by the National Guard's actions at Kent State. On May 8 in New York City, a group of angry construction workers clashed violently with a group of equally angry antiwar demonstrators. The issue was the American flag at City Hall, which had been lowered to half staff as a sign of mourning for the dead Kent State students. The construction workers wanted to raise the flag to full staff, and they won the battle—city officials raised the flag.

What caused the deep divisions that exploded among Americans in the wake of Kent State? A partial answer to this question involves understanding two long-term trends: the United States' involvement in Southeast Asia and the socioeconomic changes in American life that simultaneously were taking place.

The United States emerged from World War II as a superpower confronting another superpower, its former wartime ally, the Soviet Union. Both nations and their allies struggled to influence neutral countries in Europe, Latin America, Africa, and Asia. As we know, the resulting tensions and confrontations were characterized as the cold war. The basic bipartisan[2] foreign policy of the United States during this period was containment: a commitment to stop the spread of communism (and the influence of the Soviet Union) by all means short of total war. Regional defense alliances such as NATO and SEATO, massive economic aid and programs like the Marshall Plan, technological and advisory military aid envisioned in the Truman

---

1. "Incursion" is a word used as a euphemism for air strikes and a land invasion.

2. "Bipartisan" means supported by both political parties.

and Eisenhower Doctrines, and bilateral defense treaties like that between the United States and South Korea were all part of containment.[3]

The Japanese defeat of Western colonial powers, particularly Britain and France, in the early days of World War II had encouraged nationalist movements[4] in both Africa and Asia. The final surrender of Japan in 1945 left an almost total power vacuum in Southeast Asia. As Britain struggled with postwar economic dislocation and, within India, the independence movement, both the United States and the Soviet Union moved into this vacuum, hoping to influence the course of events in Asia.

Vietnam had long been a part of the French colonial empire in Southeast Asia and was known in the West as French Indochina. At the beginning of World War II, the Japanese had driven the French from the area. Under the leadership of Vietnamese nationalist (and Communist) Ho Chi Minh, the Vietnamese cooperated with American intelligence agents and fought in guerilla-style warfare against the Japanese. When the Japanese were finally driven from Vietnam in 1945, Ho Chi Minh declared Vietnam independent.

The Western nations, however, did not recognize this declaration. At the end of World War II, France wanted to re-establish Vietnam as a French colony, but seriously weakened by war, France could not re-establish itself in Vietnam without assistance. At this point the United States, eager to gain France as a postwar ally and NATO member, and viewing European problems as being more immediate than problems in Asia, chose to help the French reenter Vietnam as colonial masters. From 1945 to 1954, the United States gave more than $2 billion in financial aid to France so that it could regain its former colony. The U.S. aid was contingent upon the eventual development of self-government in French Indochina.

Ho Chi Minh and other Vietnamese felt that they had been betrayed. They believed that in return for fighting against the Japanese in World War II, they would earn their independence. Many Vietnamese viewed the reentry of France, with the United States' assistance, as a broken promise. Almost immediately, war broke out between the forces of the French and their westernized Vietnamese allies and the forces of Ho Chi Minh. In the cold war atmosphere of the late 1940s and early 1950s, the United States gave massive aid to the French who, it was maintained, were fighting against monolithic communism.

The fall of Dien Bien Phu in 1954 spelled the end of French power in Vietnam. The U.S. Secretary of State, John Foster Dulles, tried hard to convince

---

3. NATO is an acronym for North Atlantic Treaty Organization, SEATO for Southeast Asia Treaty Organization. The Marshall Plan called for massive economic aid to western Europe. The Truman and Eisenhower Doctrines offered military and technical aid to countries resisting communism.
4. Those in nationalist movements seek independence for their countries.

5. The Berlin Wall is a barricade created to separate East Berlin (Communist) from West Berlin. The Bay of Pigs invasion was a U.S.-sponsored invasion of Cuba in April 1961 that failed. The American role was widely criticized.

CHAPTER 10

A GENERATION
IN WAR AND
TURMOIL: THE
AGONY OF
VIETNAM

Britain and other Western allies of the need for "united action" in Southeast Asia and to avoid any use of American ground troops (as President Truman had authorized earlier in Korea). The allies were not persuaded, however. Rather than let the area fall to the Communists, President Eisenhower and his secretary of state eventually allowed the temporary division of Vietnam into two sections—South Vietnam, ruled by westernized Vietnamese formerly loyal to the French, and North Vietnam, governed by the Communist Ho Chi Minh.

Free and open elections to unify the country were to be held in 1956. However, the elections were never held because American policymakers feared that Ho Chi Minh would easily defeat the unpopular but pro-United States Ngo Dinh Diem, the United States' choice to lead South Vietnam. From 1955 to 1960, the United States supported Diem with more than $1 billion of aid as civil war between the South Vietnamese and the Northern Vietminh (later called the Vietcong) raged across the countryside and in the villages.

President Kennedy did little to improve the situation. Facing his own cold war problems with the building of the Berlin Wall and the Bay of Pigs invasion,[5] Kennedy simply poured more money and more "military advisers" (close to seventeen thousand by 1963) into the troubled country. Finally, in the face of tremendous Vietnamese pressure, the United States turned against Diem, and in 1963, South Vietnamese generals, encouraged by the American Central Intelligence Agency, overthrew the corrupt and repressive Diem regime. Diem was assassinated in the fall of 1963, shortly before Kennedy's assassination.

Lyndon Johnson, the Texas Democrat who succeeded Kennedy in 1963 and won election as president in 1964, was an old New Dealer[6] who wished to extend social and economic programs to needy Americans. The "tragedy" of Lyndon Johnson, as one sympathetic historian saw it, was that the president was increasingly drawn into the Vietnam War. Actually, President Johnson and millions of other Americans still perceived Vietnam as a major test of the United States' willingness to resist the spread of communism.

Under Johnson, the war escalated rapidly, and in 1964 the Vietcong controlled almost half of South Vietnam. Thus, when two American ships allegedly were attacked by the North Vietnamese that year, Johnson used the occasion to obtain sweeping powers from Congress[7] to conduct the war as he wished. Bombing of North Vietnam and Laos was increased, refugees were moved to "pacification" camps, entire villages believed to be unfriendly were destroyed, chemical defoliants were sprayed on forests to eliminate Vietcong hiding places, and troops increased until by 1968 about 500,000 American men and women were serving in Vietnam.

6. Johnson served in Congress during the 1930s and was a strong supporter of New Deal programs.
7. The Tonkin Gulf Resolution gave Johnson the power to "take all necessary measures to repel any armed attack against the forces of the United States and to prevent further aggression."

As the war effort increased, so did the doubts. In the mid-1960s, the chair of the Senate Foreign Relations Committee, J. William Fulbright, raised important questions about whether the Vietnam War was serving our national interest. Several members of the administration and foreign policy experts (including George Kennan, author of the original containment policy) maintained that escalation of the war could not be justified. Television news coverage of the destruction and carnage along with reports of atrocities such as the My Lai massacre[8] disillusioned more and more Americans. Yet Johnson continued the bombing, called for more ground troops, and offered peace terms that were completely unacceptable to the North Vietnamese. Not until the Tet offensive—a coordinated North Vietnamese strike across all of South Vietnam in January 1968, in which the Communists captured every provincial capital and even entered Saigon (the capital of South Vietnam)—did President Johnson change his mind. Two months later, Johnson appeared on national television and announced to a surprised nation that he had ordered an end to most of the bombing, asked North Vietnam to start real peace negotiations, and withdrawn his name from the 1968 presidential race. Although we now know that the Tet offensive was a setback for Ho Chi Minh, in the United States it was seen as a major setback for the West, evidence that the optimistic press re-

leases about our imminent victory simply were not true.

And yet America's "longest war" and the growing disillusionment that accompanied it went on. The new president, Richard M. Nixon, announced that he was committed to "peace with honor"—a double-edged policy that encompassed the gradual withdrawal of American forces and their replacement by South Vietnamese troops (Vietnamization) and the escalation of bombing of North Vietnam and neighboring areas. As you will recall, it was Nixon's announcement of the secret incursion into Cambodia that sparked the Kent State antiwar demonstrations in May 1970.

At the same time that the United States was becoming increasingly entangled in Vietnam (1945—1970), significant changes were taking place in American society. Veterans came home from World War II eager to reestablish "normal" lives—to marry, complete their education, obtain steady jobs, have children, and buy homes, automobiles, and other material goods. One result was massive suburbanization as inexpensive tract housing developments sprang up like mushrooms outside major and medium-sized cities across the nation. The birthrate almost doubled for white middle-class Americans, reversing the demographic trend toward smaller families that had begun during the late colonial era. Married women left (or were removed from) their wartime jobs by the millions, some returning to full-time jobs and others to part-time typical "female" jobs. Traditional sex roles were reinforced by popular literature and the media, and a smaller proportion of

8. This incident occurred in March 1968, when American soldiers destroyed a Vietnamese village and killed many of the inhabitants, including women and children.

CHAPTER 10

A GENERATION
IN WAR AND
TURMOIL: THE
AGONY OF
VIETNAM

women completed college degrees or sought professional education than in previous generations. Pent-up consumer demand burst forth after wartime scarcity and rationing, to be satisfied only by more and more purchases of television sets, refrigerators and other household appliances, camping equipment, clothing, furniture, and new automobiles. According to one observer, America's "affluent society" was in full bloom by the late 1950s.

There was, however, an underside to the so-called affluent society. Indeed, many Americans did not share in its benefits at all. As middle-class whites fled to the suburbs, conditions in the cities deteriorated. Increasingly populated by the poor—African Americans, Latin American immigrants, the elderly, and unskilled white immigrants—urban areas struggled to finance essential city services such as police and fire protection. Moreover, poverty and its victims could also be found in rural areas, as Michael Harrington pointed out in his classic study *The Other America,* published in 1962. Small farmers, tenants, sharecroppers, and migrant workers were not only poor, they often lacked any access to even basic educational opportunities and health-care facilities.

The "baby boom" generation of the postwar era came of age in the late 1960s, just as the Vietnam War was escalating. The shining idealism surrounding the election of John Kennedy in 1960 had been tarnished by a series of assassinations, riots in the cities, and increasing violence in reaction to the African American civil-rights

movement.[9] At the same time, college enrollments increased dramatically as millions of upper and middle-class (as well as those who aspired to be middle-class) students flocked to campuses to earn undergraduate, graduate, and professional degrees. Many of these students began questioning their parents' values, especially those connected with materialism, sexual mores and traditional sex roles, corporate structure and power, and the kind of patriotism that supported the Vietnam War. Increasingly alienated by impersonal university policies and the actions of such authority figures as police, administrators, and politicians, many students turned to new forms of religion, music, and dress and to the use of drugs to set themselves apart from the older generation.

Other young people who lacked the money or who were not brought up with the expectation of earning college degrees tended to continue in more traditional life patterns. They completed their educations with high school or before, although others attended a year or two at a local vocationally oriented community college or trade school. They often married younger than their college counterparts, sought stable jobs, and aspired to own their own homes. In other words, they rarely rejected the values of their parents' generation.

9. Assassinations included those of John Kennedy, Robert Kennedy, and Martin Luther King. City riots, beginning with the Watts riot in Los Angeles in 1965, spread across major cities for the next several years.

The issue of the draft, however, touched the lives of both groups of this younger generation. The draft, or conscription, in time of war was not new to America, nor were deferments or exemptions for various reasons. Both the Union and the Confederacy had exempted men who were well-off financially—those who could "buy" a substitute or those who owned at least twenty slaves. In World War I there were physical, mental, and financial hardship exemptions, and when ten million men were drafted for World War II, those who held jobs essential to the war effort (as well as students preparing for essential professions such as engineering and medicine) were added to the list of those exempted or deferred. The post–World War II "peacetime" draft expanded the exemption and deferment categories to include all college students up to age twenty-six and married men with children. Furthermore, those whose religious beliefs rejected military service (such as Quakers) have, historically, been offered alternative service or exempted.

As long as military needs, and thus draft quotas, were low (1954–1964), the draft was not of great concern to young men. As late as 1966, only 7 percent of high school sophomores reported that they were concerned about the draft. But by 1969, that figure had risen to 75 percent. Although women were not included in the draft, wives, mothers, sisters, friends, and lovers were deeply concerned too.

As the need for troops increased, deferments and exemptions became somewhat more difficult to obtain.

College students had to maintain good grades, graduate student deferments were ended, and draft boards were frequently unsympathetic to pleas for conscientious-objector status.[10] But the Selective Service, headed by General Lewis Hershey since 1948, was extremely decentralized and antiquated in its procedures and recordkeeping. As two observers noted, there were four thousand local draft boards with four thousand different policies. Avoiding the draft became a desperate game for many, and draft counselors and lawyers aided young men in evasions based on physical or mental impairments, legal technicalities, conscientious-objector status, or "safe" enlistments and reserve duty.[11] Of the approximately 27 million young men who reached draft age between 1964 and 1973, almost 25 million did not serve. Although some fled to Canada, Sweden, or other countries and a few remained in the United States, resisted the draft, and were prosecuted, most of these 25 million men simply avoided the draft through loopholes in the system. According to a Harris poll in 1971, most Americans believed that those who did go to Vietnam were "suckers" who could have avoided it.

In fact, those who did serve in the military and/or went to Vietnam were the less affluent, less well-educated whites and blacks. Of those who

10. Conscientious objectors are those whose religious beliefs are opposed to military service.
11. Safe enlistments are assignments to desk jobs or areas in which no actual fighting is taking place (such as Europe or the United States during the Vietnam War).

CHAPTER 10

A GENERATION
IN WAR AND
TURMOIL: THE
AGONY OF
VIETNAM

served in the military, 45 percent were high-school graduates, whereas 23 percent were college graduates. Of the high-school graduates, 21 percent went to Vietnam, but only 12 percent of the college graduates served there. Figures based on family income are equally revealing: 40 percent of men from low-income families served in the military (19 percent of them in Vietnam); 24 percent of men from high-income families served in the military (9 percent in Vietnam). Casualty figures show yet another side of the story. In the early part of the war, blacks (who made up about 11 percent of the American population) constituted 23 percent of the Vietnam War fatalities. Later this percentage fell to 14 percent, still disproportionately high.

As the arbitrary and unfair nature of the draft became increasingly evident, President Nixon finally replaced General Hershey and instituted a new draft system, the lottery. In this system, draft-age men were assigned numbers and were drafted in order from lowest to highest number until the draft quota was filled. With this action the very real threat of the draft spread to those who had previously felt relatively safe. Already divided, an entire generation had to come face to face with the Vietnam War.

In this chapter your task is to analyze the experience of members of the baby boom generation so as to understand how and why public opinion became so deeply divided about the Vietnam War.

THE METHOD

You already have had some experience with oral history. In the chapter on the Great Depression, you interviewed someone and then analyzed that interview. You also compared an individual's history with the aggregate experiences of Americans during the 1930s as portrayed by your readings. In this chapter the focus is somewhat different. Two concepts will be helpful to you here.

The first concept is *birth cohort*— those people born within a few years of one another who form a historical generation. Members of a birth cohort experience the same events—wars, depressions, assassinations, as well as such personal experiences as marriage

and childbearing—at approximately the same age and often have similar reactions to them. Sociologist Glen Elder showed that a group of people who were relatively deprived as young children during the Great Depression grew up and later made remarkably similar decisions about marriage, children, and jobs. Others have used this kind of analysis to provide insights into British writers of the post–World War I era and to explain why the Nazi party appealed to a great many young Germans.

Yet even within a birth cohort, people may respond quite differently to the same event(s). *Frame of reference* refers to an individual's *personal back-*

ground, which may influence that person's beliefs, responses, and actions. For example, in the Great Depression chapter, you may have found that men and women coped differently with unemployment or that blacks and whites differed in their perceptions of how hard the times were. You may also have found that those who were very young children during the depression did not recall as many hardships as those who were adults at the time.

In this chapter, all the interviewees belong to the generation that came of age during the Vietnam War. Thus, as you analyze their frames of reference, age will not give you any clues. However, other factors, such as gender, race, socioeconomic class, family background, values, region, and experiences, may be quite important in determining the interviewees' frames of reference and understanding their responses to the Vietnam War. When a group of people share the same general frame of reference, they are a generational subset who tend to respond similarly to events. In other words, it may be possible to form tentative generalizations from the interviewees about how others with the same general frames of reference thought about and responded to the Vietnam War.

In addition to the interviews, two other kinds of evidence are included in this chapter: photographs and popular music lyrics. Many historians are now using such nontraditional sources to give us a fuller and richer view of the past, particularly the past of people who were not well known or famous. Both posed pictures and unposed snapshots can be revealing when studied carefully. For example,

the pioneer families who settled the Great Plains often dressed in their best clothes and lined up in front of their houses to have their pictures taken to send back East to their relatives. Consider what these photographs must have revealed. The size and composition of the families, the relative modesty of their finest clothes, the limited comfort of their sod houses—in fact, the very isolation and backbreaking work of settling the plains—would be evident. Similarly, snapshots of backyard barbecues and new family cars can tell us a great deal about suburban life in the 1950s.

The final piece of evidence is "For What It's Worth," a very popular Stephen Stills song of the late 1960s. Almost every piece of music contains some sort of message. Some messages are shallow (love between a boy and a girl is a wonderful thing), but others are more profound (for example, Tschaikovsky's *1812 Overture,* which celebrates the strength and fortitude of a people and a nation). Some messages cause songs to become classics and transcend time, whereas other messages are time-bound and do not mean much to listeners years later. Yet, whether it is sophomoric or sophisticated, universal or temporally limited, there is a message in almost every song.

In the mid-1950s, popular music known as rock 'n' roll literally burst on the scene. Adults either greeted this music with disgust or waited patiently for the "fad" to pass, but young people almost universally embraced it. The rock music industry eventually became a $3 billion per year phenomenon, with 70 percent of that money

CHAPTER 10

A GENERATION
IN WAR AND
TURMOIL: THE
AGONY OF
VIETNAM

spent by people between the ages of fourteen to twenty-five. On college campuses, folk music became another popular musical form in the late 1950s. Folk music lyrics often possessed a quality that early rock 'n' roll lyrics lacked because they dealt with social issues such as poverty, racism, and war. By the mid-1960s, rock too was becoming more conscious of the world around it, and some artists merged the two musical forms into hybrid folk-rock, with lyrics laden with social comment. In analyzing the lyrics of "For What It's Worth," answer the following questions carefully:

1. What is the message of the song?
2. How is that message conveyed?
3. What is the tone of the lyrics (for example, sad, angry, strident)?
4. What events were taking place in the year in which this song was released (1967)?

THE EVIDENCE

1. Photograph of John and His Family. Left to Right: John's Father, John, John's Mother, and John's Brother.

John

[John was born in 1951. His father was a well-to-do and prominent physician, and John grew up in a midwestern town that had a major university. He graduated from high school in 1969 and enrolled in a four-year private college. John dropped out of college in 1971 and returned home to live with his parents. He found work in the community and associated with students at the nearby university.]

My earliest memory of Vietnam must have been when I was in the seventh grade [1962–1963] and I saw things in print and in *Life* magazine. But I really don't remember much about Vietnam until my senior year in high school [1968–1969].

I came from a repressive private school to college. College was a fun place to hang out, a place where you went after high school. It was just expected of you to go.

At college there was a good deal of apprehension and fear about Vietnam—people were scared of the draft. To keep your college deferments, you had to keep your grades up. But coming from an admittedly well-to-do family, I somehow assumed I didn't have to worry about it too much. I suppose I was outraged to find out that it *could* happen to me.

No, I was outraged that it could happen to *anyone*. I knew who was going to get deferments and who weren't going to get them. And even today my feelings are still ambiguous. On one hand I felt, "You guys were so dumb to get caught in that machine." On the other, and more importantly, it was wrong that *anyone* had to go.

Why? Because Vietnam was a bad war. To me, we were protecting business interests. We were fighting on George III's side, on the wrong side of an anticolonial rebellion. The domino theory didn't impress me at all.[12]

I had decided that I would not go to Vietnam. But I wasn't really worried for myself until Nixon instituted the lottery. I was contemplating going to Canada when my older brother got a CO.[13] I tried the same thing, the old Methodist altar boy gambit, but I was turned down. I was really ticked when I was refused CO status. I thought, "Who are you to tell me who is a pacifist?"

My father was conservative and my mother liberal. Neither one intervened or tried to pressure me. I suppose they thought, "We've done the best we could." By this time I had long hair and a beard. My dad had a hard time.

12. The domino theory, embraced by presidents Eisenhower, Kennedy, and Johnson, held that if one nation fell to the Communists, the result would be a toppling of other nations, like dominos.
13. CO stands for conscientious objector.

CHAPTER 10

A GENERATION
IN WAR AND
TURMOIL: THE
AGONY OF
VIETNAM

The antiwar movement was an intellectual awakening of American youth. Young people were concentrated on college campuses, where their maturing intellects had sympathetic sounding boards. Vietnam was part of that awakening. So was drugs. It was part of the protest. You had to be a part of it. Young people were waking up as they got away from home and saw the world around them and were forced to think for themselves.

I remember an argument I had with my father. I told him Ho Chi Minh was a nationalist before he was a Communist, and that this war wasn't really against communism at all. It's true that the Russians were also the bad guys in Vietnam, what with their aid and support of the North Vietnamese, but they had no business there either. When people tried to compare Vietnam to World War II, I just said that no Vietnamese had ever bombed Pearl Harbor.

The draft lottery certainly put me potentially at risk. But I drew a high number, so I knew that it was unlikely that I'd ever be drafted. And yet, I wasn't concerned just for myself. For example, I was aware, at least intellectually, that blacks and poor people were the cannon fodder in Vietnam. But I insisted that *no one,* rich or poor, had to go to fight this war.

Actually I didn't think much about the Vietnamese people themselves. The image was of a kid who could take candy from you one day and hand you a grenade the next. What in hell were we doing in that kind of situation?

Nor did I ever actually know anyone who went to Vietnam. I suppose that, to some extent, I bought the "damn baby napalmers" image. But I never had a confrontation with a veteran of Vietnam. What would I think of him? I don't know. What would he think of me?

Kent State was a real shock to me. I was in college at the time, and I thought, "They were students, just like me." It seemed as if fascism was growing in America.

I was part of the protest movement. After Kent State, we shut down the campus, then marched to a downtown park where we held a rally. In another demonstration, later, I got a good whiff of tear gas. I was dating a girl who collapsed because of the gas. I recall a state policeman coming at us with a club. I yelled at him, telling him what had happened. Suddenly he said, "Here, hold this!" and gave me his club while he helped my date to her feet.

But there were other cops who weren't so nice. I went to the counter-inaugural in Washington in June 1973. You could see the rage on the cops' faces when we were yelling, "One, two, three, four, we don't want your f---ing war!" It was an awakening for me to see that much emotion on the subject coming from the other side. I know that I wasn't very open to other opinions. But the other side *really* was closed.

By '72 their whole machine was falling apart. A guy who gave us a ride to the counter-inaugural was a Vietnam vet. He was going there too, to protest against the war. In fact, he was hiding a friend of his who was AWOL,[14] who simply hid rather than go to Vietnam.

Then Watergate made it all worthwhile—we really had those f---ers scared. I think Watergate showed the rest of the country exactly what kind of "Law and Order" Nixon and his cronies were after!

I have no regrets about what I did. I condemn them all—Kennedy, Johnson, Nixon—for Vietnam. They all had a hand in it. And the war was wrong, in every way imaginable. While I feel some guilt that others went and were killed, and I didn't, in retrospect I feel much guiltier that I wasn't a helluva lot more active. Other than that, I wouldn't change a thing. I can still get angry about it.

How will I explain all that to my sons? I have no guilt in terms of "duty towards country." The *real* duty was to fight *against* the whole thing. I'll tell my sons that, and tell them that I did what I did so that no one has to go.

[John chose not to return to college. He learned a craft, which he practices today. He married a woman who shares his views ("I wouldn't have known anyone on the other side, the way the country was divided"). They have two sons. Both John and his wife work outside the home, and they share the responsibilities of child care.]

2. "For What It's Worth," Words and Music By Stephen Stills.

There's something happenin' in here,
What it is ain't exactly clear,
There's a man with a gun over there
A'tellin' we got to beware.

Chorus
I think it's time we stop children,
What's that sound?
Everybody look what's goin' down.

There's battle lines being drawn,
But nobody's right if everybody's wrong,
Young people speakin' their minds
A'gettin' so much resistance from behin'
Time we
(repeat chorus)

14. AWOL is an acronym for "absent without leave."

CHAPTER 10

A GENERATION
IN WAR AND
TURMOIL: THE
AGONY OF
VIETNAM

What a field day for the heat,
A thousand people in the street,
Singin' songs and a'carryin' signs
Mostly say "Hooray for our side."
It's time we
(repeat chorus)

Paranoia strikes deep,
Into your life it will creep,
It starts when you're always afraid—Step out of line,
    the man will come and take you away;
You better
(repeat chorus twice)

3. Photograph of Mike in Vietnam.

Mike

[Mike was born in 1948. His family owned a farm in West Tennessee, and Mike grew up in a rural environment. He graduated from high school in 1966 and enrolled in a community college not far from his home. After two quarters of poor grades, Mike left the community college and joined the United States Marine Corps in April 1967. He served two tours in Vietnam, the first in 1967–1969 and the second in 1970–1971.]

I flunked out of college my first year. I was away from home and found out a lot about wine, women and song but not about much else. In 1967 the old system of the draft was still in effect, so I knew that eventually I'd be rotated up and drafted—it was only a matter of time before they got me.

My father served with Stilwell in Burma and my uncle was career military. I grew up on a diet of John Wayne flics. I thought serving in the military was what was expected of me. The Marines had some good options—you could go in for two years and take your chances on the *possibility* of not going to Vietnam. I chose the two-year option. I thought what we were doing in Vietnam was a noble cause. My mother was against the war and we argued a lot about it. I told her that if the French hadn't helped us in the American Revolution, then we wouldn't have won. I sincerely believed that.

I took my six weeks of basic training at Parris Island [South Carolina]. It was sheer hell—I've never been treated like that in my life. Our bus arrived at Parris Island around midnight, and we were processed and sent to our barracks. We had just gotten to sleep when a drill instructor threw a thirty-two gallon garbage can down the center of the barracks and started overturning the metal bunks. We were all over the floor and he was screaming at us. It was that way for six weeks—no one ever talked to us, they shouted. And all our drill instructors geared our basic training to Vietnam. They were always screaming at us, "You're going to go to Vietnam and you're gonna f--- up and you're gonna die."

Most of the people in basic training with me were draftees. My recruiter apologized to me for having to go through boot camp with draftees. But most of the guys I was with were pretty much like me. Oh, there were a few s---birds, but not many. We never talked about Vietnam—there was no opportunity.

There were a lot of blacks in the Corps and I went through basic training with some. But I don't remember any racial tension until later. There were only two colors in the Marine Corps: light green and dark green. My parents drove down to Parris Island to watch me graduate from basic training, and they brought a black woman with them. She was from Memphis and was the wife of one of the men who graduated with me.

CHAPTER 10

A GENERATION
IN WAR AND
TURMOIL: THE
AGONY OF
VIETNAM

After basic training I spent thirteen weeks in basic infantry training at Camp Lejeune [North Carolina]. Lejeune is the armpit of the world. And the harassment didn't let up—we were still called "scumbag" and "hairbag" and "whale---." I made PFC [private first class] at Lejeune. I was an 03-11 [infantry rifleman].

From Lejeune [after twenty days home leave] I went to Camp Pendleton [California] for four-week staging. It was at Pendleton where we adjusted our training at Parris Island and Lejeune to the situation in Vietnam. I got to Vietnam right after Christmas 1967.

It was about this time that I became aware of antiwar protests. But as far as I was concerned they were a small minority of malcontents. They were the *protected,* were deferred or had a daddy on the draft board. I thought, "These people are disloyal—they're selling us down the drain."

We were not prepared to deal with the Vietnamese people at all. The only two things we were told was don't give kids cigarettes and don't pat 'em on the heads. We had no cultural training, knew nothing of the social structure or anything. For instance, we were never told that the Catholic minority controlled Vietnam and they got out of the whole thing—we did their fighting for them, while they stayed out or went to Paris or something. We had a Catholic chaplain who told us that it was our *duty* to go out and kill the Cong, that they stood against Christianity. Then he probably went and drank sherry with the top cats in Vietnam. As for the majority of Vietnamese, they were as different from us as night and day. To be honest, I still hate the Vietnamese SOBs.

The South Vietnamese Army was a mixed bag. There were some good units and some bad ones. Most of them were bad. If we were fighting alongside South Vietnam units, we had orders that if we were overrun by Charley[15] that we should shoot the South Vietnamese first—otherwise we were told they'd turn on us.

I can't tell you when I began to change my mind about the war. Maybe it was a kind of maturation process—you can only see so much death and suffering until you begin to wonder what in hell is going on. You can only live like a nonhuman so long.

I came out of country[16] in January of 1969 and was discharged not too long after that. I came home and found the country split over the war. I thought, "Maybe there *was* something to this antiwar business after all." Maybe these guys protesting in the streets weren't wrong.

But when I got back home, I was a stranger to my friends. They didn't want to get close to me. I could feel it. It was strange, like the only friends

15. "Charley" was a euphemism for the Viet Cong.
16. "Country" was Vietnam.

I had were in the Marine Corps. So I re-upped[17] in the Marines and went back to Vietnam with a helicopter squadron.

Kent State happened when I was back in Vietnam. They covered it in *Stars and Stripes*.[18] I guess that was a big turning point for me. Some of the other Marines said, "Hooray! Maybe we should kill more of them!" That was it for me. Those people at Kent State were killed for exercising the same rights we were fighting for for the Vietnamese. But I was in the minority—most of the Marines I knew approved of the shootings at Kent State.

Meanwhile I was flying helicopters into Cambodia every day. I used pot to keep all that stuff out of my mind. Pot grew wild in Vietnam, as wild as the hair on your ass. The Army units would pick it and send it back. The first time I was in Vietnam nobody I knew was using. The second time there was lots of pot. It had a red tinge, so it was easy to spot.

But I couldn't keep the doubts out of my mind. I guess I was terribly angry. I felt betrayed. I would have voted for Lyndon Johnson—when he said we should be there, I believed him. That man could walk on water as far as I was concerned. I would've voted for Nixon in '68, the only time I ever voted Republican in my life. I believed him when he said we'd come home with honor. So I'd been betrayed twice, and Kent State and all that was rattling around in my head.

I couldn't work it out. I was an E5 [sergeant], but got busted for fighting and then again for telling off an officer. I was really angry.

It was worse when I got home. I came back into the Los Angeles airport and was spit on and called a baby killer and a mother raper. I really felt like I was torn between two worlds. I guess I was. I was smoking pot.

I went back to school. I hung around mostly with veterans. We spoke the same language, and there was no danger of being insulted or ridiculed. We'd been damn good, but nobody knew it. I voted for McGovern in '72—he said we'd get out no matter what. Some of us refused to stand up one time when the national anthem was played.

What should we have done? Either not gotten involved at all or go in with the whole machine. With a different attitude and tactics, we could have *won*. But really we were fighting for just a minority of the Vietnamese, the westernized Catholics who controlled the cities but never owned the backcountry. No, I take that back. There was no way in hell we could have won that damned war and won anything worth winning.

I went to Washington for the dedication of the Vietnam veterans' memorial. We never got much of a welcome home or parades. The dedication was

17. "Re-upped" means reenlisted.
18. *Stars and Stripes* is a newspaper written and published by the armed forces for service personnel.

CHAPTER 10

A GENERATION
IN WAR AND
TURMOIL: THE
AGONY OF
VIETNAM

a homecoming for me. It was the first time I got the whole thing out of my system. I cried, and I'm not ashamed. And I wasn't alone.

I looked for the names of my friends. I couldn't look at a name without myself reflected back in it [the wall].

One of the reasons I went back to school was to understand that war and myself. I've read a lot about it and watched a lot of TV devoted to it. I was at Khe Sanh and nobody could tell about that who wasn't there. There were six thousand of us. Walter Cronkite said we were there for seventy-two days. I kept a diary—it was longer than that. I'm still reading and studying Vietnam, trying to figure it all out.

[Mike returned to college, repeated the courses he had failed, and transferred to a four-year institution. By all accounts he was a fine student. Mike is now employed as a park ranger. He is married, and he and his wife have a child. He is considered a valuable, respected, and popular member of his community. He rarely speaks of his time in the service.]

4. Photograph of MM, Boot Camp Graduation.

MM[19]

[MM was born in 1947 and grew up in a mid-sized southern city. He graduated from high school in 1965. A standout football player in high school, he could not get an athletic scholarship to college because of low grades. As a result, he joined the Army two months after graduating from high school to take advantage of the educational benefits he would get upon his discharge. He began his basic training in early September 1965.]

I went into the service to be a soldier. I was really gung ho. I did my basic training at Fort Gordon [Georgia], my AIT [advanced infantry training] at Fort Ord [California], and Ranger school and Airborne at Fort Benning [Georgia].

All of this was during the civil rights movement. I was told that, being black, I had a war to fight at home, not in Vietnam. That got me uptight, because that wasn't what I wanted to do—I'd done some of that in high school.[20] I had one mission accomplished, and was looking for another.

A lot of guys I went into the service with didn't want to go to Nam—they were afraid. Some went AWOL. One guy jumped off the ship between Honolulu and Nam and drowned. Another guy shot himself, trying to get a stateside wound. He accidentally hit an artery and died. Most of us thought they were cowards.

I arrived in Nam on January 12, 1966. I was three days shy of being 18 years old. I was young, gung ho, and mean as a snake. I was with the 25th Infantry as a machine gunner and rifleman. We went out on search and destroy missions.

I did two tours in Vietnam, at my own request. You could make rank[21] faster in Nam and the money was better. I won two silver stars and three bronze stars. For my first silver star, I knocked out two enemy machine guns that had two of our platoons pinned down. They were drawing heavy casualties. The event is still in my mind. Two of the bronze stars I put in my best friend's body bag. I told him I did it for him.

I had a friend who died in my arms, and I guess I freaked a little bit. I got busted[22] seven times. They [the Army] didn't like the way I started taking enemy scalps and wearing them on my pistol belt. I kept remembering my friend.

---

19. Since MM's first name also is Mike, his initials are used to avoid confusion.
20. MM participated in sit-ins to integrate the city's lunch counters and movie theaters.
21. Earn promotions.
22. Demoted.

CHAPTER 10

A GENERATION
IN WAR AND
TURMOIL: THE
AGONY OF
VIETNAM

I didn't notice much racial conflict in Nam. In combat, everybody seemed to be OK. I fought beside this [white] guy for eleven months; we drank out of the same canteen. When I got home, I called this guy's house. His mother said, "We don't allow our son to associate with niggers." In Vietnam, I didn't run into much of that.

The Vietnamese hated us. My first day in Vietnam, Westmoreland[23] told us that underneath every Vietnamese was an American. I thought, "What drug is he on?" But they hated us. When we weren't on the scene, the enemy would punish them for associating with us. They would call out to us, "G.I. Number Ten."[24] They were caught between a rock and a hard place.

We could have won the war several times. The Geneva Convention[25] wouldn't let us, and the enemy had the home court advantage. To win, it would have taken hard soldiering, but we could have done it. America is a weak country because we want to be everybody's friend. We went in there as friends. We gave food and stuff to the Vietnamese and we found it in the hands of the enemy. We just weren't tough enough.

I got out of the Army in 1970. I was thinking about making the Army a career, and was going to re-enlist. But when they wanted me to go back for a third tour in Vietnam, I got out. Hell, everybody told me I was crazy for doing two.

[MM used his GI Bill benefits to obtain three years of higher education, two years at two four-year colleges and one in a business school. According to him, however, jobs have been "few and far between." He describes himself as "restless" and reports that automobile backfires still frighten him. He has been married and divorced twice.]

149   23. General William Westmoreland, American Commander in Vietnam.
150   24. "Number Ten" meant bad; no good.
150   25. The Geneva Convention refers to international agreements for the conduct of war and
151   the treatment of prisoners. The agreements began to be drawn up in the 1860s.

25

5. Photograph of Eugene Marching.

Eugene

[Eugene was born in 1948 in a large city on the West Coast. He graduated from high school in June 1967 and was drafted in August. Initially rejected because of a hernia, he had surgery to correct that problem and then enlisted in the Marine Corps.]

It was pretty clear from basic training on, no ifs, ands, or buts that we were going to Vietnam. The DIs[26] were all Vietnam vets, so we were told what to expect when we got there. They'd tell us what to do and all we had to do was do it.

I got to Vietnam in June of 1968. Over there, the majority of blacks stuck together because they had to. In the field was a different story, but in the rear you really caught it. Blacks would catch hell in the rear—fights and things like that. When we went to the movies with Navy guys, they put us in the worst seats. Sometimes they just wanted to start a fight. My whole time in Vietnam I knew only two black NCOs[27] and none above that.

We were overrun three times. You could tell when we were going to get hit when the Vietnamese in our camp (who cleaned up hooches) disappeared. Usually Charley had informants inside our base, and a lot of info slipped out. They were fully aware of our actions and weapons.

152   26. Drill instructors.
153   27. Noncommissioned officers; sergeants.

CHAPTER 10

A GENERATION
IN WAR AND
TURMOIL: THE
AGONY OF
VIETNAM

When we were in the rear, we cleaned our equipment, wrote letters home, went to movies, and thought a lot about what we'd do when we got out. I had training in high school as an auto mechanic, and I wanted to start my own business.

You had to watch out for the rookies until they got a feel for what was going on. We told one new L.T.,[28] "Don't polish your brass out here or you'll tip us off for sure." He paid us no mind and Charley knocked out him and our radio man one night.

You could get anything over there you wanted [drugs]. Marijuana grew wild in the bush. Vietnamese kids would come up to you with a plastic sandwich bag of 25 [marijuana] cigarettes for $5. It was dangerous, but we smoked in the bush as well as out. At the O.P.s,[29] everybody knew when the officer would come around and check. We'd pass the word: "Here comes the Man." That's why a lot of guys who came back were so strung out on drugs. And opium—the mamasans[30] had purple teeth because of it.

We could have won the war anytime we wanted to. We could have wiped that place off the map. There was a lot of talk that that's what we should have done. But we didn't because of American companies who had rubber and oil interests in Vietnam, and no telling what else. To them, Vietnam was a money-making thing. We were fighting over there to protect those businesses.

It was frustrating. The Army and Marines were ordered to take Hill 881 and we did, but it was costly. A couple of weeks later we just up and left and gave it back.

When I got out [in January 1970], I was a E5.[31] I couldn't find a job. So I talked to an Air Force recruiter. I got a release from the Marines[32] and joined the Air Force. I rigged parachutes and came out in 1975.

I stayed in L.A.[33] until 1977. Then I became a long-distance truck driver. I was doing pretty good when I got messed up in an accident. My truck jackknifed on ice in Pennsylvania and I hit the concrete barrier.

[Eugene has not worked regularly since the accident. A lawsuit against the trucking company is pending. He is divorced.]

28. Lieutenant.
29. Outposts.
30. Old Vietnamese women.
31. Sergeant.
32. Eugene had four years of reserve obligation.
33. Los Angeles, California.

6. Photograph of Helen at an Army hospital in Phu Bai, South Vietnam.

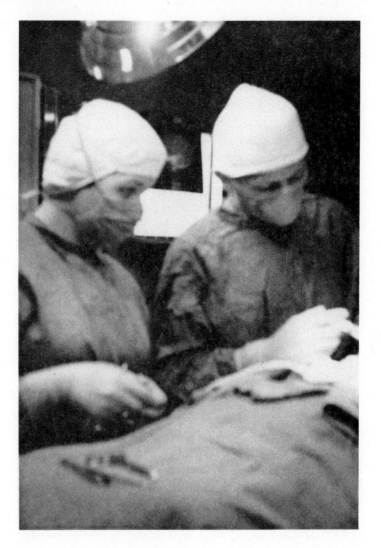

Helen

[Helen was born in 1942 in Cleveland, Ohio, and grew up there. Since grade school, she had wanted to be a nurse. After graduation from high school, she spent three years in nurses' training to become a registered nurse. She worked for three years in the operating rooms of a major medical facility in Cleveland. In 1966, she joined the Navy.]

CHAPTER 10

A GENERATION
IN WAR AND
TURMOIL: THE
AGONY OF
VIETNAM

At that point, there was nothing ideological. I simply felt I had a sound surgical background and had something to offer to the men and boys who were being made to serve our country in Vietnam.

I was assigned to the Great Lakes Naval Hospital [outside Chicago]. Although I had been trained and had experience as an operating room surgical nurse, at first I was assigned to the orthopedic wards. It was there that I got my first exposure to mass casualties [from Vietnam]. Depending on the extent of their injuries, we would see patients at Great Lakes about 7 to 10 days after them being wounded in Vietnam.

I became attached to some of the boys—they were young, scared and badly injured. I remember a Negro who in tears asked for his leg to be taken off—he couldn't stand the smell of it anymore and had been to surgery once too often for the removal of dead tissue. He was in constant pain.

On the wards, we always kept nightlights on. If someone darkened a ward by accident, it produced a sense of terror in the patients. Many were disoriented, and a lot had nightmares.

When I made the decision to go to Vietnam, I volunteered in 1968 and requested duty aboard a hospital ship. It was necessary to extend my time on active duty in order to go. I felt I had a skill that was needed and it was something I felt I personally had to do. I didn't necessarily agree with our policy on being there, but that wasn't the point.

The median age of our troops in Vietnam was 19 years old. It was like treating our kid brothers. I would have done as much for my own brothers. I know this sounds idealistic, but that's the way I felt then.

The troops got six weeks of staging, preparing them for duty in Vietnam. Most of the nurses were given no preparation, no orientation as to what to expect when you go into a war zone. No one said, "These are the things you'll see," or "These are the things you'll be expected to do."

I was assigned to the *USS Sanctuary,* which was stationed outside of Da Nang harbor. The *Sanctuary* was a front-line treatment facility. Casualties were picked up in the field combat areas and then brought by Medevac choppers to the ship. During our heaviest months, we logged over seven hundred patient admissions per month. That was at the height of the Tet offensive in January through March, 1968. I had just gotten to Vietnam.

It was terribly intense. There was nothing to shelter you, no one to hold your hand when mass casualties came in. If you had time to think, you'd have thought, "My God, how am I to get through this?" We dealt with multiple amputations, head injuries, and total body trauma. Sometimes injuries were received from our own people caught in crossfires. When all hell breaks loose at night in the jungle, a 19-year-old boy under ambush will fire at anything that moves.

How do you insulate yourself against all this? We relaxed when we could, and we put a lot of stock in friendships (the corpsmen were like our kid brothers). We played pranks and sometimes took the launch ashore to Da Nang. Occasionally we were invited to a party ashore and a helicopter came out for the nurses. The men wanted American women at their parties.

There were some people who had the idea that the only reason women were in the service was to be prostitutes or to get a man. Coming back from Vietnam, I was seated next to a male officer on the plane who said to me, "Boy, I bet you had a great time in Vietnam." I had my seat changed. When I got home and was still in uniform I was once mistaken for a police officer.

On the *Sanctuary,* we had Vietnamese patients too. But our guys were distrustful of them, especially children who had been observed planting mines (probably in exchange for a handful of rice). The Vietnamese were often placed under armed guard. I have friends who were nurses in country who harbor a real hatred for the Vietnamese.

I heard a story of a Vietnamese child running up to a chopper that was evacuating casualties and tossing a grenade into it. Everyone on board was killed in a split second; both crew and casualties, because they paused to help a child they thought needed them. A soldier I knew said, "If they're in the fire zone, they get killed." War really takes you to the lowest level of human dignity. It makes you barbaric.

After Vietnam, I was stationed at the Naval Academy in Annapolis to finish out my duty. There I dealt basically with college students—measles and sports injuries. It was a hard adjustment to make.

In Vietnam, nurses had a great deal of autonomy, and we often had to do things nurses normally aren't allowed to do. You couldn't do those things stateside. Doctors saw it as an encroachment on their areas of practice. I'd been a year under extreme surgical conditions in Vietnam, and then in Annapolis someone would ask me, "Are you sure you know how to start an IV?"[34] It was hard to tame yourself down. Also, in the civilian setting, mediocrity was tolerated. I heard people say, "That's not my job." Nobody would have said that in Vietnam. There, the rules were put aside and everybody did what they could. When we got back to the states, there was no one to wind us down, deprogram us, tell us that Vietnam was an abnormal situation. . . . It was as if no one cared, we were just expected to cope and go on with our lives. . . .

I guess the hardest thing about nursing in Vietnam was the different priorities. Back home, if we got multiple-trauma cases from, say, an automobile accident, we always treated the most seriously injured first. In Viet-

34. Intervenous mechanism.

CHAPTER 10

A GENERATION
IN WAR AND
TURMOIL: THE
AGONY OF
VIETNAM

nam, it was often the reverse. I remember working on one soldier who was not badly wounded, and he kept screaming for us to help his buddy, who was seriously wounded. I couldn't tell him that his buddy didn't have a good chance to survive, and so we were passing him by. That was difficult for a lot of us, went against all we'd been trained to do. It's difficult to support someone in the act of dying when you're trained to do all you can to save a life. Even today, I have trouble with patients who need amputations or who have facial injuries.

It is most important to realize that there is a great cost to waging war. Many men are living out their lives in veterans' hospitals as paraplegics or quadriplegics, who in World War II or Korea would not have survived. Most Americans will never see these people—they are hidden away from us. But they are alive.

Maybe the worst part of the war for many of these boys was coming home. The seriously wounded were sent to a military hospital closest to their own homes. Our orthopedic ward at Great Lakes Naval Hospital had 40 beds, and it was like taking care of 40 kid brothers. They joked around and were supportive of each other. But quite a few of them got "Dear John"[35] letters while they were there. Young wives and girlfriends sometimes couldn't deal with these injuries, and parents sometimes had trouble coping too. All these people were "casualties of war," but I believe that these men especially need our caring and concern today, just as much as they did 20 years ago.

[On her discharge from the Navy in August 1969, Helen returned to nursing. She married in 1972. She and her husband, an engineering physicist, have two children. Helen returned to school and received her B.S. degree in nursing. She is now a coordinator of cardiac surgery and often speaks and writes of her Vietnam experience. She also actively participates in a local veterans' organization. Recently, her daughter offered her mother's services to speak on Vietnam to a high school history class, but she was rebuffed by the teacher, who said, "Who wants to hear about that? We lost that war!" Both Helen and her daughter (who is proud of what her mother did) were offended.]

35. A "Dear John" letter is one that breaks off a relationship.

As you read through the interviews, try to get a sense of the tone and general meaning of each one. Then try to establish the respective frames of reference for each interviewee by comparing and contrasting their backgrounds. From which socioeconomic class does each person come? From what region of the country? What do you know about their parents and friends? What did they think was expected of them? Why?

After their time in school, all the interviewees' experiences diverged greatly. Why did some of them join the armed services? Why did John become involved in the antiwar protest movement?

Next, consider the views these people expressed. What did they actually know about Vietnam? What were their feelings about the Vietnamese people? What did they believe were the reasons for the American involvement in the war? What were their reactions to events of the times—the draft, the antiwar protesters, the Kent State killings, and the use of drugs? What did each one think about the situation of returning veterans? What do you

think each person learned from personal experiences during the Vietnam War era?

Now look at the photographs carefully. Are they posed or unposed? For whom might they have been intended? What "image" of each person is projected? How does each person help to create that image?

Both John and Mike (Sources 1 and 3) also mentioned the song "For What It's Worth" (Source 2) when they were being interviewed. Using the guidelines presented in the "Method" section of this chapter, analyze the message and tone of these lyrics as well as their historical context. What do you suppose this message meant to John? To Mike?

Finally, try to link each person's views and image with that person's background and experiences. Can you find any reasons why these individuals might have thought and acted the ways they did? Can you understand each person? These individuals have never met. Do you think they could meet together and talk about the war today? If so, why? If not, why not?

EPILOGUE

In the spring of 1971, fifteen thousand antiwar demonstrators disrupted daily activities in the nation's capital by blocking the streets with trash, automobiles, and their own bodies. Twelve thousand were arrested, but

the protest movement across the country continued. In June, the Pentagon Papers, a secret 1967 government study of the Vietnam War, was published in installments by the *New York Times*. The Pentagon Papers revealed

CHAPTER 10

A GENERATION
IN WAR AND
TURMOIL: THE
AGONY OF
VIETNAM

that government spokespersons had lied to the American public about several important events, particularly about the Gulf of Tonkin incident.

As part of his reelection campaign in 1972, President Nixon traveled first to China and then to the Soviet Union and accelerated the removal of American troops from Vietnam. "Peace," his adviser Henry Kissinger announced, "is at hand." Withdrawal was slow and painful and created a new group of refugees—those Vietnamese who had supported the Americans in South Vietnam. Nixon became mired in the Watergate scandal and resigned from office in 1974 under the threat of impeachment. The North Vietnamese entered Saigon in the spring of 1975 and began a "pacification" campaign of their own in neighboring Cambodia. Nixon's successors, Gerald Ford and Jimmy Carter, offered "amnesty" plans that a relatively small number of draft violators used. Many who were reported Missing in Action in Vietnam (MIAs) were never found, either dead or alive. The draft was replaced by a new concept, the all-volunteer army.

The Vietnam veterans who never had their homecoming parades and had been alternately ignored or maligned finally got their memorial. A stark, simple, shiny black granite wall engraved with the names of 58,000 war dead, the monument is located on the mall near the Lincoln Memorial in Washington, D.C. The idea came from Jan Scruggs (the son of a milkman), a Vietnam veteran who was wounded and decorated for bravery when he was nineteen years old. The winning design was submitted by twenty-year-old Maya Lin, an undergraduate architecture student at Yale University. A representational statute designed by thirty-eight-year-old Frederick Hart, a former antiwar protester, stands near the wall of names. All one hundred United States senators cosponsored the gift of public land, and the money to build the memorial was raised entirely through 650,000 individual public contributions. Not everyone was pleased by the memorial, and some old emotional wounds were reopened. Yet more than 150,000 people attended the dedication ceremonies on Veterans' Day, 1982, and the Vietnam veterans paraded down Constitution Avenue. Millions of Americans have already viewed the monument, now one of Washington's most visited memorials.

CHAPTER ELEVEN

POLITICS AND TELEVISION
THE PRESIDENTIAL ELECTION OF 1988

THE PROBLEM

On Sunday, October 30, 1988, the *New York Times* ran the headline "Bitter Presidential Race Heads to a Close." For months, American voters had watched the almost endless process whereby the nation would choose its next president. On the Democratic side, Massachusetts Governor Michael Dukakis had waded through several primaries as his rivals for the party's nomination dropped off one by one. By the time of the Democratic convention, the only real challenger remaining was the Reverend Jesse Jackson, an electrifying and charismatic figure to many, but a man with little chance of stopping the inevitable Dukakis nomination. For the Republicans, Vice President George Bush had an easier time securing his party's presidential nomination, following a master plan that Bush campaign manager Lee Atwater developed immediately following President Ronald Reagan's re-election in November 1984.

Many people came to agree with the *New York Times*'s description of the 1988 presidential campaign as a particularly bitter one. Yet historians of American presidential elections could point to a number of past races that were marked by an equal amount of bitterness and anger. Indeed, as early as 1800, some New England supporters of President John Adams spread rumors that, if Thomas Jefferson were elected president, he would confiscate all the Bibles in the nation and destroy them.

What set the presidential contest of 1988 apart from its predecessors was not so much the bitter nature of the campaign as the crucial role of television. As one observer said, "The next President will have been chosen in a campaign dominated as never before by television . . . this is a television election." Through television newscasts, paid political advertisements,

[317]

CHAPTER 11

POLITICS AND
TELEVISION THE
PRESIDENTIAL
ELECTION OF
1988

and debates between the presidential and vice presidential candidates, most voters received almost all the information they would ever know about the candidates from television. To many people, the fact that George Bush convincingly won the election (thus being the first sitting vice president to win a presidential election since 1836) was proof to them that he was able to use the medium of television more effectively than his rival.

In this chapter you will be examining and analyzing the evidence to answer the following three questions:

1. What role did television play in the 1988 presidential election?
2. How has television altered the presidential election process?
3. If that process has been altered by the medium of television, what are the positive and negative effects of that alteration?

BACKGROUND

Presidential campaigns as we know them are a comparatively recent phenomenon. Political organizers such as John Beckley and Aaron Burr appeared as early as the 1790s, but they reached only a small number of voters, and popular participation in presidential elections was exceedingly low. Increased suffrage in the early nineteenth century and more exciting political campaigns (the presidential contest of 1840 was a watershed in this regard), complete with campaign buttons, parades, songs, and speeches, increased voter participation markedly. But it was still considered bad form for a presidential candidate to campaign actively in his own behalf, so most were content to watch the proceedings but not participate in them. Thus almost no voters ever saw the men for whom they cast their ballots, knew little about them, and sometimes did not even know their views on certain issues. Newspapers helped somewhat, but most papers were openly partisan and actually

concealed almost as much as they reported.

As did television later, technology began to change the campaign process. The rapid growth of the railroad gave candidates the opportunity to reach the voters directly. The first presidential candidate to use the nation's railroad network extensively was William Jennings Bryan, the Democratic and Populist nominee of 1896. Although he lost to Republican William McKinley, Bryan (as one historian notes) "set such a noisy, energetic example that no candidate who followed him dared ignore it." In the 1948 presidential election, President Harry Truman logged 31,000 miles by rail, made 356 speeches, and shook the hands of approximately 500,000 voters. Later, the airplane allowed candidates to travel even faster and more widely.

Yet for all his efforts, Truman spoke directly to only a small fraction of the electorate (approximately 28.4 million people cast ballots in that election).

Far more people heard Truman's voice (as well as those of his rivals) on the radio, another technological innovation that helped change the relationship between the candidates and the voters. Using radio, candidates could enter the homes of prospective voters with their messages.

In 1923, in an effort to revive interest in the League of Nations, ex-President Woodrow Wilson took to the radio to plead his cause. Yet the radio was so comparatively new in 1923 that more of Wilson's mail dealt more with radio reception than with his message. In 1924, both President Calvin Coolidge and Democratic challenger John W. Davis bought radio time for their speeches, although it is virtually impossible to estimate how many people actually listened to them. In 1928, the first radio advertisements for presidential candidates were produced and broadcast, as was Democratic candidate Al Smith's announcement of his candidacy (perhaps the first political event staged almost exclusively for the radio, although it was broadcast only in southeastern New York).

The first president to use radio to great advantage was Franklin Roosevelt. His famous fireside chats were informative, conversational, and reassuring to a people in the depths of the depression. Whether in fireside chats or speeches, Roosevelt was a candidate and president made for radio. His well-modulated voice (as opposed to that of his fifth cousin, Theodore Roosevelt, which was thin and high-pitched), his use of memorable phrases, and his down-to-earth manner made Roosevelt an unparalleled radio candidate. Not his equal, his successor Harry Truman in 1948 was the first presidential candidate to employ a "media adviser." Both the campaigns and the candidates themselves were changing, partly as a result of technological innovations that allowed them to reach the voters directly and be heard by them. Television would vastly increase that accessibility.

In spite of its supposed newness, television is not that recent an invention. The invention of the iconoscope (the "eye" of the television camera) in 1923 made it theoretically possible to broadcast programs into homes or other places equipped with special television "sets." Experimentation continued in both the United States and England throughout the 1920s, and special events were broadcast over a very limited range to a very small number of television sets. In 1928, General Electric began semiregular telecasts from its laboratories in Schenectady, New York. Yet, whereas British television was developed by the government-owned British Broadcasting Corporation (BBC), the ultimate pioneers of television in the United States were the large radio networks, principally the National Broadcasting Corporation (NBC) and its parent company Radio Corporation of America (RCA), both of which had the revenue, scientific expertise, and contracted performers to make widespread television a reality. In 1930, NBC established an experimental television station in New York City, followed by CBS the next year.

The depression of the 1930s slowed the development of television but did not entirely stop it. In 1937, the BBC televised the coronation of George VI, and during the next year it began regular television programming. In the United States, television sets first

CHAPTER 11

POLITICS AND
TELEVISION THE
PRESIDENTIAL
ELECTION OF
1988

were sold to the general public in 1939, but sets were expensive (an RCA cost $625),[1] and only a handful of television stations broadcast anything, all in the Northeast.[2] The channeling of materials into war-related industries during World War II further blunted the growth of television.

With the end of the Second World War, television took off. Whereas there were only 10 television stations in the United States in 1947, a year later there were 127. Yet there were still very few programs to watch. In 1946, there was only about one hour per evening of programs and no daytime programming (by 1948, the evening schedules would be filled). And when baseball's World's Series was first telecast in 1947, an estimated 3.9 million people saw it (3.5 million of whom watched the games in bars, which had purchased sets to attract customers, or through the display windows of television retailers). In 1950, 7.4 million television sets were sold in the United States, and architects began to design homes with a "family room," a euphemism for a room where television was watched.[3]

The inability to broadcast over long distances meant that simultaneous transmission of television programming throughout the nation was impossible. Indeed, when the 1947 World Series was broadcast, only viewers in New York City, Philadelphia, Schenectady, and Washington D.C., were able to see it. In 1951, however, the American Telephone and Telegraph Company (AT&T) opened the first coaxial cable between the East and West Coasts, not only increasing the major networks' control over programming but allowing viewers throughout the country to watch simultaneously news broadcasts or special events. Television personalities became household names, and conversation often revolved around the previous night's television programs. A true homogeneous national culture was in the process of formation, with television as the principal agent and arbiter. By 1980, approximately 98 percent of the nation's homes had at least one television set (10 percent had three or more), and the *average* home had the set turned on roughly 6½ hours *per day*.[4]

It was inevitable that the medium of television would have a profound effect on national politics. Television clamored for news (in 1963, both NBC and CBS went to half-hour evening news programs, and by 1971, CBS News had eight hundred employees and a budget of $47 million). Also, candidates saw television as a matchless—albeit expensive—way to reach the voters directly. No longer would presidential candidates have to crisscross the country making speeches; now one speech, delivered from a television studio, could reach more people

1. In 1989 dollars, the cost would have been $4,687.50.
2. Americans who owned a television set in 1939 could have watched President Franklin Roosevelt's speech opening the World's Fair in New York. Technically, however, the first president to appear on television was Herbert Hoover, in 1927, although he was secretary of commerce at the time.
3. It was considered unfashionable to place the television set in the living room. This notion continues to the present, one result of which is that the living room of a middle-class home is barely used.

4. The average viewing time per day had reached 6 hours by 1973.

in one instant than all the people a candidate might see in his or her travels. Finally, like radio, television could allow candidates to insulate themselves from the potentially hostile press or voters while at the same time *appearing* to be more accessible. Truly, the marriage between television and presidential politics was one that both parties craved.

Yet television was an unfamiliar medium that made new demands on presidential candidates. At first, candidates purchased half-hour blocks of television time for their speeches, as Democratic candidate Adlai Stevenson did in 1952 when he ran against the immensely popular General Dwight Eisenhower. Politicians soon realized, however, that voters did not like to have their favorite programs canceled for one evening (television people use the term "pre-empted"), and so they had to devise other methods of reaching the voters. Indeed, on one particular evening during the 1964 presidential race, more television viewers watched "Peyton Place" and "Petticoat Junction" than the Republican-produced conversation between former President Eisenhower and Republican presidential candidate Barry Goldwater.

Presidential candidates also used television by purchasing one-minute or thirty-second advertisements and by getting free publicity through appearances on the networks' television news programs. Yet political figures had no experience with either method, often talking too long for a short advertisement or a short segment on the evening news (called a "sound bite"). Moreover, candidates at first failed to understand what voters who watched these advertisements or sound bites were

looking for. Voters appeared less interested in extensive, well-reasoned arguments than in how a candidate *appeared* on television—did the candidate communicate trust, vigor, decency, self-assurance, intelligence?

Thus in 1952 the Republicans hired Madison Avenue advertising executive Rosser Reeves to create General Eisenhower's television commercials. Previously, Reeves had designed advertising campaigns for Anacin, Rolaids, Colgate toothpaste, and M & M candy—the phrase "melts in your mouth, not in your hand" was his. Democrats complained that their rivals were "selling a candidate the way it [Madison Avenue] sells soap," but in 1956 they copied the Republicans with their own television campaign.

Spot advertising for presidential candidates quickly developed into an art, under the tutelage of advertising experts employed by the major parties. Negative advertising (attacking the rival candidate) was first used in 1956 (by the Democrats) and carefully skilled emotional appeals in 1964 (again by the Democrats, in the now-famous "Daisy commercial," which some believe is the most effective political advertisement ever shown on television).[5] In 1964, the Democrats spent $4.7 million on television advertising, an amount the Repub-

5. The Daisy commercial ran only once, on September 7, 1964, on the "CBS Monday Night at the Movies." In the commercial, a little girl is picking petals from a daisy and counting "one, two, three four" when a voice-over begins a countdown for a nuclear explosion. The camera zooms into the little girl's eye, which becomes the nuclear explosion, followed by a pro-peace statement by President Lyndon Johnson. The commercial was intended to focus attention on what many perceived was Johnson's more bellicose rival, Senator Barry Goldwater.

CHAPTER 11

POLITICS AND
TELEVISION THE
PRESIDENTIAL
ELECTION OF
1988

licans more than doubled in 1968 ($12.6 million). By the presidential election of 1984, both sides combined spent approximately $34 million on television advertisements.

Appearances of presidential candidates on network news programs required even greater adjustments by the candidates themselves. Unlike television advertisements that their advertising agencies produced and therefore controlled, television news demanded that candidates say all they had to say in one sound bite, the average time of which in 1984 was 14.79 seconds. What could a candidate say or do in that length of time that would make an impression on the viewers? In response, candidates began to be well-coached and began to create situations (historian Daniel Boorstin called them "pseudoevents"), principally to get on the television news. Events had to be timed properly so that tape of the pseudoevent (visiting a school, speaking to senior citizens, touring a housing project, and so on) could reach the network in time for the news. Candidates also had to simplify their appeals, at the same time looking intelligent, no easy task for the most seasoned campaign veteran.[6]

In 1960, television staged another pseudoevent, one that some believe was extremely influential in the voters' minds: the series of televised debates between Vice President Richard Nixon and Senator John F. Kennedy. It is still not clear what impact these debates had on the voters, but many observers believe that Vice President Nixon's *appearance* (thin, haggard, perspiring, with a heavy five o'clock shadow) was decisive for many voters (those who heard the debates on the radio without seeing Nixon thought he had won, whereas the reverse was true for television viewers). Yet those debates did not become a regular feature of presidential campaigns until 1976. In 1984, a new wrinkle was added when the vice presidential candidates engaged each other in one debate, a practice repeated in 1988.

By 1988, Ronald Reagan was coming to the end of what many Americans believed had been an enormously successful presidency. The domestic economy appeared healthy, federal income taxes for some groups had been reduced, and Reagan had signed the first significant arms reduction treaty with the Soviet Union. Indeed, in 1988 President Reagan's approval rating was at a record high for a president leaving office.

At first, however, Vice President Bush seemed unable to capitalize on these advantages in his bid for the Oval Office. President Reagan's personal popularity did not seem to be transferable to other office seekers (as evidenced by the defeats suffered by Republicans in the congressional elections of 1984 and 1986). In addition, some conservative Republicans distrusted Bush's embracing of Reagan, a man he had unsuccessfully opposed in the 1980 Republican primaries. Finally, in 1988 Bush's image was not very strong, leading some journalists to bring up the "wimp factor." In fact, shortly after the Democratic National

6. The candidate in 1988 who seemed best able to master the demands of the sound bite was the Reverend Jesse Jackson. What Daniel Boorstin called "pseudo events" have also been referred to by others as "media events or, in 1988, "photo opportunities."

Convention, Dukakis briefly led Bush in the public opinion polls by a wide margin.

Yet Bush was able to overcome these tremendous obstacles to beat Dukakis in the 1988 presidential race. How did Bush overcome his initial disadvantages? Although some observers believe that given the mood of the country, Dukakis had little chance of beating Bush, many other students of American politics think that Bush's masterful use of television won the election.

For all the money spent on televi-sion advertising, however, the amount of time spent creating media events for the network news and the amount of effort coaching and preparing for a televised debate, it is still not clear what impact television has had on the outcome of presidential elections. Even so, candidates and their advisers are convinced that television's impact is enormous. In 1980, Vice President Walter Mondale said, ". . . if I had to give up . . . the opportunity to get on the evening news or the veto power . . . I'd throw the veto power away." Was Mondale correct?

THE METHOD

In 1978, more than two-thirds of Americans surveyed reported that they obtained their political information principally from television. During presidential election years, modern television gives voters in three forms what for many of them may be the only political information they receive: (1) televised advertisements, produced and paid for by media experts and the candidates' parties; (2) reports broadcast on network television news; and (3) televised debates between the major presidential and vice presidential candidates.[7]

The evidence for this chapter combines several of the types of evidence you used previously: newspaper and magazine reports about television and the 1988 campaign, statistics (results of polls), samples of television advertisements, cartoons, excerpts from the presidential and vice presidential debates, summaries of one network's news coverage for October 1988. The evidence is divided into advertisements, network news broadcasts, and debates. It helps to analyze each type of evidence separately.[8]

As you examine the evidence regarding advertising, ask yourself the following questions:

7. In 1960, Congress suspended the equal time doctrine to facilitate the Nixon-Kennedy debates. If that had not been done, minor party candidates could have claimed equal time to express their views, something that television executives strongly opposed.

8. Television coverage of the nominating conventions has not been dealt with in this chapter.

CHAPTER 11

POLITICS AND
TELEVISION THE
PRESIDENTIAL
ELECTION OF
1988

1. Do observers believe political advertising was different from that of previous presidential campaigns?
2. Why do observers believe that was so?
3. Based on the limited samples of advertisements shown or mentioned by observers, do you believe their opinion is correct?
4. How did voters appear to have reacted to the 1988 advertisement?

In the late 1960s and early 1970s, many Americans, especially conservatives, attacked the news media as being biased against them. Several studies conducted between 1968 and 1980 showed, however, that television coverage of presidential candidates essentially was balanced and that the qualifications of all major candidates were well-reported by television newscasts. Based on the evidence for 1988, was television news coverage balanced? What types of stories were reported? What did observers think of the 1988 news coverage? What role did television news coverage play in the campaign?

Millions of voters watched the presidential and vice presidential debates. Judging by the selections in the evidence, how substantive were those debates? What did observers think of them? What role (if any) did these debates play in the campaign?

Once you have answered the above questions, put all your answers together to answer the three principal questions at the beginning of this chapter. For question 3, you will have to use your imagination.

Source 1 from *Gallup Report,* March 1988, pp. 6–8.

1. Public Believes Negative TV Commercials Lack Credibility.

Presidential candidates' attacks on their opponents in recent television spots draw an overwhelmingly negative response from Americans who have seen campaign advertising.

Seven in 10 (70 percent) say the criticism found in this type of advertising cannot usually be justified while only 19 percent believe the attacks are generally valid and 11 percent are unsure.

The effectiveness of negative television campaigning has been much debated during the presidential primaries. Evidence from some primaries suggests that derogatory advertising may have had the desired impact. But while the ads may have changed some votes, the survey shows that the carefully-packaged assaults generally leave a distasteful impression in the minds of many voters that could in some situations actually backfire on their sponsors.

Low regard for the credibility of negative ads cuts across all population groups. Regionally, Midwesterners are most likely to regard the charges in the ads as baseless (78 percent), Easterners least likely (63 percent).

Almost half the public (48 percent) reports seeing a great deal or quite a lot of candidate advertising, 45 percent not very much and 7 percent none. Those over age 50 report the most exposure to such ads, college graduates and Westerners the least.

CHAPTER 11

POLITICS AND
TELEVISION THE
PRESIDENTIAL
ELECTION OF
1988

Viewing of Candidate T.V. Ads

QUESTION: *So far this year, how much television advertising would you say you have seen for the candidates running for president?*

March 8–12, 1988 (Telephone)

	Great Deal	Quite a Lot	Not Very Much	None	No Opinion	Number of Interviews
National	**23%**	**25%**	**45%**	**7%**	*****	**1,003**
Sex						
Men	21	26	45	8	*	496
Women	25	24	44	6	1	507
Age						
18–29 years	24	22	45	9	*	232
30–49 years	19	23	51	6	1	416
50 and older	26	30	38	5	1	347
Region						
East	21	27	45	6	1	251
Midwest	28	23	42	7	*	267
South	27	29	41	3	*	300
West	14	19	54	12	1	185
Race						
Whites	22	25	45	7	1	887
Nonwhites	27	25	46	2	*	111
Blacks	31	24	44	1	*	84
Education						
College graduates	18	19	56	6	1	301
College incomplete	19	28	44	9	*	230
High school graduates	27	27	39	6	1	358
Not high school graduates	25	26	44	5	*	111
Politics						
Republicans	22	27	44	6	1	305
Democrats	23	23	47	6	1	323
Independents	23	25	45	7	*	348
Religion						
Protestants	25	27	43	5	*	568
Catholics	19	23	50	8	*	263

Is Criticism Justified? (Based on Those Who Have Seen Any Presidential Candidate's Advertising)

QUESTION: *When candidates criticize their opponents on T.V., is it your impression that their criticism is usually justified or not justified?*
March 8–12, 1988 (Telephone)

	Justified	Not Justified	No Opinion	Number of Interviews
National	**19%**	**70%**	**11%**	**939**
Sex				
Men	21	68	11	462
Women	18	72	10	462
Age				
18–29 years	27	65	8	213
30–49 years	20	71	9	390
50 and older	14	72	14	329
Region				
East	21	63	16	236
Midwest	15	78	7	247
South	19	71	10	291
West	23	66	11	165
Race				
Whites	18	71	11	828
Non-whites	28	59	13	107
Blacks	31	54	15	82
Education				
College graduates	19	72	9	280
College incomplete	23	65	12	212
High school graduates	19	71	10	339
Not high school graduates	18	69	13	105
Politics				
Republicans	22	67	11	287
Democrats	22	68	10	306
Independents	15	76	9	324
Religion				
Protestants	19	70	11	542
Catholics	20	71	9	245
Evangelicals				
Evangelicals	19	71	10	292
Non-Evangelicals	20	70	10	618

CHAPTER 11

POLITICS AND
TELEVISION THE
PRESIDENTIAL
ELECTION OF
1988

Sources 2 and 3 supplied by National Security Political Action Committee, Washington, D.C.

2. Transcription of Bush Television Commercial.

Bush and Dukakis on Crime

SCRIPT	DESCRIPTION
NARRATOR: Bush and Dukakis on Crime	still photographs of Bush and Dukakis
Bush supports the death penalty for first degree murderers.	photograph of Bush
Dukakis not only opposes the death penalty, he allowed first degree murderers to have weekend passes from prison.	photograph of Dukakis
One was Willie Horton who murdered a boy in a robbery, stabbing him 19 times.	photograph of Horton (a male African American)
Despite a life sentence, Horton received 10 weekend passes from prison. Horton fled, kidnapped a young couple, stabbing the man and repeatedly raping his girlfriend.	photograph of Horton with police officer
Weekend prison passes, Dukakis on crime.	photograph of Dukakis

FADE

3. Transcription of Bush Television Commercial.[9]

Dukakis on Pollution

SCRIPT	DESCRIPTION
DUKAKIS: We are going to have an Environmental Protection Agency that is more interested in stopping pollution than protecting the polluters.	film footage of Dukakis
HICKS: With a statement like that, it's hard to believe that the most polluted harbor in the country, historic Boston Harbor, is just a few blocks away from our state capitol, on Beacon Hill. I'm Cile Hicks, a state representative from Massachusetts. This used to be a beautiful harbor.	footage of Lucile Hicks with Boston Harbor in background
Now, it's a disgrace, after years of mismanagement, and a daily helping of sludge and waste. It's ironic that he wants to stop polluters.	footage of polluted Boston Harbor
Let's look at the record. In 1974, during Dukakis's first term as governor, he promised to clean up Boston Harbor. Well, nine years later, the Reagan/Bush Environmental Protection Agency had to sue Massachusetts to clean up what has been officially declared the dirtiest harbor in America.	footage of Lucile Hicks, Harbor in the background.

9. Part of "The View from Massachusetts," a television program that attacked Dukakis's record as Governor of Massachusetts.

CHAPTER 11

POLITICS AND
TELEVISION THE
PRESIDENTIAL
ELECTION OF
1988

So filthy is our once beautiful harbor that just two weeks ago, during the height of the summer season, six of our most popular beaches had to be closed by state health officials.

photograph of *The Boston Globe* newspaper clipping on beach closings

So when you hear Mike Dukakis present himself as an environmentalist, ask him why he hasn't stopped the polluters in his own state.

footage of Lucile Hicks

FADE

Sources 4 through 7 from *New York Times,* Oct. 10, 1988; Oct. 19, 1988; and Oct. 22, 1988.

4. Nominees Wage Intensified War of Attack Ads.

BY MICHAEL ORESKES

Here are a few questions a weekend television watcher was likely to encounter:

He has raised taxes and raised them again, so how good a Governor is Michael S. Dukakis?

He weakened regulations on corporate polluters, so do you believe it when George Bush tells you he's going to be the environmentalist President?

Which candidate gave weekend passes to first-degree murderers?

Which one sat by while his Administration tried to cut $200 billion from Social Security?

And there is one question viewers will not encounter: When will the Presidential candidates stop hammering each other and say why anyone should vote FOR them and not AGAINST their opponents?

HEAVY TIME FOR COMMERCIALS

The first four questions are taken virtually verbatim from the advertising of Vice President Bush and Governor Dukakis, appearing on this holiday weekend, the heaviest period yet of Presidential campaign advertising.

After a slow and shaky start by the Dukakis campaign, the war of the airwaves has finally been joined, with a vengeance, in the past few days. Presidential contenders have attacked each other in past campaigns. But there is probably no other time when both campaigns have been as relentlessly negative as they are right now.

Some of this is a result of the oft-noted nature of this year's campaign: that there are two contenders with ill-defined images that can be easily reshaped, especially for the worse.

But some of it, too, is a political style that has filtered up from below. This kind of sharp-elbow campaigning has become commonplace in races for Senate, statehouse and other offices. The ads that Mr. Dukakis began airing last week to attack Mr. Bush as a "packaged" candidate are much like the ones Democrat Thomas A. Daschle used to defeat his Republican opponent, Senator James Abdnor, in the 1986 South Dakota Senate race.

"I think people are really used to negative advertising." said Susan Estrich, Mr. Dukakis's campaign manager. "It's effective. It's become a fixture. I no longer think blame is an issue. We've moved past the point where anyone takes heat for running negative." Ms. Estrich pointed out that both campaigns have run positive spots, such as those featuring their candidate speaking at the convention. But the negative commercials are the ones being talked about, she said.

OVERCOMING EARLY DAMAGE

Indeed, one of Mr. Dukakis's big problems right now is to overcome the damage done by two negative commercials the Bush campaign fired at him after the Republican convention.

A disorganized Dukakis advertising team allowed these ads, attacking Mr. Dukakis's handling of crime and of pollution in Boston Harbor, to go unanswered for a substantial period, a cardinal sin of political advertising.

"We had a lot of creative chiefs who had their own ideas about what needed to be done," said Frank Mingo, whose New York advertising firm is handling black media for the Dukakis campaign.

Mr. Dukakis's California supporters were so distraught by the lack of action, that they made their own commercials and put them on in California

CHAPTER 11

POLITICS AND
TELEVISION THE
PRESIDENTIAL
ELECTION OF
1988

to counteract the image of a polluted Boston harbor. "Bush's Administration cut funds to clean up California's coast from San Diego Harbor to San Francisco Bay," said one ad.

At the outset of the fall campaign, the difference between the two campaigns was striking. Mr. Dukakis had a team of creative talent drawn from Madison Avenue, trying to emulate the approach President Reagan successfully used for his election drive. Mr. Bush, at the same time, had concentrated all authority for his advertising, and for much else in his message as well, in one man, Roger Ailes, his media adviser.

The result was a focused message from Mr. Bush, and a blur from Mr. Dukakis.

But the Dukakis campaign has regrouped. A new man is in charge of the Dukakis advertising. David D'Alessandro, who organized advertising campaigns for John Hancock Insurance Company. And last week the campaign struck back.

The campaign unveiled a set of spots there are now five with actors playing Mr. Bush's campaign staff. They are portrayed as cooking up attacks on Mr. Dukakis (on such issues as the furlough program under which some Massachusetts prisoners escaped) and defenses for Mr. Bush ("Get out the flag, boys," a handler sputters sarcastically in one 30 second spot). . . .

5. Dukakis Ads: Blurred Signs, Uncertain Path.

BY MICHAEL ORESKES
SPECIAL TO THE NEW YORK TIMES

WASHINGTON, Oct. 18—One major reason for Michael S. Dukakis's campaign difficulties has been an inability to produce timely, effective and consistent television advertising, judging by the laments of Democrats and the gloating of Republicans.

As seen through the eye of his own advertising, the Democratic Presidential candidate was an economic manager. Then he was a successful debater. Now, he is a concerned father.

And when it came to negative advertisements, a staple of this year's television campaign, the Dukakis spots were generally regarded as confusing or belated.

No one suggests that the advertising campaign is Mr. Dukakis's only problem. Even those who believe it is very important often suggest that the ever shifting focus of his advertising is an indicator of a larger failing in the Dukakis campaign.

One summary of the Democratic view came from Harrison Hickman, a Democratic poll taker, who said, "It's hard to talk about it in a systematic way." He added, "There are lots of nodules of Dukakis advertising, but I'm not sure there's a consistent pattern or theme that runs through it."

Mr. Hickman said the advertisements failed one basic test. "When political campaign professionals sit and look at ads they should be able to infer a strategy," he said. For example, Vice President Bush's advertising, said Mr. Hickman, was clearly aimed at creating doubts about Mr. Dukakis's record and political values while establishing Mr. Bush as both a leader and a kind man. But in the Dukakis advertising, he said, "I'm not sure you see a sequential strategy."

Janet Mullins, who is in charge of deploying advertising for the Bush campaign, went even further, saying: "It's been unfocused, erratic, borderline amateurish, a waste of money. If I were Dukakis I would not be happy with that particular part of my campaign. It just hasn't done anything to help him."

Part of the Dukakis problem was internal disorganization, campaign officials acknowledged. The campaign assembled a team of creative talent to make advertisements. But unlike the Bush campaign, where Roger Ailes has tight control over all advertising decisions, no one was clearly in charge of Dukakis advertising and little got done for months, the officials said.

Scripts, dozens of them, were written, but many were never approved. Others were approved and produced, but never aired. Two different versions of one ad, with actors playing Bush handlers, were made and the version that was used was the one that came in first. A commercial for use in the Olympics, with a teen-age gymnast doing her routine as Mr. Dukakis spoke about striving for excellence, was produced but never used. Many of the advertising people that the campaign had painstakingly recruited to give the campaign a professional style quit in frustration.

The result is that when the campaign got into full swing after the Republican convention, the Democrats were not ready for the crucial battles of the air waves.

The disorganization of the advertising team was only part of a larger problem within the campaign. In early September Mr. Dukakis decided to reorganize the campaign by bringing back his longtime aide, John Sasso, banished earlier after he said he had sabotaged Senator Joseph R. Biden Jr.'s campaign. Mr. Sasso, in turn, brought in David D'Alessandro, an advertising executive from John Hancock Insurance.

Working with Scott Miller, who runs a New York political consulting firm, and other advertising executives, they produced new advertisements. The

CHAPTER 11

POLITICS AND
TELEVISION THE
PRESIDENTIAL
ELECTION OF
1988

most controversial used a group of actors portraying Mr. Bush's campaign staff, labeled as "packagers."

The advertisements have been widely criticized as confusing. One Democrat said the best thing he could say about them was that no one could tell which side put them on.

But Mr. D'Alessandro said that the advertisements had done what needed to be done: keep open the idea of Mr. Bush as a politician being manipulated by his handlers. Mr. D'Alessandro said many critics in New York and Washington had not seen a wave of more directly negative advertising that also ran, because the packaging ads were run on network television while the more directly negative ads were run largely in local markets in key states. The other ads showed a foolish-looking Mr. Bush and attacked his record directly on issues such as education and drugs.

"People are thinking we blew our entire media budget," on the packaging ads, Mr. D'Alessandro said. In fact, he went on, about 6 percent of the overall budget, estimated at close to $30 million, was spent on broadcasting the packaging ads, as against 25 percent for ads that more directly attacked Mr. Bush.

These ads were criticized too, however, not for their ineffectiveness so much as for their poor timing. "Where was it earlier?" asked one Dukakis campaign official, "That will be the issue." The ads did not begin until weeks after Mr. Bush had started his own advertising attacking Mr. Dukakis's record on crime and the environment with devastating images of pollution in Boston harbor and dangerous-looking criminals walking through a revolving door.

After a period of relentlessly negative advertising, both campaigns this week have somewhat softened their approach, offering at least some reasons to vote for their candidate. But they also both launched new negative advertising urging a vote against their opponent.

The Bush campaign unveiled a new ad that had the unusual attribute of being made almost entirely from a tape of his opponent at a campaign appearance. The tape was of Mr. Dukakis riding around in a tank wearing his Snoopy-style helmet. As Mr. Dukakis rides, an announcer talks about how Mr. Dukakis opposes "virtually every defense system we developed," something Mr. Dukakis denies, and how he now wants to be Commander in Chief. "America can't afford that risk," the announcer says.

The same theme is struck in a more positive Bush ad that features not Mr. Dukakis but the Soviet leader, Mikhail Gorbachev. Mr. Bush and Mr. Gorbachev are shown together in a still photograph taken outside the White House as the announcer says: "This is no time to train somebody in how to meet with the Russians. This is the time for strength and experience."

The latest Dukakis ads feature Senator Dan Quayle, Mr. Bush's running mate, and his contention that he would oversee programs to stamp out drugs.

This ad will be running concurrently with another set designed to humanize Mr. Dukakis. The candidate is seen sitting or standing in a living room talking to the camera. In one, he talks about how much harder it is today to be a young parent. "I'd want my new President to be in touch with the things that are important to me and to my family," he said. "That's not a Democratic concern. That's not a Republican concern. That's a father's concern."

6. Dukakis, in TV Ads, Strikes Back in Kind.

BY MICHAEL ORESKES

After taking weeks of pounding from negative advertising by the campaign of Vice President Bush, Gov. Michael S. Dukakis of Massachusetts finally fought back yesterday in commercials of his own that accuse Mr. Bush of "dragging the truth into the gutter" and showing ads "full of lies."

One of the new ads, with the headline "George Bush's False Advertising," says the Vice President, while attacking a Massachusetts furlough program that allowed a rapist to go free and rape again, "won't talk about the thousands of drug kingpins furloughed from Federal prison while he led the war on drugs."

"One of his furloughed heroin dealers," the ad continues, "raped and murdered Patsy Pedrin, pregnant mother of two."

DEMOCRATS CRITICAL OF SLOW RESPONSE

A second new Dukakis commercial opens with a television set playing the Bush campaign commercial in which the Massachusetts Governor rides around in a tank as an announcer says Mr. Dukakis has been against virtually every new weapons system but now wants to be Commander in Chief. Mr. Dukakis turns off the set, turns to the viewers and says:

"I'm fed up with it. Haven't seen anything like it in 25 years of public life, George Bush's negative TV ads: distorting my record, full of lies, and he knows it."

Many Democrats, even within the campaign organization, have been critical of the Dukakis campaign for being slow to respond to previous Bush ads that painted Mr. Dukakis as soft on crime and weak on the environment. With just over two weeks to go, the campaign's new aggressiveness was signaled by the title given one of the new ads—"counterpunch."

CHAPTER 11

POLITICS AND
TELEVISION THE
PRESIDENTIAL
ELECTION OF
1988

BUSH AIDE SEES DUKAKIS RIDING FOR A FALL

In the ad Governor Dukakis says he was "on the record" as supporting the same weapons systems that he is said to oppose in the Bush ad showing him in a tank. Mr. Dukakis says he was sure both candidates want a strong defense. "So this isn't about defense issues," he says. "It's about dragging the truth into the gutter. And I'm not going to let them do it."

Mark Goodin, Mr. Bush's spokesman, said the new ads would do Mr. Dukakis no good. "Michael Dukakis," the spokesman said, "is trying to play his record backwards in the hopes that the American people will hear a bizarre and otherwise hidden message that would contradict a long and well-documented history of liberalism and excessive emphasis on criminal rights and the nuclear freeze movement.

"No matter how fast he spins the disk, nobody is going to hear him."

7. New York Times, October 27, 1988.

FABENS, Tex., Oct. 20—The oldtime cowboys used to call the high plains that stretch for hundreds of miles from San Antonio to El Paso "the loneliest country there is."

Even today, only ribbons of civilization along the highways and the rivers interrupt the immense, arid vistas of yucca and cottonwood, punctuated here and there by an arroyo or a mesa, and enlivened by jackrabbits and roadrunners and prong-horned antelope. This is still the Wild West, all right, but now people here have telephones, airplanes and television to keep themselves in touch.

It is from television almost exclusively, it seems, that local people have taken their picture of the Presidential campaign; the nominees don't venture out here, even though West Texas has been regarded in recent elections as an area that Democrats have to win to carry the state. This year, only Vice President Bush's message seems to be getting through.

DUKAKIS FAILURE IS NOTICED

Driving west on U.S. 90 and Interstate 10, a traveler couldn't help but notice the failure of Gov. Michael S. Dukakis, Mr. Bush's Democratic rival, to put his ideas across.

A woman in a convenience store in Van Horn asked why Mr. Dukakis did not have any television commercials. It turned out that she thought the Dukakis commercial simulating a cynical Bush strategy meeting was actually one of the Vice President's. A truck driver in Sanderson said he remembered only a single political image from television: junk floating in Boston Harbor. That came from a Bush "attack commercial."

Not one of the dozens or so people interviewed volunteered anything positive about the Massachusetts Governor when asked what he or she recalled about the television coverage of the campaign or about campaign television commercials.

That's not to say that all of them plan to vote for Mr. Bush; they don't. Grace Rodriguez, a waitress at the Cattleman's Steak House here in Fabens, just east of El Paso, said that the first picture that popped into her mind was "Dukakis riding around in that tank, looking silly," followed by "Bush's commercials hitting Dukakis on defense."

Was she going to vote for Mr. Bush, then? No, Ms. Rodriguez answered, she wasn't, because she has been "scared" of the Republican candidate for Vice President, Senator Dan Quayle of Indiana, ever since the night she watched him debating on television.

This is hunting country. Hardware stores advertise "ammo" and Chambers of Commerce put up signs of welcome to sportsmen who come to West Texas to hunt deer, javelina and doves. So it's not surprising that Mr. Bush's advertisements picturing his rival as a gun hater have gone over well here. But commercials criticizing the Massachusetts furlough policy for criminals appear to have had even greater impact.

Lucy Leyba, a gasoline station attendant in Hondo, a town straight out of a Larry McMurtry novel, drew one conclusion from what she called "that commercial that shows Dukakis letting all those people out of prison and everything." She planned to vote for Mr. Bush, she said, sniffling and adding, "If I don't die first from this cold."

Bill Cockerill also recalled the prison commercial—he called it "the revolving door commercial, implying that they come out as fast as they go in"—but he had a different reaction to it. Mr. Cockerill, the city editor of The Uvalde Leader News, said the commercial was "pretty dramatic, and probably effective if you don't know the background."

He said he judged it "ludicrously slanted" because many states, including Texas, have similar programs of releasing criminals.

CHAPTER 11

POLITICS AND
TELEVISION THE
PRESIDENTIAL
ELECTION OF
1988

Source 8 from San Jose *Mercury News,* Oct. 30, 1988.

8. Slick Ads: The Making of the President, 1988.

BY BERT ROBINSON
MERCURY NEWS STAFF WRITER

The distinctive images cascade across a television screen: dead fish bobbing
in Boston Harbor, violent criminals departing a Massachusetts jail through
a revolving door, a cop corralling smugglers who evade a California cigarette
tax.

Slick? Sure. Simplistic? Maybe. But these are also some of the most powerful political commercials in history, according to a group of disinterested
professionals who craft product advertising. In an election year without gal-
vanizing issues, this season's commercials—most of them negative in tone—
may be having unprecedented influence on voters searching for a way to
choose.

"I'm seeing a use of the medium, particularly in the Bush ads which are
very graphically powerful, that you just wouldn't have seen four years ago,"
said Geoff Thompson, director of creative services for Foote, Cone, and Beld-
ing Inc. "They have a real leadership look to them, on a par with some of
the best product campaigns."

Many of the Dukakis 30-second spots, meanwhile, look "cheesy and
cheap," Thompson said. "And since neither side is dealing with product performance issues at all, their production values go a long way toward the
only goal they seem to have."

Thompson's observations—which were echoed by three other advertising
executives who reviewed a tape of political ads for the Mercury News—
dovetail nicely with polling trends during this year's campaign advertising
season. In recent months, as an onslaught of political ads entered the nation's homes, Bush has surged strongly in front of Dukakis in every major
opinion survey.

Because people are reluctant to admit they are influenced by advertising,
those same polls have been unable to link Bush's rise conclusively to his
commercials. But the ad executives, like many political analysts, are convinced of television's crucial role: "People should be reading newspapers and
watching 'Nightline' to make up their minds," said Mike Moser, associate
creative director for Chiat/Day Inc., "We know from experience that people
aren't doing that."

Bush commercial director Roger Ailes, whose use of slow-motion cameras
and black-and-white photography struck one ad man as "very MTV," may

have refined modern political television but he didn't create it. Most knowledgeable observers say it began with Lyndon Johnson's 1964 campaign and its famous "little girl in a field of daisies" spot, which suggested candidate Barry Goldwater would lead the nation to nuclear war.

ADVERTISING AT PINNACLE

But this year, because of tactics and happenstance, political advertising has reached what many experts believe is a pinnacle.

According to Larry Sabato, a professor of political science at the University of Virginia, only a few elections can be fully defined by campaign advertising: others, like the presidential elections of 1968 or 1980, are molded by such overriding issues as war, domestic unrest, or the economy. Clearly, says Sabato, 1988 was wide open.

The gap was filled with a hot campaign technique known in political circles as "infectious advertising." That technique, refined during Sen. Alan Cranston's 1986 race against Ed Zachau, can be stated as, "Convince the public your opponent has a disease before he can prove he's well."

Such guerrilla attacks defied conventional political wisdom, which dictated that negative advertising should be used late and sparingly. Nevertheless, Cranston began flaying Zachau in June—and didn't let up until he won.

"There's no doubt that Bush took the Cranston strategy," said Darry Sragow, Cranston's 1986 campaign manager. "What I like to say is that the Democratic convention put up a blank canvas, and by the time Michael Dukakis got home from the store with the paints, George Bush had already finished two-thirds of the picture."

It helped immensely, said John Crawford, who heads his own advertising firm, that the Bush commercials were so well crafted.

WORDS VS. IMAGES

"The Republicans associate Dukakis with dead fish floating in harbors, or criminals going out of prison to wreak carnage—powerful visual images," he said. "The Democrats tend to give you a lot of written words, 'Here, read these statistics.' If people wanted to read, they wouldn't be watching television."

Crawford particularly admired the success of Bush's Boston Harbor spot in co-opting an issue—the environment—which has traditionally been Dem-

CHAPTER 11

POLITICS AND
TELEVISION THE
PRESIDENTIAL
ELECTION OF
1988

ocratic domain. In that commercial, the only visual image is provided by a camera panning the sewage pipes and polluted waters of the harbor. At the same time, an announcer intones that Michael Dukakis failed to clean this up.

Dukakis initially countered his opponent's flashy attacks with some cleverness of his own: the so-called "Packaging of George Bush" series, designed by David D'Alessandro, a veteran of John Hancock Life Insurance commercials. D'Alessandro's campaign handiwork introduced America to George Bush's handlers—portrayed by actors—who were laboring to concoct an attractive image for the vice president.

But where Bush struck chord after chord in a masterful commercial progression, Dukakis' performance seemed badly out of tune to the advertising experts.

"I was real confused the first few times I saw this," Moser said. "If you really think about it, what they're doing is using a slick commercial for Michael Dukakis to tell you that George Bush is too slick. It makes no sense."

Those ads, which aired in late September and early October, have since been removed from circulation. The advertising executives were no more impressed by Dukakis' newer, more direct responses to Bush's ads.

"He's saying, 'My opponent's doing shabby advertising. Watch this!'," Crawford said. . . .

IS FAITH UNDERMINED

One question is likely to be hotly debated after Election Day: Have this year's scathing ads undermined public faith in politics and politicians?

Already, polls have suggested that much damage is being done. A recent Wall Street Journal/NBC News survey found that nearly six out of 10 voters wish they had other choices for president.

After watching the commercials, so does Hayes of Chiat/Day. "I don't like any of these people any more," she said. "I'm not inspired to vote at all."

But Crawford retorted, "The statement that people are turned off by politics—all that says is that people are bored with the candidates and the commercials. I think (the criticism) is a rationalization.

"A good political brawl is in the great American tradition. Give 'em hell, Harry. People love it."

Source 9 from *Newsweek,* Oct. 17, 1988.

9. Well, So Much for Subtlety. . . .

VIDEO POLITICS

Dukakis's long-awaited attack ads, presenting imaginary dialogues among Bush's "packagers," were instantly controversial. Too complicated, said critics. Too inside. Voters won't get it. The Dukakis camp stuck with the concept, buying more air time to run the ads. But they also hedged their bets with a distinctly uncomplicated anti-Quayle spot.

■ "Flag" (Dukakis). Actors playing the cynical Bush handlers worry that Dukakis's health-insurance plan is "going to play real well with the middle class." They decide to "wrap" Bush up in the flag. Either much too subtle or incredibly brilliant.★★

■ "Furlough" (Bush). Stark prison scenes. Sinister inmates go through a turnstile gate. Dukakis, the ad says, gave "weekend furloughs to first-degree murderers. . . . Many are still at large." Nobody will say this spot's too subtle.★★

■ "Oval Office" (Dukakis). Dukakis can be blunt, too: "The most powerful man in the world is also mortal." A heart beats. Shot of president's chair, headlines, photos of Truman, LBJ, Ford. Yet Bush chose "J. Danforth Quayle." Packs a punch.★★★

CHAPTER 11

POLITICS AND
TELEVISION THE
PRESIDENTIAL
ELECTION OF
1988

Source 10 from *Washington Post,* Oct. 25, 1988.

10. Smoke-Filled Room.

SMOKE-FILLED ROOM

Source 11 from *Newsweek,* Sept. 12, 1988.

11. George Bush's Made-for-TV Makeover.

George Bush's campaign staffers used to wince whenever their candidate appeared on television. They feared that the vice president, prone to shrill attacks and goofy preppisms, would commit yet another embarrassing gaffe. Now, the days when Bush might blurt out "zip-a-dee-doo-da" or call ABC newsman Ted Koppel "Dan" seem little more than campaign nostalgia. Even Bush's closest advisers are somewhat astonished by the new, telegenic

George Bush—relaxed, authoritative ... even presidential. How did the man the Democrats derided for being born "with a silver foot in his mouth" become the man with the silver tongue?

Bush confidants credit the transformation to the psychological lift of last month's Republican convention, when the vice president finally emerged from Ronald Reagan's shadow. "His whole mind-set changed," says senior Bush consultant Charlie Black. "He is No. 1. He wakes up every morning thinking that this is his campaign to win, not thinking about being Reagan's vice president." At the same time, Bush has revamped the style and substance of his campaign. He has focused his message by attacking Michael Dukakis on "wedge" issues like crime and defense. And he has undergone a media makeover by some of the best political gurus in the field.

The Bush team, led by campaign honchos James Baker and Lee Atwater, has performed major surgery on their candidate's speaking style. They have all but banished the trademark misstatements and mixed metaphors by bridling Bush's tendency to ad-lib. Aides say the vice president is spending more time alone previewing his remarks, smoothing out potential tongue twisters in advance. Once behind the podium, Bush sticks to his cue cards, rarely winging it as he did in the past. And he seems to have absorbed the lessons of high-priced television consultant Roger Ailes, who has improved Bush's delivery by teaching him to speak more slowly, and in a deeper voice.

New speechwriters, such as Peggy Noonan and Bob Grady, have also been feeding Bush better material, peppered with sharp one-liners. Some of the most effective were culled from last month's well-crafted acceptance speech. When Bush talks about taxes, he invariably includes the "read my lips: NO ... NEW ... TAXES" refrain that produced thunderous applause in New Orleans. It has become so familiar that crowds often chime in.

To help ensure that the networks get a concise, punchy quote for the evening news, the Bush staff cooks up a "line of the day" to be delivered in suitably dramatic fashion. Last Wednesday's line of the day—"I am an environmentalist"—was chosen a full week in advance. Just in case reporters on the stump miss the point, the daily quotable quote is published in a one-page memo distributed to key Bush staffers and GOP party leaders all over the country. The surrogates are asked to sound the well-rehearsed theme whenever they speak on the candidate's behalf.

Good visuals: The Bush campaign is also winning the all-important battle of the backdrops. While Dukakis is often seen speaking behind a visually dull podium, the vice president is typically surrounded by enthusiastic supporters or presented in dramatic settings—like Boston Harbor. So far, the Dukakis campaign has failed to master the Republicans' understanding of

CHAPTER 11

POLITICS AND
TELEVISION THE
PRESIDENTIAL
ELECTION OF
1988

what TV news producers want and how to give it to them. "We have reels and reels of tape of the back of Dukakis's head," says Michael Rosenbaum, a CBS producer covering the governor's campaign. Rosenbaum recalls a photo op where Dukakis spoke to a group of students on a beach near San Francisco. In order to face the students, Dukakis had his back to the camera. "The only reason Dukakis was out there on the ocean was to get his picture taken," Rosenbaum points out. "So you might as well see his face." In the war of the sound bites, pictures often speak louder than words.

Source 12 is from The *New York Times,* Oct. 4, 1988.

12. Candidates and Media at Odds Over Message.

BY MICHAEL ORESKES

While the attention of most Americans was focused Thursday on the space shuttle Discovery's climb into orbit, two other infrequent events went almost unnoticed: Both Vice President Bush and Gov. Michael S. Dukakis held news conferences.

It was the first time in nearly two weeks that either Presidential nominee had spoken at any length with the herd of reporters who dependably follow them around the country. "Here we are," Mr. Dukakis told the reporters Thursday when they asked at his news conference why he rarely called such gatherings anymore. "Take advantage of the opportunity. You never know when it will happen again."

The journalists, both for publications and for broadcast outlets, are becoming increasingly frustrated about their lack of access to the candidates. Television network executives say the candidates will find it harder to get on the evening news if all they offer is a prepared theme-of-the-day, which they try to force onto the air and into newspapers by avoiding any other, distracting, comments.

'NO SUBSTANTIVE CORE'

"If the photo opportunity of the day is simply a visual with no substantive core we should walk away from it," said the NBC news correspondent Andrea Mitchell.

There is some evidence that the television cameras are turning away from the candidates, although it was not long ago that all three networks, and many newspapers as well, offered pictures of Mr. Bush visiting a flag factory in New Jersey.

Brian M. Healy, producer in charge of election coverage for CBS News, said the flag factory was really the last straw. "They're going to have to earn their way on to the air," he said.

On Friday night none of the networks used the speeches Mr. Dukakis made in Texas attacking Mr. Bush's farm policies and those Mr. Bush made in Massachusetts attacking Mr. Dukakis's criminal justice policies. ABC and NBC showed film of the candidates at their events while the anchor read a few words about their remarks. CBS did not show any pictures while Dan Rather read a few words about each candidate's day.

CBS's main coverage of the race that day was a piece on the Vice-Presidential candidates, what they were doing and how they were preparing for their debate Wednesday. On NBC, Tom Brokaw went to Chicago to interview swing voters.

Source 13 from *U.S. News and World Report*, Oct. 3, 1988.

Television turned on George Bush last week. Until then, TV's coverage of the Bush campaign had been rooted in tactical admiration: How pretty the pictures were of Bush surrounding himself with the flag and leading audiences in the Pledge of Allegiance; how clever those "visuals" were; how reflective of the values a successful presidential candidate must evoke.

The screw turned on Tuesday, when the Vice President spent time at a New Jersey flag factory telling America that "flag sales are up." Had Bush gone too far? Yep, said television unanimously. All three of the network evening newscasts hit Bush with the same club, a Dukakis sound bite attacking his opponent. "Mr. Bush," said Dukakis, "isn't it time you came out from behind the flag and told us what you intend to do?" Dukakis was talking about health care, but TV's criticism was broader. NBC's Lisa Meyers, for example, bashed both candidates, but especially Bush, for using the "kind of rhetoric that leads some to recall Samuel Johnson's observation that 'patriotism is the last refuge of a scoundrel.'" . . .

CHAPTER 11

POLITICS AND
TELEVISION THE
PRESIDENTIAL
ELECTION OF
1988

Source 14 from *New Yorker,* Oct. 17, 1988.

14.

"And as the campaign heats up, the latest poll shows the Dan Rather news team running slightly ahead of the Peter Jennings news team, with the Tom Brokaw team just two points back and gaining."

Source 15 from "NBC Nightly News," Oct. 2–31, 1988.

15. Summaries of Reports on Presidential Election.

Date	Subject	Coverage Time
October 2	Quayle campaigning	:20
	Photo opportunities—Bush and Dukakis	3:10
3	Debate and poll results	3:30
4	Upcoming Bentsen-Quayle debate	2:30
5	Upcoming VP debate–preparations	2:20
	Bush on low-income children	1:30
	Dukakis on crime and drugs	:20
6	Report on VP debate (previous night)	6:00
	Campaign in Texas	3:40

Date	Subject	Coverage Time
October 7	VP debate—who won?	5:20
	Dukakis on Quayle	5:20
	Bush on Dukakis and Willie Horton	5:20
	More on VP debate	:20
	Reaganomics and Bush	4:00
8	Bush defends Quayle	6:20
	Dukakis on Quayle	6:20
	Lack of black enthusiasm for Dukakis (photo opp. Jackson)	6:20
10	Bush leads in polls	5:00
	Bush's TV ads	5:00
	Dukakis in parade with JFK Jr.	5:00
	Election and future Supreme Court	3:10
	Quayle on becoming president	:20
11	Popular reaction to Quayle	2:30
	Dukakis's TV ads on Quayle	2:30
	Bentsen on crime	:30
12	Quayle campaigning (photo opp.)	:50
	Upcoming Bush-Dukakis debate	1:50
	Election and environmental issues	3:50
	Bush on Dukakis's prison furloughs	:30
13	Preparations for Bush-Dukakis debate	5:50
	John Chancellor on lack of warmth in campaign	1:40
	Interviews with two voters on why they will vote the ways they will	3:40
14	Debate reported (occurred previous night)	2:50
	Debate aftermath—who won?	3:30
	Polls on who won debate	2:40
	John Chancellor on debate	1:50
	Bush on whether he'll agree to third debate	:30
15	Photo opportunities—Bush and Dukakis	4:10
16	Photo opportunities—Bush and Dukakis	3:20
17	Poll shows Bush's lead increasing	4:40
	Teamsters endorse Bush but not Quayle	:20
	Dukakis strategy	1:20
18	Dukakis behind	2:20
	Bush and U.S.S.R.	1:00
	Election and U.S.S.R.	3:00
	John Chancellor on polls and TV ads	1:30
19	Polls	
	Dukakis on Bush's negative ads	2:20
	Bush's foreign policy	:30
20	Policemen criticize Dukakis on crime	2:40
	Crime issue	3:20
	Importance of Jackson to Dukakis	

CHAPTER 11

POLITICS AND
TELEVISION THE
PRESIDENTIAL
ELECTION OF
1988

Date	Subject	Coverage Time
October 21	Dukakis campaign worker resigns after starting rumor about Bush extramarital affair	
	Dukakis apologizes	2:30
	Polls	
	Bush and chemical weapons ban	3:00
22	Bush disavows literature, that alleged murderers and rapists support Dukakis	
	Bentsen popularity not helping Dukakis in Texas	7:10
	Chicago newspapers endorse Bush but not Quayle	
24	Bentsen on Republicans' negative campaign (Willie Horton)	4:00
	Some say Republican ad on Horton is racist	
	Polls and projections	1:50
25	Dukakis on Bush's TV ads	2:10
	Ineffective Dukakis TV ads	2:40
	Dukakis and Massachusetts National Guard	:20
26	Photo opportunities—Bush and Dukakis	
	Bush and taxes	2:30
	Bush TV ads	
	Campaign and deficit—reports neither candidate really addressing issue	3:50
27	Polls	2:50
	Photo opportunities—Bush and Dukakis	1:50
28	Dukakis and nuclear safety	1:00
	Bush—crime—Horton	2:30
	Campaign and drugs	3:20
30	"L" word—Dukakis says he's a liberal	3:10
	Candidates' wives (president and vice president)	4:30
31	Videotape from American hostage in Lebanon accusing Bush of negotiating with hijackers in 1985	1:00
	Projections—Dukakis and L word	3:40
	Interview with Bush (prerecorded) on several issues, including TV ads	6:10

Source 16 from *Gallup Report,* October 1988, pp. 9, 12–13.

16. Presidential Debate Has Little Impact on Contest. (Public Reaction to First Debate[10] Between Bush and Dukakis.)

As the dust settled after the first Bush-Dukakis debate, it became increasingly clear the debate had little immediate impact on the presidential race.

A Gallup Poll taken September 27–28 found the Bush-Quayle Republican ticket leading the Democrats' Dukakis-Bentsen slate by a 47 percent to 42 percent margin, virtually unchanged from the 49 percent to 41 percent GOP edge recorded in a pre-debate poll in mid-September.

More than eight voters in 10 said they had watched the televised debate (59 percent) or followed the subsequent news coverage (23 percent).

A 38 percent plurality of those who watched the debate thought Dukakis had done a better job, while 29 percent cited Bush and 31 percent felt neither candidate won. In a Newsweek Poll conducted by Gallup on the night of the debate, 42 percent named Dukakis the victor and 41 percent Bush, with only 12 percent saying neither candidate excelled. This suggests that interpretations of the event in the news media played a major role in swaying voter opinion toward Dukakis in the days following the debate.

Although Dukakis was given a slight edge as the winner, relatively few voters who either watched the debate or followed the news coverage say it influenced them to vote for either Dukakis (12 percent) or Bush (9 percent), with a large majority (77 percent) reporting their voting intentions were largely unaffected by the event.

Voters' opinions of the candidates remain about the same as they were in mid-September. The Gallup Survey shows favorable opinions of Bush outnumber unfavorable ones, 57 percent to 37 percent, while Dukakis's ratings are 52 percent-39 percent positive. These findings, however, show a halt in the steady erosion of voter confidence in Dukakis, which grew from 22 percent negative after the Democratic convention, to 32 percent following the GOP convention, to 40 percent in mid-September.

In addition, although neither candidate's trial heat standing was enhanced by the debate, the survey suggests that Dukakis may have strengthened his existing support. Currently, 20 percent back Dukakis strongly and 22 percent moderately. Before the debate his strong to moderate ratio was an anemic 16 percent to 25 percent.

---

10. In 1988, there were three nationally televised debates. Bush and Dukakis debated on September 25 and October 13, and Bentsen and Quayle debated on October 5.

CHAPTER 11

POLITICS AND
TELEVISION THE
PRESIDENTIAL
ELECTION OF
1988

Since only 42 percent of voters express strong support for either candidate—22 percent for Bush and 20 percent for Dukakis—the election outcome obviously is far from decided.

	Strength of Support					
	Sept. 27–28		Sept. 9–11		Aug. 19–21	
Bush—total		47%		49%		48%
Strong	22		22		27	
Moderate	25		27		21	
Dukakis—total		42		41		44
Strong	20		16		18	
Moderate	22		25		26	
Undecided		11		10		8
		100%		100%		100%

Bush continues to lead Dukakis among men, voters under 30, whites, the college educated and affluent, members of non-union families, Southerns [sic], Republicans, and Independents. Dukakis holds an advantage only among blacks, low-income voters, members of union households, and Democrats. The contest is a standoff among other demographic groups, including women, voters 30 and older, those without college exposure, those in the $15,000–$30,000 income bracket, and in all regions except the South.

Although white Southerners are as apt to call themselves Democrats (33 percent) as Republicans (34 percent) or Independents (33 percent), they currently prefer Bush over Dukakis by a 60 percent to 31 percent margin.

BUSH GAINS IN FIRST POST–LABOR DAY POLL

In the Gallup Poll's first post-Labor Day trial heat, taken September 9–11, the Bush-Quayle Republican ticket led the Democrats' Dukakis-Bentsen slate by a 49 percent to 41 percent margin. Prior to the GOP convention, Bush trailed Dukakis, 42 percent to 49 percent, boosting his competitive standing to a statistically inconclusive 48 percent to 44 percent edge in a poll conducted soon after the convention.

The same poll shows that Bush and Dukakis each draws considerable fire for failing "to tell voters why he would make a good president." About half the voters give Bush an excellent (9 percent) or good (39 percent) rating for substantive campaigning, while half criticize his efforts as only fair (33 percent) or poor (15 percent). Voters are equally critical of Dukakis's campaign, with 8 percent saying he is doing an excellent job; 35 percent, good; 36 percent, only fair; and 17 percent, poor.

Better Job in Debate (Based on Those Who Watched the Debate Live). THE EVIDENCE

QUESTION: *Regardless of which candidate you happen to support, who do you think did a better job in the debate—Bush or Dukakis?*

September 27–28, 1988 (Telephone)

	Bush	Dukakis	Neither	No Opinion	Number of Interviews
National	**38%**	**29%**	**31%**	**2%**	**615**
Sex					
Men	27	37	34	2	316
Women	32	38	27	3	299
Age					
18–29 years	31	46	22	1	74
30–49 years	30	41	28	1	239
50 and older	29	33	34	4	289
65 and older	31	31	34	4	156
Region					
East	27	43	28	2	134
Midwest	29	37	32	2	165
South	31	33	32	4	186
West	30	38	30	2	130
Race					
Whites	31	36	31	2	533
Education					
College graduates	29	42	28	1	213
College incomplete	28	39	31	2	117
High school graduates	27	36	34	3	215
Not H.S. graduates	41	31	25	3	62
Politics					
Republicans	42	15	31	2	194
Democrats	10	62	26	2	222
Independents	29	32	35	4	199
Household income					
$50,000 and over	27	39	33	1	136
$30,000–$49,999	34	37	28	1	144
$15,000–$29,999	24	38	37	1	140
Under $15,000	31	42	23	4	116
Religion					
White Protestants	38	29	31	2	323
White Catholics	19	45	34	2	135
Labor union					
Labor-union families	20	54	25	1	91
Non-union families	31	35	31	3	524

CHAPTER 11

POLITICS AND
TELEVISION THE
PRESIDENTIAL
ELECTION OF
1988

Debate's Influence on Voting (Based on Those Who Watched or Followed the Debate).

QUESTION: *As a result of Sunday night's debate, are you more likely to vote for Bush, more likely to vote for Dukakis, or did the debate not much affect your voting plans?*

September 27–28, 1988 (Telephone)

	More Likely to Vote for Bush	More Likely to Vote for Dukakis	Vote Not Much Affected	No Opinion	Number of Interviews
National	**9%**	**12%**	**77%**	**2%**	**852**
Sex					
Men	8	11	79	2	439
Women	10	13	74	3	413
Age					
18–29 years	10	13	77	*	118
30–49 years	10	11	77	2	361
50 and older	7	12	78	3	357
65 and older	10	13	73	4	187
Region					
East	7	15	75	3	176
Midwest	7	9	80	4	240
South	12	11	75	2	251
West	10	12	77	1	185
Race					
Whites	8	10	80	2	736
Education					
College graduates	10	9	80	1	275
College incomplete	9	10	80	1	183
High school graduates	6	13	79	2	297
Not H.S. graduates	13	16	67	4	86
Politics					
Republicans	16	1	81	2	264
Democrats	3	24	71	2	303
Independents	10	7	80	3	285
Household income					
$50,000 and over	9	8	82	1	183
$30,000–$49,999	8	10	81	1	209
$15,000–$29,999	9	8	81	2	207
Under $15,000	10	21	66	3	152
Religion					
White Protestants	10	8	79	3	442
White Catholics	8	12	79	1	191
Labor union					
Labor-union families	6	17	76	1	125
Non-union families	9	11	77	3	727

Source 17 from Transcription in *New York Times,* Oct. 6, 1988.

17. Excerpts from Vice Presidential Debate, Oct. 5, 1988.

Q. Senator Quayle, I want to take you back if I can to the question Judy asked you about some of the apprehensions people may feel about your being a heartbeat away from the Presidency.

And let us assume, if we can, for the sake of this question that you become Vice President and the President is incapacitated for one reason or another and you have to take the reins of power. When that moment came, what would be the first steps that you'd take, and why?

QUAYLE. First I'd—first I'd say a prayer for myself and for the country that I'm about to lead. And then I would assemble his people and talk. And I think this question keeps going back to the qualifications and what kind of Vice President and, in this hypothetical situation, if I had to assume the responsibilities of President what I would be.

And as I have said, age alone—although I can tell you after the experience of these last few weeks in the campaign, I've added 10 years to my age—age alone is not the only qualification. You've got to look at experience, and you've got to look at accomplishments. And can you make a difference?

Have I made a difference in the United States Senate, where I've served for eight years? Yes, I have. Have I made a difference in the Congress that I've served for 12 years? Yes, I have.

As I said before, looking at the issue of qualifications—and I am delighted that it comes up, because on the three most important challenges facing America—arms control and national security; jobs and education, and budget deficit—I have more experience and accomplishments than does the Governor of Massachusetts.

I have been in the Congress, and I've worked on these issues. And believe me, when you look at arms control and trying to deal with the Soviet Union, you cannot come at it from a naive position. You have to understand the Soviet Union; you have to understand how they will respond. Sitting on that Senate Armed Services Committee for eight years has given me the experience to deal with the Soviet Union and how we can move forward.

That is just one of the troubling issues that's going to be facing this nation. And I'm prepared. . . .

Q. Senator, I want to take you back if I can to the celebrated breakfast club after it was first revealed that you had a plan to have people pay

CHAPTER 11

POLITICS AND
TELEVISION THE
PRESIDENTIAL
ELECTION OF
1988

$10,000 a plate to have breakfast with you. You handled it with disarming, not to say charming candor. You said it was a mistake, and you disbanded it and called the whole idea off, and you were widely praised for having handled it deftly. The question I have is if The Washington Post had not broken that story and other media picked up on it. What can you tell us tonight as to why we should not believe that you would still be having those breakfasts to this day?

BENTSEN. Well, I must say—but I don't make many mistakes, but that one was a real doozy, and I agree with that. And, as you know, I immediately disbanded it. It was perfectly legal, and you have all kinds of such clubs on the Hill, and you know that. But I still believe that the better way to go is to have a campaign reform law that takes care of that kind of a situation, even though it's legal the perception is bad. So I would push very strong to see that we reform the entire situation. I'd work for that end, and that's what my friend from Indiana has opposed repeatedly, vote after vote.

MODERATOR. Senator Quayle?

QUAYLE. He disbanded the club, but he's still got the money. He is the No. 1 receiver of political action committee money. Senator Bentsen's talked about reform. Well let me tell you about the reform that we're pushing. Let's eliminate political action committees—the special interest money. There's legislation for the Congress to do that. That way we won't have to worry about Breakfast Clubs or who's the No. 1 PAC raiser. We can go back and get the contributions from working men and women and the individuals of America. We can also strengthen our two-party system, and need strengthening, and rely more on the political parties than we have in the past. That's the kind of campaign reform that I'm for, and I hope the Senator will join me. . . .

QUAYLE. Let me try to answer the question one more time. I think this is the fourth time that I have had this question And I think that—

Q. Third time.

QUAYLE. Three times that I have had this question and I'll try to answer it again for you as clearly as I can because the question you're asking is what kind of qualifications does Dan Quayle have to be President. What kind of qualifications do I have and what would I do in this kind of a situation? And what would I do in this situation?

I would make sure that the people in the Cabinet and the people and advisers to the President are called in and I'll talk to them and I'll work with them. And I will know them on a firsthand basis, because as Vice President I'll sit on the National Security Council. And I'll know them on a firsthand basis because I'm going to be coordinating the drug effort I'll know them on a firsthand basis because Vice President George Bush is going to recreate the space council and I'll be in charge of that. I will have day-to-day activities with all the people in Government.

And then, if that unfortunate situation happens, if that situation, which would be very tragic, happens, I will be prepared to carry out the responsibilities of the Presidency of the United States of America. And I will be prepared to do that. I will be prepared not only because of my service in the Congress but because of my ability to communicate and to lead. It is not just age, it's accomplishments, it's experience. I have far more experience than many others that sought the office of Vice President of this country. I have as much experience in the Congress as Jack Kennedy did when he sought the Presidency. I will be prepared to deal with the people in the Bush Administration if that unfortunate event would ever occur.

MODERATOR. Senator Bentsen.

BENTSEN. Senator, I served with Jack Kennedy. I knew Jack Kennedy. Jack Kennedy was a friend of mine. Senator, you're no Jack Kennedy.

What has to be done in a situation like that is to call in the joint—

MODERATOR. Please, please, once again, you're only taking time away from your own candidate.

QUAYLE. That was really uncalled for, Senator.

BENTSEN. You're the one that was making the comparison, Senator. And I'm one who knew him well. And frankly I think you're so far apart in the objectives you choose for your country that I did not think the comparison was well taken.

MODERATOR. Tom, a question for Senator Bentsen.

Sources 18 from *New York Times,* Oct. 7, 1988 (editorial).

18. The Bentsen-Quayle Whatever.

It was not a debate. It was not even a good news conference. It was a staged, manipulated, choreographed performance, stilted and artificial. At the end the most important question remained unanswered.

The Bentsen-Quayle whatever showed once more that the Great Campaign of 1988 is really not so much between two sets of candidates but opposing teams of political packagers, script writers, handlers, spinners and sound-bite artists.

CHAPTER 11

POLITICS AND
TELEVISION THE
PRESIDENTIAL
ELECTION OF
1988

The candidates are closely instructed in TV values. Look sincerely at the questioner for a moment, make a smart quarter turn, stare even more sincerely into the camera and give a memorized reply. Danger. Do not risk one spontaneous thought.

Neither the handlers nor the candidates are wise enough to know that the people who come across best on TV are exactly those who come across best when there are no cameras around—those who can relax a little, respect the audience and take a chance on its intelligence.

This country has become so used to rehearsed hokum that it loses its own sense of reality.

After these performances, we sit around, press and public, and analyze them in utter seriousness as if we were judging two men engaged in real intellectual encounter, not contrived contention.

We adapt the false, plastic values of the handlers. If a candidate is human enough to stammer, hesitate, correct himself or, God forbid, sweat, we ridicule him and mark him down as not good enough to represent people like us, who presumably never experience a moment's self-doubt or a bead of perspiration.

Judged as rehearsed performances, both men were terrific on memorization. Senator Dan Quayle did well enough reciting his lines that he proved conclusively that if he is told in advance what to expect and what to say, he can be taken out in polite company.

Perhaps there is more to him than that. But his handlers' high terror of allowing him an inch of leash away from memorized answers prevented us from finding out. He is not yet a skilled actor; we can see his mind furiously riffling through the memory cards. We felt sympathetic embarrassment, as sometimes when you see a child forced to tap-dance in public.

Mr. Bentsen was disappointing. He so clearly outclasses Mr. Quayle in experience and maturity that there was hope that he would show other qualities we seek in a leader, intellectual adventuresomeness, political candor.

He did not. When a tough question was put to him—such as, if fate made you President suddenly, would you carry out the policies of Mr. Dukakis with which you admittedly disagree, or your own beliefs—he simply faced the audience, gave them the old sincere, and evaded it.

Both were excellent in the evasion department. Mr. Bentsen evaded answering four questions and Mr. Quayle at least six, that counts three against Mr. Quayle for failing three times to figure out what in Heaven's name he would actually *do* if he found himself President, aside from offering a prayer, in which all America surely would join him.

Mr. Bentsen won the battle to get off the one-liner that would be repeated most often on TV. The swift knife thrust: "You're no Jack Kennedy." Not quite fair, but who cares? Was it Mr. Bentsen's rapier or his handlers'?

Mr. Bentsen "won" the evening because Mr. Quayle should not be in the same ring with him. Right now Mr. Quayle should not be in the same ring with anybody.

The unanswered question is why Mr. Bush picked this man above the many first-rate candidates he could have chosen. Was he naive enough to think that Senator Quayle, who is now a political millstone, would be a political asset? Or was it that at convention time Mr. Bush was so insecure and self-absorbed that he could not stand anybody who had a reputation and achievements independent of him? Yes, he thought he could anoint a loyal, malleable cipher as a potential President and get away with it.

But he didn't. Too many Americans see it as an insult and think less of him, though some may wind up voting for him.

Mr. Bush's misjudgment becomes the problem of the millions of voters who lean toward him but shudder at his Vice-Presidential choice.

They will have to make up their minds whether a President Bush in the White House is so much better than a President Dukakis that it outweighs the possibility of a President Quayle.

Some will say no and some will say yes, but none of them will admire Mr. Bush for presenting them with the dilemma of the campaign of 1988.

CHAPTER 11

POLITICS AND
TELEVISION THE
PRESIDENTIAL
ELECTION OF
1988

Source 19 from *Gallup Report,* Oct. 1988, p. 19.

19.   Better Job in VP Debate (Based on Registered Voters Who Watched the Debate).

QUESTION: *Regardless of which candidate you happen to support, who do you think did a better job in the debate—Quayle or Bentsen?*

September 7–9, 1988 (Telephone)

	Quayle	Bentsen	Neither/ Equal	No Opinion	Number of Interviews
National	**20%**	**60%**	**15%**	**5%**	**619**
Sex					
Men	18	63	16	3	312
Women	21	58	14	7	307
Age					
18–29 years	21	64	13	2	92
30–49 years	19	64	12	5	228
50 and older	20	57	17	6	293
65 and older	21	54	18	7	147
Region					
East	18	63	16	3	142
Midwest	18	64	13	5	166
South	24	53	14	9	189
West	18	63	18	1	122
Race					
Whites	20	60	16	4	553
Education					
College graduates	20	61	16	3	217
College incomplete	13	64	18	5	124
High school graduates	22	63	11	4	204
Not H.S. graduates	20	54	17	9	66
Politics					
Republicans	36	32	26	6	205
Democrats	7	84	6	3	187
Independents	17	64	14	5	227
Household income					
$50,000 and over	18	63	15	4	126
$39,000–$49,999	18	65	14	3	160
$15,000–$29,999	20	62	15	3	157
Under $15,000	23	59	13	5	119
Religion					
White Protestants	24	54	17	5	318
White Catholics	14	65	18	3	146
Labor union					
Labor-union families	12	76	9	3	102
Non-union families	21	57	17	5	517

Source 20 from *New York Times,* Oct. 7, 1988.

20. Bush and Dukakis Try to Capitalize on Latest Debate.

RUNNING MATES IN FOCUS
DEMOCRATS USE ADS ATTACKING QUAYLE, AND REPUBLICANS
SAY PANEL WAS BIASED
BY MICHAEL ORESKES
SPECIAL TO THE NEW YORK TIMES

WASHINGTON, Oct. 6—On the morning after the Vice-Presidential debate, the campaign of Michael S. Dukakis unveiled two new television advertisements intended to drive home the idea that Vice President Bush had picked the wrong running mate.

"Hopefully we will never know how great a lapse of judgment that really was," says one ad, featuring shots of the traumatic ceremonies in which Harry S. Truman, Lyndon B. Johnson and Gerald R. Ford were sworn in as President.

Putting the new ads on the air is a measure of the Dukakis Presidential campaign's hope that doubts about Senator Dan Quayle, Mr. Bush's running mate, will linger after the debate.

But it was only one of the quick reactions to the 90-minute encounter between Mr. Quayle and Senator Lloyd Bentsen.

'NEVER ONCE ASKED BENTSEN'

The Bush campaign was attacking its own target: the press. Mr. Bush's spokesmen were accusing reporters on last night's debate panel of being too hard on Mr. Quayle and too soft on Senator Bentsen, the Democratic Vice-Presidential nominee.

Stuart Spencer, a senior Bush-Quayle campaign adviser, complained that the four panelists asked "over and over" what Mr. Quayle would do if he suddenly became President. Mr. Quayle replied that he would pray for himself and the country and get to know his cabinet. "They never once asked Bentsen that question," said Mr. Spencer. "The media was unfair," he concluded.

The public, at least according to a CBS News Poll, disagreed. Seventy-seven percent of those who watched said the panelists were fair to both candidates.

CHAPTER 11

POLITICS AND
TELEVISION THE
PRESIDENTIAL
ELECTION OF
1988

QUESTIONS TO CONSIDER

As noted in the Method section of this chapter, it helps to examine and analyze the evidence in three segments: television advertising, television news broadcasts, and the presidential and vice presidential debates.

Concerning advertising, in source 1, a Gallup poll taken March 8 to 12, 1988 (long before either Bush or Dukakis had been selected as presidential nominees by their respective parties) seemed to show that voters did not like negative advertising in which candidates spend all their time attacking their opponents rather than talking about their own qualifications and ideas. Did people of all ages, regions, races, educational levels, political preferences, religions generally share this opinion? Can you explain any variations (if any)?

In spite of these poll results, a good deal of television advertising in the presidential campaign itself was negative. Two good examples of this are sources 2 and 3, transcriptions of pro-Bush television advertisements produced by the National Security Political Action Committee.[11] Why do you think media advisers to both Bush and Dukakis went against the results of the Gallup poll? Do the Oct. 10, 19, and 22 *New York Times* articles (sources 4 through 7) provide a clue?

Look especially at the *Times* report filed from Fabens, Texas. Re-examining the Gallup poll and the Fabens, Texas, story, what role do you believe television advertising, especially negative advertising, played in the 1988 campaign?

Source 2 is a variation of the famous and highly controversial "Willie Horton" advertisement. Some Dukakis supporters attacked the advertisement as racist, principally because it focused on an African American who received prison furloughs and, during one such furlough, stabbed a man and raped the man's girlfriend. This charge was vehemently denied by the National Security Political Action Committee, whose chairman defended the advertisement by saying, "We feel very strongly that the heinous details of this case were at issue, not the color of his [Horton's] skin."[12] Do you think the advertisement was intended to stoke racial prejudice against African Americans? Or were the Dukakis supporters' charges meant to brand Bush and his supporters unfairly as racists? How would you prove your hypothesis?

The San Jose *Mercury News* (source 8) invited several advertising executives to watch tapes of the television advertisements and then elicited their reactions. What role did those people think political advertising played? What did

11. These two advertisements are variations of the controversial "Willie Horton" and "Boston Harbor" ads which were broadcast nationwide. They are similar in content and message to those advertisements.

12. Elizabeth Fediay (chair of NSPAC) to Houghton Mifflin Company, Aug. 4, 1989, in possession of Houghton Mifflin and the authors.

they think of negative advertising? Keep in mind that these people were advertising professionals.

Finally, one editorial cartoonist (Herbert Block, known as "Herblock," source 10) offered his opinion of 1988 political advertisements on television. Did Herblock reflect the opinions of the general voters? How can you prove that your answer to that question is correct?

Regarding television news coverage of the campaign (sources 11 through 15), many critics assert that this was the presidential election in which control of the evening news passed from the networks to the candidates themselves, who manipulated television reporters into covering only well-staged photo opportunities. Do you believe this observation is true [consult especially *Newsweek,* Sept. 12, 1988 (source 11) and *New York Times,* Oct. 4, 1988 (source 12)]. If this criticism is true, how was this shift in control accomplished? How did it change television news coverage? Keep in mind that *Newsweek* and the *New York Times* are representatives of print journalism, which is normally critical of television news coverage. Were these attacks merely examples of the long-standing battle between print and television journalists?

To dramatize his difference of opinion with Dukakis over a required pledge of allegiance, in the last week of September, Bush toured a flag factory in New Jersey. What were the results of that tour? How did the media react? (See Source 13.)

While candidates *appeared* to be more available in 1988 because of carefully planned sound bites, many people believe that actually they were

less so. What is your opinion (see *New York Times* report, Oct. 4, 1988).

One cartoonist's view of television news coverage is included (source 14). How does the cartoonist stand on television news coverage of the election? Based on earlier evidence, is the cartoonist correct or incorrect? How would you prove your answer?

The summaries of the "NBC Nightly News" October coverage of the campaign can be used in a number of imaginative ways (source 15). Does it appear that NBC News favored one candidate over another? Next, look at the amount of time given to each candidate and whether the stories were likely to be positive or negative. Did television advertisements themselves become a "reportable" story? How were they treated? If one candidate received more treatment, why do you think this was so (consult earlier evidence)?

Although the debates (sources 16 through 20) were one place where voters could observe candidates on "live" television for an extended period of time, it is still not clear what role those debates played in the election. According to the Gallup polls, what is the answer to that question? Do debates change voters' minds or merely reinforce their already formed opinions? How could the Gallup polls help answer that question?

One criticism of the 1988 debates (see the *New York Times* editorial, Oct. 7, 1988, source 18) was that well-coached candidates simply ignored the questions in favor of delivering well-rehearsed minispeeches. Based on the brief excerpts from one of the three debates, is that criticism justified or not?

CHAPTER 11

POLITICS AND
TELEVISION THE
PRESIDENTIAL
ELECTION OF
1988

Indeed, what did the voters *actually see* when they tuned into the three debates?

Now put your conclusions together from the three segments. What role did television in general (and each segment in particular) play in the presidential election of 1988? How has television altered the process of choosing a president? What are the positive and negative effects of that alteration?

EPILOGUE

Like its predecessors the railroad and radio, television has had a profound effect on the American presidential electoral process and the ways presidential campaigns are organized and conducted. Potential nominees can go over the heads of party bosses and organizations and appeal directly to voters in presidential primaries. Party convention sites now are chosen so as to maximize television coverage; the conventions themselves have been drastically reorganized, with television networks and viewers in mind. Television has helped reshape presidential candidates' styles, oratory, dress, and even physical appearance, and through advertisements and photo opportunities on network newscasts, presidential candidates can directly reach virtually every voter in the nation, bombarding those voters with images, appeals, and attacks. Televised debates give voters what they believe is a matchless opportunity to learn about the candidates, see them under stress, and judge their intelligence and ideas. Finally, television has the power to identify principal issues and concerns and, when combined with poll results, report to Americans the opinions and preferences of their fel-

low voters. Little wonder many observers believe that Ronald Reagan's political success arose from his being the most telegenic president (one of his nicknames, the "Great Communicator," came principally from his televised appearances).

Although few doubt that the process of selecting a president has changed and that those changes are largely a result of network television, the extent to which television actually alters voters' behavior is still unknown. Studies of voters in 1972, 1976, and 1980 seem to show that television advertising did not change voters' minds so much as reinforce their predispositions. Yet the 1988 television advertisements were markedly different from most of their predecessors, and preliminary reports suggest that voters were more aware of the advertisements. Similarly, polls show that televised debates do not alter voters' choices significantly. It is in the area of network news reporting that television has had the most impact, especially in 1988 as the candidates themselves were able to manipulate the networks to their respective ends. By substituting images and preplanned sound bites for the reality of news reporting, candidates caught voters while their guard was down, when they *believed* they were watching news when in fact they were viewing clever minicommercial messages.

How can present and future Americans analyze the momentous choices before them, political and otherwise? They can do so only by using the knowledge and skills at their disposal to *examine* and *analyze* the evidence presented to them, by questioning that evidence, and by reaching mature and intelligent conclusions. Whether that evidence is presented in the form of speeches, debates, cartoons, advertisements, interviews, posters, films, newspapers and magazines, or televised programs or newscasts, Americans must be able to deal with that evidence skillfully and intelligently, always being able to see that evidence in its historical and contemporary contexts. To that end, we sincerely hope this book has made a contribution.

Acknowledgments continued from page iv.

CHAPTER FIVE

Source 1: "Over There" by George M. Cohan. Copyright © 1917. Renewed 1945 Leo Feist, Inc. All Rights Assigned to EMI Catalogue Partnership. All Rights Controlled and Administered by EMI Feist Catalogue, Inc. International Copyright Secured. Made in USA. All Rights Reserved. Used by Permission.

Sources 19–22: From *War as Advertised: The Four Minute Men and America's Crusade, 1917–1918,* pp. 70, 72–73, 122, 60, and 27. Copyright 1984. Reprinted by permission of American Philosophical Society.

CHAPTER SIX

Source 1: Southerners of Tomorrow. National Child Labor Committee.

Source 2: Why This Double Standard? Lewis Hine, Milwaukee Art Museum. Gift of Robert Mann.

Source 3: NCLC exhibit. Library of Congress.

Source 4: Boys on grate. Jacob A. Riis/Museum of the City of New York.

Source 5: Pennsylvania Breaker. National Child Labor Committee.

Sources 6–10, 13: Edward L. Bofford Photography Collection, University of Maryland, Baltimore County Library.

Sources 11–12: Lewis Hine, Milwaukee Art Museum, Gift of Walter and Naomi Rosenberg.

Source 14: George Eastman House.

Source 15: National Child Labor Committee.

CHAPTER SEVEN

Sources 6–11: From *Hard Times: An Oral History of the Great Depression,* by Studs Terkel. Copyright © 1970 by Studs Terkel. Reprinted by permission of Pantheon Books, a division of Random House, Inc.

Source 12: Used with permission of Ryan Harwood and Clyde and Lorene Bethel.

CHAPTER EIGHT

Source 1: From Harry S Truman, *Memoirs: Year of Decisions,* pp. 10–11, 416–423. Copyright 1955. Reprinted by permission.

Source 2: Excerpts from *On Active Service in Peace and War* by Henry L. Stimson. Copyright 1947 by the author. Reprinted by permission of Harper & Row, Publishers, Inc.

Source 5: Excerpts from *Turbulent Era: A Diplomatic Record of Forty Years, 1904–1945* by Joseph C. Grew, edited by Walter Johnson. Copyright 1952 by Joseph C. Grew. Copyright © renewed 1980 by Elizabeth Lyon, Anita J. English and Lilla Levitt. Reprinted by permission of Houghton Mifflin Company.

Source 6: From John J. McCloy, *The Challenge to American Foreign Policy,* pp. 40–44. Copyright © 1953 by the President and Fellows of Harvard College. Copyright renewed 1981 by John Jay McCloy. Reprinted by permission of the publisher, Harvard University Press.

Source 7: From James F. Byrnes, *All in One Lifetime,* pp. 282–287, 290–291, 300–301. Copyright 1858. Reprinted by permission of James F. Byrnes Foundation.

Source 8: From *The Forrestal Diaries* by James Forrestal. Copyright 1951 by James V. Forrestal. All rights reserved. Reprinted by permission of Viking Penguin, a division of Penguin Books USA, Inc.